Constructing Science in Elementary Classrooms

Norman G. Lederman
Illinois Institute of Technology

Judith S. Lederman
Illinois Institute of Technology

Randy L. Bell
University of Virginia

PEARSON

Boston • New York • San Francisco
Mexico City • Montreal • Toronto • London • Madrid • Munich • Paris
Hong Kong • Singapore • Tokyo • Cape Town • Sydney

Series Editor: Traci Mueller
Editorial Assistant: Krista Price
Marketing Manager: Elizabeth Fogarty
Editorial-Production Service: Omegatype Typography, Inc.
Manufacturing Buyer: Andrew Turso
Composition and Prepress Buyer: Linda Cox
Cover Administrator: Linda Knowles
Interior Design: Glenna Collett
Photo Research: Amy Giese, Katharine S. Cook
Electronic Composition: Omegatype Typography, Inc.

Library of Congress Cataloging-in-Publication Data

Lederman, Norman G.
    Constructing science in elementary classrooms / Norman Lederman, Judith S. Lederman, Randy L. Bell.
        p. cm.
    Includes bibliographical references and index.
    ISBN: 0-8013-3090-4
    1. Science—Study and teaching (Elementary)—United States. I. Lederman, Judith S. II. Bell, Randy L. III. Title.

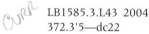 LB1585.3.L43 2004
    372.3'5—dc22

                                                                    20003057723

Printed in the United States of America

10 9 8 7 6 5 4 3 2 1   08 07 06 05 04 03

Brief Contents

SECTION I   Goals of Science Instruction   1

1   What Is Science?   3
2   Why Teach Science?   23

SECTION II   Setting the Stage   47

3   Creating a Positive Physical and Emotional Environment   49
4   Instructional Planning   81
5   Measurement, Assessment, and Evaluation of Student Learning   105
6   Gathering and Evaluating Curriculum Materials   141

SECTION III   The Teaching Cycle   169

7   Life Science   171
8   Physical Science   229
9   Earth Science   281
10   Transcendent Themes   337

Appendix A   ERIC Tutorial   355
Appendix B   Item Analysis   363
Appendix C   Professional Development   369

Index   379

Contents

Preface   xi

SECTION I   Goals of Science Instruction   1

1   **What Is Science?**   3
What Is Science?   4
Science and the Characteristics of Scientific Knowledge   7
Is There a Single Scientific Method?   12
How Objective Is Science?   12
A Few Words about Teaching the Nature of Science   19
Summary   20
Suggested Readings   20

2   **Why Teach Science?**   23
Why Require Science for All Students?   24
What Is Scientific Literacy?   27
Contemporary Reform Efforts in Science Education   28
Common Themes in the Reforms   39
Specific Comparisons between the Science Reforms   42
A Few Words about the Teaching of Scientific Inquiry   44
Summary   44
Suggested Readings   45

SECTION II   Setting the Stage   47

3   **Creating a Positive Physical
and Emotional Environment**   49

Arranging the Classroom   52

▣   BOX 3.1   Issues in Diversity:
Choosing a Classroom Design   53

▣   BOX 3.2   Issues in Technology:
One Computer, Two Computers, Three Computers, Four ...   57

Whole Group Instruction   57

▣   BOX 3.3   Issues in Diversity:
Establishing Behavior Expectations   59

▣   BOX 3.4   Learning Theory:
Keeping a Visual Record of Discussions   62

Small Group Instruction   66

▣   BOX 3.5   Managing Your Science Classroom:
Small Group Instruction   67

Beyond the Classroom   73

Summary   78

4   **Instructional Planning**   81

Instructional Objectives   82

▣   BOX 4.1   Issues in Technology:
What Did You Do in Science Class Today?   86

▣   BOX 4.2   Learning Theory:
Focus on the Affective Domain   92

The Lesson Plan   94

▣   BOX 4.3   Curriculum Connections:
1, 2 Tie Your Shoe. 3,4 Tie It Once More   100

▣   BOX 4.4   Learning Theory:
Mapping Your Plan   102

Summary   102

5   **Measurement, Assessment, and Evaluation
of Student Learning**   105

Conceptualizing Assessment, Measurement, and Evaluation   106

Developing Assessment Items: Do They Match
Your Instructional Objectives?   109

▨ BOX 5.1 Issues in Diversity:
Testing, Testing . . . 111

Developing Assessment Items: The Traditional Approach 113

▨ BOX 5.2 Issues in Technology:
Test Bank Alert! 118

Are All Assessment Items Equal? 121

Summary of Traditional Assessment Approaches 122

Developing Assessment Items: An Alternative Approach 124

▨ BOX 5.3 Issues in Diversity:
What Is Best to Assess? 124

▨ BOX 5.4 Curriculum Connections:
Portfolio Planning and Production 127

▨ BOX 5.5 Managing Your Science Classroom:
Independence! 128

How Are Alternative Assessments Evaluated? 132

Evaluation: Making Judgments from Assessments
and Measures 136

Evaluation: Determination of Grades 137

Summary 139

**6 Curriculum Materials and Their Evaluation
and Selection** 141

What's Important to You? 142

Project 2061 Curriculum Evaluation Criteria: A Summary 143

Evaluating Curriculum Materials 145

Making Sense of the Analysis 146

Revising Curriculum Materials Based on Your Analysis 147

▨ BOX 6.1 Learning Theory:
Curriculum Modification Based on
Student Prior Knowledge 151

Doing and Knowing: A Return to Criterion I 151

Finding and Selecting Instructional Materials 153

Resource Card File 154

▨ BOX 6.2 Curriculum Connections:
Integration Is in the Cards 155

▨ BOX 6.3 Curriculum Connections:
Thinking Outside the Box 159

Gathering Supplies for Science Learning   163

▪ BOX 6.4   Managing Your Science Classroom:
             Supply and Demand   168

Summary   168

SECTION III   The Teaching Cycle   169

7   **Life Science**   171

What Is Life?   171

▪ BOX 7.1   Science as Inquiry:
             Inquiry and Nature of Science Assessment Ideas   184

Form and Function   185

▪ BOX 7.2   Curriculum Connections:
             The Art of Bird Construction   193

▪ BOX 7.3   Managing Your Science Classroom:
             Distribution Deliberation   194

Life Cycles   196

Environmental Science   213

▪ BOX 7.4   Issues in Technology:
             A Picture Is Worth a Thousand Words   221

Summary   228

8   **Physical Science**   229

Properties of Matter   230

▪ BOX 8.1   Managing Your Science Classroom:
             Eyes-On versus Hands-On Activities   238

▪ BOX 8.2   Issues in Technology:
             Technology Does Not Have to Be So Technical!   244

Forces and Motion   246

▪ BOX 8.3   Learning Theory:
             The Learning Cycle   252

▪ BOX 8.4   Curriculum Connections:
             Literature Integration   253

Energy   255

▪ BOX 8.5   Nature of Science:
             Convergent versus Divergent Activities   260

Physical and Chemical Change   261

▓ BOX 8.6   Science as Inquiry:
Assessing Levels of Inquiry   266

▓ BOX 8.7   Issues in Diversity:
Special Needs for Special Students   274

Summary   277

9   Earth Science   281

The Universe: Stars and Constellations   282

▓ BOX 9.1   Issues in Technology:
Science That Is Virtually Real   293

▓ BOX 9.2   Issues in Technology:
Starry Night   294

▓ BOX 9.3   Nature of Science:
Patterns   297

The Solar System: Daytime Astronomy   297

▓ BOX 9.4   Curriculum Connections:
Just the Story   307

The Earth: Rocks and the Rock Cycle   308

▓ BOX 9.5   Managing Your Science Classroom:
Sign Up   320

Forces of Nature: Weather   320

Summary   333

10   Transcendent Themes   337

Teaching Transcendent Themes   339

Models   339

Lessons from Previous Chapters Modified to Teach Models   341

Systems   346

Lessons from Previous Chapters Modified to Teach Systems   349

Appendix A   ERIC Tutorial   355

Appendix B   Item Analysis   363

Appendix C   Professional Development   369

Index   379

Preface

There is an old adage that we have each heard at some point in our careers, "The longest walk in the world is from in front of the desk to behind the desk." When hearing this statement, usually in a methods course, the instructor typically will also walk from the student side of the desk to the teacher side of the desk. We definitely won't be telling you to anchor yourself behind your desk, as if the students are the enemy, anywhere in this book. We will be continually reminding you that the transformation from student to teacher is not automatic and it requires a lot of work, physically, emotionally, and cognitively.

All teachers need to know their subject matter thoroughly, but knowing subject matter is not enough. All teachers also need to understand students, understand how they learn, how they think, what motivates them, and how they satisfy their needs, but just knowing these things is not enough. The effective teacher successfully integrates knowledge of subject matter, students, curriculum, schools, and pedagogy. That's a lot to handle at once and it doesn't come naturally. Methods texts typically do not discuss all the types of knowledge we have just mentioned, and what is discussed is usually discussed as separate, disconnected entities that the students (that's you) are supposed to integrate toward the end of the course or after the course is over. Unfortunately, this approach does not work well and even the most well-intentioned beginning teacher dutifully learns the topics presented while continually wondering what each has to do with teaching. This methods text is organized in a very different way. The traditional topics included in a methods course are all integrated into a context of the teaching and learning of science. Instead of separate chapters on learning theory and classroom management, these topics will be discussed within the context of a teacher's planning and implementing instruction. Our approach attempts to use what we have learned about learning. People learn things best if what they are being asked to learn is placed within a meaningful context. In this case, the most meaningful context is the reason you are in a methods course in the first place—you are learning to teach science.

The text is divided into three major sections or clusters of chapters: **Goals of Science Instruction, Setting the Stage,** and **The Teaching Cycle.** The first two sections provide the theoretical and practical foundations for instruction, whereas the third section comprises the most significant portion of the text. In each section you will be asked, as much as possible, to interact with the text by doing certain activities and investigations and to critically think about what you have done. In a way, the textbook you now have in your hands will attempt to model the kind of instruction we hope you will take back to your own students.

Section I: Goals of Science Instruction

The chapters in this section present an overall view of science as a way of knowing and eventually developing an argument for why science should be included in the curriculum at all. We know it is required, but should it be required when there are so many other important things for your students to learn? The section ends with a discussion of what the best thinkers in science education have developed as goals for K–12 instruction, the primary reform documents: *National Science Education Standards* and *Benchmarks for Science Literacy.*

Section II: Setting the Stage

The chapters in this section focus on what a teacher must do in advance of teaching to set a stage that will maximize student learning. It is one thing to teach a successful lesson, unit, or year. It is another thing to set your classrooms and lessons up in advance to increase the likelihood of being successful. There is a second adage we have all heard that goes like this: "If you fail to plan, you are planning to fail." The section begins with a focus on the physical and emotional aspects of the science classroom that facilitate student learning. What follows are the mechanical logistics of lesson and unit planning.

Emphasis is placed on the importance of connecting lessons and avoiding the tendency to present individual science lessons in isolation. Naturally, if you have planned carefully what you want students to know and do, the mysterious endeavor of assessment and evaluation becomes child's play.

The teacher's most important allies while planning for instruction are instructional materials, resources, and curriculum materials. This section ends with extensive attention to such resources. Teacher resources can come in the form of brief activities or extensive sequences of lessons. Much emphasis will be placed on matching resources to the goals you have planned and developing skills for the evaluation of materials that are commercially produced. In the end, the hope is that you will be well equipped to select good materials or revise materials that are available to suit your personal needs.

Section III: The Teaching Cycle

This cluster of four chapters comprises the overwhelming majority and, in our opinion, the most significant portion of the text. Within these chapters, you will have direct experiences with subject matter concepts and themes common to national reforms. These concepts and themes are those stressed within the reforms and they are also the most commonly addressed concepts and themes within elementary-level science.

As mentioned earlier, the traditional topics of methods courses (e.g., demonstrations, laboratories, classroom management, assessment, developmental psychology, etc.) are addressed within the context of the teaching cycle. In particular, the traditional pedagogy topics (e.g., demonstrations, classroom management, assessment, etc.) will be placed within a repeating cycle of:

Goal Setting → Materials Development and Selection →
Pedagogy → Assessment → Reflection

For example, within the section on properties of matter, you will first be provided with an introduction to the depth and breadth of the topic as described in the *National Science Education Standards* and the *Benchmarks for Science Literacy.* The level of elaboration will provide you with a functional understanding of the topic that is necessary to successfully plan and implement instruction. A specific benchmark or standard will be selected for instruction and you will then be engaged in the various aspects of the teaching cycle as instruction is planned, implemented, assessed, and then followed with reflection. Examples of various materials and activities for use in the lesson are provided and these will be evaluated (pros and cons) in terms of their match with the specific instructional goal. At this point, you will be asked to consider the students, their background knowledge, and what approaches would best facilitate their achievement of the stated goal. Periodically, you will also be directed to various "sidebars" and/or "windows" that address the specifics of various instructional methods (e.g., demonstrations, laboratories, discussions, etc.). In each case, the pros and cons of the various pedagogical approaches are addressed.

Over the full range of subject matter concepts and themes, all of the traditional methods topics are addressed in depth. In addition, a concerted effort is made to model appropriate and inappropriate uses of informal education sites (e.g., museums, zoos), technology, and children's literature.

The approach of this text is unique and is designed to directly address the perennial problem of the transfer and application of methods topics to classroom instruction. By situating instructional methods in a relevant context (i.e., teaching of specific concepts and themes), it is believed that your learning will be enhanced and transfer will be facilitated. Happy teaching!

Acknowledgments

We would like to express our sincere appreciation to all of the science students and teachers we have taught and worked with throughout our careers. From them, we have learned to be better science educators.

We also wish to thank several individuals for their tireless assistance in this project. In addition to keeping us grounded in reality, they provided us with endless hours of substantive review, editing, and artwork. Lynn Bell, Randy's wife, did a terrific job with our first round of editing. We were thrilled with the beautiful illustrations Sharon Tantoco created for our book. IIT graduate assistants Eizabeth Druger and Kevin White supported us in endless ways. We thank Phil Wade for providing a great source of ideas for the geology activities in Chapter 9 and UVA graduate students Becky McNall and Karen Irving for their numerous contributions to the text. We would especially like to express our gratitude to Christine Tantoco, another IIT graduate assistant, who offered the invaluable technical assistance we needed to put the finishing touches on the manuscript.

We would like to thank the following reviewers: David T. Crowther, University of Nevada, Reno; Marion Jenice French, Kansas State University; Julie Gess-Newsome, The University of Utah; Paul Kuerbis, Colorado College; Will Letts, Charles Sturt University; Carol T. Taylor Mitchell, University of Nebraska, Omaha; Royal Van Horn, University of North Florida; and Dana Zeidler, University of South Florida.

Finally, we would like to thank Adrianne and Jessica Bell, Benjamin and Abigail Sweeney, and Bosco Lederman for loving us no matter how consumed we were with the writing of this textbook.

NGL
JSL
RLB

Goals of Science Instruction

This section will provide you with an important foundation for all that follows in the text. The two chapters in this section will help you to clarify why science is included as a basic requirement of the elementary curriculum. More importantly, it is critical that you are personally convinced of the value that science instruction has for your students' education and future. The following chapters include in-depth discussions of what distinguishes science from other academic disciplines as well as the visions of the current reforms in science education. It is our hope that this section of the text will provide you with a framework to organize the direction and nature of science instruction in your classroom. In the end we believe, as you do, that a background in the subject matter and processes of science will enrich the lives of your students.

What Is Science?

$\mathbf{S}$ome natural questions to ask before teaching science are, "What is science?" "How is it different from the other subjects I teach?" "How is it similar to other subjects I teach?" If you do not ask such questions yourself, your students are sure to ask at least the first. The answer is not as common as you may think. Many teachers, even those specifically licensed to teach science, have difficulty answering the questions we have posed. This chapter will provide you with a variety of experiences and discussions that will hopefully start you on your way to finding answers to these questions. In particular, this chapter will help you to define the characteristics that distinguish science from other subject matter disciplines. We think the background this chapter provides will enable you to more effectively *teach science* as well as *teach about science* to your students. In comparison to other textbooks that you have read, this text will ask you to complete a variety of both written and hands-on activities. It is important that you complete all of the activities.

What Is Science?

On any day, you can watch your local television newscast and hear claims made by scientists about a particular food or drug being harmful or healthy. For example, aspirin had been used as a headache remedy for many years before scientists informed us that it may be harmful to the lining of our stomachs. Taking aspirin carries the risk of possible development of ulcers. In response to this news, many companies began to manufacture alternative remedies (e.g., Tylenol, ibuprofen) that could relieve the pain of a headache without the risk of ulcers and stomach distress. More recently, doctors have found that aspirin is useful in decreasing the risk of heart disease. Consequently, many of those who had moved away from taking aspirin have returned to this old friend. Even more recently, researchers have found that ulcers are not caused by aspirin, drugs, or any of the foods known to increase stomach acid but rather are caused by bacteria or any number of other factors. At this point you may be thinking, "Why don't they make up their minds? I think I'll wait until all the facts are in." Aspirin is not unique. There are countless examples of foods and medicines (e.g., wine, fatty foods, milk, coffee) that at various times have been considered healthy and at other times have been considered harmful. Is something wrong? Are the scientists making premature claims? Should they wait until all the facts are in before making their recommendations? Actually this flip-flop of opinion is not a sign of poor behavior by scientists or bad science. It is actually symptomatic of good science.

You may now be considering a walk to your bathroom or kitchen to carefully inspect the contents of your medicine chest, refrigerator, or kitchen cabinets. Actually, we want you to walk to your kitchen or bathroom, but instead of inspecting the foods and medicines, remove the cardboard core from a roll of toilet tissue or paper towels. Now get some string, the kind you would use to wrap a package. If you do not have string, sewing thread will do. We made the tube you see pictured in Figure 1.1 using the same materials you have just gathered.

A series of actions is performed on the tube and consequences are noted. The actions and consequences are listed in Table 1.1. What is inside of the tube that can explain why the strings behaved as they did? Take a moment to draw yourself a picture of what you think the inside of our tube looks like. Using your diagram, can you predict what would happen if string C is pulled? On what basis have you made your prediction?

It's time to find out the answer! If string A is pulled, string B moves into the tube. If you predicted correctly, you are catching on. If you predicted incorrectly,

Figure 1.1 Inquiry Tube

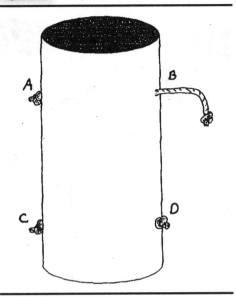

reexamine the model you imagined for the inside of the tube and revise it based on the additional data gathered by the pulling of string C.

Using the tube and string you have collected, make the model you think explains the behavior of our tube and string. After completing the construction of your model, test its accuracy by sequentially performing the actions specified previously and noting the consequences. Did your tube work the same as ours? If so, you have developed a reasonably good model of what is inside of our tube. If your tube did not work the same as ours did, see if you can change your model so that it does work the same as ours.

We really have no idea how the inside of your tube looks. Does one of the diagrams shown in Figure 1.2 represent how your tube is constructed?

Table 1.1 Actions Performed on the Inquiry Tube and the Consequences of Those Actions

Action	Consequence
String A is pulled	String B moves into tube
String B is pulled	String A moves into tube
String D is pulled	String B moves into tube
String A is pulled	String D moves into tube

Figure 1.2   Two Possible Diagrams of the Inside of the Inquiry Tube

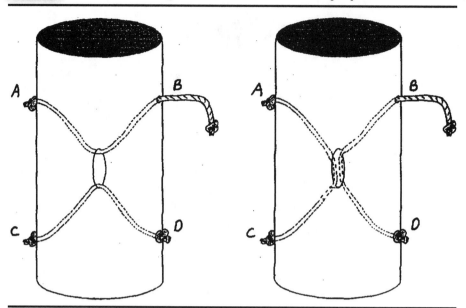

Regardless of whether either of these diagrams represents what you have constructed, would either of the two diagrams, if actually constructed, behave as the original tube we demonstrated? This leads us to a very important question. If your tube behaves the same as ours, do you definitely know how our tube is constructed? Do we know how your tube is constructed? Neither of us can say for sure how the other's tube is constructed. The only way to find out would be to look inside.

What does any of this have to do with science? Actually, it has everything to do with science. What you did during the past few minutes was to manipulate some variables (i.e., the strings), collect some data (i.e., noting the movement of the strings in response to manipulation), draw some inferences in the form of a model (i.e., speculating or hypothesizing about the construction of the tube), and then test your hypothesis or inference (i.e., constructing your own tube and matching its behavior to ours). You did what scientists do all the time. Just like the world or universe that scientists study, the original tube could not be opened to find out an absolutely correct answer to our original question.

The tube and string activity is one you can easily do with your students. We have used it successfully with students as young as third grade and are confident it can be used with even younger students. However, we need to be a bit more specific about what this activity illustrates about science and scientists.

Science and the Characteristics of Scientific Knowledge

The simplest way to describe science is as an endeavor with three interrelated but distinct aspects. Science is (a) a body of knowledge, (b) a method or process, and (c) a way of knowing or constructing reality.

Body of Knowledge

The body of knowledge of science is what most people think about when they think of science. The knowledge is the laws, theories, concepts, principles, and so on of science. Although disciplines have a body of knowledge, what distinguishes the disciplines is the specific focus of interest comprising the body of knowledge. The structure and function of living things are the focus of biology; atoms, molecules, compounds, and their interactions are of interest to chemists; the forces that govern the physical world are of interest to physicists, whereas the characteristics of a painting are of interest to the artist. In the tube and string activity, the relationships among the movement of the strings and the proposed model for what was inside the tube would constitute part of the

A collection of science books.

body of knowledge of the study of tubes. How you went about developing your knowledge of the tube involved you in a second aspect of science.

Method and Process

How scientists, or practitioners within any discipline, develop the body of knowledge is another distinguishing characteristic. Although different disciplines often use similar methods and processes, the combination of the processes and the objects of concern usually can be used to distinguish one discipline from another. For example, scientists necessarily appeal to empirical data (i.e., observations) during the development of knowledge. Mathematicians, on the other hand, do not necessarily make observations or collect empirical data. The model you developed for the content of the tube was primarily based on the manipulations of the strings and the observations you subsequently made regarding these manipulations. It would not have been acceptable for you to simply develop a model for the contents of the tube without making any observations. Also, the model you finally developed needed to be consistent with your observations. Nobody has ever told us that there is a little man in the tube directing the behavior of the strings. You could have made such a conclusion, but in the scientific way of thinking you would not have been taken seriously. This would not mean you were wrong. It just means that you would have deviated from the accepted methods and processes of science in the development of your model. Some of the more common processes used by scientists in the development of knowledge are observation, organization and representation of data, data analysis, hypothesizing, testing of hypotheses, inferences, and concluding. With all this stress on the use of processes to develop knowledge, was the knowledge you developed about the tube derived totally from empirical data? You were never able to open the original tube and so your model was not totally based on observation. This leads us to some very important and unavoidable characteristics of scientific knowledge.

Way of Knowing and Constructing Reality

As we have emphasized, scientific knowledge is necessarily developed through the use of various methods and processes. A basic assumption of the scientific way of thinking is that the world is knowable through empirical observation. However, no matter how hard scientists try, most of the time they can never collect a complete and absolute set of data on any object of interest. The tube can be used as an analogy of our universe. You were unable to open the original tube just like scientists cannot open the universe and look inside to determine all of its hidden meanings and processes. At some point, scientists must speculate and infer about what they cannot see. You did this when you developed your model of the tube. Scientists do the same thing when they speculate about the actual structure of atoms. It may surprise you, but no one has ever directly observed a single atom.

These necessary inferences and speculations imbue scientific knowledge with certain unavoidable characteristics. These characteristics, sometimes referred to as the "nature of science," are as follows:

1. Scientific knowledge is partially a product of human creative imagination.
2. Scientific knowledge is tentative.
3. Scientific knowledge is partially a function of human subjectivity.
4. Scientific knowledge necessarily involves a combination of observation and inference.

When you developed your model of the tube, the result was partially a function of your creativity and imagination. Your creativity and imagination differ from that of other individuals because of your past experiences and knowledge. Consequently, your model would not necessarily be the same as your friend's or another classmate's. Clearly, scientific knowledge has an element of subjectivity. None of these characteristics are a weakness of science. They are simply characteristics necessitated by the processes that scientists use to develop knowledge. What is especially important is that scientific knowledge is not a sterile set of objective and unchanging facts. Unfortunately, this is likely the view that was promoted in the science courses you have taken. We will be emphasizing throughout this text an approach to teaching science that is very different from what you probably experienced. We will be emphasizing an approach that is more consistent with the way science really is.

Look carefully at the picture of a fossil fragment in Figure 1.3. A fossil fragment is an actual fossil, but it is only a small portion of the complete organism. If you have a fossil fragment and would prefer to use it instead of our picture,

Figure 1.3   Fossil Fragment

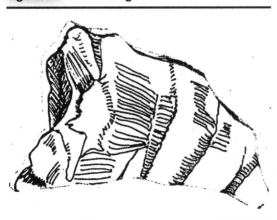

that would be fine. The only restriction is that you cannot use a fossil fragment from an organism you already know.

As carefully and accurately as possible, draw a picture of the fossil fragment. Create your drawing in the center of your sheet of paper. If you want to draw the picture on a larger or smaller scale, please note the scale (e.g., 2 ×). After finishing your drawing, please complete the rest of the fossil or organism. Fill in the missing parts of the fossil. When you have finished, ask yourself the following questions:

1. Where did the organism live?
2. How did the organism get its food requirements?
3. How did you decide how to fill in the missing parts?
4. On what basis did you decide where the organism lived?
5. On what basis did you decide how the organism satisfied its nutritional requirements?
6. Did you quickly decide what organism the fossil was from and complete your picture accordingly, or did you make totally unbiased inferences?

The activity you have just completed closely approximates what paleo-biologists do as part of their work. That is, they often collect fossil fragments and complete the organism from which it came. In this particular activity, you were given only a single fragment (actually just a diagram), whereas paleobiologists usually work with numerous fragments pieced together to form the complete organism. The dinosaur skeletons that you often see in museums have been con-structed from only various remains because the complete skeletal system is typ-ically not excavated. Nevertheless, the mental activity you performed is quite similar to what these scientists do as part of their work.

Take a moment to return to the list of four statements describing the nature of science. Which of these characteristics of science were illustrated in the fossil fragment activity? We think you would agree that both observation and infer-ence were involved. You made some very specific observations of the fossil frag-ment diagram while drawing your own picture, and then you inferred the appearance of the missing parts of the organism. While completing the diagram of the organism, your creative imagination was used. We say "creative imagi-nation" because you will find that your classmates' pictures are not identical to yours. Their pictures will differ from your picture as well as each other's because each of you expresses your creativity in different ways and each of you has a different level of background knowledge and experience. Figure 1.4 shows how a sixth-grade student completed the fossil fragment we pictured. We have also provided additional pictures in Figures 1.5 and 1.6 (fragment plus completed or-ganism) that were completed by other sixth graders when asked to perform the same task as you.

Obviously, the final pictures that were drawn have some element of sub-jectivity as well. Subjectivity was involved because the completed organism (just like the model for the internal contents of the tube) was different depending on

Figure 1.4 Depiction of Possible Organism from Which a Fossil Fragment Was Derived

1 cm

Figure 1.5 Fossil Fragment with Possible Source

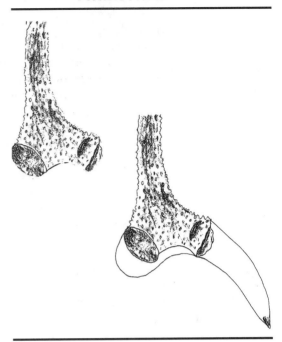

Figure 1.6 Fossil Fragment with Possible Organism from Which It Was Derived

the individual. Furthermore, it is because of the critical dependence on human beings that scientific knowledge is tentative. Therefore, all four statements about the nature of science were evident in the activity you just completed. In fact, there are several other aspects of the nature of science that we did not mention before that can now be noted.

Is There a Single Scientific Method?

Did you notice any differences between the fossil fragment activity and the tube and string activity? In the fossil fragment you simply observed and then inferred. Did you do anything else in the tube and string activity prior to inferring? The various strings were manipulated and you were asked to note the results. In a perfect world, you would have been able to manipulate the strings on our original tube prior to making your own. Nevertheless, we think you get the idea. With the tube and string activity there was an opportunity to do something to the object you were observing and note any consequences. You were able to develop some hypotheses and test your hypotheses. There was no opportunity to do this type of manipulation with the fossils. In each case, you were simulating what scientists actually do when collecting data and arriving at conclusions. However, the methods and approaches you used were clearly different. Contrary to popular belief, the sequence of processes and the specific processes used by scientists can vary from one investigation to another. *There is no single set and sequence of steps known as the scientific method.*

Although this idea is more related to science method or process, it would be a good idea to add it to the previous list of four statements describing the nature of science. The tube and string activity was more closely related to an experiment, whereas the fossil fragment activity was more descriptive. Our critical question now is, "Did either of these activities follow the scientific method?" The tube and string activity is, perhaps, close to what you were taught as *the* scientific method, but the fossil fragment is not even close. Although some scientific investigations follow procedures similar to the steps most likely listed in the science text you will be using, they are not representative of most scientific research. Scientists use a multitude of procedures and methods. These methods and procedures differ between and within scientific disciplines. The procedures and approaches that are used depend on the question to be answered.

How Objective Is Science?

Prior to beginning the fossil fragment activity, we mentioned you could use a fragment of your own. Our only restriction was that the fossil fragment not be from an organism you already knew. We wanted you to make inferences about the organism's structure, habitat, and nutrition without any bias. We wanted you to make totally objective observations. Let's consider the feasibility of our desire to have you make unbiased and objective observations and conclusions. Did you have some idea about the source of the pictured fossil fragment? That is, did you already know or try to guess the identity of the fossil fragment before beginning? Most people do this, and the subsequent completion of the organism and inferences about habitat and nutritional sources are actually biased by these preconceived ideas instead of being objective and based totally on empirical evidence. The same is true with scientists. In particular, the scientific theories and laws currently accepted by the scientific community guide scientists' data collection and interpretation. In fact, it is virtually impossible for humans to approach any situation without preconceived ideas and background knowledge. The same will be true of your students. This is an important idea but a difficult one to easily explain, so let's try an example. Read the following passage:

> The procedure is actually quite simple. First arrange things into different groups. Of course, one pile may be sufficient depending on how much there is to do. If you have to go somewhere else due to lack of facilities, that is the next step. Otherwise, you are pretty well set. It is important not to overdo things. That is, it is better to do too few things at once than too many. In the short run this may not seem important but complications can easily arise. A mistake can be expensive as well. At first, the whole procedure will seem complicated. Soon, however, it will become just another facet of life. It is difficult to foresee any end to the necessity for this task in the immediate future, but then one never can tell. After the procedure is completed, arrange the materials into different groups again. Then they can be put into their appropriate places. Eventually, they will be used once more and the whole cycle will have to be repeated. However, that is part of life. (Bransford & Johnson, 1972)

Do you know what the passage is describing or does it just seem like a paragraph of meaningless words and description? As you begin to speculate about the meaning of the paragraph, start reading it again. You have probably already started doing so. Did you notice as you read the paragraph again, with a particular idea in mind, that the individual words began to take on meanings consistent with your idea? Actually, the paragraph is about doing laundry. Now, read the paragraph again with doing laundry in mind, and notice how each of the words and phrases takes on a specific meaning that was not necessarily evident before. Suddenly, it is clear what the different groups and piles are. It also becomes clear what "lack of facilities" means.

Sometimes people think the passage is about life. If you read the paragraph with this in mind, the words and phrases take on still other meanings. The point we are trying to make is that our perceptions and interpretations of empirical data are influenced (i.e., biased) by our preconceptions of what we are seeing or investigating. Look at the diagram in Figure 1.7. Do you see a triangle between the three circular patterns?

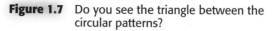

Figure 1.7 Do you see the triangle between the circular patterns?

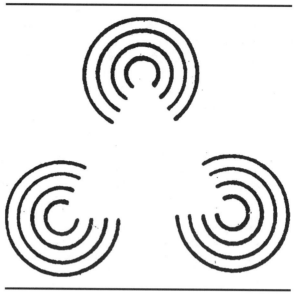

Actually, there is no triangle. Your brain perceptually completed the triangle because it expected to see a triangle between the curved lines. We do this all the time, whether we are pursuing scientific knowledge or just walking down the street. The influence of prior conceptions on observation means that science is not objective. It means that all observations are biased by our theories, laws, and beliefs. We can diagram the situation as shown in Figure 1.8.

The observations or data collected during scientific observations are influenced by our theories and laws (or beliefs) and these data then influence the development of scientific laws and theories. You can add this statement to the list describing the nature of science. You should now have six items on your list. This last characteristic may seem like a problem for scientists. After all, isn't scientific knowledge supposed to be based on empirical evidence and not on personal bias? On the other hand, if we do not have preconceptions about what we are looking at or going to see, would we see anything at all?

Have you ever driven into a supermarket parking lot immediately after a fresh snow? You are the first car there and the painted lines directing you where to park are not visible. How did it feel? Did you worry about whether you were driving in the lanes or over the parking spaces? Did you wonder where to park your car, or did you feel the exhilaration of being able to drive wherever you wanted? Once you or someone else is the first to park, everyone else parks his

Figure 1.8 **Relationship between Scientific Theories/Laws and Observations/Data**

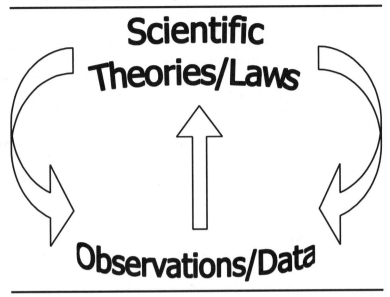

or her car relative to the first car. The point is that it is uncomfortable not having reference points. If you have ever driven through a whiteout during a snowstorm, you very clearly know what we mean.

If you carefully inspect the list of six statements concerning the nature of science, you may be led to the conclusion that all inferences derived from a set of data are okay. After all, the knowledge of science is tentative, subjective, biased, and so on. This is true up to a point. If the inferences are consistent with the data and previously developed knowledge and beliefs, highly varied inferences are fine. The key phrase in the last sentence is "and previously developed knowledge and beliefs." If you choose to do either the tube and string activity or fossil fragment activity with your students, there is at least some chance that one of your students will conclude there is a girl in the tube directing the movement of the strings or will complete an alien-like creature from the fossil fragment. Perhaps you felt a little playful during these activities and did the same. If this happens to occur in class, it will most undoubtedly create a humorous response from the other students. This is not a problem and can be used productively to illustrate additional characteristics of science and scientific knowledge.

In practice, scientists will usually select the simplest explanation for any phenomena and draw inferences that are consistent with prior knowledge and understandings. Although there may be a miniature girl in the tube, we have never noted a human being that small and there also exists a much simpler explanation for the movement of the strings. This is no different than the reason why scientists do not explain plants turning toward the sun as the result of a conscious decision by the plant. The chemical explanation is much simpler, as it does not require the existence of a complex nervous system in plants. Furthermore, nervous tissue has never been observed in plants. This may be true some day, but it is not considered true at the moment. With respect to the alien-like creature, scientists reconstruct organisms from fossil fragments using previously identified organisms as a reference point. Therefore, acceptance of an organism that looks nothing like anything we have ever seen before would be doubtful unless the amount of fragments was much greater than the missing pieces. What does this mean? It means that the subjectivity and creativity that are necessarily a part of the development of scientific knowledge are not unbridled but rather are within limits set by convention within the scientific community.

There is one more interesting thing we would like you to experience. Copy the following diagram shown in Figure 1.9 onto a blank sheet of paper. Cut out the pattern and fold it into a cube.

You should have a cube with the sides labeled *hat, bat, mat, cat,* and *fat.* One of the sides is not labeled because we did not want you to see the answer. Place the cube on your desk so that the blank side is face down. Using the observations you can make from the other sides, decide how the blank side is supposed to be labeled.

If you came up with *pat,* you correctly arrived at the intended answer. Think about the list of characteristics describing the nature of science and determine which of those items are illustrated by the cube activity. A good argument can be made that each of the six statements on your list is evident in the cube activity. Now let us consider how you arrived at the answer of *pat.* The intended pattern for the cube was that each side contains a word ending in *at,* and the first letter is a consonant beginning from the start of the alphabet. So, both *eat* and *oat* were not considered because *e* and *o* are vowels. Is this the pattern you found? Some individuals arrive at *pat* by deciding that all sides have a word ending in *at* and the actual words have a numerical relationship. *b* and *c* have no letters between them, *c, f,* and *h* have one letter between them, and *m* and *p* have two letters between them. Is this the pattern you used, or did you use an entirely different pattern and arrive at a label other than *pat*? Clearly, there are several different ways of getting the intended answer, and there is also the possibility of interpreting the data to arrive at an answer that is consistent with the data but that is incorrect. This is all consistent with how science proceeds, with the big exception being that in science we rarely get a chance to look on the bottom of the cube to find the answer.

We want you to make one final cube now. Use the diagram shown in Figure 1.10 to make a cube similar to the one made previously.

Figure 1.9   Diagram of a Word Cube

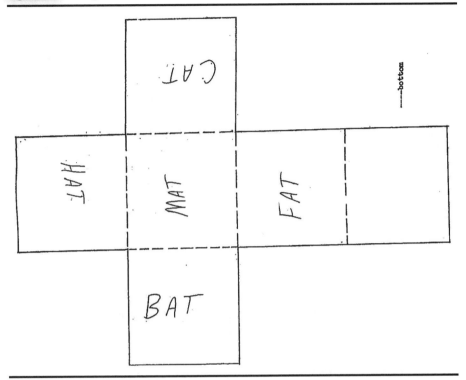

This cube should have the sides labeled with the numbers 1, 1, 2, 3, and 4. Again, one of the sides has no number on it, and this side should be placed face down on your table. As you did before, try to determine what was on the blank side before we removed the original number.

Most people decide that the blank side should have a 9. It actually was labeled with a 5. When we made this cube, we made it with the intention of there being no pattern. Interestingly, people will always find some pattern to predict what is on the blank side of the cube. Sometimes they even correctly identify the label as 5 for reasons other than what we used when creating the cube. It is quite possible to come to a solution of 5 if it is determined that all of the sides do not contain relevant data. For example, what would it mean if you decided that one of the sides with a 1 was not relevant to the solution? Then 5 becomes the solution for the blank side simply by following the sequence of numbers on the sides considered to have relevant data. When scientists make decisions concerning the inclusion of data, there is clearly some subjectivity. How are data that are very different (i.e., outliers or anomalous data) from the majority of data handled? Are they included or ignored as the consequence of

Figure 1.10   Diagram of a Number Cube

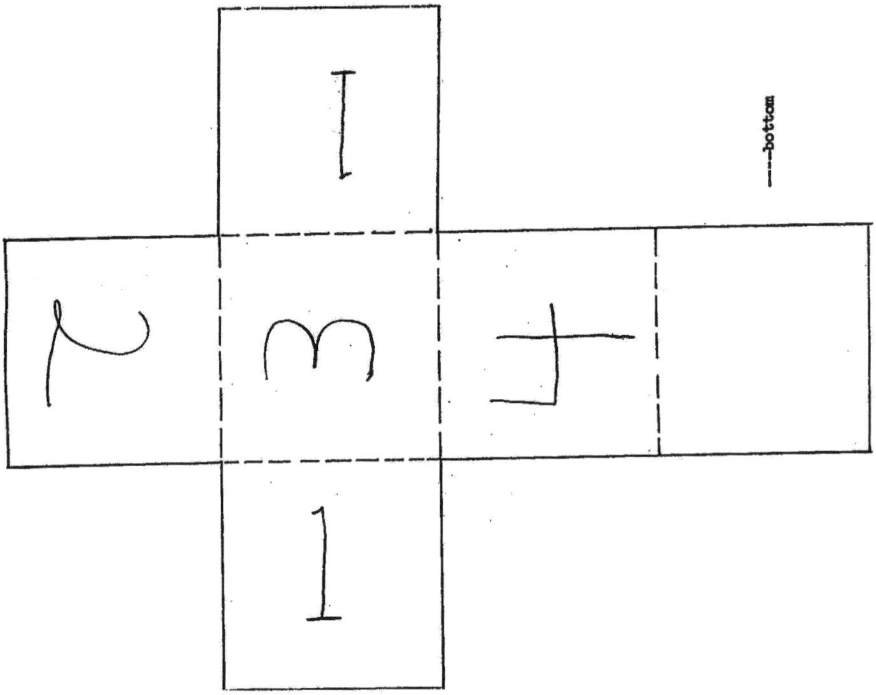

some type of error? Sometimes the deviant data turn out to be the most important. Selection of data for analysis is just another example of how creativity, inference, and subjectivity come into play when scientific knowledge is developed.

There is a more important lesson, however, to be learned from this last cube. The lesson is closely related to our previous discussion of how human beings always bring preconceptions, prior knowledge, and beliefs to every situation. It appears that one very strong characteristic among human beings is their assumption that a pattern does exist. Is it possible that there are no patterns in certain parts of nature? Perhaps; nevertheless, we always seem to be searching for patterns and eventually find them. On the other hand, would it be more correct to say that we *create* these patterns? You may feel that you already know the answer to this question. On the other hand, you may not. We want you to keep this question in mind as you proceed through this textbook. We feel that how you choose to answer this question will significantly impact how you conceptualize the teaching and learning of science.

(a)

(b)

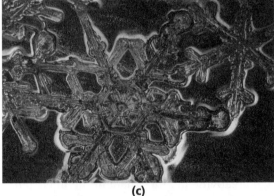

(c)

The shape and parts of a flower are examples of patterns found in nature. The veins found on a leaf are another example of a pattern found in nature. The crystalline formation found on magnified snowflakes is another example of a pattern found in nature.

A Few Words about Teaching the Nature of Science

At the beginning of this chapter, we mentioned that the instructional approach in this text may be very different from what you have previously experienced. Our approach is meant to be consistent with the way science actually is, as opposed to how it is most often presented in elementary schools. In addition, we have made every effort to use instructional approaches that research has shown to be effective. The same is true for this chapter's approach to teaching you about the nature of science. The various aspects of the nature of scientific knowledge (e.g., tentativeness, subjectivity, etc.) were explicitly addressed. The fossil activity could have been used to simply teach about fossils and the relationship between form and function. However, we explicitly included various aspects of the nature of science within the debriefing of the activity. It is very common for teachers to involve students in investigations similar to the ones we have without making the nature of science explicit. Often the assumption that students will necessarily reflect on what they have done and implicitly learn about the nature of science is made. This assumption has proven to be incorrect. If you want students to learn about the nature of science as they are also learning science concepts, you will need to include discussions about the nature of science with your discussions about the science concepts.

Summary

This chapter has attempted to answer the question, "What is science?" In doing so, we have characterized science as consisting of three basic components:

1. A body of knowledge
2. A method or process
3. A way of knowing or constructing reality

This last component (also commonly known as the "nature of science") was given the most emphasis because, unlike the other two, it is the most widely misunderstood, and its emphasis in current reforms permeates both subject matter and pedagogy. This enigmatic phrase most commonly refers to the values and assumptions inherent to scientific knowledge and its development. The values and assumptions to which we refer include tentativeness, unavoidable subjectivity, the importance of human creativity and imagination, the importance of both observation and inference, and a basis in empirical evidence. As scientists attempt to answer questions of identified importance, their observations and inferences are influenced by subject matter paradigms and personal biases held by the scientist as he or she grapples with limited data sets in an attempt to derive generalizations about the natural world.

Suggested Readings

American Association for the Advancement of Science. *Science for All Americans*. New York: Oxford University Press, 1990.

Bransford, J. D., & Johnson, M. K. (1972). Contextual prerequisites for understanding: Some investigations of comprehension and recall. *Journal of Verbal Learning and Verbal Behavior, 11,* 717–726.

Chalmers, Alan. F. *Science and Its Fabrication*. Minneapolis: University of Minnesota Press, 1990.

Chalmers, Alan. F. *What Is This Thing Called Science?* St. Lucia, Queensland, Australia: University of Queensland Press, 1991.

Driver, Rosalind, John Leach, Robin Millar, and Phil Scott. *Young People's Images of Science.* Buckingham, UK: Open University Press, 1996.

Gould, Stephen Jay. *The Mismeasure of Man.* New York: W. W. Norton and Company, 1981.

Horner, J. K., and P. A. Rubba. "The Myth of Absolute Truth." *The Science Teacher 45,* no. 1 (1978): 29–30.

Horner, J. K., and P. A. Rubba. "The Laws Are Mature Theories Fable." *The Science Teacher 46,* no. 2 (1979): 31.

Lederman, N. G., and F. Abd-El-Khalick. "Avoiding De-Natured Science: Activities That Promote Understandings of the Nature of Science." In *The Nature of Science in Science Education: Rationales and Strategies,* edited by W. F. McComas, 243–254. Dordrecht, Netherlands: Kluwer Academic Publishers, 1998.

Matthews, Michael R. *Science Teaching: The Role of History and Philosophy of Science.* New York: Routledge, 1994.

McComas, W. F. "Ten Myths of Science: Reexamining What We Think We Know About the Nature of Science." *School Science and Mathematics 96,* no. 1 (1996): 10–16.

National Research Council. *National Science Education Standards.* Washington, DC: National Academy Press, 1996.

Why Teach Science?

In the previous chapter we helped you clarify your definition of science and how it differs from other subjects studied in school. As you gain experience working in schools, you will find that time is at a premium and every teacher has a different opinion about which subjects are the most important for students to study. At the secondary level, where teachers specialize in particular subjects, the competition about the different areas is even greater. Even though you will most likely be teaching numerous subjects in a self-contained classroom, you will no doubt have to consider how much time to spend on each subject matter area relative to the others. One of the subjects you will be expected to teach is science. Although policy makers decide what to include in the required curriculum for a wide variety of reasons, we do believe that it is important, at this point, to carefully consider why science is part of the elementary curriculum. In addition to providing you with a summary of the current reform efforts in science education, this chapter will also help you develop some personal beliefs about why science should have a significant place in the required curriculum. Unless you are convinced that it is important, your attention to science may not be as dedicated as it could be. This chapter will assist you in developing some very compelling reasons for the teaching of science. If you are still skeptical about this conclusion and need some convincing, the contents of this chapter will do that as well.

Why Require Science for All Students?

Pretend for a moment that a parent has asked you why science is included in the third-grade curriculum. What would you say? Take a few minutes to make a list of your reasons, starting with the most important first. When we have asked this question of beginning and experienced teachers in the past, we have received the following reasons in no particular order of importance:

1. It helps teach critical thinking.
2. It develops problem-solving skills.
3. It develops analytical reasoning.
4. It helps students learn to think.
5. It develops logical thinking.
6. It will help students make better decisions.
7. Science is, increasingly, a part of our lives.
8. It helps to explain the world we live in.
9. Science is relevant to our daily lives.

How does your list compare to what we have listed? The first five items on our list are the most common reasons teachers, as well as others, provide as a justification for the inclusion of science in school curriculum at all levels, not just the elementary grades. It would not be at all surprising if some of these ideas showed up on the list you created. You may be interested to know that these are quite similar to the reasons that were used to justify the inclusion of science as part of the required curriculum in the late 1800s in the United States More specifically, the learning theory in vogue during that time was known as mental discipline (a.k.a. faculty psychology), which has its roots in the teachings of Plato and Aristotle. The theory postulates the existence of the following mental faculties that distinguish humans from the rest of the living world: reason, knowing, perception, feeling, free will, and memory, among others. The expression "the mind is a muscle" is the most concrete way to explain mental

Plato and Aristotle as depicted by the artist Raphael.

discipline theory and its implications for teaching and learning. Education amounted to exercising, training, and disciplining the mind. Just like a muscle, it was believed that the more we use our brains, the stronger our brains became. What was exercised in this theory of learning were the mental faculties we have listed. Therefore, the value of any particular subject matter in the school curriculum was directly related to its ability to exercise certain mental faculties and had nothing to do with relevancy or the curriculum's motivational aspects.

Plato believed that mental training or discipline in mathematics and philosophy was the best preparation for participation in the conduct of public affairs, a view that gave mathematics a longer history as a required subject in educational curricula than science. Greek and Latin continued to be required in school curricula long after their usefulness as languages had passed on the grounds that these languages improved thinking skills. Have you heard this before? Is the logic similar to what you used in justifying science to the questioning parent we mentioned before? At the turn of the century, scientific method was viewed as an effective way to develop the faculties of reason, knowing, and perception and science in general was advocated as an excellent way to develop the faculty of observation. In addition, those detailed laboratory notebooks you may have had to keep during your college courses were believed to be an excellent way to develop the faculties of observation, perception, reason, and memory at the turn of the century.

Psychologists, such as E. L. Thorndike, tested the validity of mental discipline theory in the early 1900s and found that drill or training in certain tasks did not strengthen the faculties associated with the tasks (e.g., training in estimating string lengths did not strengthen estimation skills, and developing neatness in math papers did not lead to neatness in other areas). Other studies showed that general intelligence was not influenced by students' courses of study in school (e.g., science versus humanities). More recently, researchers studying transfer of knowledge have consistently found that learning is situated, or specific, to certain contexts and does not readily transfer to other situations. Although mental discipline theory was debunked almost a century ago, we still see its remnants in movements calling for "back to the basics," cultural literacy, or those that extol the virtues of drill and practice. You will soon find that fads die hard in education.

What this means is that the justification of the inclusion of science in a curriculum on the grounds that it helps develop various higher-level thinking skills, such as logic, is erroneous. The view is intuitive but not correct. Just because your students learn to design an experiment within a science lesson does not mean that they will also approach other problems in their lives more systematically. Thus, we ask again, why should science be a required part of the curriculum at all grade levels? The truth of the matter is that science must be taught because it is the law. We are not being cynical. The lawmakers in power when such decisions were made valued science over other subjects such as Latin.

Okay, it's the law. Are there any other, more satisfying justifications you can provide to querying parents or to those students who wonder why they are being asked to learn science? Perhaps the most persistent phrase you will hear regarding the goal of contemporary science curriculum is "scientific literacy." In short, there is a fairly strong agreement among scientists, educators, and politicians that the primary goal of science education should be to produce a scientifically literate citizenry. The basis for this agreement is the recognition that science is becoming increasingly more intertwined with our daily lives and not being educated in science will condemn us to an overreliance on those who have such knowledge. That is, we will have to base our decisions on what such individuals tell us without any means of determining the validity of what we are told and, in a way, being ignorant is analogous to being in prison.

What Is Scientific Literacy?

Many definitions for scientific literacy are available, but perhaps the National Science Teachers Association (NSTA, 1982) said it best over 20 years ago in its statement about scientific and technological literacy. The NSTA defined the literate person as one who:

1. uses science concepts, process skills, and values in making responsible everyday decisions

2. understands how society influences science and technology as well as how science and technology influence society

3. understands that society controls science and technology through allocation of resources

4. recognizes the limitations as well as the usefulness of science and technology in advancing human welfare

5. knows the major concepts, hypotheses, and theories of science and is able to use them

6. appreciates science and technology for the intellectual stimulus they provide

7. understands that the generation of scientific knowledge depends on the inquiry process and on conceptual theories

8. distinguishes between scientific evidence and personal opinion

9. recognizes the origin of science and understands that scientific knowledge is tentative and subject to change as evidence accumulates

10. understands the applications of technology and the decisions entailed in the use of technology

11. has sufficient knowledge and experience to appreciate the worthiness of research in the use of technology

12. has a richer and more exciting view of the world as the result of science education

13. knows reliable sources of scientific and technological information and uses these sources in the process of decision making

Although the attributes listed by NSTA include science and the closely related field of technology, the list has served as a basis for more current statements about the aspects of scientific literacy. The list should also be familiar to you in terms of the definition of science provided in Chapter 1. The three components of science, body of knowledge, method/process, and way of knowing or constructing reality, are all visible in the thirteen components listed by NSTA. Can you identify which of the listed items are related to nature of science? In our opinion, items 2, 3, 4, 7, and 9 are closely related to what we described as the nature of science.

According to NSTA, the scientifically literate individual is a person with an in-depth understanding of scientific knowledge, the processes used to develop the knowledge, and the nature of science. Most heavily emphasized is the ability to use this knowledge to make informed decisions about the scientifically and technologically based issues that we face on a daily basis. Although there is no research to support that such decisions are improved by virtue of one's attainment of the items on NSTA's list, this list is a good starting point on the way to justifying science as part of the curriculum. In our minds, we think that science can be justified as part of the curriculum simply on the grounds that scientific knowledge empowers the individual and provides him or her with the freedom of not being overly reliant on others.

Contemporary Reform Efforts in Science Education

There have been three major attempts to reform science education during the past century, each driven by a different set of circumstances and goals. At the beginning of the 1900s, reform was primarily driven by concerns related to significant increases in industrialization, urbanization, and immigration. The second reform effort followed the Soviet Union's launching of *Sputnik* in 1957, with concerns related to national security being the primary driving force. By most accounts, neither of the previous reform efforts produced much change. The third and current effort to reform the quality of our nation's science education has been driven by economic concerns, as well as those related to our society's ever increasing reliance on science and technology. It is the current reform effort that has used scientific literacy for all students as a battle cry. There are actually two different reform efforts being masterminded by two separate scientific organizations, the American Association for the Advancement of Science and the National Academy of Sciences. The creation of the current reforms began quietly in 1985 when the American Association for the Advancement of Science (AAAS) began a long-term initiative, known as *Project 2061*, to reform K through 12 education in natural and social science, mathematics, and technology. The first publication of *Project 2061* appeared in 1989. The second reform effort in science education was initiated by the National Research Council (NRC) of the National Academy of Sciences. This reform effort is known as the *National Science Education Standards* (*NSES*) and was first published in 1996. What makes the current reform efforts different than past efforts is that they are strongly supported by two well-established scientific organizations, and it is for this reason that science educators are more optimistic about the potential effects of the current reforms.

Prior to our discussion of the two reform efforts, it is important for you to keep in mind that, for all the supposed confusion created by two separate efforts, the two reform efforts are quite parallel, with estimates of overlap being as high as 90 percent. As a teacher, you should consider the two sets of reform documents as resources that can guide your instruction and curriculum development almost interchangeably.

Project 2061

This project was launched in 1985 under the direction of F. James Rutherford. The project began during the last appearance of Halley's comet and the hope is that "today's young people will, as adults, greatly influence what life on earth will be like in 2061, the year Halley's comet next returns." Hence, the derivation of the project's name should be obvious. *Project 2061* is guided by six assertions:

1. Reform must be comprehensive and center on all children, grades, and subjects and represent a long-term commitment.
2. Curriculum reform should be dictated by our collective vision of the lasting knowledge and skills needed by our students and future citizens. Included in the knowledge and skills is a common core of learning and opportunities for learning to serve the particular needs and interests of individual students.
3. The common core of learning in science, mathematics, and technology should focus on science literacy, as opposed to preparation of students for careers in science. The core curriculum should emphasize connections among the natural and social sciences, mathematics, and technology. The connections with these areas and the arts, humanities, and vocational subjects should be clear as well.
4. School should teach less and teach it better. Superficial coverage of specialized terms and algorithms should be eliminated. This is the source of the oft-quoted phrase, "less is more."
5. Reform should promote equity in science, mathematics, and technology education, serving all students equally well.
6. Reform should allow more approaches for organizing instruction than are currently common. This diversity of approaches provides the flexibility necessitated by state and local circumstances and diversity in student backgrounds.

In 1989, *Project 2061* published its first document, *Science for All Americans*. This text set forth the vision of the project concerning the goals of science literacy. In 1993, *Benchmarks for Science Literacy* translated the vision of *Science for All Americans* into expectations (i.e., benchmarks) for what students should know and be able to do classified by grades K–2, 3–5, 6–8, and 9–12. These specified outcomes, along with the vision of *Science for All Americans*, will be of most value to you as a beginning teacher. The *Benchmarks*, in particular, will be used as a reference point whenever subject matter issues and decisions are discussed throughout the rest of this text. The total of 855 benchmarks is distributed into the following major and subordinate categories:

1. Nature of Science
   A. The Scientific World View
   B. Scientific Inquiry
   C. The Scientific Enterprise
2. The Nature of Mathematics
   A. Patterns and Relationships
   B. Mathematics, Science, and Technology
   C. Mathematical Inquiry
3. The Nature of Technology
   A. Technology and Science
   B. Design and Systems
   C. Issues in Technology
4. The Physical Setting
   A. The Universe
   B. The Earth
   C. Processes That Shape the Earth
   D. Structure of Matter
   E. Energy Transformations
   F. Motion
   G. Forces of Nature
5. The Living Environment
   A. Diversity of Life
   B. Heredity
   C. Cells
   D. Interdependence of Life
   E. Flow of Matter and Energy
   F. Evolution of Life
6. The Human Organism
   A. Human Identity
   B. Human Development
   C. Basic Functions
   D. Learning
   E. Physical Health
   F. Mental Health

7. Human Society
    A. Cultural Effects on Behavior
    B. Group Behavior
    C. Social Change
    D. Social Trade-Offs
    E. Political and Economic Systems
    F. Social Conflict
    G. Global Interdependence
8. The Designed World
    A. Agriculture
    B. Materials and Manufacturing
    C. Energy Sources and Use
    D. Communication
    E. Information Processing
    F. Health and Technology
9. The Mathematical World
    A. Numbers
    B. Symbolic Relationships
    C. Shapes
    D. Uncertainty
    E. Reasoning
10. Historical Perspectives
    A. Displacing the Earth from the Center of the Universe
    B. Uniting the Heavens and Earth
    C. Relating Matter and Energy and Time and Space
    D. Extending Time
    E. Moving the Continents
    F. Understanding Fire
    G. Splitting the Atom
    H. Explaining the Diversity of Life
    I. Discovering Germs
    J. Harnessing Power
11. Common Themes
    A. Systems
    B. Models
    C. Constancy and Change
    D. Scale

12. Habits of Mind
   A. Values and Attitudes
   B. Computation and Estimation
   C. Manipulation and Observation
   D. Communication Skills
   E. Critical-Response Skills

The specific content of the expected outcomes should be invaluable in your lesson planning and curriculum development. We strongly encourage you to obtain a copy of the *Benchmarks for Science Literacy* or download a copy from the AAAS website (i.e., www.AAAS.org). The third published aspect of the project is *Resources for Science Literacy: Professional Development* (1997). This book is a professional development tool that is designed to help educators develop curricula, select materials and activities, design instruction, and plan for assessment. The curriculum analysis tool included in this resource is highlighted in Chapter 7. In 1998, the project published *Blueprints for Reform,* a text designed to focus on systemic reform of education. Twelve expert panels were assembled throughout the nation to prepare blueprint papers on all aspects of the education system that must change to accommodate the curriculum reforms proposed by *Project 2061.* Blueprint papers for the following areas are included: equity, policy, finance, research, school

A stack of several of the books published by AAAS.

organization, curriculum connections, materials and technology, assessment, teacher education, higher education, family and community, and business and industry. In addition to those already mentioned the project has also published *Designs for Science Literacy,* which assists educators in the development of local curricula, *Curriculum Materials Resource,* which is a companion to *Resources for Science Literacy: Professional Development,* and the *Atlas of Science Literacy.*

Again, for detailed information concerning specified student outcomes (i.e., benchmarks) or any other information related to *Project 2061,* we strongly recommend that you view AAAS's website at www.AAAS.org or write to *Project 2061,* AAAS, 1333 H Street, NW, Washington, DC 20005.

National Science Education Standards

The origin of the *National Science Education Standards* (*NSES*) can be traced back to the publication of the mathematics standards by the National Council for Teachers of Mathematics (NCTM) in 1989. The National Science Teachers Association (NSTA) began to develop its own science standards but realized that, because of the diversity of the science education community, it could not continue to lead the development of national standards. Any standards that NSTA produced would be politically viewed as company rather than industry standards. In May 1991, the National Research Council (NRC) of the National Academy of Sciences was asked by the NSTA board of directors, the presidents of several scientific societies, the U.S. secretary of education, the assistant director for education and human resources of the National Science Foundation, and the co-chairs of the National Education Goals Panel to assume responsibility for the development of science education standards. In January 1996, the NRC published the *National Science Education Standards.*

At first glance, it appears that the *NSES* is a more comprehensive endeavor than *Project 2061,* but this is simply because the *NSES* is all placed in a single volume and most individuals do not know that *Project 2061* has numerous documents other than the *Benchmarks.* Both reform efforts have attempted to provide a vision for scientific literacy and a framework for the realization of the vision. The goals for school science specified in the *NSES* are to educate all students so that they are able to (1) use scientific principles and processes appropriately in making personal decisions; (2) experience the richness and excitement of knowing about and understanding the natural world; (3) increase their economic productivity; and (4) engage intelligently in public discourse and debate about matters of scientific and technological concern.

The *NSES* is based on the following four basic principles:

1. Science is for all students.
2. Learning science is an active process.
3. School science reflects the intellectual and cultural traditions that characterize the practice of contemporary science.
4. Improving science education is part of systemic education reform.

Two teachers use the National Science Education Standards to plan their curriculum.

A total of six sets of standards is delineated in the *NSES* and comprises the overwhelming majority of the published document:

1. *Science Teaching Standards* set forth criteria for making judgments about the quality of science instruction.
2. *Standards for Professional Development for Teachers of Science* set forth criteria for making judgments about the quality of professional development programs for science teachers.
3. *Assessment in Science Education* offers criteria for making judgments about the quality of assessment practices.
4. *Science Content Standards* outline what students should know, understand, and be able to do in natural science.
5. *Science Education Program Standards* set forth criteria for judging the quality of and conditions for school science programs.
6. *Science Education System Standards* provide criteria for judging the performance of the components of the science education system responsible for providing schools with the financial and intellectual resources necessary to achieve the vision delineated by the standards in the aforementioned areas.

As mentioned before, the *NSES* places in a single volume what *Project 2061* is attempting to do in multiple publications. As a beginning teacher, one set of standards that you may find to be particularly useful is the teaching standards. Such standards are not included in any of the *Project 2061* publications. A summary of these standards follows:

A. Teachers of science plan an Inquiry-Based Science Program for their students. In doing this, teachers:

1. Develop a framework of yearlong and short-term goals for students.
2. Select science content and adapt and design curricula to meet the interests, knowledge, understandings, abilities, and experiences of students.
3. Select teaching and assessment strategies that support the development of student understanding and nurture a community of science learners.
4. Work together as colleagues within and across disciplines and grade levels.

B. Teachers of science guide and facilitate learning. In doing this, teachers:

1. Focus and support inquiries while interacting with students.
2. Orchestrate discourse among students about scientific ideas.
3. Challenge students to accept and share responsibility for their own learning.
4. Recognize and respond to student diversity and encourage all students to participate fully in science learning.
5. Encourage and model the skills of scientific inquiry, as well as the curiosity, openness to new ideas and data, and skepticism that characterize science.

C. Teachers of science engage in ongoing assessment of their teaching and of student learning. In doing this, teachers:

1. Use multiple methods and systematically gather data about student understanding and ability.
2. Analyze assessment data to guide teaching.
3. Guide students in self-assessment.
4. Use student data, observations of teaching, and interactions with colleagues to reflect on and improve teaching practice.
5. Use student data, observations of teaching, and interactions with colleagues to report student achievement and opportunities to learn to students, teachers, parents, policy makers, and the general public.

D. Teachers of science design and manage learning environments that provide students with the time, space, and resources needed for learning science. In doing this, teachers:

1. Structure the time available so that students are able to engage in extended investigations.

2. Create a setting for student work that is flexible and supportive of science inquiry.

3. Ensure a safe working environment.

4. Make the available science tools, materials, media, and technological resources accessible to students.

5. Identify and use resources outside the school.

6. Engage students in designing the learning environment.

E. Teachers of science develop communities of science learners that reflect the intellectual rigor of scientific inquiry and the attitudes and social values conducive to science learning. In doing this, teachers:

1. Display and demand respect for the diverse ideas, skills, and experiences of all students.

2. Enable students to have a significant voice in decisions about the content and context of their work and require students to take responsibility for the learning of all members of the community.

3. Nurture collaboration among students.

4. Structure and facilitate ongoing formal and informal discussion based on a shared understanding of rules of scientific discourse.

5. Model and emphasize the skills, attitudes, and values of scientific inquiry.

F. Teachers of science actively participate in the ongoing planning and development of the school science program. In doing this, teachers:

1. Plan and develop the school science program.

2. Participate in decisions concerning the allocation of time and other resources to the science program.

3. Participate fully in planning and implementing professional growth and development strategies for themselves and their colleagues.

Although the teaching standards are extremely valuable for all teachers, attention is typically placed on the content standards in the *NSES*. This is the set of standards most comparable to what is found in the *Benchmarks for Science Literacy*. To ease your initial comparison efforts, the manner in which the *NSES* organizes the content standards follows.

I. Grades K–12

A. Unifying Concepts and Processes

1. Systems, order, and organization

2. Evidence, models, and explanation

3. Change, constancy, and measurement

4. Evolution and equilibrium

5. Form and function

II. Grades K–4

    A. Science as Inquiry

        1. Abilities necessary to do scientific inquiry

        2. Understandings about scientific inquiry

    B. Physical Science

        1. Properties of objects and materials

        2. Position and motion of objects

        3. Light, heat, electricity, and magnetism

    C. Life Science

        1. Characteristics of organisms

        2. Life cycles of organisms

        3. Organisms and environments

    D. Earth and Space Science

        1. Properties of earth materials

        2. Objects in the sky

        3. Changes in earth and sky

    E. Science and Technology

        1. Abilities of technological design

        2. Understandings about science and technology

        3. Abilities to distinguish between natural objects and objects made by humans

    F. Science in Personal and Social Perspectives

        1. Personal health

        2. Characteristics and changes in populations

        3. Types of resources

        4. Changes in environments

        5. Science and technology in local challenges

    G. History and nature of science

        1. Science as a human endeavor

III. Grades 5–8

    A. Science as Inquiry

        1. Abilities necessary to do scientific inquiry

        2. Understandings about scientific inquiry

    B. Physical Science

        1. Properties and changes of properties in matter

        2. Motions and forces

        3. Transfer of energy

C. Life Science
1. Structure and function in living systems
2. Reproduction and heredity
3. Regulation and behavior
4. Populations and ecosystems
5. Diversity and adaptations of organisms

D. Earth and Space Science
1. Structure of the earth system
2. Earth's history
3. Earth in the solar system

E. Science and Technology
1. Abilities of technological design
2. Understandings about science and technology

F. Science in Personal and Social Perspectives
1. Personal health
2. Populations, resources, and environments
3. Natural hazards
4. Risks and benefits
5. Science and technology in society

G. History and Nature of Science
1. Science as a human endeavor
2. Nature of science
3. History of science

IV. Grades 9–12
A. Science as Inquiry
1. Abilities necessary to do scientific inquiry
2. Understandings about scientific inquiry

B. Physical Science
1. Structure of atoms
2. Structure and properties of matter
3. Chemical reactions
4. Motions and forces
5. Conservation of energy and increase in disorder
6. Interactions of energy and matter

C. Life Science
1. The cell
2. Molecular basis of heredity

    3. Biological evolution

    4. Interdependence of organisms

    5. Matter, energy, and organization in living systems

    6. Behavior of organisms

D. Earth and Space Science

    1. Energy in the earth system

    2. Geochemical cycles

    3. Origin and evolution of the earth system

    4. Origin and evolution of the universe

E. Science and Technology

    1. Abilities of technological design

    2. Understandings about science and technology

F. Science in Personal and Social Perspectives

    1. Personal and community health

    2. Population growth

    3. Natural resources

    4. Environmental quality

    5. Natural and human-induced hazards

    6. Science and technology in local, national, and global challenges

G. History and Nature of Science

    1. Science as a human endeavor

    2. Nature of scientific knowledge

    3. Historical perspectives

As we mentioned following our summary of *Project 2061,* specific details about what the various standards actually expect of students have not been presented here. We strongly encourage you to obtain a copy of the *NSES* by downloading a copy from its website at www.NAS.edu or writing to National Academy Press, 2101 Constitution Avenue, NW, Lockbox 285, Washington, DC 20055.

Common Themes in the Reforms

You may be feeling a bit overwhelmed by all that is included in the two primary science reform documents. We are sure you are well aware that such documents exist in the other subject areas you will be teaching as well (e.g., mathematics). Fortunately, there are some common themes that transcend the various reform documents that may make you feel a bit more at ease. These themes are important and rather global in nature. They are general statements and characterizations of what is desired and known relative to teaching, learning, curriculum, and assessment, as opposed to specific content included in the reform documents. The common themes are:

1. constructivism
2. integration
3. nature of science (or nature of other subject matter area)
4. problem solving
5. critical thinking
6. relevancy
7. students' interests
8. communication
9. alternative and authentic assessment

We have already discussed the nature of science in detail in Chapter 1, and you should see it again throughout the instructional examples presented in this text. You will also see numerous references to the remaining eight ideas in the list we have provided. *Constructivism* and *integration* are, perhaps, two of the most commonly cited ideas when differences between current and past reforms are discussed. They are also two of the most widely misunderstood aspects of the current reforms, and we think it would be a good idea to quickly clarify the perspective we have taken in this text.

Constructivism is actually not a new idea. It has its roots in the writings of Giambattista Vico in 1710. It has been referred to as a teaching approach, learning theory, and philosophy. Herein lies the first misconception about constructivism. Technically it is an epistemology, which is a branch of philosophy usually referred to as the theory of knowledge. It is concerned with the nature and limits of human knowledge. More specifically, epistemology is concerned with the nature of cognitive processes, sources of human knowledge, and methods of validating ideas. Piaget is probably the most well-known contemporary constructivist. Theoretical notions and jargon aside, what constructivism boils down to is the idea that students, as well as all humans, actively construct their understandings of the world and these constructions are significantly influenced by prior knowledge, beliefs, attitudes, and experiences. According to the constructivist viewpoint, we as humans are limited in our ability to know reality in any absolute sense and are limited to our mental constructions of the world in which we live. If you need a biological description, everything that enters our brains as electrochemical impulses is somehow transformed (i.e., constructed) into the images, sensations, and knowledge we possess. All of the ideas concerning the nature of science and the development of scientific knowledge presented in the preceding chapter are examples of the constructivist perspective.

The first misconception about constructivism is that it is a teaching approach, which implies that students' construction of knowledge depends on whether the teacher uses the correct teaching approach. In actuality, students will construct knowledge whether you lecture or provide them with a hands-on

A fifth grade teacher checks in on a group of students as they work together on an experiment.

activity. The key point is whether you accommodate the fact that students are always actively constructing knowledge into your teaching approach. For the teacher, this elevates the importance of finding out what students know about a topic in advance and of consistently monitoring their understanding as instruction proceeds. It also means that if a student thinks that all gases are lighter than air, simply telling the student that he or she is wrong will not be particularly effective. The student needs to experience the behavior of a gas that is not lighter than air (e.g., carbon dioxide) so he or she can reevaluate the validity of such a view and actively revise his or her knowledge.

Closely related to the first misconception is the view that all students' answers and views are acceptable. It is believed, therefore, that the teacher should not intervene when a student arrives at a conclusion inconsistent with current scientific knowledge. The logic used is that since none of us can know reality in any absolute sense, it would be incorrect to presume one perception is any more valid than any other perception. In short, anything goes. This is not the message of constructivism. Different views of reality are not equally useful. The correct view, in a constructivist framework, is the one that is most consistent with our experiences and prior knowledge. Consequently, the teacher is perfectly justified to intervene, but the intervention should be one that places the student in a situation that causes him or her to reconsider what he or she believes. You will notice this particular view of constructivism in the instructional examples provided throughout the remainder of this text.

Integration is a second landmark of current reforms and it is as misunderstood as constructivism. To many, integration refers to the total blurring of distinctions among the various subject matter disciplines. For example, students would not know whether they were learning mathematics, science, art, or language arts. The integrated curriculum is typically organized around a real-world problem to be investigated. The philosophy behind the approach is that real-world problems are not solely concerned with one discipline or another, so there is no need to arbitrarily divide the school curriculum into the traditional subject matter areas. The goal is to achieve a school curriculum that realistically reflects the real world. However, this perception of the real world could not be further from the truth. The expansion of knowledge has necessitated specialization. Without exception, every area of study has consistently been divided and subdivided over time. These divisions may be arbitrary distinctions, but this does not argue against their necessity. There is simply too much knowledge for any one individual to know. Consequently, in the real world, there are clearly specialists, and research in science involves teams of individuals with varying specialties. The same is true in the business world. In short, the basic assumption of those who support true integration is simply inaccurate. There are also many other theoretical and practical problems associated with this type of integration. You may also be interested to know that research on the effectiveness of true integration does not support its effectiveness relative to discipline-based instruction. We say true integration, because many use the word imprecisely and are actually talking about interdisciplinary instruction.

Interdisciplinary instruction is an approach that makes clear the interactions and connections among the various disciplines, while remaining aware of the differences between mathematics, science, art, and literature. The perspective provided in the instructional examples presented in this text supports an interdisciplinary view and we think such a view is most feasible for the elementary teacher. Consequently, you will notice a strong attempt to make connections between science instruction and instruction in language arts without any attempt to blur the distinctions between the two disciplines.

Specific Comparisons between the Science Reforms

Take a few moments to review our summaries of *Project 2061* and the *National Science Education Standards.* List any specific similarities or differences that you can see, keeping in mind that we have only provided an overview of each, with few specifics. Were they more similar than different or more different than similar? Perhaps the clearest difference between the two is that the *NSES* attempts to provide standards for content as well as the rest of the educational system in a single volume, whereas *Project 2061* tries to present the same information across several publications. One advantage that the *NSES* clearly has over *Project 2061* is its clear delineation of teaching standards. *Project 2061* has a short section on science teaching in *Science for All Americans*, but it is not as extensive as the *NSES*. You may have also noticed that the content standards of each are organized a bit differently. *Project 2061* specifies four grade-level clusters whereas *NSES* specifies only three. In each case, what is listed is what students should know and be able to do upon completion of the highest grade level within each cluster. If you teach second grade, *Project 2061* may be more useful to you since it has a K–2 grade cluster, whereas the *NSES* has a K–4 cluster. You may also have noticed that the *NSES* uses grade levels to organize its content standards, whereas *Project 2061* uses general topic areas to organize its standards. There is probably no specific advantage of one organizing approach versus the other. Again, let us remind you that the specific learning outcomes were not presented in our summary. To learn more about the specific standards or benchmarks you will need to get a copy of the documents. *Project 2061* has performed a systematic comparison between the two reform documents relative to the specified content standards and has determined that there is an overlap exceeding 90 percent. So, if you remain unsure about which reform documents to use, either one will probably suffice in terms of what students are expected to know and do.

　　You may have noticed within the language of the *NSES* content standards the use of phrases such as "abilities necessary to" and "understandings about." Within the actual standards, counterparts of this language take the form of "know that" and "be able to." Similar phrases are used in the stems of the *Project 2061 Benchmarks*. This language is not used loosely and is critically important to the message of the *NSES* and *Project 2061*. Both of the reform documents specify two types of learning outcomes for students. These are what *students should know* as well as what *students should be able to do*. Although the content standards of the two reform efforts overlap much more than they differ, the most significant difference between the two is with respect to this language use when it comes to scientific inquiry. It is important to note at this point that scientific inquiry is used in three different ways within the reform documents. It is viewed as a teaching approach, a set of skills and processes to be performed, and as a cognitive outcome. Both *NSES* and *Project 2061* advocate the use of an inquiry-oriented approach to instruction. This approach is consistent with constructivism and the goals advocating the importance of problem solving and critical thinking. The two reforms also specify that students should know about scientific inquiry (i.e., the cognitive outcome). However, the *NSES* is more ambitious because it also expects all students to be able to *do* scientific inquiry. That is, the *NSES* expects all students to be able to develop a research question, develop an appropriate research design, carry out the design, and report the results of an independent scientific investigation. Although *Project 2061* values such experiences, it only specifies that students should know about inquiry as a learning outcome.

A Few Words about the Teaching of Scientific Inquiry

The teaching of scientific inquiry in terms of skills and processes to be performed is rather straightforward and has been a goal of science instruction for many years. Students need to see these skills performed and modeled by the teacher, and they then need plenty of opportunities to practice what they have learned how to do in many different contexts. However, the knowledge *about* inquiry is an instructional objective that is emphasized more in the current reforms than ever before and it presents some of the same problems we mentioned regarding the teaching of the nature of science. In particular, it is not uncommon for teachers to assume that if students are performing scientific inquiry they will necessarily reflect on what they have done and implicitly learn about inquiry. For example, if students perform an investigation that includes a control group, it is assumed that students will also come to know the importance of a control group to experimental design. It is assumed that if students perform scientific investigations that are designed in a variety of ways and never follow the same procedures, then they will implicitly learn that there is no single scientific method. In reality, this is not what occurs. The situation is no different than breathing. You have been breathing all your life, but can you necessarily explain the mechanics of breathing? Probably not, unless your area of interest is life science. If you want your students to learn about inquiry, you will need to explicitly address understandings *about* inquiry while your students are *doing* inquiry. Simply put, doing is not the same as understanding. However, it is our opinion that students are much more likely to do a better job of doing if they understand something about what it is they are doing.

Instructional outcomes pertaining to knowledge about inquiry have the same requirements as instructional outcomes pertaining to the nature of science. Both of these topics and ideas need to be explicitly addressed during instruction. Experiencing science will not necessarily promote understandings of the nature of science or scientific inquiry. As you read through the various lessons in the chapters that follow, try to keep in the back of your mind those places where understandings about scientific inquiry and the nature of science could be incorporated into what we have presented.

Summary

Our discussion of scientific literacy and how it relates to the contemporary needs of your students and future voting citizens should have helped you begin the process of developing a vested interest in the teaching of science in the elementary school grades. We think you should see its importance above and beyond preparing your students for the science courses they will take in middle school.

You are preparing your students for all of life, not just to pass a course they will take in future grades.

Although it may be reassuring to note that your views are supported by current reform documents, you may very well be wondering why you should know anything about these reform efforts because the state in which you work will no doubt have its own standards for you to follow. Although many states have chosen to develop their own content standards, they have used one or both of the national reform efforts as a guiding framework. Consequently, you will not find a significant difference between what your state requires and what is specified in either of these reform documents. In some states the deviation may be more than others, but there is a general consistency. Knowledge of *NSES* and *Project 2061* will be very useful to you as it will best prepare you to work in any state across the nation. A complete listing of publications currently available from *NSES* and *Project 2061* can be found at the end of this chapter. If nothing else, the reform documents will help you make decisions concerning the appropriateness of specific learning outcomes at the grade level that you teach. Furthermore, we will connect all learning outcomes specified in the latter sections of this text to both reform efforts whenever possible.

Suggested Readings

AAAS. *Atlas of Science Literacy.* Washington, DC: American Association for the Advancement of Science and National Science Teachers Association, 2001.

AAAS. *Benchmarks for Science Literacy.* New York: Oxford University Press, 1993.

AAAS. *Blueprints for Reform.* New York: Oxford University Press, 1998.

AAAS. *Designs for Science Literacy.* New York: Oxford University Press, 2001.

AAAS. *Resources for Science Literacy: Professional Development.* New York: Oxford University Press, 1997.

AAAS. *Science for All Americans.* New York: Oxford University Press, 1989.

National Research Council. *Classroom Assessment and the National Science Education Standards.* Washington, DC: National Academy Press, 2001.

National Research Council. *Inquiry and the National Science Education Standards: A Guide for Teaching and Learning.* Washington, DC: National Academy Press, 2000.

National Research Council. *National Science Education Standards.* Washington, DC: National Academy Press, 1996.

National Research Council. *Selecting Instructional Material: A Guide for K–12 Science.* Washington, DC: National Academy Press, 1999.

National Science Teachers Association. *Science-technology-society: Science Education of the 1980s.* Washington, DC: Author, 1982.

Setting the Stage

It is often said that, "If you don't plan, you are planning to fail." The essence of this axiom is that it is critically important for teachers to carefully consider what they are to teach and the best way to teach it. Students are as different from each other as night and day and these differences significantly impact the sense they make out of the lessons you present. Your job, as impossible as it may seem, is to maximize learning in all students. This task is daunting but not impossible. It involves serious consideration of the depth and breadth of what is to be taught (within the constraints of state and local guidelines), the context of instruction, instructional approach(es) to be used, materials and activities to be used, and how learning is to be assessed. Many of these decisions should be made before the students enter your room. We do realize that the learning and behavior of students are difficult to predict, but we also realize that it is much easier to shift gears in front of a class than it is to create something from scratch. This section will help you be better prepared for the challenges that you will face in the classroom.

Creating a Positive Physical and Emotional Environment

Flowers Are Red

(Harry Chapin, 1978)

The little boy went first day of school
He got some crayons and started to draw
He puts colors all over the paper
For colors was what he saw
And the teacher said . . . What you doin' young man
I'm paintin' flowers he said
She said . . . It's not the time for art young man
And anyway flowers are green and red

There's a time for everything young man
And a way it should be done
You've got to show concern for everyone else
For you're not the only one
And she said . . .
Flowers are red young man
Green leaves are green
There's no need to see flowers any other way
Than the way they always have been seen

But the little boy said . . .
There are so many colors in the rainbow
So many colors in the morning sun
So many colors in the flower and I see every one

Well the teacher said . . . You're sassy
There's ways that things should be
And you'll paint flowers the way they are
So repeat after me . . .

And she said . . .
Flowers are red young man
Green leaves are green
There's no need to see flowers any other way
Than the way they always have been seen

But the little boy said . . .
There are so many colors in the rainbow
So many colors in the morning sun
So many colors in the flower and I see every one

The teacher put him in a corner
She said . . . It's for your own good . . .
And you won't come out 'til you get it right
And are responding like you should
Well finally he got lonely
Frightened thoughts filled his head
And he went up to the teacher
And this is what he said . . . and he said

Flowers are red, green leaves are green
There's no need to see flowers any other way
Than the way they always have been seen

How do the words to the song "Flowers Are Red" make you feel as a student and as a future teacher? Keep these feelings in mind as you read this chapter.

Think back to when you were in elementary school. There were probably some classes that you liked a lot and others that you did not care for at all. Try to remember a specific classroom experience that you enjoyed or found particularly interesting. What was the room like? What were students doing? What was your teacher doing? Take out a sheet of paper and make a list of everything you can remember about this experience.

Now, try to recall an elementary classroom experience that was less enjoyable. Again, recall what the room was like and what the students and teacher were doing. Make a list of all of the details that you can recall about this less positive experience. Look at what you have written on your two lists. They contain items that contribute to the physical and emotional environments of the classroom. See if you can pick out the items in your lists that contribute to the physical environment. Do your lists include physical details of the classroom? You probably remember details like the layout of the room, how the seating was arranged, whether it was dark or well lighted, and so on. What about the emotional setting? Did you list the teacher's instructional style and tone when addressing students, the freedom of students to express ideas and ask questions, and the noise level of the class?

In the classroom, the combination of physical and emotional elements creates either positive or negative learning experiences. Teaching and learning do not happen in a vacuum. They are strongly influenced by the environment in which they occur. In fact, the *National Science Education Standards* includes six standards for designing and managing learning environments (as outlined in Figure 3.1). Now there may be some things in your classroom that you have no control over, such as placement and size of windows, types of desks, and number of electrical outlets. However, there are ways to deal with these limitations.

Figure 3.1   National Science Education Teaching Standards Related to the Learning Environment

Teaching Standard D

Teachers of science design and manage learning environments that provide students with the time, space, and resources needed for learning science. In doing this, teachers

- Structure the time available so that students are able to engage in extended investigations.

- Create a setting for student work that is flexible and supportive of science inquiry.

- Ensure a safe working environment.

- Make the available science tools, materials, media, and technological resources accessible to students.

- Identify and use resources outside the school.

- Engage students in designing the learning environment.

There are also ways to help maintain a balanced and healthy emotional classroom setting. This chapter offers practical suggestions for creating a supportive environment in which your students can learn.

In this chapter, you will learn how to create a supportive environment in your classroom by making the most of the physical setting, learning when and how to use whole group and small group instruction, and learning how to extend classroom facilities and learning experiences beyond the classroom.

Arranging the Classroom

If you were to visit an elementary school, you would probably notice that all of the classrooms are different, even in schools where the basic floor plan and furniture are identical. Each classroom reflects the preferences and teaching style of the teacher who "lives there." Furthermore, on any particular day, the layout of a classroom may change, depending on the unit or lesson. This is the way it should be because there is no single floor plan that is optimal for every teaching situation. One important aspect of good teaching is the ability to make modifications to the layout of the classroom in order to facilitate learning.

Choosing a Classroom Design

Consider the classroom layout in Figure 3.2. Suppose that you are a new teacher and this is the layout of your classroom. This room is equipped with typical elementary classroom furnishings, including twenty-four student desks, a teacher's desk, a round table with six chairs, six computers, a blackboard, a bulletin board, a folding table, and a bookshelf. The desks are arranged in four single rows, facing the front of the room where the teacher's desk is located. All of the other furnishings are located along the perimeter of the room. What do you think of your new classroom? Do you want to make any changes? Before you do anything, you should ask yourself, "What do I want to teach here and how can I arrange this room to teach most effectively?" The answers to these two questions determine the optimal classroom design.

Alternative Classroom Designs

Several experienced elementary school teachers created an alternative to the classroom design shown in Figure 3.2. The teachers arranged the classroom to maximize student learning and to support different teaching methods. Figures 3.3–3.5 are examples of their classroom designs.

Classroom Demonstrations. Figure 3.3 is the classroom of a teacher who prefers to do science demonstrations before having the students do individual inquiry activities. Therefore, she keeps the desks in double rows and moves the folding

Figure 3.2 Traditional Classroom Layout

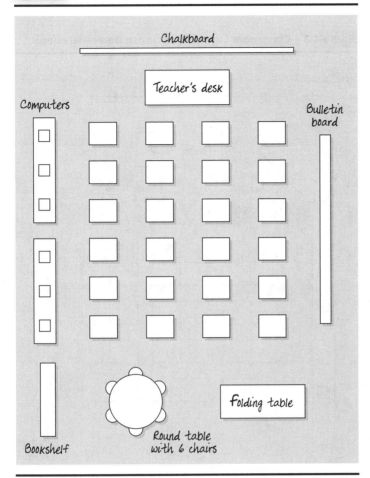

Choosing a Classroom Design

Classroom design can influence student learning and behavior. From a multicultural perspective, a recent study documented that within certain cultures boys initiate more interactions with peers than girls during classroom activities. Alternatively, in some other cultures, students do not interact at all even when placed in working groups. Being aware of acceptable culturally based behaviors is critically important. If you want to enhance student interactions, the arrangement of the classroom should facilitate student interaction and movement around the room. The more students intermingle with *all* of their classmates the more they will likely interact and overcome culturally based conventions. However, it is also important to keep in mind that some cultural values are so strong that it would be inappropriate to expect students to ignore them.

BOX 3.1

Issues in Diversity

Figure 3.3   Classroom Layout for Science Demonstrations

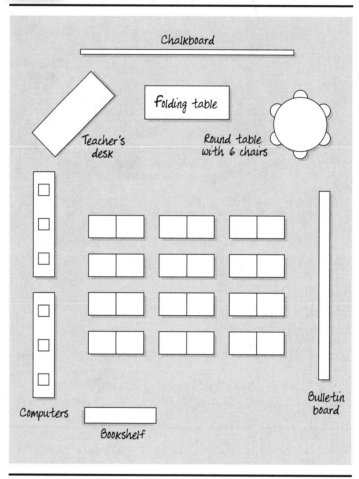

and round tables to the front of the room. This arrangement allows for maximum student visibility and sufficient surface area to do the demonstration. Her own desk is moved out of the way of the demonstration area but is still kept in the front of the room. She said that many of her demonstrations change as time passes and she likes to sit off to the side at her desk and observe the reactions of her students as these changes take place.

Hands-On Activities. Figure 3.4 is a classroom designed by a teacher who uses frequent hands-on science activities and experiments. He creates clusters by arranging desks in groups of four. He uses both the rectangular and round tables to organize and display the necessary materials and equipment for each activity.

Figure 3.4 Classroom Layout for Hands-On Activities

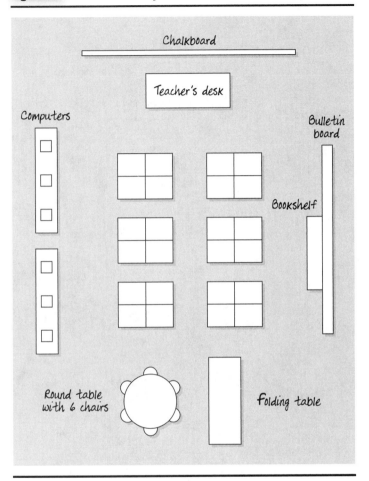

The bookcase is moved under the bulletin board to create a science reference area.

Learning Centers. The classroom design in Figure 3.5 reflects the use of learning centers for each science unit. The teacher divides her classroom into a number of stations, physically separated and different from each other. Students move from station to station within the course of a science unit. The group size varies. Six students might work at the computers while four groups of three students perform experiments at their desk clusters. Another group of three students may read at the bookcase/round table station. This leaves a small group of three students for the teacher to work with at her desk.

Figure 3.5   Classroom Layout for Learning Centers

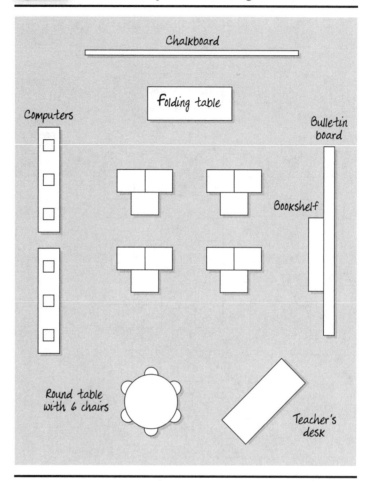

Each classroom arrangement reflects the teaching styles of the teachers and their preferences for different teaching methods. All of the teachers would likely change these arrangements to accommodate different teaching/learning experiences during the year. You may have noticed that in each case the only furnishings that were never moved were the computers. When asked why, each teacher smiled and quickly said they assumed the computers could not be moved because of the location of electrical outlets. Only one teacher considered using an outlet strip and extension cords but dismissed the idea for fear the students might trip on the cords.

Keep in mind you can always redesign what you have to enhance learning. You will also find that your preferences will change as your teaching methods

One Computer, Two Computers, Three Computers, Four . . .

How many computers will you have in your classroom and how can you adapt your lessons to the available equipment?

Many elementary school classrooms have a computer station for teacher use, as well as student workstations. Consider how many computers you have available and how you will plan for your students to use them. Whole class, small group instruction, and individual work are all possibilities.

BOX 3.2

Issues in Technology

Even if you have only one computer, you can still use it to make your instruction more dynamic, student focused, and cooperative. Creative teachers take advantage of a single computer in their classroom for demonstrations and simulations or as an individual learning center. In a classroom with one or more computer stations, lessons in which students rotate through several learning centers incorporating hands-on activities, collaborative activities, and computer activities are appropriate. When a computer lab is available, whole class instruction is possible, with all students at their own computer station working on online research, innovative inquiry projects (such as tracking the flight paths of migratory species), and multimedia presentations.

Always keep in mind two questions when planning instruction with technology: "What do I want to teach?" and "How can I take advantage of available technology to best accomplish my instructional goals?"

change and whether you plan to use whole group or small group instruction. How and why you make these decisions should always be guided by the same questions: "What do I what to teach and how can the arrangement of the classroom help me accomplish my goals?"

Whole Group Instruction

Throughout the rest of this chapter, we will address some of the important physical and emotional considerations of several specific modes of instruction. These considerations will change depending on whether you will be instructing the whole class or small groups. This section offers practical suggestions for instructing a whole group and turning your classroom into a learning environment that is both safe and engaging for students.

Preparing for Whole Group Instruction and Lecture

Think of all the times that it is necessary for a teacher to address the entire class during a typical day. Leading class discussions, performing demonstrations, and providing direct instruction are just a few of the many instances in which the teacher may need to address the entire class. Even when having students work individually or in small groups, it is generally necessary to first provide directions and expectations to the class as a whole.

There are many challenges and management issues when providing whole class instruction. How will you monitor all of your students' behavior when addressing a class of thirty students? How will you maintain student interest and assess learning? How will you encourage each student to participate in a lesson directed toward the whole group? Essentially, how will you develop and maintain a learning environment in which students feel safe interacting with you and their classmates?

Advanced preparation is the key to successful whole group instruction. Consider a second-grade elementary class in which you are conducting a lecture and discussion on the concepts of solids and liquids. Suppose your students have just finished an activity in which they were manipulating various solids, liquids, and gases. Now you want to help your students formalize their understandings of the three states of matter by reflecting on their experiences.

The first problem that you are likely to encounter is orchestrating the transition between the hands-on activity and the lecture and discussion portion of the lesson. Most students thoroughly enjoy such hands-on activities and are not inclined to stop when their attention is requested. Furthermore, the noise level is up during such activities, making it difficult for students to hear your request in the first place. In short, students' attention is distracted from the teacher. What would you do to get your students' attention and put them in the frame of mind to listen?

Experienced teachers have developed many useful ideas that help in these situations. For example, some find it useful to strike a small wind chime (or other source of pleasant but distinctive sound) when they need to get the students' attention. This method requires direct instruction and reinforcement early in the school year as students are taught to stop what they are doing and to direct their attention to the teacher when they hear the chimes. The time investment required for such training pays off handsomely throughout the rest of the year, both in terms of smoother transitions between instructional activities and less hoarseness and stress from having to raise your voice.

Even when you have your students' attention, you need to separate the students from the samples they have been working with before you begin your instruction. How would you suggest that such distractions be removed? One strategy is to simply ask students to place their samples in the middle of the table and leave them alone while they discuss their lab experiences. However, many teachers find that leaving props even remotely accessible to students leads to distractions, the very thing you are trying to avoid. Another option is to collect the samples. This works well in situations in which the samples will not be needed later in the lesson and when the discontinuity caused by collecting the samples in the middle of the lesson is not a problem. A third possibility is to move the students away from the distraction. This can be a useful technique, especially when the excitement level of the students is high and you want to make the transition to the closure of the lesson very pronounced. For example, you may wish to ask students to leave their samples at their tables and move to the front of the room (many elementary classrooms have a carpeted area for this purpose) where the closure will be conducted. This way, the samples are out of sight and reach, and you are sending a clear message that a new segment of the lesson is about to begin.

Let's say that you've chosen to have students sit at the front of the room for the final segment of the lesson. Picture your students as they move from their tables, where they have been actively engaged in hands-on exploration, to the carpet, where you want them to sit and learn in a more orderly fashion. How will you make your behavioral expectations clear but in a pleasant manner?

Establishing Behavioral Expectations. An especially effective method for establishing behavioral expectations is to have a fun phrase that you can use to cue students into the expected behavior. For example, saying "criss-cross apple-sauce" is a concise, pleasant way to let your students know that you want them to sit cross-legged on the carpet with their hands in their laps and their eyes on you. Of course, you will need to teach students what this phrase means and back it up with consistent, high expectations. Always remain alert for students who may find it difficult to settle down after the excitement of the hands-on exploration. You should begin your closure to the lesson only when students are all sitting quietly with their eyes focused on you.

As you can see, there are many concerns to deal with as you move students from the active exploration portion of a lesson to a less active closure. In our rather simplified example, you had to get the students' attention, have them put down the samples they had been working with, and move them to a different part of the room. You cued them in on your behavior expectations in a pleasant way and waited for their compliance before speaking. You now have thirty students seated on the carpet in front of you, ready to listen and participate in the lesson closure, and you accomplished all of this without raising your voice (or your blood pressure). From your students' standpoint, you have provided clear

---

Establishing Behavior Expectations

Behavior expectations of students and the students' perception of what we expect of them can vary among classrooms and across cultures. It is important to remember that children are individuals and cannot be made to fit a preconceived notion of how they are supposed to act. It is impossible to create a learning environment that is perfectly culturally matched to each ethnic group that you may encounter in your classroom. What is important is that you can identify when there is a problem for a particular child that is culturally based and that you have the tools to readily search for a solution. Multicultural knowledge is one of the many tools that teachers can use to help solve problems that inevitably arise in culturally diverse classrooms.

BOX 3.3

Issues in Diversity

instructions and high expectations for their behavior in a nonthreatening manner. There has been no yelling, idle threats, or coercion. In short, you have helped your students move from one activity to another while maintaining a pleasant learning environment of mutual respect and trust. This healthy atmosphere will go a long way toward encouraging student participation and compliance during the closure portion of the lesson.

Using an Advance Organizer. Let's say that you wish to use a questioning or discussion format to help your students synthesize what they have learned by manipulating the samples of solids, liquids, and gases in the hands-on portion of the lesson. A good way to begin your discussion is to preview the material to be learned with an advance organizer or overview of what students will be learning before you begin instruction. For example, you could start by explaining what you wish to accomplish during the lesson closure by saying, "Now that you have had a chance to play with some solids and liquids, I would like for you to share your experiences and ideas with each other. If we all participate, we should be able to learn what solids and liquids are and how they are different and alike." Advance organizers help students organize the material that is about to be presented or synthesized. Without this structure, the material may seem fragmented and students may not make the connections between the activity they have just completed and the one they are about to begin. Furthermore, starting with an advance organizer has the added advantage of helping students avoid irrelevant responses and going off on tangents.

Using Questioning Effectively. Questioning is another critical component of building and maintaining a productive learning environment during whole class instruction. Good questions increase student motivation and involvement in what might otherwise be a dull, one-way presentation of facts from the teacher to the students. Furthermore, student responses to good questions help you assess their understandings and provide you with clues for adjusting the content and pace of the lesson.

Questioning strategies are most effective when the questions are specific, planned in advance, and stimulate learning and discussion. Poorly worded or confusing questions can be frustrating for students and provide little useful information. As a student, you have probably experienced many classroom episodes in which the teacher's questions were more frustrating than helpful. How did you feel in these situations? More importantly, how can you avoid such problems in your own questioning?

For starters, the teacher should plan an organized sequence of questions to engage students and reinforce the content they are learning:

1. Who can tell me what a solid is like? (pause) Accept a couple of volunteer responses.
2. Who else observed something interesting about solids? (pause) Sarah?

A teacher conducts a discussion with the entire class.

3. What about the liquids? Can someone share their observations about the liquids? (pause) Jimmy?

4. In what ways were the liquids and solids different? (pause) Accept a couple of volunteer responses.

5. Can you think of any other differences? (pause) Zak?

6. Did anyone notice ways in which liquids and solids are alike? (pause) Accept a couple of volunteer responses.

Notice that a pause follows each question to give students time to think. This pause is known as wait time and is designed to give students time to think about the question and their answers. Only after the pause is a student name called or a volunteer selected. In this way, the teacher effectively addresses the question to the entire class before identifying which student should answer. This keeps all of the students involved in the lesson. After all, students naturally pay more attention when they know that they are likely to be called on next.

Questions should also be well sequenced and focused on the lesson objectives. These questions lead students toward the objective of identifying similarities and differences between solids and liquids by first having students relate some of the characteristics of each and then by having students describe how

Keeping a Visual Record of Discussions

BOX 3.4

How do students best process information?

Some students only need to hear information to understand, but others need to actually see the information written down before they can process it mentally. In addition, many students are more apt to answer questions if they are written down. It is important to include the use of visual aids in a lesson. This could involve writing on the board, using the overhead, or keeping chart paper and markers readily available. Recording the question after you have asked it will also help to ensure that there is adequate wait time for students to process the question and will reinforce the importance of taking notes during class.

If it is not important for the entire class to take notes, writing questions and the students' responses on the board will provide the entire class with a record of the discussion. This allows you to refer back to what was discussed at a later time and make connections from one lesson to another. Recording students' responses also provides them with validation, gives the rest of the class an opportunity to think about what was said, and encourages dialogue between students rather than just between teacher and student.

the two are alike and different. In addition, questions are brief and use vocabulary appropriate for the grade level. Students are confused and frustrated by long, poorly worded questions that use inappropriate vocabulary.

Finally, it is important to provide positive feedback to students to reinforce their participation. Students participate best when they know that their ideas are valued by both their teacher and other students. Therefore, it is critical to acknowledge students' contributions and use their ideas whenever possible. For example, once you are satisfied that students have exhausted their ideas about solids and liquids, you could sum up their responses with something like: "Wow, I'm impressed by how much you've learned today. You've told me that solids are sometimes hard, sometimes squishy, feel dry, and can have different shapes and colors. Liquids come in different colors, too, but are different from solids in that they feel wet and can be poured, and they always take the shape of the container they are in."

No single action creates a learning atmosphere. Instead, a combination of techniques and strategies work in concert. Effective teaching involves manipulating both students' physical environment (through the orchestration of transitions, removing distractions, etc.) and emotional environment (through the use of wait time, advance organizers, and effective questioning) to maintain a class environment in which students feel it is safe to participate and learn. Teachers who are able to pull this off are perceived by their students as being pleasant and supportive despite their high behavioral expectations and strong academic focus.

Demonstrations

Another common teaching situation in which the teacher addresses the class as a whole is in the use of demonstrations. Illustrating concepts, making a point, answering student questions, piquing students' interest, and initiating inquiry lessons are just a few of the many appropriate uses of demonstrations. Also, it is sometimes necessary to use a demonstration when safety or cost considerations prevent the teacher from allowing students to perform a particular activity themselves.

Think of a situation in which you asked a friend or relative to teach you a complicated task, such as how to use an unfamiliar computer program. Even though your mentor may have been an expert, the demonstration may have been less than informative. Perhaps your mentor moved along at a pace that was hard to follow, showed you too many options in too little time, or just talked so much that you could not ask questions as they arose. You were probably more confused after the demonstration than before and left with a sinking feeling of inadequacy. Obviously, this is not the way you want your students to view your demonstrations. Like all forms of instruction, good demonstrations don't just happen. They require careful planning and attention to the physical and emotional environment. The following steps will help you plan and manage the physical setting and emotional environment in order to use the demonstration to its full potential.

1. *Prepare for demonstrations by organizing and constructing materials.*

Let's say you want to use a particular apparatus to introduce the concept of buoyancy to your fifth-grade students. Perhaps you learned of the apparatus known as a Cartesian diver at a recent state science teachers' convention. Your idea for the lesson is to start out with a demonstration of a working Cartesian diver, then have students construct and experiment with their own versions. Eventually, you intend for them to be able to explain how the Cartesian diver works and to apply the principle of buoyancy that governs the diver to other "swimming" objects, such as fish and submarines.

Your first step is to construct the apparatus, which is not difficult at all. All you need is an empty two-liter soda bottle, an eyedropper, and a source of clean water. Begin by removing the label from the empty soda bottle and filling it with water. Next, draw a little water into the eyedropper and place it into the water-filled soda bottle. Carefully adjust the amount of water in the eyedropper until it just floats. Finally, screw the lid to the bottle on tightly. Now try out your Cartesian diver by squeezing the sides of the bottle. This will increase the pressure of the water inside the bottle and should cause the eyedropper to sink. Releasing the pressure on the sides of the bottle should allow the dropper to rise again.

You will not need to teach for long before you realize that Murphy's law is especially applicable for classroom demonstrations. Anything that can go wrong is apt to go wrong, especially if you are unfamiliar with how a particular device works. There is nothing less impressive to students than a demonstration that does not work. Therefore, it is imperative to thoroughly try out every apparatus you plan to use in a demonstration prior to the lesson. If your Cartesian diver does not behave as described, you will need to further adjust the amount of water in the eyedropper. If the dropper does not sink when the bottle is squeezed, draw up a little more water into it. If it does not float well or does not rise when the bottle is released, squeeze out a drop or two of water. Keep adjusting the water until you are confident that you can make the diver sink or float at will.

2. *Enhance the visibility of the apparatus.*

Now that you have a working Cartesian diver, you are ready to use it to demonstrate buoyancy to your class. To begin the lesson, hold up the Cartesian diver in front of your students and ask them to describe what they see. Of course, you are careful to keep your fingers out of the way, so that students have a clear view of the diver inside the bottle. Likely, students sitting near you will raise their hands to indicate they want to respond, but those sitting toward the back of the room may be squinting and jockeying for a better view. What does this indicate? What would you do in this situation?

Visibility is a prime consideration when performing demonstrations. It is very frustrating for students to try to learn from a demonstration they cannot see well. Use oversized props whenever possible, and be willing to move around the room when oversized props are not available. The two-liter soda bottle Cartesian diver is not small, by any means, but your students' reaction to your initial question should be an obvious clue that its size is insufficient. The obvious solution is to move across the room so that students in the back will be able to see the Cartesian diver more easily. As you walk, hold the Cartesian diver out from your body and elevate it above your students' heads to enhance visibility. Upon arriving at the back of the room, you may want to hold the Cartesian diver in front of a background that contrasts with the diver to further enhance its visibility. A clean whiteboard or blank wall will do nicely.

3. *Ask students to make observations.*

When all the students have obtained a good view of the apparatus, you may want to ask for their observations. Making observations is a basic skill in science and it is a good idea to take advantage of opportunities for students to practice observing. A common problem in these situations is that some of the more impatient students may call out answers out of turn. This is a significant problem, because overeager responders may overpower and discourage more timid students from participating. A simple reminder to raise hands before answering, supported with proper reinforcement (ignoring call-outs, while allowing those with raised hands to speak), is often all that is needed to quell the chaos.

Once students realize you are serious about not accepting call-outs, you are likely to see half your class eagerly waving their hands in the air. It is gratifying to see so many students eager to participate, but look closely and you will likely see a few holdouts. Getting a wide range of students to respond is an important way to increase participation in the lesson. Students achieve more when their interest is high and when they actively participate in discussions rather than sitting passively during a lesson. Therefore, you will probably want to call on some of the nonvolunteers. On the other hand, ignoring students who are anxious to respond could have a negative impact on their enthusiasm. What would you suggest as a solution to this dilemma?

One possibility is to mix things up a bit by calling on both volunteers and nonvolunteers to offer their observations. In doing so, you are sending the message that you value all students' participation without ignoring those who are anxious to share what they know. As you do this, keep a mental tally of those who volunteered but did not get to answer. That way, you can give these students other opportunities to participate later in the lesson.

Soliciting observations from a class of fifth graders is often like opening floodgates—the answers pour forth in amazing quantities! Keep track of student responses by writing them on the board. This helps you acknowledge that every student's response is important and helps students recall all of the various comments.

4. *Label new objects or concepts.*

Eventually, the students will be unable to supply any new observations. This is a good time to explicitly label the Cartesian diver. Teachers sometimes forget to label the new objects or concepts in demonstrations. Then the students have difficulty following the lesson or referring to the object or concept when answering questions. You could have identified the Cartesian diver at the beginning of the demonstration. However, sometimes it is more effective to wait until after students have made some careful observations before you apply the label. A certain amount of curiosity is developed as students try to figure out what the device is and what it will do, and this can help maintain interest. In this lesson, soliciting students' observations of the Cartesian diver served two purposes: (1) Students were encouraged to look closely at the apparatus before they saw it in action, and (2) the resulting list of observations served as a description of the Cartesian diver.

In labeling the Cartesian diver, you may want to emphasize the second point by drawing a circle around the list of observations and labeling it "Cartesian diver." Say the words and have your students repeat them as you write them on the board. The goal is to make the new term familiar to students so that they will feel comfortable using it throughout the rest of the lesson.

5. *Perform the demonstration.*

By now you may be wondering if you are ever going to actually show students how the Cartesian diver works. That is the next step in this process, but we hope you can see how important it is to prepare students for this moment through careful planning and attention to their physical and emotional settings. You certainly could have started the lesson simply by holding the Cartesian diver up in front of the class and giving it a squeeze. However, had you done so, many of your students would likely have felt frustrated by not being able to see what you were doing, and many others would have missed the point of the demonstration. Some may have been unimpressed because they were given the "punch line" with no buildup. Others may have sat passively throughout the lesson without participating. In short, your demonstration would have been all wet!

However, through careful manipulation of the physical environment (enhancing the visibility of your demonstration) and the emotional environment (valuing and affirming student responses, attention to timing, etc.), you have avoided these problems. Your students are now prepared for the big moment when you squeeze the bottle and make the diver sink. Most likely, you will find that the effort you have taken to prepare students for this moment will pay off throughout the lesson as you solicit further observations on the action of the Cartesian diver and have students construct and experiment with their own Cartesian divers.

Small Group Instruction

You will likely find that having students work in small groups will be among your most powerful instructional modes. Small groups have between two to five students who work primarily with one another at a pace that is independent of other students in the class. The critical distinguishing characteristic is that students are working primarily with just the students in their own group. In addition, each group sets its own pace independently of the rest of the class. Within such an instructional organization, students' opportunities to interact with one another are maximized. Students usually feel more comfortable offering opinions and ideas to their peers in small groups as opposed to volunteering answers to the teacher in front of the entire class. Think about yourself as a student. Did you feel more comfortable working with your classmates or did you prefer to answer questions and give reports in front of the entire class? Educational psychologists will tell you that the reason for this is that working in small groups with peers, versus the whole class dynamic, is a low risk situation. There is less fear of making a mistake within a small group than in front of the teacher and the entire class.

On the other hand, some individuals do not like working in small groups with peers because they often feel a lack of direction and prefer feedback from the teacher instead of classmates. After all, it is the teacher who will be assigning grades. As with any instructional or classroom organization, having students work in small groups has its trade-offs. However, small group instruction provides an excellent vehicle for teaching science through the use of small group work, laboratory activities, and discussion groups.

Students work together on an experiment in a small group.

Small Group Work

Suppose that you are teaching a lesson about the difference between observation and inference and you want to utilize small groups and a shoe box activity. Assume you have distributed sealed shoe boxes with mystery objects inside. The students will work in small groups to determine the contents of the shoe box. They are allowed to make their determination in any way other than opening the box. As the activity proceeds, you will ask your students to list their observations and inferences. This activity poses little risk to students' confidence, since

Small Group Instruction

Frequently, girls find it difficult to speak out or exhibit academic behaviors in a gender-mixed setting. They will often defer to boys, either because of the boys' assertiveness or because of their own timidity. Girls will sometimes only display their knowledge in groups that are all female. Most teachers are not aware of this tendency and will insist that all groups be gender mixed, which unintentionally inhibits girls' ability to participate and learn on an equal basis.

BOX 3.5

Managing Your Science Classroom

it is clear that there is no way for them to know what is inside the shoe box. Additionally, it is an activity that students typically enjoy. To maximize the effectiveness of the lesson, you will want to carefully plan the number of students per group and the process that will be used to complete the activity.

The first step in planning a small group activity is to decide how many students to place in each group. In this particular activity, students have been paired up. How would you decide how many students to put in a group for this activity? Take a moment and write down a list of considerations. Your list probably contains issues such as the following:

1. The number of students in my class.

2. The number of boxes I want to make.

3. Maximizing the number of student-generated ideas about what is in the box.

4. Creating a range of abilities in each group.

5. Creating groups that work well together.

All of these ideas are important to consider. Certainly the number of students in your class is important. The fewer groups you have the easier it will be for you to manage groups working at different rates. Naturally, in order to have fewer groups you will need to have more students in a group. The number of boxes you need to make will depend on the availability of time and materials. You will want to maximize the number of ideas generated in each group by including an appropriate number of students with a wide range of interests and abilities. Finally, we want to make sure that the students in each group work well together or at least have the potential of working well together. This does not mean that you can only put friends together in each group. One advantage of group work is that your students will get to know each other better. This also does not mean that you should force two students who are mortal enemies to work together. This might be counterproductive.

In deciding on the number of students to include in the groups, also consider the level of activity that will be assigned for each member of the group. Given the nature of the shoe box activity, there really is not enough to actively involve more than two students. While one student is gathering data from manipulating the shoe box, the other can record the observations and inferences. The two students can easily rotate responsibilities several times. If more than two students were placed in the group, there would always be a time when one or more students were just sitting, watching, and waiting. We are also concerned about the possible detrimental emotional effects of having too many students in a group. With too many students in a group, not all students will have their ideas heard or be able to manipulate the shoe box. In short, individual students will be intentionally left out by the others. Some students may even learn to leave themselves out. This is a situation that teachers should work hard to avoid. We want an environment that fosters learning for all students and increases the likelihood that all students' ideas and needs will be respected and considered. Naturally, when the teacher calls the class together as one large group, she will want to be sure to acknowledge the ideas from all of the groups equally.

There is one final point we would like to make concerning the shoe box activity. It has to do with the distribution of materials. Should the students have the boxes on their desks while you provide instructions for the activity? It will save some time if you pass out the boxes while giving instructions. However, if this activity is going to be successful, the shoe boxes will need to be mysterious and it is this mystery that can cause problems while you provide students with instructions. Therefore, it would probably be easier for you to distribute the boxes after the instructions have been provided. One last consideration: Would you have the students leave their seats to get the boxes from another location in the room or would you walk around the room and pass out the shoe boxes? Is there another way to distribute the shoe boxes? We are not going to offer any suggestions now. We just want you to think about what you would do in the situation described.

Conducting Laboratory Activities

Suppose that during a series of lessons on earth science you have your students investigate the chemical and physical characteristics of various rock samples. Each group of four students has a small box of approximately fifteen rocks and their task is to record visible characteristics such as color, luster, smoothness, and size on a data table. In addition, the students will test for content of calcium using vinegar and rock hardness using a scratch test. To maximize the success of the laboratory activity, the teacher needs to clarify her expectations for each student's role in the group and provide a safe environment.

In this situation, students are placed in groups of four. There is plenty for the students to do and there will be no reason for students to sit passively as peers do the "real" work. There is nothing about the task that requires only one student to handle the rocks while only one student handles the recording of data. In fact, the activity will proceed more efficiently if several students divide up the work. The key point to this type of organization is that all students can feel useful to the group and feel that their views or contributions are needed. However, it is important to consider that some students may prefer to handle the rocks and make observations while other students will prefer to simply record data. Should you allow students to perform only those tasks that they like? What are the advantages of such an approach? What are the disadvantages? In this particular case, what would you do if none of the students wanted to record data?

One of your first considerations should be the instructional objectives of the activity. This particular activity will do much more than teach students about the various characteristics of rocks. It also gives students an opportunity to experience and develop various aspects of a scientific investigation. Recall what we said about science in Chapter 1. The important aspects of scientific inquiry are data collection, recording and organizing data, making inferences, developing and testing hypotheses, and data interpretation. The activity described here has numerous potential opportunities for knowledge in addition to learning about the characteristics of rocks. In order to maximize student learning, it would be important for all students to experience all aspects of the activity. Consequently, it would be a good idea, pedagogically, to have students rotate roles. Have each student collect data from manipulating the rocks and also have each student record, organize, and interpret data. By having students rotate tasks, you can ensure that every student has at least some time doing the tasks that they like. There would be nothing worse than having a student spend the whole time performing a task that he or she did not like. How much do you think this student would learn from the activity? Do you think this student would have much appreciation for the complexity of rocks? We are not saying that students need to have fun all the time or that having fun is the only goal you should have for your students. Maximizing student learning should be your primary goal at all times. What we are saying is that it is actually beneficial to students' ability to learn if they enjoy what they are doing.

When students finish their data collection tasks, it will be important for the students to discuss their results and reach group consensus. It is not uncommon for certain students to dominate these discussions in the same way. If allowed, certain students might also dominate who does what during an activity. Setting up some clear rules for students to follow and providing students with clear instructions about how to reach group consensus can help alleviate some of the problems. For example, you may require that each student provide at least four observations and/or conclusions about the rocks. Naturally, you will need to carefully monitor the behavior of all groups. In doing so, be a little flexible in the beginning as students adapt to the rules you have set. They will get better with time and you need to consider this as you monitor student behavior.

In planning a laboratory activity, safety is a critical issue. In this activity, you may prefer to use vinegar instead of dilute hydrochloric acid to test for calcium. Whenever students are heating, mixing, or combining chemicals that have the potential to bubble or splatter, students should be wearing safety goggles. In fact, we recommend the use of goggles whenever students are using chemicals or any materials that would be dangerous to their eyes. If the materials can be damaging to clothes, laboratory coats (or large shirts donated by parents) are recommended as well. Although students may resist wearing goggles at first, they never resist wearing white lab coats.

Teachers often think about safety primarily in terms of legal issues. The focus is often on what to do to avoid a lawsuit. Although legal issues are important, we recommend additional precautions. How would you feel if a student injured his or her eyes even though you were not legally to blame?

Small Group Discussion and Problem Solving

There are many instructional activities other than laboratory experiences or hands-on activities that are facilitated by having students work in small collaborative groups. A major emphasis in current science education reforms involves students in discussing controversial issues and achieving group consensus on potential solutions for societal problems. In such cases, establishing small collaborative groups is much more effective than having the class work together as a single unit.

Obviously, the individuals who constitute a particular group are critical to the potential success of the entire group. If individual members are unable to work together in a productive manner, little work will be accomplished. Consequently, when forming small groups, teachers need to pay close attention to students' abilities and personalities. The following example demonstrates several issues and offers potential solutions to issues that teachers typically face when attempting to ensure the formation of collaborative groups.

Suppose you want your students to consider the effects of acid rain on the community and environment. Students will be told that there is an acid rain problem in their community and will be asked to research and consider possible solutions to the problem. Solutions are to carefully consider potential effects on community members' employment and lifestyles. In this activity, students will be expected to use library resources, computer simulations, computer databases, and laboratory investigations specifically related to the effects of acid rain.

As you have learned from the shoe box activity presented earlier, the number of students in each group will need to be determined. Given the variety of activities that groups need to perform, five to six students per group should be about right. There are enough students to accomplish the necessary tasks while at the same time there are enough tasks to involve all group members in a productive manner. However, who these five to six students are is equally important.

Students are unique individuals with different interests, academic backgrounds, abilities, and personalities. You will need to consider the best possible mix for each group. Some students may have aggressive personalities and may dominate group discussions and activities. Other more timid students will be happy to let them do so. It is not necessarily wrong to group aggressive and timid students together. However, if you do so, you will need to consider how to avoid the unproductive dynamic of a few students doing the activity while the rest of the group watches. One solution is to assign roles or rotate responsibilities within a group. In this way, each student in the group has a responsibility and each student must also learn to depend on his or her peers. This will help ensure a collaborative spirit within the group.

A teacher assists two students working together on a computer.

You may be wondering whether grouping students by mixed or homogenous abilities is better for learning. This is a question that has not been answered in any definitive way. However, creating groups of mixed abilities is usually unavoidable and ability grouping is difficult for the classroom teacher to validly achieve. In addition, students will quickly develop the perception of which students are in the "smart" group and which are in the "slow" group. In our opinion, whatever value can be claimed for ability grouping is far outweighed by the potential emotional scars it can create.

To summarize, the problem the teacher faces is how to form groups of differing students who can work effectively together. Before a teacher has had the chance to get to know his or her students, randomly assigning students to groups works as well as anything else. However, as the year proceeds, you should be more familiar with your students and have a good idea of who can work better with whom. Quite often, the dynamics of the group as a whole are much more important than the dynamics existing between two particular students. An effective approach to use at the beginning of the year is to explicitly teach students how to cooperate with their peers and how to reach productive consensus when disagreements exist. Teachers often assume that students know how to cooperate and will do so as soon as they are put into groups. This is not the case and there are numerous cooperative behavior-building activities that have been developed by supporters of cooperative learning techniques. We will illustrate several of these within the subject matter sections organized around the teaching cycle. Regardless of the approach, the key point to remember is to compose groups that can effectively work together. "Effectively" refers to groups of students who acknowledge the value of each other's opinions and are willing to compromise when disagreements arise.

Suppose you have formed student groups and they are working independently around the room. You notice in one group that one of the students begins at the computer and refuses to give any other group member a chance to use it. The other students want a chance to search the Web for information, but the student at the computer insists that the others can tell him what site address to open and he will do it. What would you do? Is this group cooperation? How do you suppose the other students feel? How would you characterize the emotional environment in this group?

One thing you would need to do for this group is to intervene in some way. This group is clearly not functioning in a collaborative manner. Our recommendation is that your intervention be neutral at first. Ask the group how things are going. Ask if everyone has had a chance to work at the computer. Let the students indicate the nature of the situation and let the students decide on a solution. This is a much better initial approach than intervening with a solution to a problem that you have already decided exists. Can you think of anything that could have been done to prevent this situation? As suggested earlier, you could have assigned students roles and set up a schedule for rotation of roles during the activity. As the year moves along, you can have students assume the responsibility for ensuring that everyone is equally involved by allowing them to assign roles and rotation schedules.

Beyond the Classroom

So far we have restricted the physical teaching environment to a self-contained classroom. This is where most teaching and learning will be taking place. However, there will be situations when you will find that the classroom is too restrictive an environment, limiting the size, space, and resources that are necessary for your students to learn and do science. It might become necessary to find other places and spaces in which to teach. You will need to choose alternative learning environments, not because they offer a change of scenery, but because you will be able to teach more effectively in those places. Most importantly, your students will be able to learn more effectively in these alternative learning environments. As you plan your lessons, you should not only be asking yourself what is the best way to teach a concept but also where is the best place to teach that particular concept.

There are many benefits to taking science instruction beyond your classroom walls to other areas of the school grounds or into the community. By making connections to students' lives outside the classroom, you will be able to reinforce the relevancy of science and give them concrete examples of science applications. If you want your students to value science and realize the important role it plays in their everyday lives, you have to show them how and where science concepts are applied.

The School Laboratory

Often teachers only consider the "Big Field Trip" when they want to extend science learning beyond the classroom, demonstrate relevancy, or make community connections to their curriculum. Actually, much of what you will be teaching in your classrooms can be experienced firsthand by simply walking outside the classroom door! The school building itself offers countless resources. Take a moment and consider all the different ways you could use a typical school building to help you teach science. The school kitchen can be a wonderful place to investigate the physical and chemical properties of matter. An elementary school classroom is probably neither adequately equipped nor safe enough to have students investigate chemical changes, but the school kitchen may be the perfect place to have students explore these concepts. Consider a simple cookie recipe. Students could examine and compare the physical characteristics of the different ingredients, apply measuring skills, observe the changes as the ingredients are mixed together, and predict what will happen to the dough as it bakes. Often they will use words such as *melt, dissolve, mix,* and *combine* to describe what they see happening. You could use this opportunity to discuss what these words mean to them and gain insight into their understanding of these concepts. In the kitchen your students can also experiment firsthand with change of state by freezing pops or ice cream, melting cheese on little pizzas, and boiling broth for soup or milk for hot chocolate. Often we only discuss water with students when talking about changes of state. Because you can probably assume most students are familiar with water as a liquid, solid, and gas, this can be a starting point. In addition, the kitchen classroom can be used to make many more connections to equally familiar substances, while providing students with the opportunity to be actively involved in the process, not to mention the added bonus of eating the experiment at the end of the lesson!

Where else in the school building did you consider teaching? Did you include the lavatories? Many classrooms don't have sinks. Rather than excluding experiments that would require sinks, move your class into a lavatory. Not only will you have sinks and water available but you'll also have all the paper towels you'll need for cleaning up right there at your fingertips. Sometimes the most valuable resource missing from a classroom is space. What would you do if you wanted to test the aerodynamics of paper airplanes, explore Newton's laws of motion, conduct an egg drop contest, or any other activity that would not be possible to do within the space of an average classroom? You might consider going outside to use the schoolyard, but what if it is raining or freezing cold on the day you schedule your lesson? Hallways, gymnasiums, and cafeterias can provide the space and surface area you will need without having to worry about the unpredictability of weather conditions or seasonal restraints. You can also use more than one place in a school to teach a science concept. For example, you can have your students go on energy transformation scavenger hunts. The school's central office, kitchen, library, nurse's office, and furnace room are all places where they will find energy being transferred from one form to another. While teaching about sound, you can have your students compare the acoustics in their classroom to the acoustics in the auditorium, gymnasium, cafeteria, and schoolyard. Observing the different filing systems in the school office and library can be an introductory lesson to classification systems in your life science unit. Have the students compile a technology inventory by finding where and how computers are used in their school. This report can also include interviews with administrators, faculty, staff, and other students about their daily use of technology.

A class conducts a science experiment outside in the schoolyard.

Stepping Out

There is no better method for teaching about the environment than having students study it directly. Regardless of whether a school is located in an urban, suburban, or rural area, the schoolyard and surrounding neighborhood provide a living laboratory to explore and investigate. Weather and daytime astronomy are the most common units for teachers to address outdoors, but do not limit yourself to these obvious connections. A simple puddle can become a focus for a lesson on reflection, density, or evaporation rates. Add a few drops of oil to its surface and begin a wondrous discussion when a rainbow of colors appears. During the same lesson, your students can blow bubbles and again observe the rainbow of colors on the surface of the soap film. A sidewalk crack can reveal a tiny world inhabited by ants and other insects, grasses and dandelions, little pools of water, and pebbles of various sizes and shapes. Students could make sketches of their sidewalk cracks, observe interactions between the living and nonliving elements, and record changes that occur within them over a period of time. This mini ecosystem can be much more fascinating and revealing to young children than any classroom study of some faraway place. After all, they are actively engaged in a real investigation occurring in their very own neighborhoods.

Byrd Baylor's book, *Everyone Needs a Rock*, gives readers ten rules for finding their own perfect rock. You could use this story as an introduction to an outdoor field trip to hunt for rocks. Students will inspect, feel, smell, and compare a number of rocks before they make their selections. While hunting, they will begin to realize the variety and diversity of rocks that can be found in their own neighborhood. Back in the classroom, students can present their rocks and explain why they chose them. You now have a ready-made rock collection to use as you continue your geology unit.

Many of the concepts you will be expected to teach are abstract and difficult for students to understand. Introducing these concepts through familiar activities conducted in familiar places can help children construct meaning from them. A playground can provide the equipment and experiences to teach and learn difficult physics lessons. A swing is not just an example of a pendulum that moves in a cyclic manner. It is also a pendulum students can experience firsthand. They become part of it. Their bodies move back and forth, and they experience cyclic motion directly. They feel speed, acceleration, and change of direction. Children can also experience speed, acceleration, and inertia on a playground slide. The effects of frictional forces on motion can be difficult to understand. Take your students and a box of toy cars outside to the playground. Allow them to "play" with the cars on the slide. Now ask them what they think will happen to the motion of the cars if you throw sand on the slide. Give them the opportunity to test their predictions. Ask them what will happen if you coat the slide with oil, sandpaper, or leaves. Once again, let them test their ideas. Ask them if there is any connection between the surface of the slide and the motion of the car. They will begin to construct a relationship between surface texture and speed from their own observations and tests.

Taking It on the Road

Sometimes the best place to teach a science lesson is not in or near your school at all. A field trip to an informal science resource such as a museum, zoo, aquarium, environmental center, or planetarium might offer the best opportunities to supplement and enhance your science instruction. Do you remember taking field trips with your class as a child? What do you remember about those trips? Write down the details that come to mind about any one of them. You probably listed the place, grade, teacher, and the fun of going off for a special day. You may have even remembered the weather, whom you sat next to on the bus, and where you stopped for lunch, but do you remember what you learned on that trip? Often field trips are only focused on introducing students to new places and not necessarily to new ideas. Making students aware of community resources is an important component of their education. Young students should be aware of the treasures to be found in a natural history museum and the wondrous diversity of the living collections in zoos and aquaria. However, a teacher is overlooking valuable teaching and learning opportunities if these visits are not also linked to the science curriculum. Informal science trips should not simply be entertaining days away from school. Instead, they should offer unique experiences to extend and enrich your students' understanding of science.

This chapter deals with physical and emotional learning environments. We suggest you consider the informal site as an extension of your classroom and that you take advantage of all the special resources it has to offer. Announce to your students as the bus pulls up to a science center entrance that today this center is their school and the exhibits in it will be their classroom. You will reinforce the educational focus of the trip and generate an excitement to learn in this wonderful new place!

A field trip experience can be an effective method to introduce, extend, or assess a science unit. The best time to plan a field trip is not immediately before you plan to teach the related unit. Often popular programs and workshops fill up quickly and, if you wait, you may not be able to get the dates you want. Suppose you plan to teach an astronomy unit in February and you would like to bring your class to a planetarium program to introduce the topic to them. If you wait too long, you may not be able to get the dates or programs that best fit your instructional plans. Bringing your class at some other time may still be an interesting experience for them, but they will not consider it an extension of their formal classroom education. A more appropriate solution may be to reconsider the placement of the trip within your unit. You could connect the content of the planetarium program to material your students will be learning later in the unit. In this way, the visit will extend and enhance the astronomy unit instead of introducing it.

You should also consider the following points as you plan a science field trip:

- Contact the education department for information about the facility, suggestions for appropriate programs for your students, and corresponding teacher's guides. Make sure you describe any special needs that your students may have and ask what accommodations can be made for them. Most centers will be able to provide adaptive instructional materials for students with disabilities.
- Visit the center before your field trip. Make a list of the exhibits that best fit your science curriculum. Many facilities will offer free admission to teachers.
- Plan pretrip activities with your class to prepare them for the visit. These should connect classroom instruction to the informal science trip. You should also include pretrip activities that introduce students to the center itself.
- Brief students prior to the trip about expected conduct and teamwork. Remind them that they will be in a learning environment.
- Design and assign specific learning tasks for students to complete on the trip.
- Plan posttrip activities to review what was experienced and to assess learning.

As you can probably tell by now, field trips are resource intensive. That is, they require a great deal of your time and effort to design and implement. A trip that is well planned and implemented can be a dynamic learning experience that could never be duplicated in a classroom and will never be forgotten by your students.

Summary

In this chapter we have stressed organizing classrooms in terms of physical environment, student dynamics, and instructional orientation. The primary theme that permeates each of our discussions is that all students should have equal access to science learning in an environment that has minimal personal and emotional risk. Whether instruction is taking place in small or large groups, or inside or outside the classroom, students are individuals in a social structure. In a large or whole group setting, many students choose to remain anonymous or are intimidated into anonymity. It may seem that placing students within small groups of peers is a solution to this problem. However, the members of this small group are a critical concern because, even in a group of five, personal dynamics are a factor. The message we have attempted to communicate is that teachers must carefully consider the background and characteristics of individual students and how these factors interact within the larger social structure.

Instructional approach is often considered separately from the physical and emotional environment. However, it is our view that these are inseparable. If a teacher is presenting a lecture to thirty students from the perspective that there is only one correct answer, some students will fearlessly offer responses to the teacher's questions, while others will do whatever they can to hide. Such situations are created by the instructional approach and represent high risk to many students. Alternatively, an instructional approach that is student and inquiry oriented empowers students. For most students, this is a situation with low risk, and they may feel more comfortable participating. The key point is that how a teacher facilitates learning directly influences the social and emotional environment of the classroom.

The physical environment is clearly related to safety issues. In addition, the physical setting, both within and outside of the classroom, also impacts student access to learning and instruction. If only a few students can manipulate material objects because of seating arrangements or limited resources, their cognitive and affective learning is significantly impacted. What a student learns about density from actually holding two equal volumes of different materials is qualitatively different from what is learned from watching someone else do the manipulation. The attitudes a student develops about science are qualitatively different if the student is allowed to draw inferences from data as opposed to learning someone else's inferences.

We take the phrase "science for all" seriously. If science is truly for all, teachers must pay special attention to the physical and emotional environment of the classroom in addition to the subject matter being presented.

Instructional Planning

Once you begin your teaching career, you will most definitely look forward to summer vacation. Your anticipated vacation will not be indicative of any displeasure with your teaching position, it is just part of human nature. We all appreciate a much needed and well-deserved rest after an intensive nine months of work. Vacations are not unique to teachers. As a student, you have no doubt taken many vacations. Think back to your last vacation. How did you decide where to go? How far in advance did you select a location? Whether you simply went home to visit parents and friends or to Disneyland, such decisions were probably made well in advance. Or are you one of those people who just gets in the car and drives? Do you know anyone who does this and just stops somewhere along the way? If you are like us, you have a destination planned in advance. If you do not know where you are going, how will you know when you get there?

Planning vacations is not all that different than teaching. You should have some idea of what you want students to know and be able to do in advance. After all, teaching should be a systematic and purposeful activity of facilitating students' movement from one place to another. By "place" we are referring to knowledge, beliefs, values, skills, and so on. This movement occurs more efficiently if there is a plan. This chapter presents strategies to help you design effective instructional plans. These plans will help guide classroom activities and specify how you will help students develop the knowledge, skills, and attitudes desired. It is these plans that will enable you to know when your students get there.

Instructional Objectives

Let's consider the development of a plan, regardless of topic. What would be the first thing to do? The answer should be obvious. You need to decide what your students should know and be able to do after the lesson is complete. This is analogous to deciding on a vacation destination. In educational terms, these decisions are called **instructional objectives.** These decisions are also sometimes referred to as behavioral or performance objectives. Regardless of the label, the purpose is always the same. Objectives specify what students should know and be able to do. Let's look at an example.

Imagine that you are teaching a sixth-grade class and the topic is the human body. The following is a possible objective:

> Students will know the main parts of the human heart.

Does this objective specify what students need to know or be able to do? An initial approach to answering our question might be to first consider how you would assess whether students know the main parts of the heart. Would you ask them to label or identify the parts on a diagram? Would you ask them to make a list? Would you ask them to explain the function of the parts of the heart? These are all very real possibilities, but they are also very different. What one student defines as "know" may be very different from what one of his or her classmates defines as "know." Hopefully, you have already figured out our point. Is there a better word than *know* for specifying what it is students should gain as a consequence of the lesson? As a hint, you may want to refer to the words we used when discussing how students might be assessed. Wouldn't "label," "list," or "identify" be less ambiguous than "know?" So, a different and more effective version of the sample objective could be:

> Students will be able to identify the main parts of the human heart.

The specific student behavior described is commonly called the **performance component** of the objective. Perhaps it is now clear why instructional objectives are sometimes called performance objectives. Is our new objective, with its performance component, as specific as it can be? Does it provide guidance, as all objectives should, for the systematic planning of instruction? What is meant by "identify" might be different depending on whether students are provided with a diagram or a model. That is, will they identify the parts with the aid of a diagram to jog their memories or identify, perhaps in the form of a list, strictly from memory? We are confident that you have noticed that the context and conditions under which students are asked to identify makes a difference. So, to be even more specific, let's revise the objective further to:

Given a diagram, students will be able to identify the main parts of the heart.

The phrase "given a diagram" provides more guidance than we had before because it tells us under what conditions and/or context the students are expected to exhibit the specified performance component. Such a phrase within an instructional objective is commonly called the **condition component.** The condition component typically refers to such things as what materials students will use to complete the task; how they will accomplish the task (e.g., from memory, from the textbook, or working in groups); and where the performance will take place (in the classroom, in a museum, or in the library). The condition component of the objective helps the teacher keep the outcome fair. For example, students who have been given the ambiguous task of studying a diagram of the heart might interpret the task as being able to label a diagram using a list of terms, while the teacher expects them to label the various parts from memory. In summary, the condition component provides very specific guidelines to the teacher regarding instructional activities. Because the students will eventually be expected to label a diagram of the heart, classroom instruction should provide the students with experiences in doing so.

Is our objective specific enough now? We have one more question. Take a moment to list the main parts of the human heart. What did you list? One of us listed the right and left ventricles. Another listed the two ventricles and the two atria. Finally, one of us listed the two ventricles, two atria, vena cava, and aorta. So, just what is meant by "main?" Again, we have a word in our objective that leaves too much room for interpretation. Luckily, this is easily fixed by the following change:

Given a diagram, the students will be able to label the two ventricles and two atria.

With the addition of a phrase that clarifies what is meant by "main," the objective is now more definitive in its specifications than before. The portion of an objective that specifies how well a student must perform the desired task is commonly called the **criterion component.** In this particular case we have specified that it is the ventricles and atria that must be identified and the assumption is that this will be done with 100 percent accuracy. A criterion component could have been written that stated the students will identify three of the four chambers of the heart. Again, this would specify the expected level of performance students would need to exhibit.

What follows are several examples of well-stated instructional objectives. However, each objective may not contain all three components we spoke about (more about this later). Read each objective and identify the **performance, condition,** and **criterion** components.

1. Given a model of the human skeletal system, the students will identify two bones.
2. The students will be able to explain the function of the heart ventricles.
3. The students will be able to compare and contrast igneous and metamorphic rocks, citing two similarities and two differences.
4. The students will be able to construct, using provided materials, a series circuit that can light a lightbulb.
5. The students will be able to define an acid as a substance with a pH value of less than 7.

Objective 1 clearly contains all three components and is most similar to the examples we provided relative to the human heart. Objective 2 is a good objective but may seem to be inadequate because there appear to be no condition or criterion components. However, these two components are implied. There is no need to state whether the student is using a paper and pencil or must explain orally, unless you want to be overly specific. The criterion is implied to be 100 percent. In general, objectives may not contain a condition or criterion component when conditions are obvious or the expected level of performance is 100 percent. All objectives, however, must contain a performance component. Objective 3 contains a performance component and criterion component, but no condition component is necessary. In objective 4, the criterion component is that the lightbulb will light, and in objective 5, a particular definition of an acid is desired. In truth there are several other correct definitions that could have been provided.

If you have noticed that well-written instructional objectives seem very similar to assessment items, you are correct. Remember that although the primary use of instructional objectives is to guide the planning of instruction, a secondary purpose is to aid in the assessment of student progress. This makes sense since the best assessment of instruction would be to see if students know or are able to do what you specified prior to instruction. How well students do on such assessments is also an indirect assessment of your own teaching.

Reform Documents and Instructional Objectives

The examples we provide in this book should make it clear that our position is that planning and instruction should be based on the *National Science Education*

Standards, Benchmarks for Literacy, and/or state reform documents. A quick perusal of the aforementioned documents should make it clear that the standards and benchmarks included in them do not reflect the required components of instructional objectives that we discussed in the previous section. This causes consternation to some teachers who do not realize that the science education reform documents were never meant to be curricula. Their purpose is to inform curriculum development, but what does this mean for your planning and instruction?

Perhaps it is best to think of individual benchmarks and standards as goals from which you may develop specific objectives. Consider, for example, the following grades 3–5 benchmarks:

> Students should know that the earth is one of several planets that orbit the sun, and the moon orbits the earth.

Could you use this as an instructional objective? Hopefully, by now you recognize that more detail needs to be added to transform this benchmark into a useful objective. You probably noticed that the benchmark includes neither a condition nor a criterion component. However, you probably also remember that it is acceptable for these to be implied when they are obvious. In this case,

A teacher uses the Benchmarks *book to plan his curriculum.*

the implied condition is after instruction and the implied criterion is 100 percent. There is another more critical problem with using this benchmark as an objective as it is written. The problem has to do with specificity of the expected outcome. For instance, what is meant by "students should know"? Does it mean that they can state that the earth is one of several planets, label a diagram, or draw a picture? Each of these could be taken as evidence that the student "knows" the content of the benchmark. What about the meaning of "several" in the benchmark? *Several* generally means more than two, but do students have to know all of the planets, most of the planets, or just three of them? Does it make a difference which ones they know? The point here is not to criticize the benchmark, but to point out that it is not in a form that is consistent with instructional objectives. To put it into a useful form that can guide instruction, it needs to be made more specific:

> The student will be able to draw a picture of the inner solar system including the sun and all four of the inner planets (Mercury, Venus, Earth, and Mars).

You may have noticed that the second part of the benchmark dealing with the moon's orbit was not included in our objective. This was purposely omitted in order to make a point. Some benchmarks contain more than one concept and,

Issues in Technology

What Did You Do in Science Class Today?

BOX 4.1

How will your students answer the question: "What did you do in science class today?" If they respond, "We worked on the computers today," have you accomplished your science objectives? Many teachers fall into the trap of "gee whiz" technology use in the classroom, in which the technology bells and whistles are what the students remember most.

Technology can be used to support appropriate pedagogy by fostering inquiry learning and activities in which students are engaged in doing science. Although computers and other forms of electronic technology can be integrated into the classroom in many ways, matching your learning objectives to appropriate technology is critical in designing and planning effective lessons. Always keep your learning objectives in mind as you think about how to incorporate technology into your lessons.

Think about how the unique features of particular technologies can support your learning outcomes. For example, microscopes extend the visual senses for students allowing them to see small things. A digital camera might be an excellent tool to document plant growth or the life cycle of a butterfly. Simulation software can help your students visualize abstract phenomena.

Then, when your students are asked about what they did in science class, they are more likely to respond, "Today we learned about the different kinds of volcanoes. You should have seen the amazing pictures of Mount Saint Helens we saw on the computer!"

at times, several concepts. You may find that objectives are more useful for planning and evaluating instruction if they are written simply and do not include too many concepts simultaneously. You may also find that some ideas take several lessons to teach whereas others are more quickly addressed. Consequently, we suggest that when you are trying to address either benchmarks or standards that contain several important concepts, you write individual objectives for each of the main concepts or ideas.

Our next example is from the *NSES* K–4 Life Science Standard. Rather than do it ourselves, this time we want you to write an instructional objective (or objectives) that addresses the following standard:

> Each plant or animal has different structures that serve different functions in growth, survival, and reproduction. For example, humans have distinct body structures for walking, holding, seeing, and talking.

Bloom's Taxonomy

Our original example of an objective about the parts of the human heart eventually included a focus on the ventricles. Objective 2, in the set of five sample objectives, also mentions ventricles. However, do you notice any differences in terms of what will be expected of students? The sample objective only expects students to identify the ventricles on a diagram. Objective 2 expects students to explain the function of the ventricles. Which would be easier for you to teach? Which would be easier for your students to learn? The first objective really only requires that students have good enough memories to remember the location of the ventricles. Objective 2 requires an understanding of how the ventricles work. Although you may be tempted to think that the memory-based objective is easier for you to teach and for students to learn, this may not always be the case. Some students have poor memories and perform much better on conceptual tasks, whereas for others the reverse in true. The main point we want you to remember here is that the tasks we require of our students differ with respect to the complexity of mental processing or skills that students need to exhibit.

Benjamin Bloom developed a taxonomy, or classification, of instructional objectives in 1956. He divided all educational outcomes into three broad domains: cognitive, affective, and psychomotor. The **cognitive domain** specifically refers to students' knowledge and thinking processes. It is around this domain that most instruction focuses. The **affective domain** focuses on students' values, attitudes, and beliefs. Although this domain may not directly contribute to a student's evaluation, most teachers and administrators believe the affective domain to be as important as the cognitive domain. The **psychomotor domain** is concerned primarily with students' gross and fine movements. This domain is critically important in physical education courses, for example. However, it should not take you long to realize how important physical skills such as coordination are to the performance of many science-oriented tasks.

The Cognitive Domain. Much of what teachers attend to in their planning and classroom instruction is focused on what they want students to know, understand, and think about the content of the subject matter they are teaching. In Bloom's Taxonomy, these concerns fall within the cognitive domain, which contains six levels of increasing complexity: knowledge, comprehension, application, analysis, synthesis, and evaluation.

Knowledge. The knowledge level in Bloom's Taxonomy emphasizes recall or recognition of information stored in one's memory. For example, a teacher who is teaching a unit on experimental design might want students to be able to recall the definition of a hypothesis. Keep in mind that well-written objectives should be specific. Many terms, including *hypothesis*, have several possible definitions. Hypothesis is commonly defined as an educated guess. A more useful definition for hypothesis is that it is a proposed answer to a scientific question. Since there is more than one way of defining the term, a knowledge-level objective should include the desired definition:

> Students will be able to verbally state the definition of a hypothesis as a proposed answer to a scientific question.

On the other hand, a recognition objective might require students to recognize this same definition from a list of possibilities in a multiple-choice question. An important characteristic of knowledge-level objectives is that the retrieved information is basically in the same form as it was stored; no processing of the information is necessary. For example, if a sixth-grade teacher taught her students that a variable in an experiment is the one factor that an experimenter varies between the treatment and control groups, then an appropriate knowledge-level question would be to ask, "What do you call the factor that an experimenter changes between the control and treatment groups?" To answer the question, students would simply have to remember the information in the same basic form as it was learned.

Comprehension. The comprehension level in Bloom's Taxonomy involves a student transforming information into a form that makes sense to that particular student. In other words, comprehension-level objectives require students to understand rather than simply memorize definitions and concepts. For example, the teacher just mentioned might want her sixth-grade students to be able to explain why only one variable is typically altered in an experiment. Her objective might look like this:

> Students will be able to use their own words to write out an explanation for why only one variable is typically altered in a scientific experiment.

By requiring students to explain the concept in their own words, the teacher is requiring students to make sense of the concept rather than simply memorizing it. Another type of comprehension-level objective would be to have students provide an example of an experimental variable. Again, students must demonstrate their understandings of the concept to accomplish this task. By focusing on conceptual understanding, comprehension-level objectives provide a precursor to higher levels of learning, and it is clear that students must understand a concept before they can use it to solve or analyze problems.

Application. The application level in Bloom's Taxonomy involves using information in a novel context. More specifically, students are asked to apply their knowledge to a new situation or problem. Application problems often have a single preferred solution, despite alternative ways of solving the problem. Once students understand the single-variable concept, the teacher in our previous example could address the application level by having students select and alter a variable in an experimental design:

> Students will be able to select a variable and develop an experiment to test the effect of the variable on the results of an experiment.

The teacher could first have the class generate a list of factors that could influence the growth of a bean plant. Then she could have individual students select a variable (or variables) to investigate and develop a research design to test the effects of altering the variable. In this case, it would be important for students to have the freedom to choose more than one variable. Students could accomplish the task without applying their understandings of the concept if the teacher explicitly instructed them to select only one variable from the list.

Analysis. The analysis level in Bloom's Taxonomy involves breaking a complex situation or concept into its constituent parts, with the emphasis on finding the underlying structure. Analysis differs from application in that it requires the taking apart, rather than the putting together, of a complex solution. It goes beyond comprehension in that it involves working backward from a solution or event and explaining how all of the parts work together to produce an effect, rather than simply providing a description of a solution or event. In the example of the sixth-grade inquiry lesson we have been using, an analysis objective could be written that requires students to analyze the results of an experiment:

> Given a graph of plant growth over time, students will be able determine the relative effectiveness of four different fertilizer treatments.

Synthesis. The synthesis level in Bloom's Taxonomy focuses on putting together existing understandings to create a product that is new and unique. Of the six levels in Bloom's Taxonomy, synthesis places the most emphasis on creativity. In fact, the definition of synthesis itself implies the creation of something new. Designing an investigation can be an example of either the application or synthesis category, depending on the level of originality reflected in the work. If the design is valid but adds nothing to previous work and/or instruction, the student is considered to be operating at the application level. If, on the other hand, the student puts together ideas in new and unique ways to create an experimental design or procedure, then he or she would be operating at the synthesis level. An example of a synthesis level objective for our sixth-grade teacher would be:

> Given the formula for calculating speed, students will use their knowledge of the measurement of time and distance to create a procedure for determining the average speed of a ball when rolled across the room.

Notice that the objective requires students to apply their understandings of the formula for speed and the measurement of distance and time to synthesize an entirely new procedure. Notice also that the whole (determining the speed of a rolling ball) is more than just the sum of the parts (understanding the formula for speed and knowing how to measure distance and time). It is this extra part that puts this objective in the synthesis category.

Evaluation. The evaluation level of Bloom's Taxonomy involves making decisions on open-ended topics and using sound reasoning to substantiate these decisions. Evaluation differs from analysis in that it requires some sort of value judgment. Good evaluations require that the criteria for judgment be clearly identified. In science, these criteria may focus on accepted norms and procedures, such as using a control group for comparison in an experiment or replicating the results of an investigation. In keeping with our sixth-grade teacher example, an evaluation objective might focus on deciding on the best procedure to use in an investigation:

> Students will be able to justify, using two reasons, their selection of a best choice for measuring the growth of a bean plant from among the three methods suggested by the class.

Just as often, however, the criteria for judging issues and procedures in a science class stem from cultural and societal values. This is especially true in regard to controversial scientific issues that form the connection between science and society. An example of an evaluation-level objective along these lines is:

> After completing a series of lessons on the costs and benefits of protecting endangered species, students will be able to write an essay defending their decision on whether the spotted owl should be protected, providing at least two arguments in favor of their position.

Note that a central component of each of these examples is the necessity of making a judgment. It is the act of making an evaluative judgment that sets the evaluation category apart from the other levels of Bloom's Taxonomy.

Take a moment to assess your understanding of the different levels of Bloom's Taxonomy of the cognitive domain. Identify each of the following objectives as being at the knowledge, comprehension, application, analysis, synthesis, or evaluation level.

1. The student will be able to explain why control groups are included in many experiments.
2. The student will be able to define photosynthesis as the process by which plants produce food from sunlight, water, and air.
3. Given the materials and the research question for an experiment, the student will be able to create a valid procedure for answering the question.
4. The student will be able to list three examples of things that grow.
5. Given the pooled data set from the class, students will be able to construct a graph depicting plant growth rate as a function of experimental treatment.
6. Working in groups of three, students will be able to create a set of criteria for deciding which fertilizer is best.
7. Given the pooled class data set for plant growth, students will be able to use their criteria for best fertilizer to judge which fertilizer provided the best results.
8. Given a centimeter ruler, a yardstick, a protractor, and a compass, students will be able to select the proper measurement tool to determine the lengths of familiar objects to the nearest millimeter.

The Affective Domain. Teachers are human and we are all committed to both the emotional growth and academic growth of our students. The affective domain does not encompass the whole area of emotional growth, but it is more heavily weighted in this area than the cognitive domain. Quite simply, we all want our students to like the subjects we teach, to like school, and to appreciate and enjoy learning. Although such feelings may not directly contribute to academic achievement, in a sense, they may have more lifelong effects than the learning of a specific subject matter. The affective domain can be represented in a much simpler hierarchy than the cognitive domain. There are three basic levels: complying, responding, and valuing.

The following three objectives represent the three primary levels of the affective domain:

1. Students will complete homework assignments 80 percent of the time.
2. When offered an opportunity to gain extra credit, students will choose to complete the extra credit assignment.
3. Students will voluntarily (without being asked) bring to class subject-related materials they have found at home.

As you can see, the affective objectives provided are fairly generic as opposed to being specific to any particular topic. However, it should be clear how each could be adapted to any particular content unit. Objective 1 is written at the level known as **complying.** When students are complying, they value a subject enough to complete all assignments and requirements. At a very basic level, completing assignments shows that the student does value the subject and/or class.

Focus on the Affective Domain

BOX 4.2

What interests your students? What makes them value what they are learning? When planning a lesson, be sure to take into account students' interests and backgrounds. For example, if many of your students are involved in soccer or basketball, be sure to incorporate these sports into your science lessons. This allows you to make a connection between an abstract science concept and something in the students' own lives, making the concepts more concrete through the connection to students' experiences and interests. When students can make a connection between what they are learning in school and the rest of their lives, they are more likely to engage in class discussions and actually learn and remember the concept being taught.

Objective 2 shows a slightly greater level of commitment on the part of the student. In this case, the student values the subject or class enough to voluntarily complete an extra credit assignment. This level of the affective domain is known as **responding.** In objective 3, the student has taken the initiative, without prompting by the teacher, to voluntarily bring to class subject-related materials from home. This is known as **valuing,** and it is indicative that the student sincerely values the subject or topic being taught. Affective domain objectives should be written for every unit or topic, along with cognitive objectives. They do not necessarily need to be related to student assessment and grading. In fact, the accomplishment of valuing-level objectives can quickly be reduced to either the complying or responding levels when credit is given for student-initiated work.

The Psychomotor Domain. The psychomotor domain relates specifically to students' physical skills and is typically divided into the two major categories of **gross** and **fine** movement. Science typically involves many fine motor skills, especially hand–eye coordination, during laboratory activities. Students will need such skills when making measurements with meter sticks, thermometers, and balances. They will also need such skills while using microscopes and preparing slides for viewing. The list is extensive, and these are just a few examples that will occur in your class.

An example of a science objective that you might write for a third-grade science class would be:

> The student will be able to connect wires, batteries, and bulbs while making a circuit.

This objective involves fine motor skills and is important to many activities you may do during a unit on electricity. Note that there is overlap between this objective and the cognitive objectives we discussed previously. The student must know how to connect the batteries, bulbs, and wires. This is the cognitive aspect

Two students work together to build a circuit.

of the task. However, whether the student can physically manipulate the materials in the appropriate manner is the psychomotor aspect. Psychomotor objectives normally contribute to the teacher's assessment of a student's academic progress. However, you will need to be particularly careful when working with students who have physical disabilities that prevent the completion of certain physical tasks. Although many physical skills are critical to science, it would be inappropriate to penalize a student for not being able to perform a task that is simply impossible given the student's physical condition. On the other hand, performance tasks in science classes can provide students with opportunities to practice and improve their fine motor skills. You will want to consider whatever adaptations you can to assist students with disabilities so that they can equally experience learning activities.

Objectives are written for each student with the expectation that each objective will be achieved by each student. However, student achievement of individual objectives, as stated, should not be the sole basis for the determination of student grades. The level of achievement of objectives by students in a class is directly related to the teacher's decision about whether to proceed to the next topic or unit.

The Lesson Plan

It's time to put what we have learned about objectives to use. The evolution of shoes has taken us to a situation in which many shoes do not have laces. For those shoes with laces, it is often considered fashionable not to tie the laces. Suppose you are planning a lesson designed to teach your students how to tie their shoes. This is not a science lesson, but the logistics of teaching the topic and skills will help us illustrate many of the important aspects of planning a lesson. The first step, as we have been discussing, is to develop instructional objectives for the lesson. Take a few minutes to think about what you would focus on during the lesson and what you would expect students to be able to do, and possibly know, after the lesson is completed. These expectations should be written in the form of instructional objectives.

Naturally, there is no way that we can know exactly what you decided, but your objectives should be something similar to the following examples:

1. Given a shoe with laces, the students will be able to tie the shoe using a bow knot.
2. Students will be able to state two reasons why it is important to tie their shoes.

The objective you wrote most similar to example objective 1 most likely did not specify the type of knot students would be able to use. We chose to specify the knot type because this is the most common knot used to tie shoes and because it is as easy to untie. We feel that an important part of tying shoes is also the ability to easily untie the knot you have used. Just as a review, in what domain of Bloom's Taxonomy is objective 1? Did you write an objective in the cognitive domain, as we have done with objective 2? In this particular case, we wanted students to know why the skill we are teaching is important as opposed to just having them learn the skill. If students understand the importance of the skill, they will be more likely to use the skill outside of school. Some of you may have included a time limit as part of the criterion component for the skill-oriented objective, though we chose otherwise.

Before we continue, it is important to remember that the objectives you, or we, have written are not set in stone. Objectives are written to guide the plan-

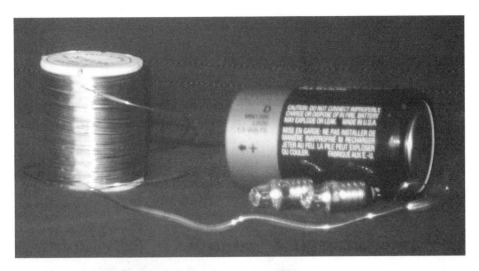

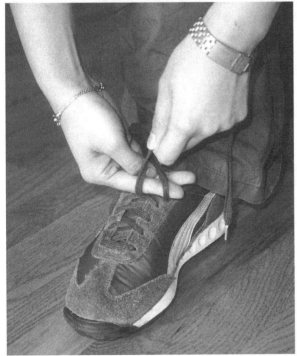

A close-up of the materials used to build a circuit: a wire, a battery, and light bulbs (above).

A student practices tying her shoe (left).

ning of instruction, but it is not at all uncommon for teachers to revise, add, or delete objectives during the planning process. For the sake of the plan yet to be written, we will start with the two objectives we provided previously. Assuming that your lesson will last approximately 60 minutes, the task can be quite daunting. Many beginning teachers find it useful to break the lesson into smaller blocks of time, based on instructional purpose, much like the sections of an essay (i.e., introduction, body, and conclusion), prior to beginning detailed planning. If you are an extremely organized person, you may find this step unnecessary, but for now let's proceed in this manner.

Hopefully, your list and sequence of lesson segments look something like this:

1. Introduction: Establish the importance of tying shoes
2. Demonstrate procedures: Teacher-centered experience
3. Guided practice: Students are slowly directed though each step of the task
4. Independent practice: Students practice task independently and at own pace
5. Closure

These five segments should provide the students with the necessary experiences to accomplish the objectives and assess learning. The time allotted to each step may vary depending on the difficulty and/or novelty of each segment. Take some time now to write your own lesson to accomplish the objectives using these five lesson segments. Remember that it has to fit within a 60-minute time frame.

Did your lesson include the following elements in the indicated lesson segments?

Introduction

- Something to capture students' attention
- Assessment of students' background knowledge
- Student involvement, for example, asking students why they think knowing how to tie shoes is important, what safety issues are involved, and what they want to know about shoe tying
- Background information and/or diagrams on the board or overhead
- Plans for giving and getting feedback, for example, writing student responses on the board or overhead
- What you will do if desired responses to questions are not received
- Time estimate for this section of the lesson plan

Demonstrate Procedures

- Questions to assess students' understanding as you demonstrate procedures
- Visibility of demonstration
- Involvement of students during demonstration
- Using students who already know how to tie shoes
- Translation of directions, such as right and left and crossing of laces
- List of items to be written on board or overhead
- Role of students during demonstration

- What you will do if desired responses are not received
- Time estimate for this section of the lesson plan

Guided Practice

- Grouping decisions
- Using students who already know how to tie shoes
- Questions to assess student understanding as they practice
- Materials planning and distribution
- Monitoring of the students' progress
- What you will do if desired responses are not received
- Time estimate for this section of the lesson plan

Independent Practice

- Grouping decisions
- Review of directions
- Using students who already know how to tie shoes
- Teacher monitoring of students' progress
- Questions to assess student understanding as they complete the task
- What you will do if desired responses are not received
- Plan for early finishers
- Time estimate for this section of the lesson plan

Closure

- Grouping decisions
- Collection of materials and cleanup
- Planned questions related to instructional objectives
- What you will do if desired responses are not received
- Follow-up assignments
- Time estimate for this section of the lesson plan

If your plans included most of these issues, then give yourself a pat on the back for a job well done. More likely, you focused primarily on the content to be covered and not the pedagogy used to facilitate student understanding. Most beginning teachers develop content outlines like these instead of what we call instructional plans. Hopefully, you realize that lesson planning requires a lot of behind-the-scenes effort that is not at all obvious when you watch an effective teacher present a lesson. Take our list of considerations and try to revise your lesson plans. Depending on what you included in your plan, you may need to add even more details. Table 4.1 contains an example of a lesson plan for the original objectives.

Table 4.1   Instructional Plan Template

Instructional Objectives: Given a shoe with laces, the students will be able to tie the shoe using a bow knot. Students will be able to state two reasons why it is important to tie your shoes.

Lesson Segment	Materials	Instructional Sequence	Feedback to/ from Students	Time Estimate
Introduction	N/A	Teacher, with shoelaces untied, walks across front of the room and fakes tripping. Teacher does this several times, while glancing down toward shoes, until a student mentions untied shoelaces. If there are no unsolicited comments, the teacher asks a student in the front row if he or she notices anything wrong and/or directs student attention to shoes.	Q/A Verbally acknowledges responses	7 minutes
		Once students have recognized that the teacher's shoes are untied, the teacher asks, "Why is it important for me know how to tie my shoes?"	Verbally acknowledges responses	
		Teacher continues to record students' suggestions until the following are listed: • So you won't trip on laces • To help keep your shoes on • So you won't ruin shoelaces • So you can do it yourself without help • If students fail to mention any of these in the allotted time, teacher will provide.	Teacher records answers on the board	
		The teacher quickly follows with the question, "How many of you know how to tie your shoes?" Teacher notes which students can tie their shoes for future reference, then states "The topic for today's lesson will be how to tie your shoes."	Verbally acknowledges responses	
Demonstration	Large poster board drawing of shoe with large laces, labeled 1 and 2	Teacher gathers students around her on the floor and shows poster board model of shoe. Teacher asks a student identified in previous section as being able to tie shoes how to begin. Teacher continues to use student input as appropriate as teacher models the following steps: • Take one lace in each hand • Cross the two laces		8 minutes

Table 4.1 Continued

Lesson Segment	Materials	Instructional Sequence	Feedback to/ from Students	Time Estimate
		• Loop lace 1 through resulting loop • Pull tight • Make a loop with lace 1 and hold at top of shoe • Loosely wrap lace 2 around the loop, creating a second loop • Push the middle of lace 2 through the second loop to form a third loop • Grasping the top of the first loop in one hand and third loop in the other hand, pull in opposite directions to tighten The teacher demonstrates all of these steps again and then asks students if they want to try it.	Teacher demonstrates each step using poster board model	
Guided Practice	Students were instructed the day before to wear lace-up shoes	Teacher asks students to untie one of their shoes. Teacher asks volunteers to sequentially provide each of the 8 steps. If teacher does not receive expected response, teacher provides the necessary information. Teacher demonstrates each step and helps students to follow along using their own shoes.	Verbally acknowledges student responses	15 minutes
Independent Practice	Lace-up shoes	Teacher instructs students to pair up with the person sitting next to them. Teacher instructs one student in each pair to provide the steps needed to tie the shoe while the other partner follows these directions. Once the shoe is tied, students switch roles so that both partners have a turn at tying their shoes. Teacher calls on several students to explain the directions for the task and asks clarifying questions, such as "What does the person not tying the shoe do?" "What does the person not giving the directions do?" Teacher tells students to begin. Teacher circulates among the student pairs to monitor progress and help as needed. Teacher asks procedural questions, such as "What do you do next?" Early finishers: Teacher challenges students to tie their partners' shoes.	Q/A	20 minutes

(continued)

Table 4.1   Continued

Lesson Segment	Materials	Instructional Sequence	Feedback to/ from Students	Time Estimate
Closure	N/A	Teacher has students return to their places at the front of the room. Teacher asks for a volunteer to come forward to tie the poster board shoe and then calls on individual students to direct each step. The teacher then refers back to the list of reasons to tie shoes that is on the board and asks students to discuss with the person next to them which are the two most important reasons. Teacher asks a couple of volunteers to share their decisions. And, finally, the students are instructed to practice their shoe tying at home.	Q/A	10 minutes

Evaluation Plan:
- Verbal responses from students
- Visual monitoring of students
- Next-day assessment of ability to tie shoes

Curriculum Connections

1, 2 Tie Your Shoe. 3, 4 Tie It Once More

How can the concept I am teaching be reinforced in other classes?

When planning a lesson, remember to check with other subject area teachers to share your ideas and find out what they are planning to teach in their classes. While having a conversation about your upcoming lessons you may identify meaningful opportunities to collaborate and integrate your topics so that they are covered in both classes.

BOX 4.3

For example, during a lesson on forces, you may talk to the physical education teacher and find that students are currently learning how to throw a baseball. You can make references to this activity in your class, and the physical education teacher can refer to the science that students are learning in his or her instruction as well. This will reinforce their knowledge about forces and, more importantly, will help students understand that knowledge is not discrete but can be applied to any area of their lives.

Ideally, meeting with other subject area teachers should be done regularly. Practically speaking, this is not always possible since most teachers' schedules are already packed. A good time to meet may be at the beginning of each term or whenever you find yourself planning the next unit you will be covering in class.

As you can see from the sample plan, our conception of instructional planning is a detailed and systematic description of the content that will be taught, as well as the instructional approaches and logistics used to teach the content. Experienced teachers hardly ever write instructional plans with such detail. However, if asked, effective teachers can provide the details that we have written. It is simply not necessary for them to write plans with such detail because they have most of the information about subject matter and pedagogy in their heads. Notice that we qualified our last statement with the label "effective teachers" as opposed to experienced teachers. Years of experience do not directly translate into effectiveness. Some teachers use their experience and others just accumulate experience. There are teachers who have taught for twenty years and there are teachers who have taught the same year twenty times. The research on effective teaching supports instructional planning as a critical factor to classroom effectiveness and student learning. Whether the plans are actually written is a different issue.

You will find, as you become more experienced, that the detail we have suggested is no longer necessary. You will no longer have to write down how you will handle student responses because you will fall into teaching routines that will consistently pay attention to getting feedback from students and giving feedback to students. You will no longer have to think about being sure to check for student understanding of instructions before sending them off to work on an inquiry-based activity. You will do this automatically. In many ways, much of what we have discussed will hopefully become analogous to driving a car. Driving is quite complex if you consider all that must be done or thought about. However, after a while, you do much of what is needed automatically. What the research indicates is that teachers eventually perform many essential pedagogical practices as if they were natural reflexes. These pedagogical procedures are often called teaching routines. These routines do not mean that you will eventually be able to effectively teach without thinking. Instead, the routines will help you streamline your teaching so that you can more readily attend to unexpected situations as they occur during the course of instruction.

As a beginning teacher, you must first develop your routines and preferred approaches to instruction. Our recommended plan is also a technique to help you think through lessons in a detailed manner. Our planning approach is heuristic to help you develop the perspective of a teacher whenever you think about instruction. Eventually, you will be able to wean yourself away from writing such detailed plans, and a more abbreviated instructional plan, with key phrases and words to jog your memory, will be all that is needed. For now, however, we recommend that you write your plans in sufficient enough detail that a substitute teacher can teach the same lesson in the same manner from reading your plans.

We have provided a particular template, or form, for instructional plans. There is nothing special about the form we have provided. However, we have

Learning Theory

Mapping Your Plan

It is important to know where you are going, but it is just as important that the students realize where they are going, as well as where they have been.

Your students need the opportunity to rethink what they know and connect past ideas to new knowledge. One way to achieve this is by creating a classroom-size concept map focused on a particular unit, or units, that you are teaching. The unit title or theme could be the central item on the concept map. Related topics could be linked to the main idea. The concept map should be large and displayed in a prominent area of the classroom. New ideas can be added as the unit progresses.

BOX 4.4

Connections to other subjects can be included by using different colored paper to represent different types of connections. For example, suppose you are teaching an astronomy unit. Astronomy would be the central idea in your concept map. Connecting ideas may include the moon, planets, and stars. As your unit proceeds, you can continue to connect more ideas to the subtopics, such as constellations, galaxies, or orbits. Interdisciplinary connections can also be linked into your concept map. You may have read a book to your class about the mythology behind a constellation. This mythology concept could then be connected to the particular constellation on the concept map. The literature concept should be a different color to enhance the interdisciplinary relationship. Green could be used for science concepts, red for literature, and blue for math. This colorful concept map can then be referred to throughout the unit!

found that teachers, in general, have found this format to be particularly useful. Our experience tells us that if we provide no template, teachers want a template, but if we provide a template, teachers are concerned about having to follow the template provided. Our advice is that you follow whatever template is comfortable for you to use during instruction. In this case, "comfortable" means a plan format that is easily viewed during instruction and a form from which you can quickly access the information you need, whether it be subject matter or pedagogical, during instruction. The key point, however, is that whatever planning format you use, it should contain the specific items that we have asked you to consider and use.

Summary

What follows is an overall summary of what we have included as essential considerations during instructional planning. In our opinion, this summary is an excellent "cheat sheet" that you can use to cross-check while planning lessons.

Important Planning Considerations

1. Include all planned questions and desired responses
    a. Consider what you will do if the desired response is not received
    b. Consider what you will do with the students' responses
2. Key points to stress in discussions should be specified
3. You must include an assignment somewhere in the plan
4. You must have a specific evaluation section at the end of the plan
5. Include all handouts, overheads, and lab descriptions and materials lists
6. Method-specific inclusions
    a. Films, videos, and/or computer programs
7. Prediscussion
8. Handout to focus the students' attention
9. Postdiscussion
    a. Demonstrations
10. Introduce and set context (predemonstration discussion)
11. Show setup of demo materials
12. Planned questions
13. Postdemonstration discussion
    a. Inquiry-based activities
14. Preactivity discussion
    a. Demonstration and discussion of procedures
    b. Safety precautions
    c. Cleanup procedures
    d. Plan for early finishers
    e. Question-and-answer session to assess student understanding
    f. Grouping plan
    g. Materials distribution
15. During the activity
    a. Planned questions
    b. Monitoring plan
    c. Review of safety precautions
    d. Reminder of cleanup procedures
    e. Cleanup
16. Postactivity discussion with planned questions

The foregoing outline specifically emphasizes the level of detail that is required for the "instructional strategies" portion of the lesson plan. Do not forget that successful instruction must also include the following general attributes:

1. Planning with specific objectives in mind
2. Appropriate strategies and methods
3. Logical flow of materials
4. Appropriate level of material
5. Introduction that is clear, concise, and attention getting
6. A variety of activities
7. Frequent and high-quality questioning
8. Periodic review
9. Closing summary
10. *Your personal touch* to produce a dynamic presentation!

Measurement, Assessment, and Evaluation of Student Learning

$\mathbf{A}$ grade is . . . ?

> A grade is an inadequate report of an inaccurate judgment by a biased and variable judge of the extent to which a student has attained an undefined level of mastery of an unknown proportion of an indefinite amount of material.

As a first-year teacher, Norm Lederman was greeted by this quotation written on the faculty lounge blackboard. At the time it was humorous and, unfortunately, true in many instances. We felt that the quote serves as a good reference point for this chapter. It is our sincere hope that the words written on the faculty lounge blackboard will simply remain as a humorous quote instead of a realistic description of your approach to student grading.

As you read each of the instructional segments in Chapters 9 and 10, you will notice that there is a concerted effort by the teacher to gather knowledge of student thinking and reasoning throughout all aspects of the lesson. Following the lesson, considerable time is also spent deliberating the direction of future lessons as well as the gathering of information to find out what the student has learned. In short, assessment and evaluation have been considered to be a significant aspect of the **teaching cycle.** When all is said and done, teachers need to find out how successful their instruction was at helping students develop desired understandings. The information they collect is critical for teacher self-evaluation as well as for the evaluation of student performance.

Measurement, assessment, and evaluation are critical responsibilities for all teachers and should not be taken lightly. Assessment and evaluation are so intertwined with the instructional process that the *National Science Education Standards* (*NSES*) have specified a set of assessment standards. Similarly, we have decided to devote a full chapter to assessment and evaluation, a chapter consistent with the vision of *NSES*. We have often heard the axiom, "Once you close the door to your room, you can do whatever you like." However, what a teacher does with respect to measurement, assessment, and evaluation cannot be hidden by closed doors. The contents of this chapter will help you develop a level of confidence in your assessment and evaluation approach that you will not see any need for hiding "behind closed doors." In particular, you will learn how to develop valid assessment items and make valid decisions (evaluations) based on students' performance on your assessment items.

Conceptualizing Assessment, Measurement, and Evaluation

You have just received a grade of 68 on a science test. How do you feel about the grade? Would you tell your friends you did poorly, okay, or great? What information would you need to make a decision on how well you did? How well students have performed on a test or any other task is a question that students may ask of themselves or may be asked by their parents. It is also a question that you will need to ask as a teacher. When considering what information a student needs to determine whether 68 was a good or bad score, the student may wonder: "How many points was the test worth?" "How did the other students do?" "What was the average score in the class?" " How do I usually do on science tests?" Although these are all very important questions, the student is probably not equally interested in the answers to each of these questions. The student probably has particular criteria in mind that help determine whether his or her score was good or poor. Other students in the class might not agree. One student might be most interested in the class average, whereas another would be more interested in how many points were on the test.

This short mental exercise can be used to clarify some terminology, such as *measurement, assessment,* and *evaluation,* that you will hear throughout your career as a teacher. You can look these words up in a dictionary or an education book on measurement and assessment and find a variety of definitions. The critical distinction you will need to be aware of as a teacher is the difference between a measurement and an assessment and the decision about the meaning of both measurement and assessment. We will be using the terms *measurement* and *assessment* as synonymous (although some may disagree). The score of 68 is a measurement or an assessment of a student's understanding of science, as measured by the particular test or task the student completed. It is not uncommon for the test or task to be called an assessment instrument, activity, or task. The decision about the meaning of the 68 is an evaluation. **Evaluation** is a judgment that teachers and students make about the quality of learning that is represented by a numerical score. It is very common for teachers to transform numerical grades into letter grades (e.g., A, B, etc.). This transformation is an evaluation of the meaning of the numerical score. We say that this practice is very common because there are some states (e.g., New York) in which the numerical score is what is reported on the report card as a grade. In such cases, the assessment, or measurement, is equivalent to the evaluation. We could also say that no evaluation or judgment was made by the teacher. Of course, this assumes that the numerical score reported has not been adjusted up or down.

Let us now return to the various questions you may have asked yourself in response to the original question of whether a score of 68 was indicative of a good or poor performance. A careful examination of your response to the question can be used to tell us something about your view of evaluation. When teachers are asked to make judgments about the level of a student's performance, a reference point is needed. We all need some frame of reference to make such decisions. In this case, the reference point may be the total points available, the performance of other students, or a comparison with how the individual student usually performs. If you were primarily concerned with how many points were available or what percentage of the total points was achieved with a score of 68, your views are consistent with a belief in criterion referencing. **Criterion referencing** is an approach to evaluation that is based on a preset criterion for what score or percentage of points constitutes a certain grade. The most common example of the criterion-referenced approach is the 90, 80, 70, 60 and 50 percent scale corresponding to letter grades of A, B, C, D, and F. In this case, the teacher has set up an a priori decision for what the various levels of performance mean. A criterion-referenced approach does not require quantification of student performance. Alternatively, clearly stated outcomes can be determined, as in the case of performance standards, and the quality of a student's performance is determined by checking his or her knowledge against the level of knowledge expected. The significant distinguishing characteristic of a criterion-referenced approach to evaluation is that student performance is evaluated against an a priori (determined beforehand) reference point.

It is more likely that you experienced a different approach to evaluation than the criterion-referenced approach while in college. In particular, how well you did was probably strongly based on how well your classmates performed. Consequently, in terms of our question at the beginning of this chapter, you may have wanted to know what the average score in the class was or how the other students did. This approach is characteristic of a **norm-referenced** approach. A reference point exists for making evaluation decisions, but instead of it being an a priori set of expectations, the reference is the performance of the other students in the class. This is the traditional process of curving or scaling to determine grades. A score of 68 would be considered as good, okay, or poor depending on the scores of the other students in the class. If the class mean was 58, then a score of 68 is anything but poor. Norm referencing can be accomplished using the class level as a reference group, or it can involve a much larger group, typically known as a norming group. The standardized tests that you have taken over the years (e.g., SAT, GRE) are all based on very large norming groups. A score of 1120 on the SAT exam is determined to be good or poor by the average score a student of your age and grade level is likely to obtain. If the average score on the SAT is around 1000, then a score of 1120 is considered to be a fairly good score. The level of your SAT performance is expressed in the form of a percentile rank, which is one way of indicating how well you did compared to others taking the test. The important point (no pun intended) is that the meaning of your score is determined by how well other students do on the same exam as opposed to any a priori set of expected knowledge outcomes. When considering how you feel about norm-referencing and criterion-referencing approaches, you may want to consider the following question. Would you prefer that your family doctor attended a medical school that evaluated performance using a norm-referenced or a criterion-referenced approach? What are the implications for the quality of medical care you may receive? Is this a relevant example or is the field of education different than the field of medicine?

You may not have responded to our question about the meaning of 68 in either of the ways discussed thus far. You, as well as many other elementary teachers, may have focused more on how the student had done on previous tests and/or tasks. More than a focus on a particular score, the focus would most likely be on the percentage of points usually obtained by the student. In our particular example, a student who usually achieves at the 30 percent level would have been considered to have done quite well if the 68 points were out of a possible 90. Such an approach to evaluation uses the individual student's previous performance as a reference and is typically called **self-referencing.** This approach to evaluation is primarily concerned with the progress a student is making relative to himself or herself as opposed to an a priori standard or with respect to the performance of other students. A self-referenced approach is often used with special needs students, but it is also very common in the lower grades. As with criterion referencing and norm referencing, self-referencing has both positive and negative attributes. Take a moment to consider the pros and cons of this approach. Have you ever been graded in a course based on the progress you made? Did this approach affect your effort in either a positive or negative way? Should a student who begins the year with very little understanding of science but ends the year with a moderate to high understanding receive the same grade as a student who begins and ends the year with a high level of understanding? Should the first student get a higher grade? Hopefully, you have realized that deciding on an approach to evaluate student achievement is no easy task. However, evaluation does remain an important and unavoidable task in our educational system.

Developing Assessment Items: Do They Match Your Instructional Objectives?

As you recall from Chapter 4, the first place to start when planning to assess student achievement is with your instructional objectives. As we have mentioned before, instructional objectives are absolutely necessary for quality instruction and assessment. The following are two examples of instructional objectives actually written by a sixth-grade teacher, along with a test item designed to assess student achievement for each objective:

1. **Objective:** Given a diagram of a cell, the student will be able to identify five of the cell parts discussed in class.

   Test Item: Name five of the cell parts we discussed in class.

2. **Objective:** The student will be able to list five carnivores and five herbivores.

   Test Item: Explain the nutritional relationship between carnivores and herbivores.

At what level in Bloom's cognitive domain would you classify the first objective? Do you still remember? If you are thinking the objective is at the knowledge level, you are correct. The student is simply expected to label or identify five cell parts on a diagram. The student should be able to do this from memory recall and the objective does not specify the student knowing anything other than the name of the organelle. What about the test item designed to assess the student knowledge specified in the objective? Is there a substantive match? Remember, the test item and the objective do not have to use the same wording, but the two should be consistent in terms of what the student is expected to know or do. The test item for the objective asks students to name five cell parts. At what cognitive level is the test item? It appears to be at the knowledge level because a student could certainly name cell organelles from memory recall. With this in mind, is there a substantive match between the objective and test item? You should have concluded that there is not a match. The test item requires slightly more from the student, even though it is at the same cognitive level. The test item expects students to recall the names of organelles without having a diagram to jog their memories. If we assume that instruction was based on the written objective, as it should be, it would be reasonable to assume that many students might have trouble with the test item. Quite simply, this would be a case of the test item being unfair because it is asking for knowledge above and beyond what was included in instruction. An appropriate test item for the stated objective would be to present the students with a diagram that includes cell parts and asks them to label five of these parts.

At what level in Bloom's cognitive domain would you classify the second objective? Again, we have an objective at the knowledge level. Presumably, classroom instruction would have included a discussion of various organisms along with a categorization of the organisms as carnivores or herbivores. It is implied that the student would be asked to list five carnivores and five herbivores on some type of assessment task, most likely a quiz, homework assignment, or test. Naturally, a student would be able to do this from memory. What is your opinion of the written test item? At what level is the test item? Is there a substantive match between the test item and the objective? It should be clear that the test item requires much more than memory recall. It is asking for an explanation of the relationship between carnivores and herbivores. Therefore, the student needs to know more than is specified in the objective. The test item would be classified at the comprehension level and is clearly a mismatch with the test item.

In each of the examples presented, there was a mismatch between instructional objective and associated test item. As a teacher, you always want to accurately assess student understanding relative to what was taught and to what you planned to teach. Without accurate information, you will not be able to adequately assess your own instruction or plan subsequent instruction. If test items do not match your instructional objectives, student performance on assessment tasks will either be lower or higher than is actually the case. The deviation will be an artifact of the mismatch and not an accurate measure of student knowledge. There is no substitute for checking each assessment item, whether it is a test item or a project, against the objective(s) it is designed to assess. However, time is at a premium for teachers. There is at least one effective shortcut that will let you know if there are potential problems with assessment tasks. Naturally, you will then have to investigate these potential problems further. The shortcut that we are referring to is called a table of specifications. This table comes in various formats, but we have found the following format, which ac-

Table 5.1   Table of Specifications and Objectives

Topic	Knowledge	Comprehension	Application	Analysis	Synthesis	Evaluation
Inertia	2	1, 3, 5				
Speed		4, 8	12, 13			15
Velocity	6, 7	9	10			
Force		11, 14	16	17		
Newton's Laws	18, 19	20	21			

tually involves the development of two tables, shown in Tables 5.1 and 5.2, to be the easiest to create and analyze.

Prior to developing an assessment instrument, a table of specifications that charts each of the instructional unit's objectives should be created. The table is developed by numbering the instructional objectives sequentially and then placing these numbers in the appropriate cell of a table that includes both subtopics and cognitive levels in Bloom's Taxonomy. Table 5.1 is a hypothetical table for a unit on forces and motion. The subtopics, for which objectives have been written, are placed along the left side of the table and the columns of the table represent the cognitive domain in Bloom's Taxonomy. Objectives that are written for the affective and/or psychomotor domain are easily placed in similar tables. We have chosen to represent the cognitive domain in our example because this is the domain that is most commonly assessed when determining student achievement. However, we strongly believe that students should be educated within all domains during science instruction.

Table 5.1 clearly indicates that a total of twenty-one instructional objectives were written for the unit on forces and motion. The unit addressed five

---

Testing, Testing . . .

How do you modify exams for students with learning disabilities?

This is often done by special education teachers, and it is important to know which students in your class have IEPs (individualized education plans). However, it is also important to remember that a learning disability does not equal lower-level-thinking questions. All students, no matter what their level of special needs, **BOX 5.1** should be challenged to think within all of the cognitive domains from Bloom's Taxonomy. This does not mean the questions need to be presented in a complicated manner that is difficult to understand. A task can be straightforward in nature and also assess higher-order thinking.

Issues in Diversity

Table 5.2   Assessment Items

Topic	Knowledge	Comprehension	Application	Analysis	Synthesis	Evaluation
Inertia	1, 3, 5	15	17	19A		
Speed	2, 6, 7	8, 10	4, 9			Project 2
Velocity	11, 12	13, 16	14	15		
Force		18, Project 1	19, 20			
Newton's Laws	21, 22	23, 24	25			

subtopics and the objectives were distributed equally across the subtopics. It should also be clear that the level of instruction, assuming it was consistent with the levels of objectives, typically reached the application level with the exception of inertia, and sometimes went beyond the application level. For this unit, the teacher has decided to assess student understanding using a combination of a test and two projects. All assessments for the unit are now included in a second table (see Table 5.2). Although our tables have been developed for the complete unit, it is perfectly acceptable to develop tables for individual assessments within a unit.

Table 5.2 was developed by listing the number associated with each test item in the appropriate location, as we did with instructional objectives in Table 5.1. In the case of the two projects, these are simply listed by name and number. As you recall from the sample objectives and associated test items we presented several pages ago, one potential problem with assessments is a mismatch in the cognitive levels of objectives and assessments. The development of a table of specifications can alert you to such a mismatch. Carefully inspect the items in Tables 5.1 and 5.2. Do you note any mismatches? Hopefully, you noticed that there are two assessment items for the topic of inertia that extend into the application and analysis levels (i.e., 17 and 19A, respectively). In contrast, the instructional objectives for inertia do not extend beyond the comprehension level. We can assume that items 17 and 19A will be too difficult for most students and should be revised. Do you notice any other mismatches? You may be thinking that there is a problem for the topic of speed because assessment items have been written at the knowledge level, but there are no objectives written at the knowledge level. Recall that Bloom's Taxonomy is a hierarchy, and if students have been taught at the comprehension level, they should be able to answer assessments at the knowledge level. We will leave it to you to consider any other potential problems highlighted by your analysis of the two tables.

As we mentioned before, a table of specifications is simply a shortcut to noting potential problems. It does not provide all the information you need as a teacher. In particular, there is one very important piece of information omitted from such tables. They do not specify which objectives are associated with which assessment items. For example, it is possible that objective 2 is unrelated to assessment items 1, 3, and 5. All the table tells us is that these assessment items are at the same cognitive level as objective 2. The table of specifications only provides you with a shortcut to the identification of potential problems with assessment. The only definitive way to identify problems is to check each assessment item against the particular objective(s) it is designed to assess. Therefore, even if your table of specifications looks like a good match with your assessment items, there may still be a problem that will surface after students have taken the test or completed the assessment task. Later in this chapter, we will discuss what your options are if you notice a mismatch after your students have taken a test or completed an assessment.

Developing Assessment Items: The Traditional Approach

Several years ago, the "traditional approach" portion of this section's title would not have been necessary. However, current reforms and contemporary knowledge about how students demonstrate what they have learned have spawned a much wider variety of assessment approaches than the typical test item. These alternative approaches are often called alternative or authentic assessments. This nomenclature is often used inappropriately. Authentic assessment is a principle we should all follow, regardless of the means for assessing students. It simply means that we have students demonstrate what it is we are trying to assess. If you want students to have the ability to make a wet-mount microscope slide, have them actually make a wet-mount slide instead of asking a multiple-choice question about the process. Paper-and-pencil tests or tasks can be authentic depending on the knowledge and abilities that are being assessed. The phrase "alternative assessment," when correctly used, refers to assessments other than the traditional paper-and-pencil questions (e.g., the two projects listed in our table of specifications). This section will focus on the traditional and familiar types of questions.

True–False Test Items

The following are actual examples of true–false items used on teacher-made exams:

      _____ 1. Water expands when heated.

      _____ 2. π is equal to 3.14.

      _____ 3. The chemical digestion of starch begins in the mouth.

Try to answer each of the questions. What did you decide? The key used by the teachers who created these questions had each one as being "true." Do you agree with the teachers' answer keys? It is true that water generally expands when heated, as is true of most forms of matter. However, water behaves a bit differently between the temperatures of 0 and 4 degrees Celsius. Between these temperatures, a given amount of water actually decreases in volume. You may be familiar with the reverse of this phenomenon. Water expands when it turns to ice.

When using π in mathematics and science classes, a value of 3.14 is used by convention. However, teachers should be sure to discuss with students that this is just a rounded value, and π is not equal to exactly 3.14. Interestingly, there is a state that has mandated by law that π is equal to 3.14. Regardless of the law, the mathematics community would beg to differ. Starch digestion does begin in the mouth when you are eating something like bread. However, starch digestion does not begin in the mouth when you are eating uncooked vegetables. This is one of the reasons why vegetables can provide roughage to your diet.

The point we are trying to make with each of these sample questions is that there is an exception in each case. If a student answered true for each of the foregoing questions, we would not know whether he or she was aware of the exceptions and, in the case of question 2, would not know if the student knew that 3.14 is an approximate value created by convention. If a student answered false to any of these questions, we would not know if he or she was aware of the exception or actually possessed a deeper misconception. In short, true–false questions are difficult to write for anything but very low-level subject matter that has definitive answers. As the examples we provided illustrate, there are even exceptions to some low-level ideas. Also, if students have no idea what the answer is, they still have a 50 percent chance of guessing correctly.

Are true–false questions all bad? What are some of their strong points? Each question is typically short and can be written and answered quickly. Therefore, you can put many of these on a test and assess a greater proportion of subject matter in a given amount of time. Scoring is also quickly done, preserving your valuable time.

Modified True–False Items

If you are worried about the students' ability to guess correctly and you also want to gather a bit more evidence about student understanding, there is a reasonable modification to the true–false test item. In this case, a portion of the question is underlined. If the students decide the item is false, they are instructed to change the underlined portion so that the item is true. This approach de-

A toad is one example of an amphibian, and an iguana is one example of a reptile.

creases the rate of guessing correctly without having any knowledge. Here are some examples of questions from actual tests for you to review:

1. Salamanders belong to the class <u>Reptilia</u>.

2. Spiders are <u>insects</u>.

3. A snake is not a <u>reptile</u>.

4. When a cold front passes through an area, the wind direction <u>changes</u>.

Take a few moments to answer the four questions. Question 1 should have been answered as false, and Amphibia should have been used to replace Reptilia.

In our opinion, this is a good test item because students often confuse reptiles and amphibians because of their similar appearance. If your goal is to have students learn the difference, this question will help you discriminate those who understand from those who do not.

How did you answer the second question? Spiders are often confused with insects but are actually arachnids; however, you could have also replaced insects with animals, cold-blooded, carnivorous, or eight-legged and still have been correct. Notice that question 1 provided a qualification (i.e., class) for the underlined segment, whereas question 2 did not. Therefore, multiple answers are technically correct for the second question. This question could be improved by using more careful wording that would specify the type of answer preferred (e.g., class). Item 3 is false as written because snakes are reptiles. However, the instructions for modifying false items are to revise them so that they are true. How would you do this? Which of the following would be acceptable revisions for "reptiles?": mammal, plant, amphibian, mollusk, worm, fish, polygon, ice cream cone. . . . The list of correct answers is endless. The problem with this question is the use of the negative (i.e., *not*) prior to the underlined portion.

Finally, question 4 defeats the purpose of the modified true–false question in terms of guessing. Because the underlined portion of the item is a dichotomy, there remain only two responses, *changes* and *does not change*. The chance of guessing is still 50 percent. Overall, modified true–false test items do provide some advantages over the regular true–false question (i.e., lower guessing success and more information about student understanding). However, the other advantages and disadvantages previously discussed remain.

Completion and Short-Answer Items

One sure way to significantly decrease students' chances of guessing successfully is to use the **completion** or **short-answer** type of assessment item. This approach still has the advantage of being easy to grade and many can be included on a single examination. Look at the following examples and see if there are any other advantages and disadvantages to such assessment items:

1. The person who invented the microscope was _____.
2. A substance has a volume of 3.3 cc and a density of 8.7 grams/cc. Its mass in grams is _____.
3. _____ exists at room temperature as a _____ and boils at _____ °C.

If you attempted to answer question 1, you probably noticed that more direction is needed. Is the correct answer the individual's name, nationality, or occupation? In a sense, all responses are potentially correct. Consequently, without very careful wording multiple correct answers are a possibility. This usually relegates these types of assessment items to knowledge-level cognition. We feel that item 2 is a good item because the expected response is very clear, including the appropriate units of measure. However, if the calculation of density involved multiple steps, such an approach to assessment would not be very informative. We say this because you would not be able to assess student understanding of each particular step in the problem. Since the completion-type assessment item only focuses on the final answer, you will be unable to provide partial credit to students who simply make a mistake in arithmetic during one of the steps.

Finally, you might have found yourself getting confused trying to answer item 3. There are simply too many blanks to be completed in this question. What makes matters worse is that the test item begins with a blank. If you think this item is confusing, imagine trying to answer the following item that was included in an introductory college-level biochemistry course:

> The hydrolysis of a polypeptide by chymotrypsin involves the formation of a _____ in which _____, _____ and _____ amino acid residues participate, the catalysis being initiated by the _____ of the _____ residue.

We recognize that your knowledge of biochemistry may be limited, but just reading the question should illustrate our point. Even students with a strong background in biochemistry find this question confusing. If there are too many blanks within the question, students do not have a strong enough frame of reference or context to discern what is being asked. We strongly suggest that completion-type items include no more than two to three blanks, with one or two being optimal. Remember that the goal is to assess what your students know, not to trick or confuse them.

Completion items are easy to construct and they do not rely as much on students' writing skills as essay items. However, they are almost too easy. There is the temptation for some teachers to randomly select passages from textbooks and other reading materials the students have read and simply omit random words. All too often, the words removed are trivial or peripheral to the science idea being assessed. The items you select for the blanks should be significant words that are directly related to the science concept being assessed.

Multiple-Choice Items

The **multiple-choice** type of question is perhaps the most widely used of all test items. Again, it is easy to grade and many items can be included on a test because they typically do not take students a long period of time to answer. The issue of guessing arises again, as this item type provides a selection of responses from which students choose an answer. However, the chances of guessing are vastly lower than true–false items because there are usually four or five answers to choose from. If written carefully, multiple-choice items can assess both high- and low-level types of outcomes. What do you think about the following sample item?

_____ Who wrote *The Origin of Species* in 1859?
   a) Darwin
   b) Carl Sagan
   c) Jane Goodall
   d) Watson & Crick
   e) Neil Armstrong

You most likely know that choice "a" is the correct answer. Let us consider what might happen if you did not know Darwin wrote the book in question. With the exception of choice "a," all of the people mentioned worked far more recently than the publication date of *The Origin of Species*. It would be possible for you to eliminate these choices as a possibility simply by knowing that *The Origin of Species* was written a long time ago. The question you need to ask yourself as a teacher is what information do you want your students to use when eliminating choices? In our opinion, eliminating the choices in the preceding question would be based on knowledge other than what this question is trying to assess. It would have been much better to replace these choices with the names of other, less contemporary scientists who worked in the same field as Darwin.

If multiple-choice items are written with plausible distracters (i.e., response choices), then they are effective at assessing a variety of cognitive outcomes, spanning various cognitive levels. They also permit the recognition of patterns

Issues in Technology

Test Bank Alert!

BOX 5.2

Coming up with good test questions can be a challenge. Sometimes you need some ideas to jump-start your creativity. Fortunately, most publishing companies include test questions with their curricular materials, and if you are lucky, they also may provide their bank of test questions on a CD-ROM. Test bank resources are also available on the Internet.

These resources can be useful as you create tests for your students, but you will want to keep several factors in mind. The questions provided in the test bank are unlikely to be a perfect match with the content you addressed in your class. Test questions need to be carefully selected and modified to match your objectives. Students might be confused by test questions that use different wording than you used in your instruction. Also, you'll want to pay particular attention that the reading level required by the questions is consistent with the reading ability of your students.

As you can see, test banks are helpful for constructing tests, but they do not eliminate the need for you to make thoughtful decisions.

in incorrect responses. For example, you may notice that most students answering a question incorrectly tend to choose the same distracter. This information may inform subsequent teaching as it provides some clear data about how students interpreted your instruction.

Matching Items

Carefully read and attempt to answer the following assessment item:

Directions: On the line to the left of each expression/word in Column A, write the letter of the expression/word in Column B that best fits.

Column A	*Column B*
1. _____ Chlorophyll	A. Respiration
2. _____ Photosynthesis	B. Transpiration
3. _____ Water Given Off	C. Carbon Dioxide Is Used
4. _____ Oxygen Used	D. Green Plants

How did you answer the question? You may have chosen the following sequence of responses: D, C, B, A. This is the sequence of answers that the teacher intended students to choose. However, you may have noticed that D is a correct choice for all items. Because the instructions do not specify that an answer cannot be used more than once, either set of responses should be graded as correct. Indeed, if any response can be used more than once, there is a variety of other response sets that are correct for this question. **Matching items** are an effective way to assess student knowledge of lower-level outcomes (e.g., definitions) without having to write a full question for each. However, the wording of choices must be done very carefully. Also, as you have already noticed, the wording of your directions should be clear. If the directions are not clear, students cannot be held accountable for not understanding your intended meaning.

There is one other important issue related to matching items. Have you noticed any problem created by the fact that there is the same number of items in each of the columns? Think about it. If we assume that the question and directions were more carefully written to avoid multiple correct answers, what happens after a student has answered the first three items? The final answer is determined because there is only one choice remaining. This creates a problem because the student will get the last question correct or incorrect depending on whether there is a mistake in the previous answers. Consequently, the student will not get item 4 correct or incorrect based on his or her knowledge of that particular question. The solution to this situation is clear. Simply make sure there are more potential responses in Column B than Column A. We suggest that Column B contain approximately one-third more responses than there are items in Column A.

Essay Items

Extended essay questions requiring in-depth answers are much more common to the upper elementary grades. The primary reason for this is that a student's ability to respond correctly is significantly related to the student's ability to read and write. Completion and short-answer items, as well as any of the other assessment items discussed, are more amenable to younger students who have not yet developed strong reading and writing skills. However, essays are perhaps the most efficient way to assess higher-level understandings of students while affording them flexibility of expression. In short, it is the best way to gain in-depth knowledge of what your students know. As a beginning high school biology teacher, one of us included the following question on an exam:

> The squid is a mollusk that has been used extensively in neurological research because of its highly visible axons. You may recall that a squid propels itself through the water with a highly coordinated contraction of muscles. A large ganglion, with many branching neurons, is responsible for such contraction. The neurons that extend from this ganglion innervate various parts of the squid's musculature, meaning that the stimulatory impulses emanating from the ganglion travel varying distances to their respective effectors. Given that the impulses are initiated simultaneously and that they must arrive at their effectors simultaneously (so that coordinated contraction can occur), offer a description of the histological anatomy of the squid's nervous system. In other words, what relative structural characteristics are necessary, within the nervous system, for coordinated muscle contraction?

How would you react if confronted with this question? We have all taken tests with questions like this before. The text is long, full of unfamiliar vocabulary, and leaves you wanting to ask, "What is the question?" The question presented was simply trying to assess student understanding of the influence of nerve cell structure on the speed of nerve impulses. The problem is that rather than just ask the question, the teacher attempted to be highly technical and ended up creating a highly complex and abstract question. Again, the purpose of assessment is to find out what students know and are able to do, not to confuse and frustrate them.

Well-constructed essay questions are not easy to write but are well worth the effort. They allow your students flexibility of expression as opposed to having to fit responses or explanations into constrained response formats. Unfortunately, students can not complete many essay questions in a given amount of time and so this assessment approach is limited in terms of assessing all the science ideas or concepts included in a single unit of instruction. Essay questions are also not easy to grade and are often criticized for not being an objective assessment of student knowledge. However, essays can be as objective as the other types of assessment items if a scoring guide is carefully constructed. If it is clear what you are looking for in students' answers, you and a colleague should arrive at the same assessment of a student's response. If you choose to use essay questions to assess student understanding, we recommend that you follow these guidelines:

1. Before scoring any papers, review the material relevant to the question.
2. List the main points that should be addressed in a correct response, along with associated point values.
3. Read a sampling of students' responses to obtain a general idea of the quality of answers to be expected.
4. If there is more than one essay question to be scored, read through all answers to one question before scoring the next question.
5. Read through each answer once and then a second time for factual details.

Undoubtedly, you have noticed that essay questions are labor and time intensive. We suggest, however, that you attempt to use such questions occasionally. They will not only give you a different view of student understanding but will also help students develop both reading and writing skills.

Are All Assessment Items Equal?

In order to answer this question, first practice writing the six types of assessment items we have discussed. Your assignment is to write an assessment item, using each of the six types, for each of the following three objectives. This should give you a total of 18 assessment items, six for each objective. Here are the objectives:

1. The student will be able to identify the characteristics of scientific inquiry.
2. Given a specific research question, the student will be able to identify a valid strategy to answer the question.
3. The student will be able to identify two beneficial and two negative aspects of two different approaches to answering a question or problem.

Each of these objectives is specifically related to scientific inquiry, one of the most strongly advocated emphases of current reform efforts in science education. Consequently, you will be expected to teach your students about inquiry, as well as assess their knowledge of inquiry. This is a good chance to start developing your approach to assessing this important instructional objective. Although objective 1 addresses inquiry in general, objective 3 will require you to place your assessments within the context of particular questions or problems. The question or problem you use for context is your choice. Now, it is your turn. Try to write assessment items for each of the three objectives using each of the six types of assessment items discussed.

If you sincerely tried to complete the assigned task, you may be feeling a bit frustrated, in addition to having had a chance to practice your assessment writing skills. We must admit that there was a hidden agenda to our task. Some assessment items lend themselves better to certain types of instructional objectives than others. If you did not try to complete the assigned task, you will still be able to see our point but without the accompanying frustration. If you look at the set of instructional objectives in terms of Bloom's Taxonomy, you should note that the first objective is at the knowledge level and the objectives that follow sequentially increase in cognitive level with objective 3 being at the highest level. Essay questions should have been the easiest to write for the set of objectives, although it may have seemed unnecessary to write an essay question for objective 1. This objective hardly takes advantage of the potential value of an essay question. On the other hand, you probably found it extremely difficult to write true–false or multiple-choice questions for objective 3. If you did not attempt to write assessments, try to write some now—don't just take our word for it. Our primary message is that true–false, modified true–false, and matching questions are not well suited for higher-level objectives, whereas essay questions are. On the other hand, essay questions are not necessary for assessing lower-level objectives. When deciding how to assess student knowledge, you will need to carefully consider what type of item is the best for assessing what you tried to teach. It would not be appropriate to decide in advance the types of questions you will ask or to only use certain types of questions regardless of instructional objectives. The decision of what assessment approaches to use is closely related to the learning outcomes you are attempting to measure.

Summary of Traditional Assessment Approaches

We have discussed quite a bit relative to traditional assessment items. Before we move on, here is a summary of some of the key points to remember about the advantages and disadvantages of the six types of assessment items discussed.

True–False Items
1. easy to write
2. easy to grade
3. short in length (which allows many items on a test)
4. limitations:
   - 50 percent chance of guessing correctly
   - absolute words (e.g., *never, always*) normally indicate that item is false
   - restricted primarily to lower-level knowledge

Modified True–False Items
1. student is required to rewrite false statements so that they are true
2. reduces probability of guessing

3. limitations:
   - except for 50 percent guessing success, has same problems as true–false items

Multiple-Choice Items

1. most widely used test item form
2. can be used for a wide variety of cognitive levels
3. easy to grade
4. limitations:
   - plausible distractors are difficult to construct
   - guessing can be a problem if there are too few distractors (less than four)
   - too many distractors increase emphasis on student reading ability (more than five)

Matching Items

1. actually a variation of multiple choice
2. easy to grade
3. easy to write
4. limitations:
   - normally restricted to lower-level knowledge (e.g., knowledge, comprehension)
   - proper construction is critical
   - be sure that the number of response choices is greater than the number of statements
   - be sure to specify whether answers can be used more than once

Completion or Short-Answer Items

1. usually recall or calculations
2. easy to write
3. easy to grade
4. limitations:
   - use of more than two blanks per question can be confusing
   - there is a tendency for teachers to copy statements from textbooks and delete random phrases
   - multiple answers are usually appropriate

Essay Items

1. easy to construct
2. excellent for assessing higher levels of knowledge

3. limitations:
  • difficult to objectively grade but you can alleviate the problem
  • difficult to include many essays on a single test and this limits assessment of all concepts in unit

Note: Be sure to construct a model answer or outline prior to scoring. Then assign point values to appropriate content within your outline or model answer.

Developing Assessment Items: An Alternative Approach

During the past decade, educators have realized that traditional assessment techniques, like those we just illustrated, are often not appropriate for the measurement of instructional outcomes. Consequently, recent reforms have introduced terminology such as *authentic, alternative,* and *performance* assessments. Although these terms are often used synonymously, they are not the same. The primary purpose of all science assessments is to get an accurate measure of student understanding of the scientific concept, process, or idea under consideration. An *authentic* assessment is one that most accurately assesses what a student is expected to know and/or be able to do. If you want to assess a student's ability to focus a microscope, asking the student to recall the procedure on a paper-and-pencil test is not very authentic. A more authentic measure would be to have the student actually focus a microscope during a

Issues in Diversity

What Is Best to Assess?

BOX 5.3

If your students have diverse backgrounds, you may be wondering if they will do better on alternative assessment tasks than on traditional tests. The intent of alternative assessments is to provide students with the best opportunity, or medium, for them to express what they know and can do. Often traditional testing approaches are biased to those who read and write well. Alternative assessment tasks will probably give you a more accurate picture of what your students know and can do because they focus on the ability of students to apply knowledge in real-world situations. However, it does not mean that more traditional test scores will show a dramatic rise concurrent with gains evident on alternative measures. Performance differences on open-ended assessments (as opposed to multiple-choice tests) may even be greater for some students. This may be the result of those students spending more time being drilled on basic skills, rather than being exposed to rich ideas and problem-solving activities that are a trademark of alternative assessments.

laboratory practical. Authentic assessments are those that are closely aligned with the knowledge or skill expected of the student. As a consequence of current knowledge about student learning and reform efforts, authentic assessments are often considered to be those that are more firmly based in the daily life experiences of students. It is certainly possible for a traditional assessment to also be authentic. Often this has not been the case and the quest for authentic assessment has led to the use of alternative and/or performance assessments. *Alternative* assessment is a general term that refers to all assessments other than traditional approaches. Having a student focus a microscope is an example of a *performance* assessment. For our purposes, we will consider any assessment approach other than a traditional paper-and-pencil test item as an alternative assessment.

The Laboratory Practical

Quickly look ahead to the teaching cycle example related to physical and chemical change presented in Chapter 8. Would it have been possible for Ms. Patla to have taught her students about physical and chemical changes using a different set of activities and then chosen to use the described laboratory practical as an assessment of what they had learned? Hopefully, you answered "yes." The hands-on and minds-on stations designed by Ms. Patla are unique in that they can be used to teach students about physical and chemical change, as well as assess knowledge of physical and chemical change. Naturally, some of the wording and instructions at each station would need to be altered to correspond more to an assessment than to an instructional activity. In addition, how students rotated from station to station might need to be altered, depending on whether the assessment was viewed as an individual or group activity. Nevertheless, student responses to the task at each station could be used as an authentic assessment of student understanding. Why do we say this laboratory practical would be considered to be *authentic*? The student has been asked to directly interact with the materials and phenomenon, and he or she has been asked to characterize each as a physical or chemical change. The students have been given an opportunity to directly experience the phenomenon in question as opposed to reading a description of it. Finally, many of the phenomena experienced at the set of stations are closely related to students' everyday experiences.

If Ms. Patla used the laboratory stations as an assessment, would you also describe the assessment as a *performance* assessment? How will you decide? A start would be to think about each station and decide if part of the assessment of student knowledge involves doing something. However, just doing something is not enough. If the "doing" indicates student knowledge of the science ideas or skills of interest as well (e.g., focusing a microscope), then the assessment is of the performance type.

Portfolios

Portfolios have become widespread in their use as a type of alternative assessment. An increasing number of school districts and states have adopted portfolios as alternatives to report cards, graduation requirements, or even as evaluations of preservice and in-service teachers. However, they are much more complex than the single assessment of a small set of instructional goals or objectives that we have described so far. Portfolios are a collection of various forms of evidence with a particular purpose or focus in mind. They are more than a comprehensive collection of all of a student's notes, assignments, tests, projects, and so on. In short, a portfolio can be considered as a means by which a student can "make a case" or provide evidence for his or her learning. It is not a scrapbook. Contrary to the content and organization of the student folders that many teachers currently use, a portfolio includes a selected sample of student work that is systematically assembled as evidence for the students' learning and knowledge with respect to a particular set of instructional goals. These goals can be as global as course or curriculum goals or as specific as unit goals.

When using a portfolio assessment, some decisions need to be made at the very beginning. Because the portfolio is put together with a particular purpose in mind, consider the following questions: What will the portfolio be used for? What will the included documents provide evidence about? Will the portfolio be designed to show progress or will only the student's best work be included? What forms of evidence will be included? How much evidence is needed? Because the portfolio is being developed and organized as evidence for student learning, should the student have some input into the answers to these questions? Should the teacher make all the decisions about what should be included and what should not, and about what should count as evidence and what should not? There are no definitive answers to these questions, but careful consideration is required. Discuss these questions with your colleagues. What do they think?

Although portfolios differ widely, there appears to be a core of items included as evidence. **Artifacts** are any documents produced in the normal course of work by students (e.g., tests, projects, assignments, etc.). **Reproductions** are documents of typical classroom events that are not usually recorded. For example, you may have your students working on a bulletin board for the classroom as part of instruction. Once the bulletin board is removed there is no record of it. A photograph of the bulletin board may be included in a student's portfolio as evidence for his or her learning of a particular topic. **Attestations** are documents about a student's work from someone other than the student or teacher. For example, a student may have participated in a science fair and has received feedback forms from the judges. Or your student may have worked with the school custodian on a recycling project and he or she has a letter of commendation from the custodian. Finally, **productions** are documents that are prepared especially for the portfolio by the student. Productions may include goal statements that provide support for the accomplishment of the portfolio goal,

Curriculum Connections

Portfolio Planning and Production

Using alternative assessments, such as portfolios or visual representations, provides an opportunity to make the assignment interdisciplinary in nature. Portfolios could easily be considered both a record of scientific knowledge and application and a record of writing skills. Because they often include a good amount of written documentation, portfolios provide students with an opportunity to work on their language arts skills while simultaneously applying the science they have learned. Similarly, when students create visual representations of their scientific knowledge, they are also being given the opportunity to put their artistic skills into practice.

BOX 5.4

In more long-term projects such as portfolios, students can certainly learn a lot more than science in completing the assignments. This also means the additional time needed to complete these alternative assessments can be divided between the different subject area teachers involved in the project. An example would be a long-term research project for a science class in which a lot of writing would need to be done. In addition to being evaluated on the science that it covers, it could also be worked on and assessed in English class in terms of the writing quality and structure. Assessments such as portfolios provide a valuable opportunity to integrate other subject areas into a science lesson.

reflective statements that discuss how the portfolio contents provide evidence for personal growth, and captions attached to each included document that describe what it is and why it is evidence.

Interviews

Conducted in the style of a conversation, a teacher asks each child or a small group of children questions about the activity in which they are engaged. These questions are directly linked to the lesson's learning objectives. A general series of questions might include:

- How did you begin your activity?
- Why did you do that?
- What did you see?
- Why did this happen?
- How is this related to what we did earlier in class?
- What do you think will happen next?
- What did you learn?
- What do you still want to know?

There are a number of advantages to this method of assessment. Shy or less confident students are often more comfortable in individual or small groups settings. They are more likely to express themselves freely and share their ideas

A kindergarten teacher interviews a student to assess his progress.

during these safe conversations. Teachers also have more freedom during these interviews to modify their lines of questioning to adjust to the responses of students, customizing each interview to suit the needs and style of each child. Therefore, the interview provides the teacher an opportunity to find out what each individual student knows and provides the student with greater flexibility to communicate what he or she knows.

Managing Your Science Classroom

Independence!

How can you manage the rest of a class when you are busy assessing just a few students with interviews?

One way to minimize classroom problems is to provide interesting activities for the other students while working with your selected students. Such activities should be engaging and also contribute to student learning. They should not just be "fillers," but rather they should be activities that all students will eventually have to complete because they are important for their learning of future concepts. At first, it will be difficult to use interviews for assessment without experiencing some management problems. However, students will eventually learn your behavioral expectations for this assessment approach, and it will provide you with the time and freedom to make observations of student behaviors or to conduct interviews.

BOX 5.5

Visual Representations and Pictures

Students can be given illustrations or asked to draw their own pictures to show their understanding of concepts, order of events, or relationships. Pictures can be cut out from old magazines and newspapers in class or at home or can be downloaded from computer clip art programs on classroom computers. Always remind students that it is not their artistic ability but their understanding of science that is being assessed in these assignments. Examples of assessment tasks that use illustrations are:

- Order pictures of the stages of the life cycle of a butterfly.
- Arrange pictures of living organisms to reflect their relationship in a food web.
- Draw a picture of what happened during a lab.
- Draw a picture of your results.

Students work on creating a visual representation of the science content they are studying.

- Draw the parts of a water cycle and use arrows to show how they are related.
- Make a collage of items that use energy to work.
- Make a collage of different marsupials.

Interviews and visual representations are particularly useful when assessing learning in primary-level grades. Traditional methods of assessment are often limited in K–2 classrooms because the information given by young children depends on their language arts abilities and often does not reflect the actual science learning that has occurred.

Concept Maps

This category of assessment involves the consideration of central themes, ideas, and/or concepts and juxtaposing them to show interrelationships. Because this type of assessment involves broad knowledge of concepts and processes, concept maps are especially useful methods to assess learning at the end of curriculum units. Concept maps provide students with the opportunity to express their understanding of relationships between concepts and processes through schemes that include an ordering of concepts linked by verbs or phrases and arrows that indicate the flow of the relationships. They provide the teacher and students with insight into students' knowledge as well as insight into their understanding of the knowledge. Figure 5.1 presents an example of a concept map created by a young child.

Teachers can direct the construction of the maps by first providing the students with the main concept and a list or paragraph of terms to be included in the map. For example, at the end of a unit on motion, students could be directed to construct concept maps that include the following terms: *force, speed, acceleration, deceleration, friction, mass, weight, distance, time, balanced forces,* and *unbalanced forces.*

Concept map assessment tasks can be made more challenging by providing only a main concept. Students are instructed to design their own maps from their understanding of information presented during a unit about this main concept. This open-ended approach should only be assigned after students have become familiar with concept map construction and have had practice creating more directed forms. Pairs or small groups of students can share their individual maps and submit a single entry for a group grade. The rich discussion that occurs as students pool their information and arrange the relationships among concepts and processes can make the assessment task a valuable learning experience.

Journals

Writing across disciplines is considered a valuable application and extension of language arts skills as well as a useful tool to assess the understanding of other

Figure 5.1 Concept Map

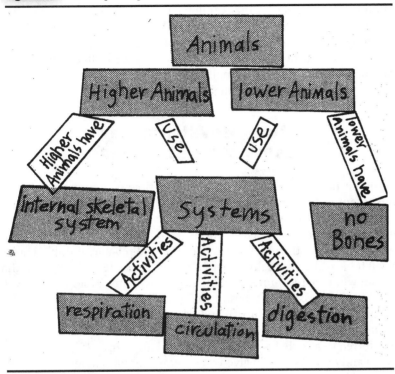

subjects. Keeping a journal can be a valuable tool for teachers and students to assess their learning of science. Journals can be used during science classes to record observations, calculations, drawings, charts, questions, conclusions, concept maps, and so on. In this way, it becomes a science log of information gathered during each science class.

Students can also be given a different "question of the day" to consider and answer in their journals that is directly linked to the daily topic, such as:

- How did your cup of water change as the temperature changed?
- What happened when you shined a light on your snail?
- Why did your toy truck roll faster on the wood floor than the rug?

Journal entries can also answer the same questions each time:

- What did you learn today in science class?
- What do you still what to know?

In all of these situations, students are provided with a means to formulate their thinking and reflect on their understanding of science. Teachers can use this information to assess student learning and evaluate the effectiveness of their own teaching. Grading all student journals on a daily basis would be much too time consuming. Teachers can randomly collect three to five journals daily for consideration or incorporate journal grading and reviewing while conducting individual student interviews throughout a unit.

How Are Alternative Assessments Evaluated?

Although alternative assessments provide a feasible way to more validly assess certain student outcomes, they are not without problems. How does a teacher score an alternative assessment? How do you grade a portfolio or what a student says during an interview? Clearly, the type of answer key you need to create will look nothing like the one you used for that old reliable multiple-choice test. What will it look like? Actually, what you need to create will not be all that different from what we recommended for essay-type items. Basically, you will need to decide two things: What types of things are you looking for related to the instructional goals (i.e., indicators), and what value is placed on the various levels of quality you are likely to see? The answers to these questions are commonly referred to as **rubrics** in the educational literature. Rubrics are not easily developed and used. We could give you several examples to look at, but that approach would not be particularly useful. The best way to learn about rubrics is to practice developing a few yourself. What we would like to do now is get you started.

In Chapters 1 and 2, scientific inquiry was specifically addressed as an instructional outcome. We emphasized that students need to know about inquiry as well as be able to do inquiry. These are both very different and complex instructional objectives. Let's focus here on the ability of students to do inquiry. The assessment of student ability to do inquiry cannot be done with a traditional form of assessment. We could ask students about the different aspects of inquiry (e.g., data analysis). We might even give them a question to be answered and ask how they would proceed. This approach would be headed in the right direction, but would it be authentic in the way we have defined authentic assessment? The answer is probably not. The most authentic way to assess students' ability to do inquiry would be to have them actually do inquiry. The assessment will be performance based and it would fit into our definition of an alternative assessment. As you have already guessed, we will need to develop a rubric for our assessment.

Here are your parameters and a few hints. Assume that you are developing a rubric for a fifth-grade class. Because scientific inquiry as an instructional goal is achieved over the long term, it would be best to view your rubric in terms of what you would expect students to be able to do by the end of the school year. You also need to consider that students will vary in how well they exhibit the indicators you have noted. This is where you are able to distinguish how well students are doing relative to the standards (i.e., indicators) you have set. For example, you may include "analyzing and interpreting data" as one aspect of inquiry. When considering this aspect of inquiry, you should develop indicators that illustrate different levels of quality that a student may exhibit. How many levels is totally up to you. It is now time to start. Develop your fifth-grade rubric for the performance of scientific inquiry. When you are finished, compare the rubric you created with the sample we have created in Table 5.3.

The rubric you created is most likely much simpler than the one we created. There is no need to get concerned. We have been working with rubrics for many years and you are just learning about the topic. Our rubric divides scientific inquiry into four general areas: **Framing the Investigation, Designing the Investigation, Collecting and Presenting Data,** and **Analyzing and Interpreting Results.** Below each of these aspects, we have written in *italics* an explanatory definition of the aspect. We have decided to create six levels of indicators for each aspect of inquiry. How many did you use? The bold line between the third and fourth levels for each aspect is what we consider a distinguishing point between acceptable and unacceptable. This demarcation is not an essential component of developing a rubric. It is more of a reflection of what we are seeing across the nation. An increasing number of states and school districts are developing cutoff levels for various content standards that have been developed at the state and district levels. You may find this type of cutoff useful in the determination of grades for tasks that are assessed using alternative approaches.

As you compare your rubric to ours, we want you to focus on some very important aspects of a well-designed rubric, not that ours is perfect. The indicators, regardless of level, should be as clear and concise as possible. Rubrics do not have to be complex. The example we have presented is complex because scientific inquiry is complex. The indicators should be easily noted or documented by a teacher when observing students' work. In addition, the better the rubric, the more easily it is consistently used by individuals other than you. Would you and your friend provide the same evaluation of a student's work if you evaluated it independently using our rubric? Can you say this about your rubric? Hopefully, you can see that the rubric is really not any different than developing a scheme for the evaluation of an essay test item. The main thing to keep in mind as you practice is that the purpose of the rubric is to provide you with a clear and functional framework to guide your evaluation of alternative assessment tasks. The ultimate goal is to allow you to accurately, fairly, and consistently evaluate the work of all your students.

Table 5.3   Sample Scoring Rubric for Performance of Scientific Inquiry

	5th Grade: Framing the Investigation (F) *Use observations/concepts to formulate and express scientific questions/hypotheses to frame investigations.*	**5th Grade: Designing the Investigation (D)** *Describes designs for scientific investigations to provide data that address/explain questions/ hypotheses.*	
6	a) Explains the origin of the question and/or hypothesis based on background that is relevant to the investigation. b) Expresses a clear question and/or hypothesis with advanced support for thinking. c) Formulates or reframes a question and/or hypothesis, which can be answered or tested using data, and provides focus for a scientific investigation.	a) Records logical procedures with an obvious connection to the student's scientific knowledge. (Teacher guidance in safety and ethics is acceptable.) b) Communicates an organized design and detailed procedures. c) Presents a practical design appropriate for answering the question or testing the hypothesis with evidence of recognition of some important variables.	6
5	d) Links background to the question and/or hypothesis. e) Expresses a clear question and/or hypothesis with detailed support for thinking. f) Formulates or reframes a question and/or hypothesis that can be answered or tested using data gathered in a scientific investigation.	d) Records logical procedures that imply a connection to student's scientific knowledge. (Teacher guidance in safety and ethics is acceptable.) e) Communicates a general plan including some detailed procedures. f) Presents a practical design for an investigation that addresses the question or hypothesis and attempts to provide a fair test.	5
4	g) Provides some support or background (prior knowledge, preliminary observations, or personal interest and experience) that is relevant to the investigation. h) Expresses a question and/or hypothesis with some support for thinking. i) Formulates or reframes a question and/or hypothesis that can be explored using data in a simple scientific investigation.	g) Records logical procedures with only minor flaws. (Teacher guidance in safety and ethics is acceptable.) h) Communicates a summary of a plan and some procedures but generally lacks detail. i) Presents a practical plan for an investigation that substantially addresses the question or hypothesis.	4
3	j) Provides a background that is either irrelevant or missing. k) Expresses a question and/or hypothesis that is not supported. l) Formulates or reframes a question and/or hypothesis that provides limited opportunity for data collection.	j) Records generally logical procedures having flaws. (Teacher guidance in safety and ethics is acceptable.) k) Communicates an incomplete summary of a plan with few procedures. l) Presents a practical plan related to the topic that minimally addresses the question or hypothesis.	3
2	m) Not applicable. n) Expresses a question and/or hypothesis that is not understandable. o) Formulates or reframes a question and/or hypothesis that cannot be explored through a simple scientific investigation.	m) Records that are significantly flawed. (Teacher guidance in safety and ethics is acceptable.) n) Communicates an incomplete summary of a plan that is difficult to follow. o) Presents a plan somewhat related to the topic that may not address the question or hypothesis.	2
1	p) Not applicable. q) Does not express the purpose of the investigation as either a question or a hypothesis. r) Not applicable (see q).	p) Records procedures that are wholly inappropriate. q) Communicates a plan or procedure that cannot be followed. r) Presents a plan that is impractical or unrelated to the topic.	1

Table 5.3   Continued

	5th Grade: Collecting and Presenting Data (C) Conduct procedures to collect, organize, and display data.	*5th Grade: Analyzing and Interpreting Results (A)* Analyze results to develop conclusions.	
6	s) Records accurate data and/or observations consistent with complex procedures. t) Designs a data table (or other format) for observation and/or measurements that is efficient, organized, and uses appropriate units. u) Transforms data into a student-selected format(s) that is most appropriate to clarify results.	s) Reports results and identifies simple relationships (e.g., connecting one variable to another). t) Explicitly uses results to address the question or hypothesis and illustrates simple relationships. u) Not applicable.	6
5	v) Records accurate data and/or observations completely consistent with the planned procedure. w) Designs a data table (or other format) for observations and/or measurements that is organized and uses appropriate units. x) Transforms data into a student-selected format(s) that is complete and useful.	v) Reports results accurately and identifies obvious patterns (e.g., noting a pattern of change for one variable). w) Explicitly uses results to address the question or hypothesis. x) Not applicable.	5
4	y) Records reasonable and sufficient data and/or observations generally consistent with the planned procedure. z) Designs a data table (or other format) useful for recording measurements or observations. aa) Transforms data (e.g., graphs, averages, percentages, diagrams, tables) with teacher support and with minimal errors.	y) Summarizes results accurately. z) Responds to the question or hypothesis with some support form results. aa) Not applicable.	4
3	bb) Records reasonable data and/or observations consistent with the planned procedure with some obvious errors. cc) Designs a data table (or other format) that is inadequate for recording measurements of observations. dd) Does not transform data into a teacher-recommended format.	bb) Summarizes results incompletely or in a misleading way. cc) Responds to the question or hypothesis without support from results. dd) Not applicable.	3
2	ee) Records insufficient data and/or observations inconsistent with the planned procedure. ff) Uses a teacher-supplied data table with minimal errors. gg) Not applicable.	ee) Summarizes results inaccurately. ff) Provides a response(s) to the question or hypothesis that is unrelated to the investigation. gg) Not applicable.	2
1	hh) Records data and/or observations unrelated to the planned procedure. ii) Does not correctly use a teacher-supplied data table. jj) Not applicable.	hh) Omits results in summary. ii) Does not respond to the question or hypothesis. jj) Not applicable.	1

Evaluation: Making Judgments from Assessments and Measures

Developing assessment items or tasks and presenting them to your students (either in the form of a test or assignment) is only part of your teaching responsibility. The real work begins once you get the tests or tasks back from your students and complete the scoring. It is now time to make a judgment about what the score means. We have previously referred to this step as evaluation, and it is the primary reason for the assessments you have had your students complete. The first issue related to evaluation is how the scores will be used. No doubt this decision was made before the assessments were even developed, but we have yet to discuss the two primary types of evaluation.

Although assessments and evaluations are most commonly used to provide feedback to students and parents in the form of a grade or verbal description, there is another purpose that is equally important. The current reforms in science education and emerging knowledge about teaching and learning have clearly emphasized the importance of students' prior knowledge and understanding. In short, instruction that considers the principles of constructivism focuses heavily on assessing the prior knowledge of students and using this knowledge to guide instruction. Assessment and evaluation of student knowledge, whether they are questions during class, tests, quizzes, projects, or homework assignments, are primarily used to guide subsequent instruction and/or class planning and are examples of **formative evaluation.** This type of evaluation can be used for purposes of grading students. However, more often than not, the only purpose is to provide feedback the teacher can use to enhance subsequent instruction. Do you remember the days when you took a spelling or mathematics pretest on Monday and a posttest on Friday? The pretest was a formative evaluation. Your teacher probably used the pretest to guide his or her instruction during the week as well as provide you with feedback on your own initial knowledge. The pretest scores may have contributed in some way to your grade in the subject, but this was not the main purpose. The posttest, on the other hand, was used to provide the teacher with a final evaluation of your knowledge of the material. The posttest is an example of **summative evaluation.** Some common examples of summative evaluations are unit tests, chapter tests, quizzes, and so on. You may have already noticed that the format of both summative and formative evaluations is the same. The critical difference is in how the evaluations are used. Formative evaluations are primarily used to inform subsequent instruction and course development, whereas summative evaluations are a final assessment of what students have learned.

Regardless of how you plan to use your assessments and evaluations, it is important that the assessments provide an accurate measure of student understanding. Inaccurate assessments can result in evaluations that are equally inaccurate. Have you ever taken a test that included questions on topics that were never covered? Have you ever been asked to complete an assignment for which you were not provided adequate instructions? What would your score on either the test or assignment mean? Would it provide your teacher with accurate data on what you knew about the particular subject matter?

We have already discussed one approach to ensuring that your assessments are consistent with instructional objectives. That approach was a shortcut called a table of specifications. We also mentioned in our discussion of the table of specifications that there are mismatches that may remain hidden no matter how careful you are. These mismatches do not appear until after students have completed assessment items or assessment tasks. Consequently, after you have determined students' scores, there are further steps you can and must take to further ensure that the scores are to be trusted. It is not too late to correct problems, even though the students may have already taken a test. It is not too late provided corrections and adjustments are made prior to the evaluation step. Remember, poor assessments can only result in poor evaluations of student performance.

Perhaps the simplest final check a teacher can do after students have taken a test is to determine how many students correctly answered each assessment item or calculate the average percentage of points achieved on assessment items providing variable point values. As a general rule of thumb, if more than 50 percent of your students have incorrectly answered a particular assessment item (or fewer than 50 percent of the points were achieved on the average for variable credit items), there is a problem. The problem may be with the assessment item or it could relate back to the quality of your teaching. In either case, you may want to eliminate this assessment item or adjust students' scores for these items. If 50 percent is too lenient for you, a cutoff of 60 percent can be used. The choice is yours, but remember the primary goal is for your assessment item to be a fair measure of student learning.

Evaluation: Determination of Grades

As we have mentioned throughout this chapter, there are two primary approaches to evaluation currently used in schools: criterion referencing and norm referencing. A third is self-referencing, but it is not as commonly used and, we predict, will decrease in use within the climate of learning standards and educational accountability. As a quick review, criterion referencing is determining grades using a priori levels of performance as a reference point, and norm referencing uses the relative performance of students in comparison with their classmates as a reference point.

Evaluating student performance is a relatively straightforward task in a criterion-referenced system. You simply add each student's scores on all assessment items and then compare the total against a preset point total or percentage. This is the traditional 90 percent, 80 percent, 70 percent, 60 percent for grades of A, B, C, and D. The specific criterion levels you set are a professional decision you will need to make, or your school district may have a particular written policy that specifies criterion levels for specific grades. As a new teacher, the primary problem you will have in using a criterion-referenced system will be your ability to develop fair assessments. The reason most teachers (beginning and experienced teachers alike) give for not using a criterion-referenced approach to evaluate is lack of confidence in their ability to consistently develop assessment items or tasks. They simply do not want their students to achieve less than they should because of poor assessments. We maintain that careful and consistent construction of a table of specifications, followed by item analyses after assessment, will allow you to remove or adjust unfair assessments. If this argument is not convincing, there is always the norm-referenced approach to evaluation.

Norm referencing is done in a variety of ways, ranging from informal to systematic. The first step, whether determining grades for a course, unit, or a single test, is to develop a frequency distribution for student scores. Figure 5.2 is an example of a frequency distribution for students' scores on a 90-point test in a class of 35.

Each *x* indicates a student score. For example, four students achieved a score of 71 on the exam and the highest score was 89. The most common approach to norm referencing, or curving, is an informal procedure called the **inspection method.** The teacher simply eyeballs the distribution of scores and looks for natural or convenient break points. For example, the six top-scoring students would receive an A with the scores ranging from 87 to 89. We did the easy one. Which students would receive a B? How far down would you go? Is the natural break point at 81, 79, or 77? Actually, the four students receiving grades of 74 and 75 achieved above 80 percent. Shouldn't they get Bs? You will need to make

Figure 5.2   Frequency Distribution for Student Scores

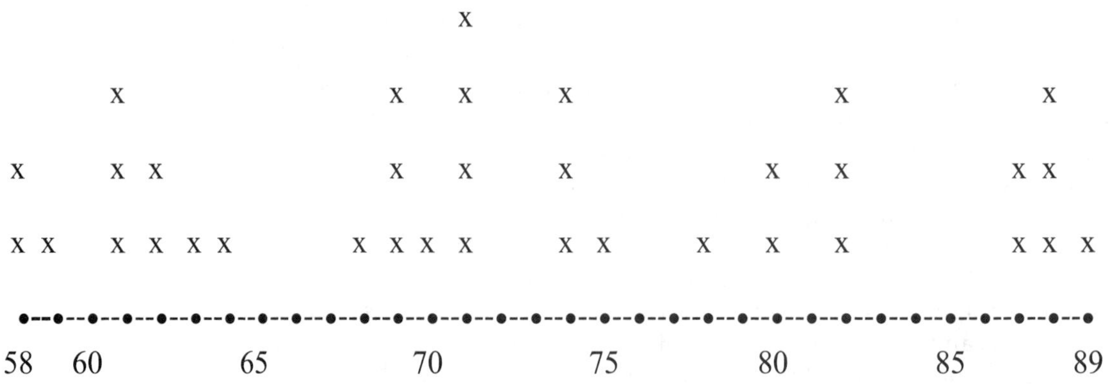

some hard decisions regarding the relative importance of total percent achieved versus break points. Personally, we would extend the B range all the way down to 74, but this is because we are supporters of a criterion-referenced approach, and we place much value on the percent correct achieved by the students. However, this is supposed to be an example of norm referencing. Where do you stand on this matter?

There appear to be several other natural break points toward the lower end of the distribution (i.e., 68, 64, 61, and 59). The question that looms is whether your final grading scale will include A–F. A typical norm-referenced approach would give the students toward the lower end of the distribution Ds and Fs. However, keep in mind that 70 percent is a score of 63 on this exam. When searching for natural break points does not yield easy decisions, teachers find themselves referring to percentages, or asking themselves if they are giving too many As, Cs, or Fs.

Naturally, your goal as a teacher should be to reduce the number of students receiving Fs and Ds as much as possible. In the ideal world, all of our students would get either As or Bs. Unfortunately, none of us live in the ideal world. Although as teachers we are an extremely important influence on the lives of our students, we are but one of a multitude of influences. Try as we may, the best we can hope for is a minimization of poor student performance. It is unrealistic to think that a quality science education alone will eliminate less than desirable student achievement. Do not misunderstand our meaning. We are not advocating that we should give up because all students will never succeed regardless of what we do. We are just trying to buffer our recommendations with some harsh reality. We strongly believe that every teacher should approach every student with the expectation that the student can achieve at the highest level.

Summary

This chapter presented a firm foundation on a wide variety of topics related to the assessment and evaluation of student performance. Of utmost importance was the stress placed on being sure that the content and type of assessment should be as consistent as possible with the desired outcome you stated for student learning in your instructional objectives. Sometimes this assessment can be done with multiple-choice questions, whereas at other times a long-term project is needed. We also stressed the importance of evaluating the quality of your assessment items. All too often it is the assessment item that is at fault rather than a shortcoming in students' learning. Finally, we discussed the determination of grades (i.e., evaluation). If you are feeling a bit overwhelmed at this point, we totally understand. Assessment and evaluation are complex and difficult, but they are serious business to students, parents, and teachers.

As you continue your journey of development as a teacher, you will no doubt face many hard decisions related to the assessment, measurement, and evaluation of student learning. These tasks never become easy. However, please continue to use the quotation presented at the beginning of this chapter as a reference point. Remember that all evaluation requires a reference point. The further your assessment and evaluation practices move away from the reality described in the quotation, the higher your grade.

Gathering and Evaluating Curriculum Materials

In Chapter 2, we defined *curriculum* as a combination of the subject matter to be taught and the instructional approach used. As a beginning teacher, you will most likely be using a curriculum designed by someone with many more years of experience than yourself. In addition, you will be using curriculum materials (i.e., textbooks and associated resources) that were also selected by someone else. As you become more experienced, you will be called on to help in the selection process. Depending on where you teach, this may come sooner than you think. The process of selecting textbooks and associated materials is a very important decision because it significantly influences both the subject matter and instruction that students experience. For most teachers, the primary curriculum resource is the textbook.

It is unfortunate that most teachers tend to teach directly from the textbook. Rather than using the textbook as a resource, it is used as the curriculum. It is regrettable that this approach transfers all the responsibility of deciding what students are to learn and how they are to learn (i.e., presentation of subject matter) to textbook publishers and developers. This would be fine if the textbook happens to be a perfect match with the goals of your school and the students in your class. Because there is no way a textbook publisher can know the important details about your particular teaching situation, this is usually not the case. On the other hand, we do think that having good materials to support your instruction is absolutely necessary, and these materials usually come in the form of a text and associated materials such as laboratory or activity books.

All teachers have some input into the textbooks that are adopted by their school districts and/or schools in their personal area of expertise. This input comes in a variety of forms. In some states, there is a textbook adoption list from which teachers can select their preferred texts. In other states, the selection is much more open and teachers can pretty much select whatever textbooks they wish within the constraints of their particular district or school. These constraints range from cost considerations to the aforementioned adoption lists that may have been created at the district or school level. Whatever the mechanism you will face, it is our opinion that your selection of textbook and supporting materials should be an informed choice and it should be guided by your professional knowledge about subject matter and pedagogy. After all, you will have to live with your decision for several years (usually about five) before you will be allowed to change textbooks. You should be selecting textbooks or materials for reasons that extend well beyond visual appearance and aesthetic appeal. The following chapter will provide you with a systematic approach that you can use in the selection of the curriculum as a whole or in the selection of associated curriculum materials. The chapter will conclude by providing you with a variety of resources for curriculum materials, as well as a useful way to organize the materials you have collected.

What's Important to You?

If you have not thought about what you prefer in instructional materials before now, this is a good time to start. If nothing else, the process will help you clarify your instructional philosophy and views about student learning. Take a moment to make a list of what you would look for in the textbook and associated resource materials for use in your classroom. Other beginning teachers whom we have worked with created lists like the following:

1. Reading level
2. Vocabulary
3. Glossary of terms

4. Activities for students

5. Summary questions at the end of chapter

6. Instructional goals and objectives

7. Illustrations coinciding with text

8. Teacher's guide with answers

9. Tests and other assessments

10. Supplementary resources

How does your list compare? It is probably not exactly the same, but we guess there is probably some overlap. Neither your list nor the one we have provided is *the* right list, but such lists do serve to clarify what you think is important when considering the teaching and learning of science. Although it is true that there is no single set of characteristics that all curricula or instructional materials should contain, there are certain central attributes that can be derived from the research on teaching and learning. *Project 2061* has developed an evaluation procedure that incorporates these central attributes.

As we have mentioned before, *Project 2061* is the science education reform effort developed by AAAS. In an effort to inform teacher evaluation and selection of curriculum and instructional materials, AAAS has spent almost five years developing a systematic evaluation tool. To date, this evaluation tool is the most extensive one available to teachers. Although developed with *2061 Benchmarks,* this evaluation tool can be used with the criteria that follow, along with a brief explanation of each criterion as well as a complete listing of *National Science Education Standards,* any state-developed standards, or any other identified instructional goals. Specifically the *2061* analysis tool enables the teacher to examine the instructional materials with respect to how well they address (substantively and pedagogically) the instructional goals identified for student learning. A summary of the AAAS explanation of the criteria can be found at the AAAS website (www.aaas.org).

Project 2061 Curriculum Evaluation Criteria: A Summary

Criterion I: Content Match. There is a subject matter match between the material and the particular goal, benchmark, or standard. Does the instructional material address all aspects of the intended instructional goals? Does it go beyond or fall short of these goals?

Criterion II: Identifying and Maintaining a Sense of Purpose. The material clearly identifies, or has students identify, why they are doing what they are doing in an interesting, motivating manner. Does the material convey an overall sense of purpose and direction that is understandable and motivating to students?

Criterion III: Taking Account of Student Ideas. The material recognizes the importance of the knowledge and ideas students bring to instruction. Does the material identify what students need to know to understand the instructional goal and how to identify students' conceptions, commonly held misconceptions, and ways to address common misconceptions?

Criterion IV: Engaging Students with Phenomena. The material engages students directly with scientific ideas. Does the material provide students with firsthand experiences with scientific phenomena when appropriate?

Criterion V: Developing and Using Scientific Ideas. The material provides evidential support for scientific ideas and opportunities to apply scientific knowledge. Do the materials build an evidentiary base for the scientific ideas and provide students with opportunities to use the knowledge?

Criterion VI: Promoting Student Thinking. The material promotes higher-level thinking and self-monitoring of progress. Does the material encourage students to ask questions, express their ideas, and monitor their own learning of the instructional goal?

Criterion VII: Assessing Student Progress. The material adequately assesses the intended goal. Does the material include assessment tasks that match the instructional goal, including higher-level applications? Are these task integrated throughout the material?

Criterion VIII: Enhancing the Learning Environment. The material helps the teacher provide a creative learning environment. Does the material help the teacher create an open and safe classroom environment that promotes curiosity, inquiry, and creativity of all students?

Take a moment and compare your list of expected items in curriculum materials with those included in the *Project 2061* evaluation tool. Are they similar? Would you add anything from the *Project 2061* list to your own list? One very useful aspect of the *2061* evaluation criteria is that they are derived from the empirical research on teaching and learning. This does not mean that the concerns you listed as important to you should be ignored. You will need to feel comfortable with the materials you select for use with your students. However, you will also want to ensure that the materials you use contain aspects that are typically related to improved student achievement.

The *2061* evaluation approach can be used with either existing materials that you are evaluating relative to specified learning goals, or it may be used to help you create materials for use with your students. You may be in a school or district that has no elementary-level science textbooks and part of your job will be to develop and piece together all the science materials that will be used to teach science. In such cases, the 2061 approach can be used as you develop materials. The questions posed by the evaluation procedure can be used to ensure that the materials you create have certain attributes.

Evaluating Curriculum Materials

The best way to begin to understand a process, whether it is in science or curriculum evaluation, is to do the process. So far, all we have done is talk about the process. It is now time for you to experience and practice the process. If you are currently working in a school, use the curriculum materials your supervising teacher is using. If you are not currently in a school-based practicum, select an elementary-level curriculum from the curriculum library or resource center in your department or college library. Your methods teacher is also a great source for such materials. Pick a unit from the materials you have selected and carefully read through both the student and teacher materials (if you have the teacher's edition). As you do this, consider what benchmarks (from the *Benchmarks for Science Literacy*) the materials do a good job of addressing. There are 855 benchmarks, but this task is not as ominous as it may seem. For example, if you pick a unit on rocks and minerals, the best place to find relevant benchmarks would be in Chapter 3, The Physical Setting. In addition, you may also find some relevant benchmarks in Chapters 1, 7, 8, 9, and 10. There is no need to look through the total set of benchmarks. Identify the two benchmarks you think your materials do the best job addressing. If you do not have access to *Benchmarks for Science Literacy* or prefer to use the *National Science Education Standards* or your state's content standards, the procedure would still be the same. Chances are high that your state standards are based on either the *Benchmarks,* the *National Standards,* or a combination of the two. As you review the materials, choose two benchmarks or learning outcomes that you feel are best addressed.

Now comes the hard part. Use the eight *Project 2061* criteria and evaluate how well the materials address each criterion for each of the two identified learning outcomes. This will require a careful reading of the materials but will provide you with a very detailed analysis of how well the materials actually address the learning outcomes you have identified. Most often, teachers never go beyond the initial superficial analysis you performed to identify the two benchmarks. This is why publishers are able to claim that all of their texts are consistent with national reforms. Completing this process will help you avoid the problem of your materials falling short of their intended purpose during instruction. Then you, as the teacher, will not have to scramble to collect additional materials to supplement what you have. It is much easier to note shortcomings and adjust in advance than in the middle of teaching a unit. How well the materials actually address each of the criteria will vary, so you might want to develop a simple scoring guide or rubric to use as you evaluate the curriculum materials.

Making Sense of the Analysis

After completing the analysis, you may be surprised by how the curriculum materials you chose fared. First, it is important for you to keep in mind that if, for example, the materials were produced before the *Benchmarks* were created, it would be quite a coincidence if there were a good match. After all, the materials could not have been created using the *Benchmarks* as a guiding framework. Also keep in mind that it may be possible to revise the materials so that they more completely address the learning outcomes you have specified. However, this is not always the case and you may simply need to search for or develop more adequate materials.

Perhaps the most important criterion on the list of eight is Criterion I: Content Match. We say this because one of the primary reasons curriculum materials and instruction fail is the lack of consistency between instructional goals and instruction or the lack of consistency between materials and the learning outcomes they are supposedly designed to promote. This idea should not be new. You probably recall from our discussion in Chapter 4 about planning how important it is for there to be consistency between instructional objectives, instruction, and evaluation. Here is an example to illustrate what we have been discussing. Suppose the materials that you analyzed had students classifying the shoes they were wearing based on lacing style. This is a whole class activity designed for fourth grade. Since you are using the *Benchmarks for Science Literacy* for the analysis, you identify the following benchmarks from the section on Diversity of Life, Grades 3–5 as an apparent match with the materials:

1. A great variety of kinds of living things can be sorted into groups in many ways using various features to decide which things belong to which group.
2. Features used for grouping depend on the purpose of the grouping.

If you carefully read these benchmarks and compare them with the emphasis in the curriculum materials, it becomes evident that benchmark 1 is only partially addressed. The activity has students sorting shoes into categories, but there does not appear to be any emphasis on the idea that a variety of features could have been used to sort the shoes or the higher-level concept that groups of living things can be formed based on similarities and differences. The curriculum materials have specified a particular sorting characteristic and have not communicated to students that other characteristics could have been used to validly sort or group the shoes. There is absolutely no mention of the relationship between the purpose of sorting and the particular feature used for sorting, so benchmark 2 is not really addressed either.

The pile of shoes above could be sorted in many different ways by a group of students.

Revising Curriculum Materials
Based on Your Analysis

At this point, you would need to decide whether the materials are so far removed from what you intended students to learn (assuming the *Benchmarks for Science Literacy* was your reference point) that they are inappropriate or whether the materials can be revised to address more adequately what you intended. What do you think? Can the materials be adjusted without too much of a time investment or should you search for better materials? We think that a simple revision of the materials can more directly align instruction with benchmark 1. By allowing the students to develop their own sorting features, the students can quickly see that various features can be used. Naturally, the students would also need to realize that grouping the shoes is meant to be analogous to what scientists do with living things. On the other hand, if the benchmark that you are attempting to teach is, "Some animals and plants are alike in the way they look and in the things they do, and others are very different from one another" (a benchmark specified for grades K–2), you would conclude that the materials are inappropriate in terms of both grade level and content. It would not be easy to revise the presented activity to address the intended content and the best approach would be to search for better instructional materials or to develop something of your own.

Let us assume that you have decided to revise the sorting activity we have just described so that it directly matches the benchmark that states, "A great variety of kinds of living things can be sorted into groups in many ways using various features to decide which things belong to which group." However, please remember that the curriculum analysis procedure we have been using is designed for sets of curriculum materials as opposed to individual activities. Since the example we are using consists of just one activity, the actual revisions you will make will probably a bit more complex. You may have already noticed that of the eight *Project 2061* criteria, seven are pedagogically based. Indeed, another way to view the set of criteria is that the first one considers the critical match between curriculum materials and learning outcome, whereas the remaining criteria focus on aspects of instruction that will influence the likelihood that students will learn the subject matter included in the curriculum. Consequently, the revisions you make related to Criteria II–VIII may seem to be less substantial than those associated with a mismatch on Criterion I.

Let us consider what you found in your analysis relative to Criterion II. Did the materials you looked at do a good job of letting the students know or having the students consider why they were being asked to learn what was being presented? Quite often curriculum materials present students with a variety of activities, which might be quite engaging, but students have no sense of purpose for doing these activities. The activities do not seem to be leading to a solution to a problem or directing students toward answering a question of interest. It does not matter whether the purpose is communicated to the students by the teacher or students are asked to derive the purpose themselves, but unless a sense of purpose is evident and maintained throughout a unit, student achievement is compromised. As the teacher, it is possible for you to enhance existing curriculum materials through revisions that clearly communicate a sense of purpose. Is this missing from the materials you reviewed? Is it possible for you to do this with the materials you reviewed?

For the sorting activity we described earlier, lack of attention to Criterion II can be corrected if the teacher precedes the activity with a class discussion about the tremendous diversity of living things in the world. Students could even be asked to make a list of the living things they see every day on their way to school. Alternatively, the teacher could begin the unit without even mentioning living things but instead focusing on the types of music in which students are interested. Whatever the approach, instruction would eventually focus on the human (or scientific) need to organize the complex set of living things in the world into a more manageable form. With such an introduction, the sorting activity we described has a very clear purpose. Even if the original activity would be enjoyable to students, the addition of instructional activities and approaches that provide a sense of purpose would enhance the instructional integrity of the sorting activity with respect to the benchmark. This sense of purpose would also need to be maintained through a careful consideration of the activities that followed the shoe sorting activity.

Criterion III involves taking into account student ideas and preconceptions. Once again, review your selected curriculum materials, this time using Criterion III. The material should recognize the importance of the knowledge and ideas students bring to instruction. Does the material identify what students need to know to understand the instructional goal and how to identify students' conceptions, commonly held misconceptions, and ways to address common misconceptions? If the instructional materials you reviewed do not address student thinking, then you will need to add strategies to the material that will include this. Let's go back to the sample activity on grouping shoes that we have been reviewing and revising to show you what we mean. This activity does not address students' ideas or their prior knowledge of classification. Benchmark 1 states that living things can be sorted into groups using various features. When soliciting the students' ideas, you will not only want to find out what they know and think about grouping in general but also what features they consider to be important when creating their groups.

In the introduction of the lesson, you can have a discussion with the students about grouping. You can ask if any of them have collections, such as rocks, stamps, dolls, or toy cars, and why certain items belong in the group or collection. You may show them a sample of a collection of your own. Ask the students why they think these items all belong in a collection. Then ask them if it was possible to make more groups of items within the collection. This line of questioning will

A group of rocks is an example of one type of collection.

reveal students' background experiences with groups and their conceptions about criteria for grouping. If at this point you find that your students have no experience with classification or too many misconceptions about classification, then you will probably want to reconsider teaching this activity as planned and revise it to address student misconceptions first. For example, although students may be able to put shoes into groups, they may not be able to distinguish between good criteria and bad criteria. That is, if they believe that all grouping criteria are equally valid, this will affect how well they will understand the classification criteria for living things later on in the unit.

When you cross-check your curriculum materials against Criterion VI, you are looking to see if the material provides students with opportunities to express their ideas and evaluate their own progress. This information will not only inform the students of their progress but will also provide you with feedback about their progress. Does your instructional material include suggestions for ways in which students can routinely express, clarify, justify, and represent their ideas? You will probably find that most instructional materials only include opportunities for students to express their ideas at the end of a lesson or activity as an assessment and that these suggestions are seldom provided routinely. However, it is possible for you to weave more student feedback opportunities into the material. In the shoe grouping activity, there were no suggestions for ways in which students could express their ideas about classification during the lesson or other ways in which students could check their progress as they proceed through the activity. Can you think of suggestions you might add to this activity to make it better meet Criterion VI? Again, effective questioning can be added to the material to provide opportunities for students to express their ideas. For example, once the students are in their groups sorting the shoes, it is possible for you to circulate around the class and ask questions. These work groups also present an opportunity for students to express their ideas and get feedback from their peers. Therefore, a suggestion or reminder to do this could be included in the materials.

Also included in the instructional materials could be the suggestion to have the students present their final shoe grouping decisions to the class, thereby providing them with an opportunity to defend their ideas. One aspect of Criterion VI that we have not addressed here is the provision of opportunities for students to monitor their own progress. By now, you should begin to see that there are methods that can be used to adjust most curriculum materials to meet the various components of an evaluation criterion.

Through our examples, you should have also realized that if curriculum materials do not fair well against the *Project 2061* evaluation criteria, there is still hope. Virtually all curriculum materials have valuable aspects even if they also have numerous critical shortcomings. It is possible to salvage materials that initially do not fare well. You may have also noticed that the sample revisions we provided seemed very much like revisions to a lesson plan. This is because seven of the eight criteria provided by *Project 2061* are pedagogically based. You will

Learning Theory

Curriculum Modification Based on Student Prior Knowledge

What do your students know before they walk into your classroom?

When planning your lessons and modifying curricula, it is important to think about varying levels of student knowledge and experience. Students come from a wide variety of learning backgrounds. This includes their own life experiences and interests as well as having different teachers who have taught them different science concepts. It is possible that some of them may not have had any formal science instruction, and it is just as possible that some of them have already done investigations or activities similar to the ones you are planning. In addition, some students may already have a personal interest and passion for science, whereas other may have never developed an interest in it. Keep this in mind when selecting and modifying curriculum materials. As you begin your teaching career, you may not know as much about your students' knowledge and experience as you would like. However, the more experience you gain, the more accurately you will be able to anticipate your students' backgrounds and interests.

BOX 6.1

soon find that publishers of curriculum materials vary significantly with respect to the pedagogy that is suggested or explicitly included in their published materials. However, as you may recall, curriculum typically includes both subject matter content and pedagogy.

Doing and Knowing: A Return to Criterion I

There have been numerous reforms in science education over the past century. However, the *Benchmarks for Science Literacy* and the *National Science Education Standards* differ in at least one very important way from previous reforms. In particular, when it comes to scientific inquiry (as well as some other areas), the reform documents distinguish between what students need to be able to *do* and what they need to *know*. It is especially important that you know the difference between these two forms of learning outcomes when you are deciding whether there is a subject match between the curriculum materials and the particular goal, benchmark, or standard as described in Criterion I.

In the "Science as Inquiry" section for grades K–4 of the *National Science Education Standards,* you can find two separate categories of standards: abilities necessary to do scientific inquiry and understandings about scientific inquiry. Under the former, you will find the following:

1. Ask a question about objects, organisms, and events in the environment.
2. Plan and conduct a simple investigation.

3. Employ simple equipment and tools to gather data and extend the senses.

4. Use data to construct a reasonable explanation.

5. Communicate investigations and explanations.

Under the latter category, the following understandings *about* inquiry are specified:

1. Scientific investigations involve asking and answering a question and comparing the answer with what scientists already know about the world.

2. Scientists use different kinds of investigations depending on the questions they are trying to answer. Types of investigations include describing objects, events, and organisms; classifying them; and doing a fair test (experimenting).

3. Simple instruments, such as magnifiers, thermometers, and rulers, provide more information than scientists obtain using only their senses.

4. Scientists develop explanations using observations (evidence) and what they already know about the world (scientific knowledge). Good explanations are based on evidence from investigations.

5. Scientists make the results of their investigations public; they describe the investigations in ways that enable others to repeat the investigations.

6. Scientists review and ask questions about the results of other scientists' work.

If you carefully look at the two lists concerning scientific inquiry, it should become clear that the first set specifies outcomes that indicate what students need to be able to do, whereas the second list specifies what students are to know about scientific inquiry. For example, items 1 and 2 on the first list indicate that students should be able to develop a research question and then plan and conduct an investigation to answer the question. However, items 1 and 2 on the second list focus more on students knowing that investigations involve asking questions and further specify that students know about the different types of investigations. The two sets of outcomes are very different, and these differences have significant implications for the content of curriculum materials.

Curriculum materials that have students asking questions that are then used to plan scientific investigations would have a content match with items from the first list, the "to do" list. However, for a content match to exist for the items on the second list, the "to know" list, there would need to be some activities that require students to discuss or articulate the basic characteristics of a scientific investigation. Although it may be intuitive that doing and knowing go together, it is not unusual for students to be able to do a scientific investigation but not know anything about what they did and why they did it. Quite simply, doing is not the same as knowing. There were numerous curriculum reforms in the 1960s that had students performing scientific investigations with the expectation that they would also learn about scientific inquiry. The results of research focusing on the effectiveness of such curricula consistently showed that students did not understand much about scientific inquiry even though they could perform scientific investigations.

What this all means is that when you are considering whether curriculum materials have a content match with learning outcomes, particular attention should be given to whether the outcomes specify performance of a particular behavior or knowledge about certain behaviors. In our view, both are important, but not all curriculum materials recognize that performance and knowledge are not the same.

As you choose your instructional materials, keep in mind that curriculum materials address both subject matter to be taught and the instructional approaches to be used. Therefore, there should be a match between your intended outcomes and both the content and pedagogy of the curriculum you decide to use. A careful analysis of curriculum materials is required to determine if such matches exist. To help you make this analysis, *Project 2061* has developed a criterion evaluation instrument. The *2061* analysis tool enables teachers' examination of instructional materials with respect to how well they address, substantively and pedagogically, the instructional goals identified for student learning. Often curriculum materials fall short of meeting one or more criteria. It is possible to revise instructional materials to more completely address the desired learning outcomes. However, in some cases it may not be possible or appropriate to satisfactorily adjust the materials. In those cases, you may decide not to use the materials at all and seek out other materials instead. It is also quite possible that curriculum materials have not been officially adopted by your school district, and appropriate materials may not be readily available. In such cases, the curriculum analysis tool should be quite useful in making sure you consider important aspects of the curriculum materials that you will personally develop. In the long run, it will be up to you as the teacher to make the final decision about what curriculum materials to use in your classroom.

Finding and Selecting Instructional Materials

It is one thing to know how to evaluate the quality of curriculum materials, but it is another to know where to find materials in the first place. Good teaching depends on using many resources, but few teachers start their careers with a head full of perfect activities for every possible science lesson. Where do good teachers get all their ideas for science lessons and activities? The answer is nearly everywhere! Effective teachers are always planning and thinking about their lessons. Therefore, they find ideas for their classrooms in nearly every imaginable (and unimaginable) place. Whether it is a TV program, a science teachers' convention, a college class, or a museum, the world is full of great ideas that can be used when teaching.

One place where teachers often get their ideas is from the classes they themselves take, or have taken.

One of your goals for this class is to develop a set of great ideas for teaching science that you can use in your own classroom. Having a set of attention-grabbing demonstrations and activities is important for both beginning and experienced teachers. The night before starting a new unit is no time to begin searching for an appropriate introductory activity. Now, before you need them, is the time to begin developing a set of activities for your science instruction. The following sections of this chapter will help you develop a resource card file that you will refer to again and again throughout your teaching career. We will also suggest sources for great teaching ideas, as well as provide a list of supply sources (both everyday and science specific) that can help you turn your ideas into reality.

Resource Card File

One way to collect ideas is to develop a file of resource cards. You will definitely want to start resource card files for every unit you will be teaching, and you may also want to have a file for other good ideas you run across. Your cards can contain ideas on a variety of activities that will enhance learning—introductory demonstrations, supplementary readings, bulletin boards, educational games or software, videos, projects, laboratory activities, field trips, and so on. Note that, because you include only the most important information on your resource card, you will find it more quick and convenient than a copied article. By using a resource card file, you will not have to read through an entire article to figure out why you once thought an idea might be useful.

Resource card formats vary, but the following information will be useful on your resource cards.

Descriptive Title

Topic: *Provide some description of the science (or other) topics where this idea is useful.*

Standards/Benchmarks: *Identify the standards and/or benchmarks that support this idea.*

Source: *Specify the source of the activity. If the source is original, be sure to indicate that you are the source; if the source is from the Internet, be sure to include the Internet address as well as any information about the author should that Internet address no longer be active.*

Idea: *The idea section is typically short and gives a quick overview of the general idea that is envisioned.*

Use: *Provide a general plan of how this lesson goes and how this lesson is integrated with other ideas in a unit.*

Materials: *What would you need in order to do this activity? If you need specific materials for each student, be sure to label that you need them for each student. If you need them for each group of students, label that. Be clear about the amounts of specific chemicals, materials, and so on that are needed to do the activity.*

Modifications: *At least three modifications of different types: different materials, different topic, different classroom organization.*

Integration Is in the Cards

What about curriculum integration ideas?

When creating resource cards, do not forget to think about possible integration ideas that might work with the activity. Be sure to consider the possibility of collaborating with another teacher at the school because it will provide an opportunity to make a curriculum connection to other subjects you might be teaching in your classroom. Record your ideas in the "modification" section of the card. Even if they are not applicable now, they could be useful for future lesson planning sessions.

BOX 6.2

Curriculum Connections

It is also a good idea to attach a copy of articles or worksheets that you might want to have available if you were to use this resource. Before you decide to use any instructional materials or resources, you should carefully decide if they meet your needs. Figure 6.1 provides a specific example of a well-written resource card.

Do not forget the eight criteria discussed at the beginning of this chapter:

Criterion I: Content match

Criterion II: Identifying and Maintaining a Sense of Purpose

Criterion III: Taking Account of Student Ideas

Criterion IV: Engaging Students with Phenomena

Criterion V: Developing and Using Scientific Ideas

Criterion VI: Promoting Student Thinking

Criterion VII: Assessing Student Progress

Criterion VIII: Enhancing the Learning Environment

Use these criteria to evaluate the quality of the resource card example provided. Keep in mind that if an instructional idea does not fare well when compared with the evaluation criteria, it does not mean the idea or materials should be tossed into the nearest trash receptacle. Quite often slight revisions can turn a poor activity into one of high quality. The evaluation criteria will provide you with a guide for the types of revisions that may be needed.

As we mentioned before, most beginning teachers do not have a large store of instructional materials and ideas. The following four sections will provide some sources for your resource card ideas.

Professional Organizations and Their Publications

National Science Teachers Association (NSTA)
1840 Wilson Boulevard
Arlington, VA 22201-3000
Phone: 703-243-7100
www.nsta.org

NSTA is the largest organization in the world committed to promoting excellence and innovation in science teaching and learning for all. Its current members include science teachers, science supervisors, administrators, scientists, business and industry representatives, and others involved in science education. Its national and regional conventions provide innovative ideas and opportunities for professional development. NSTA also publishes three great journals for K–12 science teachers:

Science and Children is a four-color journal written for and by teachers at the preschool, elementary, and middle levels. Published eight times a year, it

Figure 6.1   Resource Card Example

Statistics: M&Ms and Spreadsheets

Topic: Organizing and analyzing data in spreadsheets

Standards/ Benchmarks: The following *Benchmarks* are from Chapter 9, The Mathematical World: Grades 3–5:

- Tables and graphs can show how values of one quantity are related to values of another. (page 218)
- Graphical display of numbers may make it possible to spot patterns that are not otherwise obvious, such as comparative size and trends. (page 223)
- Summary predictions are usually more accurate for large collections of events than for just a few. Even very unlikely events may occur fairly often in very large populations. (page 228)

Source: Niess, M. L. (1992). "Mathematics and M&Ms." *The Computing Teacher, 20*(1), 29–31.

Idea: This activity uses M&Ms candies to introduce students to using a spreadsheet for data analysis and graphing.

Use: This is an introductory lesson on graphical data analysis. The teacher provides each student (or pair of students) with a bag of M&Ms, for which they record the numbers of each color of candy on 3 × 5 cards. Then in groups of eight, students place the cards in a spreadsheet fashion as directed by the teacher. This floor spreadsheet is used to instruct students in a variety of spreadsheet concepts (including labels, numbers, and numbers resulting from formulas). The teacher instructs students to create necessary formulas and play the role of the computer by placing values resulting from calculations on top of the formula in the floor spreadsheet. The teacher follows this lesson by having students create an actual spreadsheet on the computer. Finally, students create a pie chart of the average numbers of each color of M&Ms candy and answer the question: What is the probability of selecting a red candy from any given M&Ms bag?

Materials for individual students: bag of M&Ms
10 3 × 5 cards
crayon

for groups of students: floor space for simulated spreadsheet
extra 3 × 5 cards

for whole class: computer lab (and/or)
demonstration computer and projector

Modifications:
1. Visit the M&Ms site to find out the actual percentages of colors in bags of various M&Ms: www.m-ms.com/us/about/products/index.jsp
2. Use the M&Ms data to demonstrate the advantages and disadvantages of different types of graphs (e.g. bar graphs, line graphs, and pie charts).
3. Rather than working in small groups, have students create one index card spreadsheet for the whole class.

presents peer-reviewed feature articles describing activities and instructional approaches. Here is a sampling of articles from one issue of *Science and Children:*

- Teaching Tropisms
- Library of Conservation
- Teaching with Dewey on My Shoulder
- A Workshop Approach
- Worldwide Weather
- Studying Our Skin
- Evening Skies (seasonal star maps)
- Resource and Software Reviews

Science Scope is a professional journal written for and by middle-level science teachers. Published eight times per year, *Science Scope* contains peer-reviewed articles providing creative activity ideas that often include reproducible student worksheets. *Science Scope* also includes monthly departments, such as Scope on the Skies (myths and information about the night sky), Tech Trek (using technology in the classroom), Science on Display (ideas for exhibiting science), After the Bell (extracurricular science activities), Editor's Roundtable (issues facing educators today), Relevant Research (selected with the middle-level educator in mind), Scope's Scoops (brief summaries of recent scientific research), Happenings (announcements of programs and events), and Instructional Reviews (reviews of trade books). Many issues contain a poster with facts and activities on a variety of subjects.

The Science Teacher is a professional journal for secondary school science teachers. It highlights articles incorporating assessment, cooperative learning, interdisciplinary studies, and problem solving. Recent favorite activities include "Oil-Spill Ecology" (October 1998), "Quake Search" (December 1998), and "Nature Network" (April 1999). In addition to *feature articles,* it includes Science Briefs (the latest scientific discoveries), *Idea Bank* (helpful classroom hints), Taking Note (upcoming events), and Reviews (the latest books, videos, and software).

The Council for Elementary Science International (CESI)
http://unr.edu/homepage/crowther/cesi.html

The Council for Elementary Science International (CESI), a division affiliate of the NSTA, is an international professional organization for teachers (pre-K through 8th grade) who have the responsibility to teach science to children, elementary and middle school science educators, and pre-service teachers who will become Pre-K–8th grade teachers. The mission of CESI is to promote excellence and equity in K–8 science education. CESI membership includes a professional journal, newsletters, and opportunities to learn and collaborate with colleagues at breakfasts, luncheons, make and take sessions, workshops and presentations, and mini conferences usually held at national and regional NSTA conventions. CESI is the elementary affiliate of the National Science Teachers Association. The CESI website provides more information about activities and membership.

School Science and Mathematics Association
Arthur L. White, Executive Director
School Studies and Mathematics Association
The Ohio State University
238 Arps Hall, 1945 N. High Street
Columbus, OH 43210-1172
Phone: 614-292-8061
www.ssma.org

The School Science and Mathematics Association (SSMA) is dedicated to improving instruction at all levels in and between science and mathematics by providing leadership in the field. Its primary work and publications address the needs of all of those involved in the science and mathematics teaching and learning processes. SSMA focuses on issues relating to teacher education, research, and K–12 teachers.

SSMA's journal, *School Science and Mathematics,* emphasizes issues, concerns, and lessons within and between the disciplines of science and mathematics in the classroom. Although the articles published in *School Science and Mathematics* tend to be more scholarly than those found in *Science Scope* or *Science and Children,* the journal strives for a useful balance between research and practice. For example,

Curriculum Connections

Thinking Outside the Box

What's out there as an educational resource besides science?

Don't forget to look beyond the science resources listed here to people, places, and things available in your own community. Ideas that can be applied in a science classroom are not found only in science-related venues. Community parks or lakefronts may offer natural resources that could be used on a field trip. A trip to the supermarket may result in supplies for a science lab or an idea for how a science concept can be applied to your students' lives. Ideas for a science lesson can be inspired by a visit to an art or history museum. These venues often have valuable resources for science teachers as well. One example of a museum that is geared toward an interdisciplinary approach is the Exploratorium in San Francisco, which is devoted to "science, art, and human perception." They can also be found on the Internet at www.exploratorium.edu. Remember, science can be found everywhere. Do not forget to practice what you preach.

BOX 6.3

in addition to technology reviews and book reviews, the April 1999 issue included the following articles:

- "Decision Making and STS Education: Exploring Scientific Knowledge and Social Responsibility in Schools and Science Centers Through an Issues-Based Approach"
- "Student Reactions to Standards-Based Mathematics Curricula: The Interplay Between Curriculum, Teachers, and Students"
- "A Vision Educators Can Put into Practice: Portraying the Constructivist Classroom as a Cultural System"

The Internet

The Internet has become a source of abundant educational resources, some worth using and some not. You can track down lesson plans and educational activities using an Internet search engine. Appendix A provides a guide for searching databases on the Internet.

At this time, the maintenance of many websites over the long term is not dependable. You should never assume that a website you visit now will still be available your first year of teaching. The larger the host organization or institution is, the greater the chance that its site is still in existence. The following websites give you a good place to start and should be around for awhile. They also provide up-to-date links to other useful sites.

National Science Teachers Association

www.nsta.org/onlineresources/links

Under "Resources for Teachers," you will find a variety of informational websites and lesson plan sources.

National Aeronautics and Space Administration Educational Resources

http://education.nasa.gov

The purpose of this site is to help involve the educational community in NASA's endeavors to "inspire American students, create learning opportunities, and enlighten inquisitive minds." You will find space-related curriculum support materials, as well as Internet, video, television, and multimedia resources.

WebQuests, Hosted by San Diego State University

http://edweb.sdsu.edu/webquest/webquest.html

A WebQuest is an inquiry-oriented activity in which most or all of the information used by learners is drawn from the Internet. WebQuests are designed to support learners' thinking at the levels of analysis, synthesis, and evaluation. This site links you to many examples of WebQuests, as well as providing instruction for creating your own WebQuests.

AskERIC Virtual Library

http://ericir.syr.edu/Virtual

The Educational Resources Information Center (ERIC), administered by the National Library of Education, is a database of abstracts of education-related literature and conference reproductions. Its virtual library is full of lesson plan ideas and web links to supplemental information, as well as special project ideas and television series companion materials.

The Gateway to Educational Materials (GEM)

www.thegateway.org

The GEM project is a consortium effort to provide educators with quick and easy access to the substantial, but uncatalogued, collections of educational materials found on various federal, state, university, nonprofit, and commercial Internet sites. Through it, you can access literally thousands of K–12 lesson plans.

Publications

Scientists and science educators have written a variety of books focused on making science more accessible to children. The following resource books are just a few of our favorites (and don't forget this book! The Teaching Cycle section is full of activities):

Great Explorations in Math and Science (GEMS) Teacher's Guides
   Based at the Lawrence Hall of Science, University of California, Berkeley, GEMS has developed and published more than sixty teacher's guides and handbooks for pre-K through tenth grade on a wide range of science and mathematics topics. The guides feature clear, step-by-step instructions, complete background information, lists of resources, assessment suggestions, and literature connections. GEMS supports the *National Science Education Standards* and other leading math and science guidelines. For more information, see its website at www.lhs.berkeley.edu/GEMS.

Hands-On Nature: Information and Activities for Exploring the Environment with Children, Jenepher Lingelbach, Ed. (Vermont Institute of Natural Science).
   With its important biology and ecology messages, this book contains sound and timely environmental science, interesting activities, and ways to relate scientific ideas to other subjects.

Whizbangers and Wonderments: Science Activities for Young People, Joseph Abruscato (Pearson).
This book includes activities in life, physical, earth, and space sciences, as well as ecology, technology, and invention.

Science Is . . . , Susan V. Bosak, Douglas A. Bosak, and Brian A. Puppa (Firefly Books).
Packed with ideas, fascinating facts, experiments, projects, puzzles, games, and stories, this book covers everything from kitchen investigations to outdoor explorations.

Teaching Physics with Toys: Activities for Grades K–9, Beverley A. P. Taylor, James Poth, and Dwight J. Portman (McGraw-Hill).
This book provides complete instructions and teaching techniques for teaching basic physics principles through simple activities that use popular children's toys like Legos, Tomy push-n-go fire engine, magnet cars, balloons, bouncing balls, and others. The activities are grouped by appropriate grades, (i.e., K–3, 4–6, and 7–9). Each activity provides the teacher with a list of key science topics.

Teaching Chemistry with Toys: Activities for Grades K–9, Jerry L. Sarquis, Mickey Sarquis, and John P. Williams (McGraw-Hill).
The content of this guide focuses on chemistry concepts appropriate for elementary and middle school. The is similar to *Teaching Physics with Toys: Activities for Grades K–9.*

Janice van Cleave has produced a series of resource books on almost every science topic. Some examples include:

Janice van Cleave's Astronomy for Every Kid
Janice van Cleave's Ecology for Every Kid
Janice van Cleave's Play and Find Out About the Human Body: Easy Experiments for Young Children
Janice van Cleave's 202 Oozing, Bubbling, Dripping and Bouncing Experiments
Janice van Cleave's Guide to the Best Science Fair Projects

National Education Technology Standards for Students: Connecting Curriculum and Technology, International Society for Technology in Education.
This book includes curriculum examples and scenarios, as well as learning activities by grade level.

Science on the Internet: A Resource for K–12 Teachers, Jazlin V. Ebenezer and Eddy Lau (Prentice Hall).
This book is a compilation of time tested, useful, and informational science websites grouped by category. It also includes a list of tutorial sites to help you become Internet literate.

Other Resources

Science textbooks, of course, usually contain activity ideas. Keep in mind, however, that these activities are not always inquiry based. Therefore, they may require modifications to fit both your teaching style and students' needs.

Experienced teachers have great insights about what works in the classroom and what will require extra effort. Build relationships with more experienced teachers and learn from them. In addition, do not downplay your own experiences. Think about the science lessons you have observed in the past, whether in school or on television.

Gathering Supplies for Science Learning

How do you actually begin the process of ordering science supplies for your classroom? One way to start would be to go through your textbook and other activity books, find all the demonstrations and activities you would like to do, and gather the necessary supplies. Do you see a problem with this approach? If you have had a chance to look at the lesson development examples in the teaching cycle section of this book, you probably recognize that this is backward. In this approach, the activities are driving the content you teach rather than the other way around. Purposeful instruction starts with goals and objectives. All activities should support these goals and objectives.

The first step should be to determine the units, goals, and objectives you will teach throughout the year. Then find activities that will help students meet the goals and objectives and *then* begin gathering supplies. To complete this entire process in one sitting is a daunting task. A unit-by-unit approach will make your job more manageable.

Example from a Real Classroom

The following is a list of science units from a real fourth-grade class in Virginia:

- Structure of the Earth
- Rocks and Minerals
- Electricity
- Solar System (Sun, Moon, Earth) and Gravity
- Plants
- Ecosystems

In the Rocks and Minerals unit, the four major goals for students were as follows:

1. To participate in hands-on activities and enjoy science.
2. To understand rock classification.

3. To understand the difference between rocks and minerals.

4. To understand the rock cycle.

Cookie Activity. This activity is used to introduce the concept of rocks and minerals and the idea that rocks are made of many different kinds of minerals. Supplies include different types of cookies, such as oatmeal raisin, chocolate chip, and chunky peanut butter, and a variety of rock and mineral specimens.

Discovering Minerals in Sand. To further develop the analogy from the cookies and discover that sand contains different minerals, students sort minerals in sand. Supplies include sand, toothpicks, a magnifying glass, and graph paper.

Mineral Identification. Students practice identifying mineral specimens by performing common tests to determine their properties. They use the identification key in their textbook. Supplies include the following, organized by the test to be performed:

Hardness test: glass plates, steel nails, storage containers, hammer, newspapers, and pennies

Streak test: storage containers, streak plates, and newspapers

Acid test: glass plates, magnifiers, steel nails, storage containers, vinegar in dropping bottles, newspapers, paper towels, and safety goggles (for practicing the test, sugar, cornstarch, and baking soda)

Luster test: magnifiers, storage containers, and newspapers

Magnetism test: a magnet

Growing Sugar Crystals. This activity shows students that crystals grow from solutions. Fast cooling results in smaller crystals, and slow cooling results in larger crystals. Supplies include sugar, water, hot plate or microwave oven (for heating water), nails, string, and jars or clear plastic cups.

Rock Cycle Recipe. In this activity, students create the three major types of rock in the rock cycle by pressing white and dark chocolate shavings together to form sedimentary rock, partially melting the sedimentary rock to form metamorphic rock, and thoroughly melting the shavings together for igneous rock. Supplies for each group include bars of dark chocolate, bars of white chocolate, potato peelers, one electric skillet or hot plate, and aluminum foil.

Rock Cycle Bulletin Board. Students create a bulletin board about the rock cycle as a culminating activity for the unit. Supplies include construction paper, stencils for lettering, rulers, scissors, paste, and small rock samples (igneous, metamorphic, and sedimentary).

As you can see, gathering materials for all of these activities consumes a lot of time. Teaching in a hands-on manner requires extra work, but the results are worth it. Be sure to store your supplies in an organized manner for ease of future use. Ideally, you can store supplies together by unit in large plastic bins. In a few years, your supply stock will grow and be tailored to your teaching style. Then you will need only to replace consumables.

Indispensable Supplies

Although the proper way to think about choosing activities and collecting materials is to start with goals and objectives, there are some materials useful in a variety of activities that you will want to have on hand in your classroom:

Rulers
Glue
Paste
Scissors
Eyedroppers
Slides and cover slides
Thermometers
Hand lenses

Some of the indispensable supplies needed in any science classroom.

Magnets

Measuring cups

Clear, plastic cups

Matches

Candles

Straws

String

Wax paper

Aluminum foil

35-mm film canisters

Two-liter bottles

Popsicle sticks

Classroom plants and pets

Potting soil

Newspapers for protecting desks from messes

A variety of small bottles and jars for storing specimens

Plastic bags with zipper closures

Old electric skillet to use as a heat source for activities

Flashlights

A wide variety of nature identification books, such as the Golden Nature Guide series.

Although not absolutely necessary, collections of natural items provide ways to challenge students and increase their interest. You can collect things like tree leaves and cones, seeds, insects, rocks and minerals, fossils, bird feathers, and seashells. Collecting all these items yourself would be difficult, so you can have students bring in items they find. As they identify the items they have donated, they will also be learning. The items would then become part of the long-term class reference collections and, in a few years, your classroom collection should be fairly complete.

Supply Companies

A number of companies specialize in providing science materials to classrooms. Here are a few of the common ones:

Carolina Biological Supply Co.
2700 York Road
Burlington, NC 27215
Phone: 800-334-5551
Fax: 800-222-7112
Website: www.carolina.com

Nasco
Phone: 800-558-9595
Website: www.nascofa.com

Central Scientific
CENCO
3300 Cenco Parkway
Franklin Park, IL 60131
Phone: 800-262-3626
Website: www.cenconet.com

Flinn Scientific, Inc.
PO Box 219
Batavia, IL 6010
Phone: 800-452-1261
Fax: 630-879-6962
Website: www.flinnsci.com

Edmund-Scientific
101 East Gloucester Pike
Barrington, NJ 08007-1380
Phone: 800-728-6999
Website: www.edsci.com

Kits

Kits provide ideas for activities. They also have the advantage of already containing the teacher's manual and all of the handouts and supplies necessary. They save you the time it would take to gather these materials yourself.

One commonly used series of kits is the STC (Science and Technology for Children) kits, which come packed with enough materials to do inquiry-based lessons with an entire class. They include both teacher and student handbooks to support instruction. Another series is the FOSS (Full Option Science System) kits, which have the added advantage of being available in both English and Spanish versions.

Although kits have advantages, not everything about them is beneficial to the beginning teacher. Despite their claims, they may not promote critical thinking or be truly inquiry based. Fortunately, you can usually modify the activities in the kits to make them more inquiry based. Also, many kits appear to have adopted the philosophy that you can teach science effectively even without the proper background knowledge. Such kits do not provide much in the way of background information for the topics they cover, which can be a serious detriment to teachers who have not had opportunities to learn these topics.

Supply and Demand

Whenever you do an activity that requires a lot of supplies, materials management in your classroom can be hectic. Furthermore, the logistics of storing all of your science materials can present a dilemma.

BOX 6.4   A good way in which to organize your science supplies is to sort them by activity. Some teachers also include a master copy of the handouts in the bin. The bins that work best are shoebox-size plastic containers with lids. They are easily stackable, and most are clear so that you can see the contents. An index card can then be attached to the front of the bin with the name of the lab and a list of the materials inside the container. Often teachers use many of the same materials in different activities. In this case, you can either purchase duplicate supplies or store the most often used supplies in their own bins. Therefore, when you want to do an investigation that requires glue, you can read the card to discover that the glue necessary for the lab is in the general-purpose bin. If your supplies are neatly organized, the setup and cleanup of labs become a much more organized task. When your materials are well organized, your students will also find it easier to retrieve needed materials, as well as return them to their proper location once finished with them.

Summary

If you have completed the activities in this chapter, you should now have a better understanding of how to determine the quality of curriculum and instructional materials with respect to your instructional goals. You also should have the resources to facilitate your science instruction. For instance, you have a list of sources to find good science teaching ideas and, hopefully, you have joined the National Science Teachers Association so that you can receive one of their excellent journals. You have begun to develop a resource card file specifically tailored to the science topics you will be teaching, and you will add to the file throughout your education program and teaching career. Finally, you have a list of essential supplies and places to purchase science teaching materials. Of course, you will want to add to these lists as you gain experience in teaching the various topics covered in elementary science. Finally, remember that even the best resources do not teach themselves. It takes a caring teacher to turn good resources into great lessons.

The Teaching Cycle

The "rubber meets the road" in this section of the text. The instructional vignettes will provide you with numerous opportunities to use the knowledge gained in previous chapters to carefully consider the interaction of subject matter, pedagogy, and student learning.

The next four chapters comprise the most significant portion of the text. These chapters will provide you with direct experience of subject matter concepts and themes common to both the National Science Education Standards and *Project 2061*. These concepts and themes are those stressed within the reforms and they are also the most commonly addressed concepts and themes within elementary level science. All concepts and themes are directly referenced to the appropriate benchmarks and standards.

The traditional topics of methods courses (e.g., demonstrations, laboratories, classroom management, assessment, developmental psychology) are addressed within the context of *The Teaching Cycle,* a repeating cycle of:

Goal Setting → Materials Development/Selection →
Pedagogy → Assessment → Reflection

The level of elaboration on each subject matter topic is intended to provide you with a functional understanding that is necessary to successfully plan and implement instruction. Specific benchmarks or standards are selected for instruction and you are then engaged in the various aspects of The Teaching Cycle as instruction is planned, implemented, assessed, and then followed with reflection. Examples of various materials and activities for use in the lesson

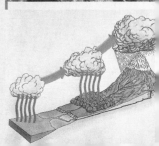

are provided and these are evaluated in terms of their match with the specific instructional goals. Throughout this section, you will be asked to consider the students, their background knowledge, and what approaches would best facilitate their achievement of the stated instructional goals. Reflective Boxes discuss the various instructional methods (e.g., demonstrations, laboratories, discussions).

Life Science

What Is Life?

"What is life?" seems like a simple question, but is it really? Take a moment to jot down your definition of life. If you feel that something as complex as life cannot be confined to a simple definition or sentence, then make a list of the characteristics that you believe describe all living things. Your definition or list should include those things that are unique to living things. In other words, what makes living things different from nonliving things? Your list or description most likely contains "movement." Things that move without an apparent external force (e.g., push) are often considered alive. For example, if you or one of your friends has a pet hamster, noting that it runs around a wheel on its own (without being wound up like a toy, for example) is an obvious characteristic that the pet is alive. If your pet hamster, or even your friend, lies around all day, you might even joke about whether your friend or your hamster is really alive! In response, your friend might say, "I'm dead tired." If you are a fan of monster movies, as we are, you may remember the climactic seen in *Bride of Frankenstein* when the newly created female companion for the original monster opens her eyes and moves her arm. In response to these actions, Dr. Frankenstein gleefully screams, "She's alive!" At this point, we probably have convinced you that "movement" should be on your list of characteristics of life. Is the plant in your home alive? If so, is it moving? You may quickly respond to our apparent challenge by declaring that the plant is alive, even though it might not be so easy to identify that it is capable of movement. We would eventually expect you to defend your conclusion by telling us that the plant turns its leaves toward the light, but what about a cactus? Is it alive?

Let's investigate the idea of movement in a little more detail before discussing the other characteristics on your list. Get a cereal bowl. The wider and more shallow the bowl, the better. Fill the bowl about one-third full with milk. Next, get some food coloring. We would prefer that you have four different colors.

Do you have everything you need? Good, let's begin. Place a single drop of each color of food coloring in your bowl of milk, equally spaced around the edge. Using the face of a clock as a model, you could place yellow at twelve o'clock, green at three o'clock, blue at six o'clock, and red at nine o'clock (see Figure 7.1). Take a toothpick and touch it to the milk in the center of the bowl. What happened? Now, dip the end of your toothpick in some liquid dishwashing soap. Touch the milk with the soapy end of the toothpick in the same place as you did before. Wow! Did you see that? We are not going to tell you what actually happened because we really want you to try this activity. It is an excellent activity to do with your students, regardless of their grade level. We probably are not giving too much away by admitting that a lot of movement occurs when the detergent-coated toothpick touches the milk. Do you consider the milk and the food coloring alive because they seemed to move on their own? The movement noted in this activity is a result of a moderately complex chemical interaction between the milk and the detergent. The actual explanation is not important with respect to our current discussion. The important question, however, is considering whether this movement is an indication of life. If you consider the variety of situations you encounter every day in which you see movement, it becomes immediately clear that movement, in and of itself, is not a distinguishing characteristic of life.

Let us now return to the remaining items on your list of the characteristics of life. Some of the most common items that individuals list as characteristics of life include made of cells, reproduction, growth, metabolic activity, life cycle, ability to respond to its environment, and movement. Growth of an object is usually a good indication that it is alive. In this sense, growth refers to a change in size,

Figure 7.1 Bowl of Milk and Food Coloring

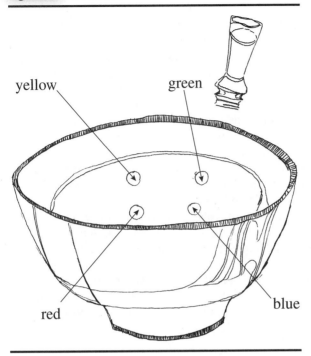

yellow

green

red

blue

volume, structure, or appearance over time. Some may prefer to use the term *development* in addition to growth, but let's not make things more complicated than necessary. The cactus we mentioned earlier grows very slowly in size and volume over time. Your pet dog or hamster also grows during its lifetime. Technically speaking, growth is the result of the continual addition, replacement, and modification of the cell(s) that make up the living organism. We need to be careful, however, because growth is similar to movement in that it, in and of itself, does not constitute life. Just about any craft or novelty store now sells small packages labeled "grow a frog," "grow a fish," and so on. These packages contain sponge-like forms and the instructions simply tell you to put the form in a glass of water and watch it grow. Within twenty-four hours, the small sponge-like form has grown into a much larger version of its original shape. Is this object that grew through the absorption of water alive? I think you would agree that it is not. You may also remember growing crystals or even rock candy during your childhood. This was accomplished by simply placing a string (in the case of rock candy) in a highly concentrated sugar solution. Over an extended period of time, the sugar in the solution accumulated on the string to form rock candy. Is this type of growth indicative of life? By now, you get the point. Nonliving things can exhibit either movement or growth for reasons other than because they are alive.

Another item on the list provided is made of cells. Indeed, if we asked you why some of the examples of growth we gave are not indicative of life, you might have answered by referring to the source of the growth. Eventually, statements relating to whether cells were involved would likely surface. Quite simply, cells are small packets of materials (both liquid and solid) that are found in all living things. If we look at small portions of living things under a microscope, we would see that they are made of numerous compartments or cells (see Figure 7.2). Cells were first observed by Robert Hooke in 1665. Actually, he observed the remains of cells (cell walls) that were left in nonliving cork material. What Hooke saw were numerous small empty compartments that he named cells. The first descriptions of living cells were actually made by Leeuwenhoek (Lave-in-hook) while looking at water from a rain barrel under a microscope. The difference between Hooke's cells and those that are living is the presence of a combination of solid and liquid material (i.e., protoplasm) that through a complex series of processes controls the activities of the cell. Thus far, we have discussed two of those activities, growth and movement.

To be more specific, cells grow, move, and perform a variety of activities through a combination of chemical reactions that break apart and put together complex substances. The breaking apart and putting together of chemical substances is commonly referred to as *metabolic activity.* You may be familiar with the word *metabolism.* It is commonly used in all of those advertisements related

Figure 7.2 Cork Cell

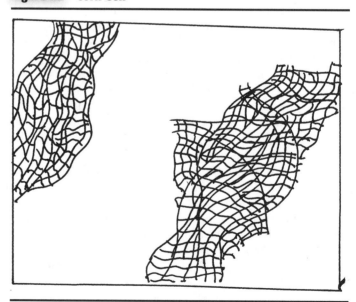

to weight loss and body building. If you have a low metabolism, you will find it very easy to gain weight. If you have a high metabolism, you can eat more without gaining weight. In the case of living organisms, metabolic activities are internally controlled by the cells that make up the organism. The instructions that control these processes are contained in the genetic material (DNA) found primarily within the cell's nucleus.

In the case of rock candy, growth is the result of a nondirected interaction between the sugar water and the string. With time, any concentrated sugar solution will deposit crystals. In the case of a living cell, growth is controlled by internal instructions that meet the requirements of the cell and the organism in which it resides. For example, cells of living organisms do not grow without limitation like the giant cell seen in the movie *The Blob*. Cells have prescribed limitations on their growth, whereas nonliving crystals (e.g., rock candy) are largely controlled by the amount of sugar available in the water. The cells that make up your pet hamster's nose do not change in size or structure as a consequence of feeding your hamster more.

Reproduction is closely related to growth, and living organisms have the capacity to reproduce. Reproduction can take one of two forms. In one instance, a new organism is produced. In a second instance, old and worn-out cells are replaced within an existing organism. Without the ability to reproduce new organisms, each type of organism would eventually disappear. This is because all living organisms have a life cycle in which they come into existence, grow, mature, and eventually die. The intimate relationship between reproduction and life cycle is consistently noted among living organisms. Nonliving substances are sometimes inappropriately said to reproduce when broken into smaller pieces. After all, if you break a large piece of granite into many smaller pieces with a sledgehammer, the number of granite pieces increases. This is equivalent to someone reproducing by cutting their fingernails or hair. This type of reproduction is not linked to any kind of life cycle, nor is it controlled by any mechanisms (metabolic activity) inherent to the rock, hair, or fingernails. This use of the term *reproduction* is a common misnomer.

The second type of reproduction is the more common. It involves the replacement and repair of cells that are part of a larger, living organism. This reproduction does not result in a new organism but allows the living organism to continue through its life cycle. The cells of the human digestive system and skin are continuously replaced, whereas those of the nervous system are usually never replaced. The most concrete example of cellular reproduction is the healing that takes place after you have cut your finger. New skin cells replace the damaged cells within days. The broken granite in the example that we described earlier has no mechanism through which it can repair itself.

Whether they are human beings or bacteria, living organisms have the capability of responding to changes in the environment. These responses may be quick, like the removal of your hand from a hot stove, or they can be slower, like the eventual migration of bacterial cells from a region of darkness to one in which there is light. In such cases, the response may or may not be a conscious one, but ultimately it is controlled by metabolic activities at the cellular level. A rock possesses no ability to respond in a conscious or controlled manner to any changes in the environment. A rock left outdoors will eventually and uncontrollably erode as a consequence of environmental conditions.

The seven characteristics of life that we have discussed may be fewer than those you have included on your personal list. Indeed, if you open up a series of life science textbooks, you will find many lists that differ from ours and yours. It would be incorrect to assume that any single list, including ours, is the correct one. The varied descriptions of life reflected in these lists are simply the result of how difficult it is to describe or define something as complex as life. The important point to note is that if you look around your room, you can find numerous nonliving objects that possess one or more of the attributes we have attributed to life. The possession of one or more of these characteristics of life is not enough to constitute life. Rather, living organisms must possess a combination of all of the characteristics that we have listed.

Defining life is, perhaps, the best example of what we meant in Chapter 1 when we stated that scientists create or invent knowledge rather than discover knowledge. Life is a concept that scientists have invented to describe one aspect of the natural world. However, as we stated in Chapter 1, all scientific knowledge is tentative. Viruses and certain other microorganisms do not necessarily adhere to what have commonly been considered characteristics of life. Consequently, scientists still debate whether viruses are alive and whether the definition of life needs to be changed. More recently, we have been intrigued by the possibility of life existing on other planets. In an effort to answer this question, we have sent spacecraft to planets such as Mars to investigate the existence of life forms. It is important to note that these investigations are performed from the perspective of life as we conceive of it. For example, we take measurements of oxygen and carbon dioxide levels as indicators of metabolic activity, but it is possible that life forms exist with metabolic activities totally foreign to any we have seen before. Such life forms may remain unnoticed because our observations have been biased by our current conceptual framework. The nature of science strikes again.

The Teaching Cycle

Mr. Evans is beginning his first unit on life science in a second-grade class. He is enthusiastic about this unit because it will focus on ideas and experiences that are directly relevant to his students' lives. Consequently, he is enthusiastic that his students will be successful at learning the subject matter and will enjoy the lessons. Mr. Evans also feels that his unit on life science will be an excellent way to help his students develop important inquiry skills, such as questioning, observation, inference, and data analysis. He feels they will also learn about inquiry. For example, they will learn the importance of keeping careful records of data collection and that different people will interpret the same data in different ways. They will be working with things they can experience while coming to school in the morning and leaving in the afternoon. The relevance of this material to students' everyday lives is particularly important to Mr. Evans because he has heard in the science reforms that many students view phenomena that occur in science class as being independent of the world outside of school. He has also heard that students construct their own understandings from what they experience and not necessarily from what they hear.

Goal Setting

Prior to planning instruction, Mr. Evans knows that it is important to set specific learning goals for his students. This will help him to select activities and assess student learning. He feels a little uneasy about setting appropriate goals for his students because science was not his primary field of study in college. Consequently, Mr. Evans typically refers to the recommendations of the *National Science Education Standards* and the *Benchmarks for Science Literacy*. The K–4 standards of the *National Science Education Standards* state under Characteristics of Organisms:

> Organisms have basic needs. For example, animals need air, water, and food; plants require air, water, nutrients, and light. Organisms can survive only in environments in which their needs can be met. The world has many different environments, and distinct environments support the life of different types of organisms. (p. 129)

In the *Benchmarks for Science Literacy,* the Cells section includes the following for K–2 students:

> Most living things need water, food and air. (p. 111)

And for students in grades 3–5:

> Some living things consist of a single cell. Like familiar organisms, they need food, water, and air; a way to dispose of waste; and an environment they can live in. (p. 111)

In terms of science inquiry, the *National Science Education Standards* under Science as Inquiry stresses the ability to do scientific inquiry and acquiring understandings about scientific inquiry. In the *Benchmarks for Science Literacy* are the following K–2 nature of science benchmarks:

- People can often learn about things around them by just observing those things carefully, but sometimes they can learn more by doing something to the things and noting what happens. (p. 10)
- Describing things as accurately as possible is important in science because it enables people to compare their observations with those of others. (p. 10)

It is clear to Mr. Evans that his second-grade students will be moving toward these standards and benchmarks rather than actually achieving them. In particular, both the standards and the benchmarks appear to start with the various characteristics and needs of living organisms rather than a definition or description of life itself. Mr. Evans feels that before his students can achieve the understandings stated in the reforms, they must first have an understanding of what constitutes life.

Mr. Evans realizes that the goal of students understanding what constitutes life is too general to guide instruction and assessment. Consequently, Mr. Evans decides on the following objectives for his introduction to life science:

- Students will be able to state at least seven characteristics of living organisms.
- Given appropriate examples, students will be able to distinguish between those that are living and those that are nonliving and defend their choices.
- Students will be able to state that it is important in science to compare their observations with those of others.

It is important to note that Mr. Evans has included objectives that focus on both foundational knowledge and application of this knowledge. These objectives clearly specify what students should know and be able to do following instruction. Therefore, they provide appropriate guidance for both instructional planning and student assessment.

In addition to the preceding objectives, students will be learning to carefully observe and draw conclusions based on their observations while doing scientific inquiry. However, such instructional outcomes take a long time for students to master and subsequent activities will continue to address these knowledge and skills.

Materials Development and Selection

As Mr. Evans begins to consider how he can facilitate the growth of his students' knowledge about living things, it becomes critically important that he identify some concrete activities. The most obvious and visible attribute of living organisms is the ability to move independently. Mr. Evans decides to focus on movement because it will be most accessible for students in the second grade. Mr. Evans tries to stretch his students' understanding as much as possible, but he is also keenly aware that certain learning outcomes are not developmentally appropriate.

While looking through several resource books, he notices a demonstration that can be done on the overhead with mercury, potassium dichromate, and nitric acid. A chemical reaction is created that causes the mercury to wriggle around on the overhead giving the appearance of a living organism. Although this demonstration appears to be highly motivational to students of varied grade and ability levels, it involves the use of two toxic chemicals (i.e., mercury and potassium dichromate) and a third that is highly caustic (i.e., nitric acid). It is an impressive demonstration, but Mr. Evans thinks it best not to take the chance of using such dangerous chemicals in his classroom. In addition, he would rather provide the students with something they can experience more directly as opposed to a demonstration. Although demonstrations are powerful instructional strategies, students' construction of knowledge is enhanced through concrete experiences that allow them to physically manipulate objects as well as ideas.

Mr. Evans finds another activity that will allow the students to directly manipulate materials. This activity involves the use of club soda and raisins. Raisins are placed in a cup with club soda and are then observed to float and sink as the bubbles adhere to the surface of the raisins and then eventually burst. The students are asked to determine if the moving raisins are living or nonliving. This approach will allow the students to freely experiment with the materials. Although this activity appears to be safe and will allow the students to directly manipulate laboratory materials, Mr. Evans has several concerns. He is worried that the students may be confused because the raisins can technically be considered to be alive and this may detract from the primary purpose of the activity, which is to reinforce the idea that the raisins' movement is unrelated to any life activity. The description of the activity suggests that pushpins can be used instead of raisins and the pins will move more readily than the raisins. This will solve the problem anticipated by Mr. Evans, but now there is the concern of his second graders playing with pins.

Finally, Mr. Evans decides that he can use small pieces of pasta to produce the same effect. At last, he has devised a variation on the published activities that will be safe and will allow the direct involvement of students. He also decides to use a second activity involving wind-up toys to allow students to further investigate whether movement, in and of itself, constitutes life. Mr. Evans is pleased to have found and developed two activities that directly involve students in the investigation of movement. The activities clearly match the intended focus of the lesson and allow a safe and developmentally appropriate treatment of the subject matter.

Pedagogy

Since this lesson is an introduction to a new topic (i.e., life science), it is especially important for Mr. Evans to assess students' prior knowledge on the topic. In fact, Mr. Evans usually approaches any topic by finding out what students know or have experienced related to the topic so he can build on students' background knowledge. Students' learning is significantly influenced by their prior experiences and understandings. The lesson begins with Mr. Evans requesting his students to make a list of all the living things that they saw on their way to school today. He also has them create a list of the nonliving things they observed. By beginning the lesson in this manner, Mr. Evans has also quickly involved the students in an active way. This will help focus their attention and interest in the rest of the lesson. Nevertheless, he does not want this task to occupy more than five to seven minutes of class time so he is sure to ask several students what they are to do. He knows from experience that students may not know what they are expected to do even though clear directions were provided. In addition, he is careful to quickly circulate around the room as students begin to be sure that everyone is off to an appropriate start. Students of this age, or any age for that matter, often take much more time than is necessary to take out needed materials, such as pen and paper.

Mr. Evans does not have a specific number of items he wants students to have on each list, but he wants each student to have enough items so that the subsequent class discussion and task will have a sufficient amount of data with which to work. He is going to have students look for patterns that the items on each list have in common, as well as patterns of differences between the lists. If the students do not have a sufficient number of items on each list, their ability to successfully complete the task will be compromised. As Mr. Evans circulates around the room, he waits until all students have two lists of approximately ten items before calling the writing task to an end.

Mr. Evans calls the class back to order and asks for volunteers to share some of the items on one of their lists. As he selects from the students who have volunteered to share, he is careful to call on an equal number of boys and girls. As students share their listed items, Mr. Evans records these on the board in the form of two lists. He knows that supplementing students' verbal responses with a visual listing on the board will reinforce the content of the shared items. Some students will tend to focus more on things that are written on the board rather than those that are only verbally stated. Mr. Evans is very receptive of students' responses, as the purpose at this point is simply to involve students and get some sense of their background experiences and knowledge. It is important for Mr. Evans to solicit contributions from as many students as possible because the class will be using the two lists on the board during the rest of the lesson. He has chosen to have all students eventually use the same two lists so the class can work with a common frame of reference instead of a variety of lists. Still, it is important for each student to have some sense of ownership of the lists. He could have simply, and more quickly, provided two lists for the students, but this would have ignored the importance of students' background knowledge and experiences in the development of the lesson. Although Mr. Evans has made the development of these lists student centered, it is critically important that the two lists contain items that show movement. This is important because the major portion of Mr. Evans's lesson focuses on movement as a characteristic of life. Therefore, he is ready to question the students about whether they saw cars and birds if these are not offered by any of the students. Even student-centered lessons are orchestrated by teachers behind the scenes.

Mr. Evans has the students work in pairs by turning to a neighbor and discussing the similarities among the items on the list of living things and the list of nonliving things. He also wants them to discuss the differences between the two lists. Can you anticipate any problems with this procedure? In particular, we are wondering how you would have approached the dividing of students into discussion groups. Is two in a group enough? Do students turn to their left or right when choosing a partner? Is there an even number of students in the class?

As before, Mr. Evans asks several students what they are expected to do. After he is satisfied that the students know the task, he lets them get to work. This time he provides a specific time limit of 15 minutes and he circulates around the room as the students work. As Mr. Evans circulates, he has several questions that he is prepared to ask in order to assess student understanding of what is being done. These questions are very general and simply ask students to state and explain the similarities and differences they have identified within and between lists. Establishing verbal contact and physical proximity with students during independent work is very important to Mr. Evans. He knows that students will be more likely to stay on task and ask questions if he is close by. He has also noticed that students tend to ask more clarifying questions if he takes the initiative to ask them questions as they work.

Mr. Evans carefully assesses the progress of the students as he circulates relative to the 15-minute time limit. He is especially concerned with whether 15 minutes is enough time or whether too many students will finish the assignment before the 15-minute period is over. The last thing he wants is to have students who have completed the task early sitting around with nothing to do. Mr. Evans calls the class to order and solicits volunteers to describe the similarities and differences noted. He records student responses on the board in three columns. The columns are similarities among the living items, similarities among the nonliving items, and differences between living and nonliving items. As he records responses on the board, Mr. Evans is careful to have students explain their reasoning. He asks for a reason regardless of whether he agrees or disagrees. There is no pattern in his request so that he does not cue students about his feelings toward their responses. He then asks the other students in the class if they agree or disagree. The desire is to reach a class consensus for each response listed. From an instructional standpoint, Mr. Evans finds this approach an excellent way to maximize student involvement and to gather additional feedback on student knowledge. Students often answer correctly for the wrong reasons. It is very important to Mr. Evans that his students begin to develop an understanding of the relationship between observations, evidence, and conclusions.

Fortunately, the class has agreed that movement is one thing that distinguishes living things from nonliving things, so Mr. Evans does not have to use his planned set of questions to raise this issue. In response, he tells the class that for now they will focus on the idea of movement. Mr. Evans walks around the room and places a wind-up toy in front of each student. The toys are varied, but most are mice and farm animals. Mr. Evans has been careful to use toys that are not biased toward one gender or another. As he passes out the toys, he asks the students to list additional examples of living things that move. These are things that they did not necessarily see on their way to school. Mr. Evans wants to keep the students actively engaged in the time it takes him to pass out the toys. He could have saved time by having the students come to the front to get the toys out of a box. Would this have created any problems? How would you have distributed the toys?

The students are instructed to wind up the toys and observe the subsequent behavior. Each student is expected to carefully observe his or her toy and record whatever they see. They are also told to investigate a bit by seeing how the toy reacts to an obstacle that is placed in its path. The purpose of this activity is twofold. Mr. Evans wants students to focus on movement and he is also setting up some foundational experiences for future class discussions on whether reacting to the environment is a characteristic of life. Mr. Evans gives the students five minutes to play and explore with their toys. This is followed by another full class discussion of what the various toys did and how they behaved in response to obstacles. He also discusses the importance of making careful observations during scientific investigations with his students. Mr. Evans asks the class at the end of the discussion whether the ability to move is a characteristic that distinguishes the living from the nonliving. Several students answer that it is and he responds with the question, "Does that mean your toy is alive?" The class unanimously agrees that the toys are not alive. Mr. Evans was fairly certain he would get this response, but he asked the question to make sure that the students focused on the connection between the toys and the previous class discussion. It would not be uncommon for the students to not look for connections between the wind-up toys and the previous discussion about the characteristics of living and nonliving things. In short, he is having the students explicitly make the connection between their observations and conclusions.

Although Mr. Evans was hopeful that one of the students would question the seriousness of the activity as a test of the issue at hand, no one does. Therefore, Mr. Evans tells the class that the toys are obviously not alive because the students wound up a spring and made them move. He says that they need to look at a situation in which there is no clear human involvement, such as winding a spring. The students are told that they will be doing an investigation involving a cup, club soda, and pasta. Each student is told to get some pasta and a cup of club soda from the front of the room. To keep things orderly, he has students come to the front of the room by rows and get some pasta fragments (which have been placed in a small bathroom cup) and a clear plastic cup of club soda. Mr. Evans remains at the front and pours the club soda for students as they come to the front. Are there any concerns you have about the distribution of materials? Is there a better way to accomplish the distribution of the pasta and club soda? The students are told to carefully observe the pasta for ten minutes when they return to their seats. Mr. Evans tells the students not to touch or interfere with the pasta and that they should write down whatever they see for the full ten minutes.

As usual, Mr. Evans circulates and verbally interacts with students by questioning them about what they have observed. The students thoroughly enjoy watching the pieces of pasta ascend and descend in the club soda as bubbles attach to their surface and eventually burst. Mr. Evans knows it will be difficult to call them to attention when the time comes. Consequently, he warns the students that they have only two minutes left to observe. This way, Mr. Evans's attempts to get the class reorganized will not be unexpected. After two minutes, the class is called to order and Mr. Evans engages the students in a conversation about what they observed. As the discussion proceeds, several students appear to be distracted by the wind-up toys and cups of club soda and pasta that remain on their desks. How could this have been avoided? In response to the distracted students, Mr. Evans remarks that the toys and cups should be placed at the upper right corner of their desks. He follows the discussions of what they observed by asking, "Are the pieces of pasta alive?" The students that volunteer a response state that the pasta is not alive. Mr. Evans questions them further by asking for their reasons. The students have difficulty answering this question but seem to agree that the movement of the pasta fragments does not mean that they are alive. The students seem to feel that something else is missing. Mr. Evans asks for further clarification by directing students' attention to the fact that they did not interfere or do anything to the pasta as they did with the wind-up toys. Some of the students say that the bubbles had something to do with it but are uncertain what that is. They also think it is important that the bubbles did something to the pasta instead of the pasta moving by itself. At this point, Mr. Evans reinforces the idea that careful observations are critical to science. He also emphasizes that the various contributions the students are making do not mean that some students are wrong, but rather different individuals may have different interpretations of the same data. None of this is uncommon to science. Mr. Evans asks if there is a way to test the bubble idea. He asks, "Is there a way for us to see if the bubbles caused the movement of the pasta?" He also asks, "Are you sure it was the bubbles and not the water?" One of the students suggests placing the pasta in water to see what will happen. Mr. Evans does so in front of the class and asks the students to report their observations. The students do so and are quickly able to conclude that the bubbles must be important. Mr. Evans reinforces this idea by asking the students if they ever saw their mother or father cook spaghetti. Several students had and Mr. Evans has them describe their observations of the spaghetti remaining at the bottom of the pot at first, but how it eventually begins moving around when the heated water boils. This discussion may appear to be a digression, but Mr. Evans knows that getting students to understand science as inquiry takes a long time and must be addressed throughout the year. Consequently, this discussion, which is only partially related to the focus of the lesson, helps to establish critical groundwork for one of his long-term instructional objectives.

Mr. Evans brings the discussion to a conclusion by getting the students to restate the idea that movement alone does not distinguish living things from nonliving things. He asks the students for additional examples to illustrate the point, and he offers the example that the school bus that brought them to school was moving but is not alive. In contrast, a student who walked to school was also moving and he or she is alive. Mr. Evans has carefully chosen examples that are relevant and gender neutral. The students again exhibit the belief that there is something else related to movement that is missing from nonliving things, such as the pasta and the bus, but they are unable to say what it is that is missing. Mr. Evans concludes by telling students to spend some time at home looking at the class lists of characteristics of living and nonliving things and think about whether any of these things could be the missing item. He also tells the class that they will be investigating more characteristics of life in future lessons.

Assessment

As an assessment of student learning, Mr. Evans tells the students to look around their yard, neighborhood, or home at the end of the day and list five living and five nonliving things that move. It is important that students can identify living and nonliving things that move because the day's lesson established that movement is not a distinguishing criterion. This encourages the students to only associate movement with living things and would be an assessment that is inconsistent with the focus of the lesson being assessed. Mr. Evans feels this approach to assessment is much better than simply requiring the students to

Inquiry and Nature of Science Assessment Ideas

How can you assess knowledge of inquiry and nature of science in this lesson?

One possible way to assess knowledge of inquiry is to add another component to the assignment. In addition to listing five living and five nonliving things, students could record the observations they made of these objects and explain how these observations led them to their conclusion. Thus, the assessment could ask students, "What data do you have to support your answer?"

BOX 7.1

An informal assessment of nature of science could also be included in the lesson. It would be important to stress that scientists' opinions can differ and ideas can change, just as they did in the class. Not all students may have agreed with the classifications, and some students may have also changed some of their original answers after talking about them with the class. Because scientific knowledge is tentative and because there is an element of subjectivity in science, scientists do the same thing. Science's definition of life has changed over time. In addition, the way in which organisms have been classified continues to change. Students could be asked to describe how the activity illustrated tentativeness of scientific knowledge or how individuals interpret the same data in different ways.

make a list during a class quiz. The approach of using a quiz is not grounded in students' everyday experiences. The approach used by Mr. Evans is much more authentic in terms of the desired learning and his students' lives. Mr. Evans has decided to not assess inquiry or nature of science at this time. As mentioned before, Mr. Evans feels that both of these objectives are important but will take a long time for students to achieve.

Reflection

At the end of the school day, Mr. Evans usually takes time to mentally review the day. This is something he did much more informally and automatically during the start of his career, but he has found it so useful that he now reflects on the day's activities in a much more systematic and formal way. Most of us wonder whether we are doing a good job and how we can improve. This is what reflection is all about and Mr. Evans uses it to investigate ways that he can improve. He has been teaching for fifteen years but realizes that there is always room for improvement.

Mr. Evans was particularly pleased with the science lesson because he thinks the students have a reasonably good understanding of the idea that movement has something to do with whether something is alive but that the situation is much more complex. The students recognize that nonliving things can also move, but there is something missing from the nonliving things that is present in the living things. It seems that the students are in a good position for the subsequent lessons he has planned regarding growth, metabolism, life cycle, and response to the environment. He was also pleased with how well the students attended to the various activities he had planned. They were actively involved, but they were thinking as opposed to just playing. He was worried that they might just play with the toys and learn little because the toys were too familiar. On the other hand, he wanted the initial activity to be very familiar and accessible to his second-grade students.

In retrospect, it seems that it might have been better if he had taken the students on a short trip on school grounds to generate the initial lists of living and nonliving things. This would have allowed the class to begin with common lists instead of the varied lists constructed from students' memories of their trips to school. It would have also given Mr. Evans more control of what would be included on the initial lists. It is difficult to predict what students will notice as they come to school and Mr. Evans had forgotten to tell students the day before to carefully look around as they came to school the next day. Taking a short walk around the school campus would still have grounded the list in students' experiences and would also have saved class time. Whether your school is in an urban or rural environment, there are plenty of examples of living and nonliving things. In fact, Mr. Evans is now considering using such a class trip as a quick review when he and his students return to their discussion of the characteristics of life.

Suggested Literature Connections

Alexander and the Wind-Up Mouse by Leo Lionni, Random House, Inc., New York, 1969.
   This story about the friendship between a toy mouse and real mouse can be used at the beginning of the lesson to generate a class discussion about the differences between living and nonliving things and tap prior student knowledge about the characteristics of life. The characters in the book can be referred to during the assessment and students can be asked to compare them.

How Dogs Really Work! by Alan Snow, Little, Brown, and Company, Boston, 1993.
   Dog anatomy and physiology are cleverly translated into humorous mechanical drawings and explanations. Ask students how these illustrations compare to the real dog.

Form and Function

Pick up a sheet of paper or tear one out of your notebook (any size will do) and throw it out in front of you as hard as you can. Watch it as it falls to the ground. Now take the same piece of paper and fold it into a glider shape with a pointed front end and triangular sides. Throw it out in front of you the same way you threw the flat sheet. Did it move differently as it fell? Now pick up your paper glider and crumple it to a tight ball and throw it one more time. Once again, you should have noticed a difference in the way it moved through the air. Why was there a difference each time? You were always working with the same piece of

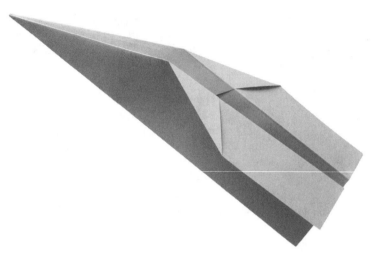

Paper folded into the shape seen above allows it to function as a paper airplane.

paper—its composition and mass never changed. What had changed? Yes, it was its shape! Changing the shape of the paper changed the way it moved through the air. Its function changed when its form changed.

There are many things both natural, like birds and insects, and human-made, like airplanes and rockets, that move through the air with the grace and ease of your glider. Can you think of similarities in the forms of these clearly different items that allow them to function in similar ways? You may be thinking about their streamlined body shapes, pointed conelike front ends, wings, or smooth surfaces. In these examples, similar forms functioned in similar ways.

The relationship between form and function is reflected in nearly all aspects of nature. Understanding these relationships can also give us insight into the behavior of living things. Look at the following pictures of animal skulls (see Figure 7.3). What kinds of foods do you think the animals to which the skulls belonged might eat? What led you to these conclusions? You probably looked at the form or structure of the different teeth to help you determine their function. The sharp, pointed incisors look like they could tear and cut through meat. The thick, broad, flat molars look like they could grind tough plant fibers. In the same way we can look at the beaks of different birds and predict what kinds of foods they probably eat and do not eat. A duck's spoon-shaped bill would not be able to pick berries and seeds and a sparrow's tiny pointed beak could not effectively scoop up fish. By looking at the shape alone, we may not be able to know exactly what it is that the animal can eat, but we can get some ideas about the general categories of things that are and are not possible for it to consume given its structures.

Figure 7.3   Examples of Animal Skulls

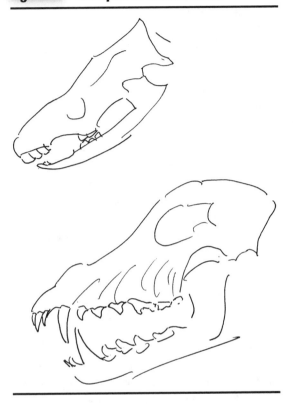

It might be a good idea for us to stop at this point and caution you about going too far with these connections. So far we have only been using form and function relationships to make inferences about what we think these animals eat. Without making direct observations, we do not really know for sure if our inferences are correct. Teeth or beak shape are not the only factors that influence an animal's eating behaviors. The size of the mouth opening, the length of the jaw, the position of the head in relation to the rest of the body, and the other living organisms in the surrounding habitat should also be considered. What we know about nature is a combination of both inference and observation. If this discussion sounds familiar, it should! This is one of the many things we were talking about during the discussion of the nature of science in Chapter 1. By looking at human teeth alone, you would never guess the variety of foods that we eat. The fact that we have developed tools such as knives, forks, spoons, and food processors to change the size and consistency of the food compensates for not having large canines or sharp incisors. Think of the last few meals you ate.

How easily could you have eaten all the food on your plate if you had just depended on the structure of the teeth in your mouth? In the case of humans, as well as many animals, we have the ability to add direct observations to our inferences. Sometimes, however, that just is not possible. Take dinosaurs, for instance. Their fossil remains are all we have to make inferences about how dinosaurs functioned. However, we will never be able to directly observe them so we will never be able know for sure if our predictions are correct.

As another cautionary note, it is necessary to use language carefully. It is important not to confuse form and function with need and adaptation. Living things do not intentionally grow parts so they can accomplish particular tasks or certain objectives. Giraffes did not grow long necks so that they could eat the leaves at the tops of trees. Rather, they are able to eat the leaves at the tops of trees because they have long necks! Remember the wolf in the story about Little Red Riding Hood? When she remarked about his long teeth, the wolf replied, "The better to eat you with my dear!" He didn't grow these teeth just because he wanted to eat Little Red, but having this particular set of canines certainly could help him accomplish the task.

The Teaching Cycle

The students in Mrs. Santos's fifth-grade class are in the middle of a unit on birds. They have already reviewed bird anatomy and physiology. At this point in the unit, she is confident that the students are familiar with the common characteristics of all birds and now she wants the students to learn more about the variations of bird species. Although all birds have beaks, wings, and feathers, their shapes and sizes can vary greatly from one bird species to another. This lesson on variation also provides an appropriate forum for discussing the concept of form and function. Mrs. Santos's science curriculum consists of several units that seem to have no apparent connections. As a fifth-grade teacher, her school system requires her to teach units on forces and motion, flowering plants, birds, and rocks and minerals. She wanted to find some common themes that would connect each of these units in some way for her students. After checking the *National Science Education Standards,* she found the section on Unifying Concepts and Processes and read that these could be used to provide students with a meaningful conceptual framework for scientific ideas. This was just what she was looking for, common themes that could be woven through all her units to connect them and build scope and sequence into her yearlong curriculum. She decided that the relationship between form and function could be illustrated within each of her required science units. Mrs. Santos also developed a reading center to correspond with the themes of her science units. She tried to fill each center with a combination of fiction and nonfiction trade books, poetry, and activity books. They come from her personal collection of books as well as the public and school libraries. She encourages her students to also add their own books to the classroom reading center. She makes an effort to include books that meet the needs of the students in her class, including the variety in their reading levels, skills, and interests. For this particular unit, the center is aptly called "Birds' Words" and includes a copy of *Peterson's First Guides to Birds* and a collection of Audubon drawings. She feels the illustrations in these books will reinforce the concepts of bird diversity as well as the relationship between form and function.

Goal Setting

In this particular lesson, Mrs. Santos will address form and function by focusing on the relationship between the structure and function of birds' beaks. As a guideline, she again refers to the grades 5–8 standards of the *National Science Education Standards,* which state:

> Living systems at all levels of organization demonstrate the complementary nature of form and function. Important levels of organization for structure and function include cells, organs, tissues, organ systems, whole organisms and ecosystems. (p. 156)

Mrs. Santos also feels the activity she has planned for this lesson clearly reflects aspects of the nature of science. She tries to take every opportunity to explicitly point out these connections in her science lessons whenever possible. In the *Benchmarks for Science Literacy,* within the nature of science chapter, she finds the following benchmark for grades 5–8 to support her planned instruction:

> Scientists' explanations about what happens in the world come partly from what they observe, partly from what they think. Sometimes scientists have different explanations for the same sets of observations. That usually leads to their making more observations to resolve the differences.

She found the following nature of science standard for grades 5–8 within the *National Science Education Standards:*

> Science requires different abilities depending upon such factors as the field of study and the type of inquiry. Science is very much a human endeavor, and the work of science relies on basic human qualities, such as reasoning, insight, energy, skill, and creativity—as well as on scientific habits of mind, such as intellectual honesty, tolerance of ambiguity, skepticism, and openness to new ideas.

In this lesson Mrs. Santos wants her students to recognize that the behavior of the whole organism (in this case, birds) is dependent on the form and function of its individual parts. She sets the following objectives for her lesson:

- Given a specific beak as a example, students will be able to infer the type of food the bird eats and defend their inferences.
- Given a specific food type, students will be able to describe the shape of a beak that can eat it and defend their descriptions.
- Students will be able explain the role of creativity in the development of scientific explanations.
- Students will be able to describe how all scientific ideas, although partly inferred, are also based on observations of the empirical world.

Mrs. Santos has purposely selected objectives that direct students to relate both form to function and function to form. She decided to design separate objectives for these two concepts. She has learned through experience that objectives that address too much are harder to meet and difficult to assess. The simplicity of her objectives will make assessment and diagnosis of what students have and have not learned easier.

Material Development and Selection

As we said in the introduction to this lesson, Mrs. Santos weaves the concept of form and function through all of her science units. As a result, it is presented each time within a different context and through a variety of instructional methods and learning experiences. This addresses the range of the individual differences of the students in her class. Learning style diversity is also taken into account as she selects and plans the activities for her lessons.

Mrs. Santos often uses children's literature or poetry to introduce a lesson. She selects a book from the "Birds' Words" reading center to read to the class. *Hey, Al* by Arthur Yorinks is a favorite story of many of her students and she knows it will quickly draw them into the lesson. Today she will use it to begin the discussion of the relationship of form and function to a bird's body parts.

During this lesson, Mrs. Santos also wants her students to construct bird beaks that can be used to eat particular types of foods. She wants her students to be selective about the materials they use for their constructions and so she must make available to them a broad assortment of materials from which to choose. Since she began teaching four years ago, Mrs. Santos has collected a variety of materials and assorted items to use for these types of activities. Many of the items are recycled from other projects. She brings materials from home, and parents and friends will often add to her collection.

Mrs. Santos knows the more prepared she is before the lesson the more smoothly the lesson will run. Consequently, students will have more time for their science investigations and less time will be required for materials distribution and cleanup. At the beginning of the school year, Mrs. Santos went to a local shoe store and asked them for 12 empty shoe boxes. She uses these to assemble and organize materials for her science investigations. Each shoe box always contains a roll of tape, a pair of scissors, a stapler, and some colored markers. She then adds different items to these units as they are called for in different science activities. She tries to have the shoe box units and any other necessary materials ready at the beginning of each lesson. However, she does not have a very large classroom and has little available surface area to display materials for science activities. Consequently, she keeps a folding table in the back of her room and only opens it up when she needs it for a science lesson. Her students have come to connect this table with interesting science experiences and have nicknamed it TOES, which stands for "Table of Exciting Science."

Mrs. Santos plans to divide her class of twenty-four students into eight groups of three, so she will need eight different examples of bird food. She bought walnuts, hazelnuts, sunflower seeds, raisins, and cranberries at a local market a few days before the lesson. She chose these not only because of the differences in their sizes and surface textures but also because they do not need to be refrigerated and she can add them to the classroom setups several days before the actual lesson. She considered using candies such as gummy worms to represent earthworms and chocolate sprinkles to represent ants but decided against this idea. The students will be excited to be handed cups of candy and will probably want to eat them. Your lesson ends before it even begins if your students eat your activity! Besides, one can never predict food allergies and the last thing you want is to have a student have an allergic reaction to your lesson. Because she is always concerned about allergies, she checks with the school nurse at the beginning of each school year to find out if any of her students have allergies and, if so, what it is they are allergic to. For this activity, she decides to use rubber bands to represent worms and whole black peppercorns to portray insects. She puts several samples of each of the eight food types into separate paper cups and adds them to the eight shoe boxes, one for each team of students. These sets will be easy to distribute and will also be easy to collect at the end of the lesson. She plans to instruct students to put all of the food back into the cups, return them to the shoe boxes, and return the shoe boxes to TOES (the materials table). Later, she can easily remove the cups of foods from the shoe boxes and replace any missing materials so that the boxes will be ready for the next activity.

Pedagogy

Before the lesson begins, she has the students take out a blank sheet of paper and a pencil. She does not want to interrupt their concentration by taking them out later. She then reads them the book, *Hey, Al.* This is a story about a man and his dog. They are flown to a beautiful island in the clouds inhabited by birds. Life was wonderful there for them until the day they woke to discover that they were turning into birds! When she is finished reading, she asks her students to close their eyes and imagine what they would look like if they, too, turned into birds. Now this is a funny request and she knows the students will laugh at the thought of themselves as birds. To keep them focused on the task, she proceeds to ask them a series of guiding questions: What is your beak like? What is its shape? What size is it? What color is it? What size are you? Are you a big bird like an ostrich or a tiny one like a hummingbird? What color are your feathers? What is the shape of your wings? How long is your tail? Are the feathers in your tail the same color as the rest of your body? How about your feet? What shape do they have? How does their size compare to the rest of your body? She uses a soft, quiet voice and asks the questions slowly. She has found that this tone helps to create a more thoughtful classroom mood in which the students can more easily concentrate. She waits at least ten seconds between questions to give them time to think and add detail to their images. Can you think of another method to settle the children down and get them focused?

She includes some examples of birds but she is careful not to mention specific birds when asking questions about beaks. She will want as much variety as possible for this body part as she continues the lesson and she does not want to influence her students' selections. She knows that some students are likely to limit their choices to her examples and she is especially concerned that this lesson builds on students' prior experiences and knowledge. She intentionally asks questions only about structure and appearance because this is what she wants her students to concentrate on during this part of the lesson.

She then tells the students to open their eyes and draw the birds they just imagined themselves to be. She reassures the students who have difficulty drawing that their drawings don't have to be fancy; they just have to include all the basic parts of the bird. As she moves around the room, she encourages their efforts and asks them if they forgot anything when and if she notices omitted parts. At the same time, she is assessing how well they remembered the basic characteristics of birds, concepts that had been addressed in previous lessons of this unit. Next she asks for three volunteers to draw the beaks of their birds on the blackboard at the front of the room. She wants to use these drawings to begin a discussion about the relationship of form and function. As she moves around the room she takes note of the beaks the students are drawing, which enables her to select three volunteers who drew three very different beaks. As this example demonstrates, with a little planning teachers can still have control of a seemingly random process and remain focused on the objectives of the lesson. As we have mentioned before, teachers do control even the most constructivist of lessons. What are the rest of the students doing while the three volunteers are completing their drawings on the board? What would you do to keep their attention? Mrs. Santos asks them questions about the different beaks. Who drew a very tiny beak? How many of you drew a great big beak? Did anyone draw a beak shaped like a spoon? A hook? A needle? A ladle? She reminds the students to raise their hands and not just yell out answers. Besides managing behavior, she feels the visible show of hands helps students realize the diversity of beaks imagined by their fellow classmates. When the blackboard drawings are completed, Mrs. Santos points to each and asks what foods the students think a bird with that beak could eat and why. Under each drawing she makes a list of the foods the students suggest along with their reasons for these suggestions. Mrs. Santos is careful not to criticize students' reasons, but she challenges students to refer to form or shape to justify their answers. At this point in the lesson, Mrs. Santos takes a few moments to emphasize that scientists develop their explanations using both evidence gained from observations as well as creative inference. She is careful to explicitly emphasize that the scientists' explanations, as well as the students', should not be based on opinion without any evidence. Now she asks the students to make similar lists for their own beak drawings. She asks them how and why they made their food choices. Again, the students cite structure as the rationale for their answers. Mrs. Santos summarizes the student-generated remarks by saying that the form of the beak is related to its function.

Mrs. Santos then reminds students about their previous science unit on flowering plants. She asks if anyone can recall something from that unit that involved the same concepts. A few students remember the lesson that related to the form and function of plant parts. Mrs. Santos tells the students that they will continue to discover this interesting and important relationship throughout this unit on birds as well as in their next unit on rocks and minerals.

The first part of this lesson illustrated the relation of form to function. Mrs. Santos now wants to establish the complementary nature of this relationship. She first has the students list all the types of foods they can think of that birds eat. Starting with the student in the first seat, she then goes around the room and asks each student to name one example of a bird food that is on their list, adding that they cannot repeat a food that has already been named. This approach will ensure that students listen to each others' examples. She repeats this activity once again, only this time she starts with the student in the last seat so he or she is not limited by other students' examples (as was true during the first round of the activity). As the most common bird food, categories such as seeds, nuts, and berries are named. The students are then forced to think more carefully about the different kinds of things birds eat. Fish, worms, and insects eventually come to mind. As the selections continue to get used up, students become more resourceful and will start to name specific types of foods such as strawberries, blueberries, cranberries, hazelnuts, walnuts, peanuts, and so on. Mrs. Santos selects two of the student responses, an earthworm and nectar, and asks the students to describe the type of beaks that could eat these foods. During this discussion, the students explain that very differently shaped beaks are needed to eat these very different foods. Mrs. Santos is pleased with the direction of the discussion and decides to move to the next activity.

The Art of Bird Construction

Is it possible to integrate science and art?

An activity in which students construct their own bird is also a good place to integrate science and art. This will allow even more flexibility in terms of the time spent on the project, since it can be worked on both in science and in art class. A discussion of the color of different birds could also be added. Color can serve a **BOX 7.2** function in terms of the bird's survival and it is also an important component when creating artwork. The construction of the beaks and the materials used could also become more elaborate if done as a part of art class. Since the final beaks are meant to be three-dimensional models, an art component could be a discussion of different sculpting or modeling techniques that could be used to create their beaks. In science, the function of different types of beaks could be discussed.

This lesson also lends itself to integration within different science disciplines. Studying structure and function by studying birds is certainly a life science topic. However, a physical science connection could be added if the discussion also included the physics of how different wing and beak structures work.

Curriculum Connections

In order to divide her twenty-four students randomly into eight groups of three, she passes around a container of colored buttons. There are eight different colors of buttons in the container and there are three buttons of each color. The three students with the same colored buttons form a team. Mrs. Santos typically groups students randomly because she thinks it is important for all students to have an opportunity to work with each of their other classmates during the year. The students are directed to move into their groups quickly before any further instructions are given. Once they are all seated in their new groups, Mrs. Santos informs them that each group represents a research and design team hired by a company called Bert's Beak Boutique. Their assignment is to design a beak that is particularly suited to a certain type of food. She then passes out the cups of bird foods that she prepared earlier. Each group receives a different food for which they must design and construct a beak. Mrs. Santos shows them the array of materials she gathered for them at TOES (the materials table) to use for their constructions. She cautions them to select wisely and only take what they need. Each group can use no more than three different building materials. By limiting the number of materials, the students will more carefully consider their planning and Mrs. Santos's supplies will not be depleted as quickly.

She tells them they have 30 minutes to complete their construction, clean up their work areas, and return any unused materials to the front table. She also tells them that they must be able to explain why they designed and constructed their beaks the way they did. Having the students be aware from the start that they will have to defend their construction plan is extremely important when doing this kind of activity. Without this accountability, students could consider this an arts-and-crafts activity and lose sight of the science objectives.

At the end of the 30 minutes, Mrs. Santos calls on each team to describe their food, present the beak they constructed to eat it, and defend their design choices. Mrs. Santos summarizes the presentations by pointing out that all of the groups designed the shape

Managing Your Science Classroom

Distribution Deliberation

Is the determination of material distribution really that important?

Yes! Notice that in each of the lessons discussed thus far, it was important to take into consideration how materials should be distributed. This may seem like a small detail, but it has a major effect on the amount of time an activity may take, the focus of the students, and the amount of control you have over the materials being used. Such details may seem minor, but they need to be thought about when planning a lesson to help ensure that the lesson runs smoothly and efficiently, to ensure that the students' opportunity to learn from the lesson is maximized, and to avoid any potential safety problems.

BOX 7.3

It is extremely critical to plan ahead to ensure that any safety risks are minimized. We sometimes take it for granted, but students often deal with potentially harmful materials and it is important that their distribution be done as safely as possible.

of their beaks to correspond to the task of eating different foods. They all reflected the relationship of form and function. As she concludes the lesson, Mrs. Santos reviews all the different activities that were presented. She asks the students how each part of the lesson is related to the concept of form and function.

Assessment

Mrs. Santos's lesson involved many group discussions and activities. From the feedback she received from the class as a whole, she feels confident that they met the learning objectives. However, she also needs to assess what individual students have and have not learned. Therefore, she plans an assessment that requires them to work independently. Mrs. Santos used Eyewitness software about birds with her students when she first introduced this unit. Thus, her students are already familiar with the program. She decides to use this once again to assess students' learning of form and function relationships. The illustrations and photographs of birds in this program are very clearly presented, and a wonderful variety of birds is included. Students have the ability to rotate the graphics, isolate certain structures, and enlarge their size. This interactive guide to birds provides a three-dimensional investigation that the books in the reading center cannot provide. The school has a computer lab and there are enough computers for all of the students. She scheduled her class to use the lab on the same day as this science lesson. Her students have been using these computers since kindergarten and they are very comfortable in this lab. She instructs her students to select one of the birds that is included in the program. She then asks her students to choose one of the bird's parts, other than the beak, and describe how it reflects form and function. They compose their descriptions on the computer and print out a copy to give her at the end of this session. As a homework assignment, students are asked to take a copy of what they wrote home and explain how their explanation was derived from both observation and personal creativity. The students are also asked if this is similar to what scientists do when developing explanations and are expected to provide an example to support their position.

Reflections

Mrs. Santos was introduced to journal writing in her college methods course. She considers it a professional responsibility to reflect on her daily teaching experiences and she finds it useful to enter these reflections in a journal. She often refers to past journal entries when she prepares to teach a unit that she has covered in previous years. The journal entries help her to remember details from successful lessons and prevent her from repeating mistakes. Her entry today includes the following:

- some of the comments made by students during the lessons
- students' comments about the fun they had drawing themselves as birds
- sketches of the students' beak designs

She also makes a note to herself to add hand lenses to the shoe box sets. She wants the students to become better observers and the lenses will remind both her and them to

examine items more carefully. She thought that if they were in the boxes today the students may have taken a closer look at the textures and details of the bird food. She is not sure that this would have influenced their construction plans but at least they might have taken this detail into consideration. She remembers that she has a class field trip to the local Audubon preserve scheduled in two weeks and she writes a reminder to call their education department next day to check their reservations.

Life Cycles

We are all familiar with cycles, which are regularly repeating events or sequences of events, but have you ever considered how common cycles are to everyday experience? We experience cycles in the rising and falling of the tides and the changing of the seasons. We observe that water cycles through different forms as water in the oceans evaporates and eventually condenses into clouds. Water in its liquid form then falls to earth as rain and eventually makes its way back to the sea. The moon passes through familiar phases as it completes its cycle of 28.5 days. Even our sun will cycle through distinct stages as it completes its cycle of existence, eventually returning to the gas clouds of space from which it came. Surely, cycles are evident everywhere we look. It is not surprising, then, to find that they play a critical role in life itself.

All living beings progress through definite stages. They come into existence, grow, mature, reproduce, and eventually die. Organisms take on new appearance and behavior as they progress through their life cycles. Thus, a dragonfly larva has little resemblance to the adult it will eventually become. This is not really surprising, since the dragonfly larva lives underwater, while the adult lives its life in the air. Each is adapted to its own particular environment.

The differences an organism experiences as it progresses through its life cycle are not restricted to appearance alone. If you have ever dug up a cicada larva (or grub), you know that it avoids light in its underground habitat. In contrast, the winged adults sing out their mating songs in the sun. This is only one example of how organisms exhibit different behavior as they progress through their life cycles. Differences in behavior include what the organism eats as well. For example, newborn humans drink only milk, while adults can eat a variety of foods. Caterpillars eat day and night in order to satiate their huge appetites for vegetation but graduate to sipping nectar as adult butterflies. Just like the differences in appearance the dragonfly experiences throughout its life cycle, these differences in how larvae and adults behave and eat are important for survival because they allow the organism to take advantage of different resources during different stages of its development.

In all their various forms, life cycles are interesting to students and provide excellent opportunities for observation and discovery. Furthermore, we have

seen that they are ubiquitous to all life and are important for survival. Life cycles certainly present a fascinating topic for the elementary classroom. Next, we will consider some life cycles of common plants and animals in more detail.

Plant Life Cycle Examples

Although the changes in appearance and behavior of insects and amphibians are commonly known, we seldom consider the fact that plants also undergo incredible changes during their life cycles. These changes are evident in the plants you are likely to find in your own backyard or neighborhood. We will consider two common examples here, the first being a typical flowering plant (see Figure 7.4).

Figure 7.4   Life Cycle of a Cherry Tree

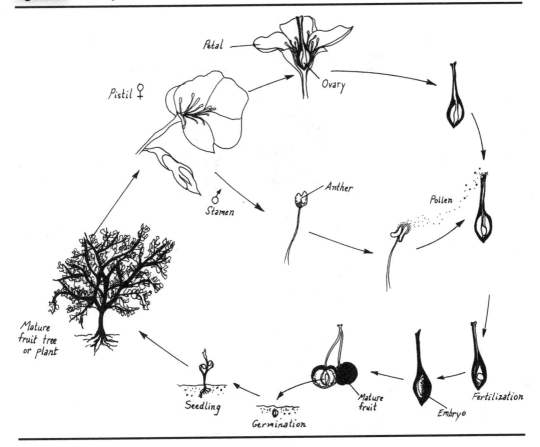

Although there are many familiar flowering plants that could be used to illustrate life cycles, we will use a cherry tree as an example. The life cycle of the cherry tree begins with the sprouting of a seed. The resulting seedling grows until it is mature enough to produce flowers. If you have ever examined cherry flowers (or other fruit tree flowers), you may have noticed that each flower has two kinds of stalked structures surrounded by its petals. These stalked structures are the male and female parts, called the anther (an-ther) and pistil (pis-tle), respectively. The anther contains pollen and the pistil contains eggs. When the pollen is mature, it is carried by insects or wind to the pistil. Fertilization occurs after the pollen reaches the tip of the pistil and grows a tube down to the eggs located in the ovary at the base of the pistil. Sperm (contained within the pollen) travels from the pollen to the eggs. The fertilized egg matures into a cherry seed and the ovary containing the seed develops into the fruit. The cherry seed is distributed by birds or other animals that consume the fruit but cannot digest the seed. If the seed is deposited in a suitable place for the cherry tree to grow, it eventually sprouts, beginning a new cycle.

Figure 7.5   Life Cycle of a Fern

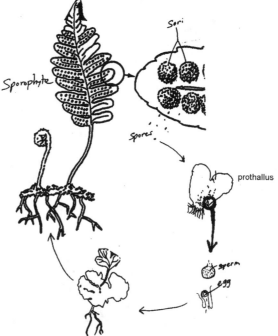

Ferns undergo even more pronounced changes during their life cycles (see Figure 7.5). Ferns are commonly found in moist, shady areas. Alternatively, you can purchase fern fronds at a florist shop. When you look at the fern fronds, which most people are familiar with, you are looking at the stage of the plant that produces reproductive spores. Fern spores are bundled in tiny sack-lack structures called sori on the underside of the fern frond. Sori come in a variety of shapes and can be very interesting to observe with a magnifying lens. Not all fern fronds have sori, but if you look at several different plants, you are likely to find some.

After the spores have been dispersed by wind to a place with the right combination of moisture, light, temperature, and space, spores can develop into a flat, heart-shaped plant known as the prothallus. It is unlikely that you have ever seen a prothallus. They are tiny and not easy to find among the leaves and other debris scattered along the forest floor. The prothallus grows male and female reproductive structures on its bottom side, which contain sperm and eggs, respectively. When the conditions are right, the microscopic sperm swim in the thin layer of moisture coating the prothallus's underside. If the sperm contacts a mature egg, fertilization may result. The union of the sperm and egg forms a new fern plant that grows on top of its parent prothallus. The young fern bursts through the prothallus, sinks roots into the soil, and lifts a frond into the air. The prothallus then withers, leaving only the familiar fern plant in its place.

Animal Life Cycle Examples

The life cycles of animals commonly raised in classrooms may be more familiar, and possibly more interesting, than those of plants. Consider the insects, for example, which follow several different developmental patterns. In one pattern, the newly hatched insect looks like a miniature adult. Development primarily involves getting larger, without any major changes in appearance. There are few behavioral differences between larvae and adults, with the important exception that only the adults mate and reproduce. The grasshopper is an example of an insect with this kind of life cycle. Grasshoppers hatch into immature nymphs, which resemble mature grasshoppers without wings. As the nymph grows through several stages, it gradually develops wings and becomes an adult (Figure 7.6). This type of life cycle is known as incomplete metamorphosis.

Other types of insects, such as honeybees and butterflies, develop through four distinct stages. This process is called complete metamorphosis. In these insects, the egg hatches into a larva, which generally spends most of its time eating. Eventually, the larva enters a resting stage called the pupa. During this stage, the larva is literally transformed. When it emerges as an adult, its appearance and behavior are completely different from that of the larva it used to be (see Figure 7.7).

Figure 7.6   Life Cycle of the Grasshopper

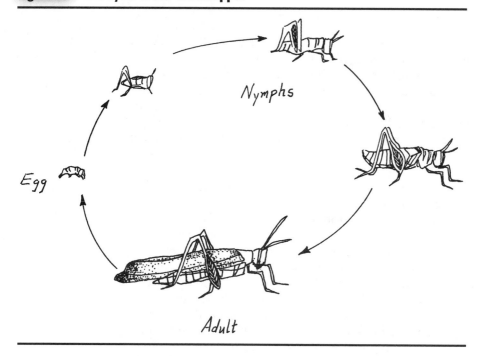

Nymphs

Egg

Adult

Figure 7.7   Life Cycle of the Butterfly

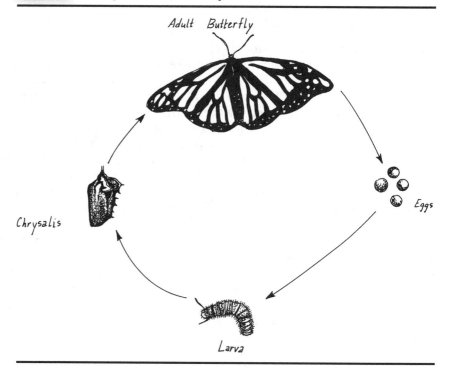

Adult   Butterfly

Eggs

Chrysalis

Larva

Figure 7.8   Life Cycle of the Frog

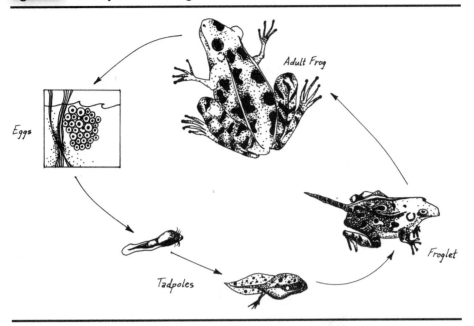

Insects are not the only animals that develop through this type of metamorphosis. Some amphibians undergo complete metamorphosis as well. The frog is a common example of this type of amphibian. Most frogs living in temperate climates have two life stages, one in water and the other on land. The female lays eggs in the water, which are immediately fertilized by the male (see Figure 7.8). The eggs hatch into gilled larvae, commonly known as tadpoles. Tadpoles feed on algae and other forms of vegetation. As the tadpoles grow and develop, they gradually lose their gills and tails and simultaneously develop lungs and legs. The adults have the ability to live on land (although they must keep their skin moist) and feed primarily on a variety of insects, worms, and spiders.

As you have seen in these few examples, there are many variations to the life cycles in familiar plants and animals. Even greater variation in life cycles exists in less familiar organisms, such as algae, fungi, and slime molds. Maybe you have never considered this, but even human beings cycle through various stages of development. How would you describe the human life cycle? Does it involve distinct stages, as in complete metamorphosis, or would you describe it as a more gradual maturation, like the silverfish? Take a moment to jot down your version of the human life cycle and then compare it to the one seen in Figure 7.9. Where are you in the cycle of life?

Figure 7.9   Life Cycle of Humans

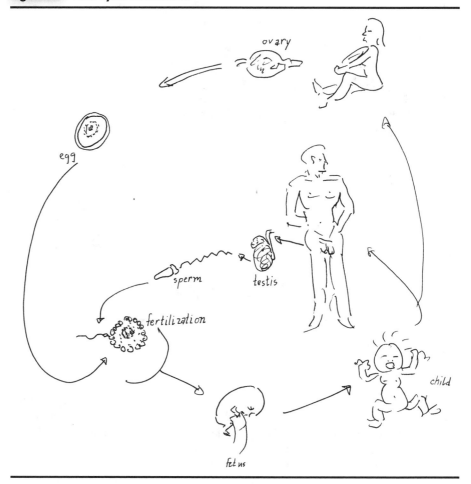

The Teaching Cycle

One thing that will quickly become apparent in your lesson planning is that there is a constant interplay between goal setting and reflection. Your choice of instructional objectives and activities for a particular lesson will often be influenced by your assessment of student learning and behavior in previous lessons. Therefore, in some instances, it may be difficult to distinguish whether the teaching cycle begins with goal setting or whether it begins with reflection. What matters, though, is not whether you are able to identify where reflection ends and goal setting begins but that you effectively use information gained from previous lessons to inform subsequent planning.

Goal Setting

Mr. Anderson has just finished grading the last of his sixth-grade students' poster projects and he is very pleased with the results. This unit on life cycles and metamorphosis has been very popular. Mr. Anderson thought back on the trepidation he felt when Vicki first suggested that they raise butterflies in class. After all, neither he nor any of his students had ever completed such a project before. However, he could not ignore how enthusiastically his students embraced Vicki's suggestion and soon found himself filling out a science supply company order form for a butterfly rearing kit. It did not take long for the kit to arrive and soon the north window ledge of the classroom was graced with a butterfly house containing 32 painted lady caterpillars.

Although many of his students would have been happy simply watching the caterpillars as they gradually developed into butterflies, Mr. Anderson wanted to take advantage of the learning opportunities that the project afforded. Upon reviewing the relevant sections of the *Benchmarks for Science Literacy* and the *National Science Education Standards,* he learned that these reform documents emphasized general aspects of life cycles (being born, growing, reproducing, and dying). Additionally, the benchmarks and standards recommended that students learn that the details of life cycles are different for different organisms.

> *Section E, Flow of Matter and Energy*
> *Benchmarks for Grades 3–5*
>
> Over the whole earth, organisms are growing, dying, and decaying, and new organisms are being produced by the old ones.
>
> *NSES Content Standard C*
> *Life Cycles of Organisms, grades K–4*
>
> Plants and animals have life cycles that include being born, developing into adults, reproducing, and eventually dying. The details of this life cycle are different for different organisms.

He knew that students would be interested in seeing the caterpillars pass through the various stages of their life cycle and believed that this would provide excellent opportunities to address the benchmarks and standards recommendations. Additionally, watching the butterflies progress through their life cycle over the next few weeks would provide numerous opportunities for students to apply their observation skills and reflect on prior experiences. Mr. Anderson knew that making accurate observations was an important inquiry skill that was heavily emphasized in the benchmarks and standards.

Since this would be a long-term project, it would be important for students to carefully record their observations for subsequent analysis. Therefore, he introduced the process of journal keeping, instructing his students to spend several minutes of free time each day recording the caterpillars' behavior and appearance. Students needed guidance in deciding what types of information to write down at first, and it seemed that he was constantly reminding them to include the date and time with their journal entries. However, they eventually caught on, and soon their journals were filled with pictures and prose depicting the caterpillars' appearance, development, what they liked to eat, at what times they appeared to be resting, and so on.

Mr. Anderson knew that students would want background information on butterflies that their observations alone could not provide. He could simply tell them the answers to many of their questions, but he remembered from his education courses that instruction is more effective when students are actively involved. Therefore, he stocked his classroom with reading material on butterflies and moths from the library and used bookstore. At least twice per week, as the caterpillars were growing, he chose one of these books for reading time. Mr. Anderson developed a system for checking these books out and was pleased with how popular they were among his students. He also encouraged students to search the Internet for information on the life cycles of butterflies and moths during their weekly visits to the computer lab. It was fun to watch the students excitedly share their newly discovered butterfly information and pictures with each other.

A teacher helps a student research her science project on the Internet.

While these activities were open ended and lacked formal assessment, he could tell from the ensuing discussions that students were learning a lot about the life cycles of butterflies and moths. Mr. Anderson certainly knew that he had learned a lot. The challenge that lay ahead was to help students piece together the knowledge they had gained into a meaningful conceptual understanding of the life cycle.

The first step toward this goal was to have students construct a poster on the life cycle of the painted lady. This provided an opportunity to use what they had learned from their observations, readings, and Internet surfing. Students consistently included all four stages of complete metamorphosis (egg, larva, pupa, and adult). Additionally, many had included more specific terms for the life cycle of butterflies (*egg, caterpillar, chrysalis, and butterfly*). The posters included pictures of the painted ladies and what they ate at each stage of their development, as well as descriptions of their behavior. The posters were impressive indicators of student learning and would make good additions to the students' portfolios.

Mr. Anderson believed that there was more to understanding life cycles than being able to depict butterfly metamorphosis. Thus far, students had focused on a single, specific example of a life cycle. What he wanted them to do next was to more generally apply what they had learned from their experience with the painted lady butterflies. What could they learn about life cycles that would be relevant to their lives?

One of the concepts of life cycles that was emphasized in the books he read and websites that he visited was that the various changes an organism undergoes during its life cycle allow it to occupy different roles, or niches, in its environment. This is especially true of organisms that undergo complete metamorphosis, like the butterfly. Thus, the caterpillar eats a completely different food (often leaves or other vegetation) than the adult butterfly, which typically feeds on nectar. Students already had information recorded in their journals about what the painted lady caterpillars and butterflies eat, but he doubted whether students had considered the ecological significance of their observations. Mr. Anderson believed that this issue needed to be explicitly addressed during the next day's lesson. He, therefore, wrote the following objective:

> Students will be able to describe at least three ways metamorphosis is beneficial to painted lady butterflies.

The second concept that he wanted students to learn was that life cycles are common to all organisms, from algae to zebras. Some life cycles, as in the case of butterflies, are more prominent than others, but all life is characterized by cycles of development. Mr. Anderson decided that students could learn this concept by working in pairs to construct life cycle posters of familiar plants and animals, like corn, cats, and dogs. Thus, his second objective for the lesson was:

> Students will be able to construct a poster that effectively describes the life cycle of an organism of their choice (other than the butterfly).

Mr. Anderson was certain that students would find this activity interesting and that it would be an effective way to illustrate the universal nature of life cycles. He hoped that by emphasizing the ecological significance and universal nature of life cycles in tomorrow's lesson, students would find relevancy beyond what they had observed and learned from rearing the painted lady butterflies.

Finally, Mr. Anderson realized that students could learn an important lesson about science by reflecting on their butterfly observations during the past few weeks. Previously, while browsing through the *National Science Education Standards,* Mr. Anderson noticed an inquiry standard relevant to the butterfly investigation his students had completed:

> Different kinds of questions suggest different kinds of scientific investigations. Some investigations involve observing and describing objects, organisms, or events; some involve collecting specimens; some involve experiments; some involve seeking more information; some involve discovery of new objects and phenomena, some involve making models. (*NSES,* Science as Inquiry, Grades 5–8)

The key point of this standard is that science uses a variety of methods; it is not limited to the familiar experimentation or to "The Scientific Method" to which people commonly refer. Mr. Anderson knew that if students were to learn this concept, he would need to explicitly focus attention on it. Otherwise, students would be unlikely to learn this important scientific inquiry concept, even though they had been engaged in "doing science." Therefore, he added a third objective to his list for the lesson:

> Students will be able to explain that all scientific investigations do not follow a specified sequence of steps.

Materials Development and Selection

Having decided on two behavioral objectives for the next science lesson, Mr. Anderson began to consider the types of activities he could to use to help students achieve these outcomes. He felt that a classroom discussion centered on their journals and posters would be a good way to introduce the concept of the benefits of life cycles. He could start by returning their posters and reviewing the concept of metamorphosis they depicted. From there, it should be easy to move the discussion to the benefits of metamorphosis. Mr. Anderson wanted students to refer to the data recorded in their journals when discussing these benefits. This would reinforce the utility of their recorded observations. He was certain that if he compiled data from the students' journals on the board, it would be relatively easy for them to see how the process of metamorphosis benefited the painted lady butterflies.

Mr. Anderson was not sure whether there would be time to address the second objective in tomorrow's lesson or whether it would have to be postponed to the next day. Addressing the second objective would provide an "elastic clause," or way to adjust the lesson should the benefits of the metamorphosis activity and discussion run longer than expected. To address the second objective, Mr. Anderson wanted student pairs to construct posters depicting the life cycles of organisms other than the butterfly. Working in pairs would provide opportunities for sharing and cooperation while students extended their understandings of the life cycle concept to other organisms. After the posters were completed, they could be used as props while the student pairs shared what they had learned about the organism they chose to research. The ubiquitous nature of life cycles should become evident as the various posters are shared with the class, providing that the student pairs all gave reports on the life cycles of different organisms. Therefore, it would be important for Mr. Anderson to provide some guidance for which organisms the student pairs chose to research in order to ensure that enough different kinds of life cycles were reported. On the other hand, he did not want to assign specific organisms for students to research, as this might stifle some of their enthusiasm for the task. When attempting to teach in a manner consistent with constructivism, teachers must often balance their desire to base instruction on students' interests and knowledge with curriculum requirements. In the end, Mr. Anderson decided to make a list of the interesting organisms prior to teaching the lesson and to use the list to suggest alternatives when different pairs of students wanted to research the same organism.

Although Mr. Anderson believed that his students would find it easy to come up with ideas for their posters from brainstorming alone, he knew that it would be important to have other sources of information available as well, such as magazines and encyclopedias. He also intended to have students conduct research on the Internet for information on their chosen organisms during the class's next scheduled visit to the computer lab. Mr. Anderson had increasingly found the Internet to be useful for such work, as long as students were given plenty of guidance in searching for and selecting appropriate information and pictures.

Pedagogy

Mr. Anderson returns the students' posters at the beginning of the next day's science lesson. He explains how pleased he is with their efforts and that they should seriously consider including these posters in their portfolios. He then introduces today's lesson on the importance of life cycles.

Mr. A: These posters are great! You've obviously learned a lot about painted lady butterflies and metamorphosis in the past few weeks. What I'd like for you to do in today's lesson is to extend this learning a bit. One of the things we're going to consider is how life cycles, particularly metamorphosis, can be beneficial to an organism. After that, we'll start a project that will help you answer the question, "Are butterflies the only organisms that have life cycles?"

Mr. Anderson asks Adrianne if he can use her poster as an example. She agrees to this, so he tapes her painted lady life cycle poster to the board. He asks students to refer to their own posters and journal notes as they review what they know about life cycles.

Mr. A: So, what do scientists call the painted lady's life cycle? . . . Sam?
Sam: Metamorphosis.
Mr. A: OK. [Mr. Anderson writes the word "metamorphosis" on the board above the poster.] And what does the word "metamorphosis" mean?
Sam: To change, I think. Like when the caterpillar changes into a chrysalis and then a butterfly.

Mr. A: Good. So metamorphosis means to change or transform. Can anyone tell me what the two types of metamorphosis are? . . . Sally?

Sally: I don't exactly remember . . .

Mr. Anderson pauses for several seconds to give Sally a chance to think about the question a little more. He knows that students often benefit from having more time to process a question and compose an answer. When it is clear that Sally will not come up with an answer on her own, Mr. Anderson provides the following hint.

Mr. A: One refers to total transformation, the other is less complete . . .

Sally: Oh yeah! Complete and incomplete metamorphosis.

Mr. A: Now, which type of metamorphosis did you observe in your painted lady butterflies? . . . Jessi?

Jessi: The complete kind.

Mr. A: And why do think it's complete metamorphosis?

Jessi: 'Cause the caterpillars look totally different from the butterflies, even though they're both painted ladies.

Mr. A: Do the rest of you agree? [The class nods in agreement. Mr. Anderson then writes "complete" on the board beside the word "metamorphosis" that he had written earlier.]

Mr. A: For this next question, I want you to get out a sheet of paper. Write your name on the paper and prepare four column headings, like this. [Mr. Anderson writes "egg," "larvae," "pupae," and "adult" as separate column headings on the board.] Now, using your journals and posters, fill each column with as many observations as you can about the painted lady butterflies that we reared. For each stage, you can include observations about appearance, behavior, and what the painted lady ate (if anything). Try to come up with several items for each list and feel free to discuss your ideas with a neighbor. Plan to be finished and ready to share your results in about five minutes. If you have any questions, raise your hand so that I'll know to come by to help.

For the next several minutes, Mr. Anderson circulates around the room to offer help where it is needed. From past experience, he knows that close proximity to his students reduces opportunities for them to misbehave and, thus, serves as a low-key form of behavior management. Circulating also makes it easy for him to monitor student progress and offer encouragement or assistance when necessary. It only takes a few minutes for students to list several observations under each heading. Mr. Anderson then returns to the front of the room and addresses the class.

Mr. A: Who would like to share their observations about eggs? . . . Ellie?

Ellie: Well, we noticed that the eggs were greenish. They were also round and kind of clumped together.

Mr. A: [Mr. Anderson lists these observations under the "egg" column.] What about eating or other behavior?

Ellie: Eggs don't eat or move around, Mr. Anderson!

Mr. A: I agree, but don't forget that the embryo inside the egg could be eating and moving.

Bill: But we didn't observe that.

Mr. A: Good point. Did any other groups have something to add to our list of egg observations? . . . Susan?

Susan: The eggs were attached to a leaf.

Mr. A: Right! I had forgotten about that. [Mr. Anderson records Susan's observation.]

For the next several minutes, Mr. Anderson solicits and records the students' observations for each stage of the life cycle of the painted lady butterflies. When completed, each column has between five and ten listed observations. Mr. Anderson reminds students to add to their own lists whatever class observations they had failed to consider. Next, he refers to the class observations compiled on the board.

Mr. A: Now, I want you to consider all of the observations that we've listed here on the board to answer this next question. This is a very interesting question and one that is important to consider now that you know about the stages of metamorphosis and the life cycle of painted lady butterflies. What good is metamorphosis? I want you to see if you can think of any reasons for how the process of metamorphosis might be beneficial, how it might be a good thing for butterflies. Feel free to discuss possible answers with other students at your table. Be prepared to share what you think in about five minutes.

Mr. Anderson writes "Benefits of metamorphosis" on the board. He circulates from table to table to listen as students discuss their ideas but offers no help. After a few minutes, he begins calling on volunteers from each table to share what they have decided.

Ellie: We noticed that the painted ladies look a lot different at each stage. The eggs are small and hard to see. The caterpillars are easier to see because they're bigger and move around, but they also have spines that may help protect them from being eaten. The chrysalis can look a lot like a leaf hanging from a twig, so it's hard to see, just like the eggs. And the butterfly is very easy to see, but it can fly to get away from its enemies.

Mr. A: OK, so what would you say is a reason that these differences are beneficial to the painted lady?

Ellie: It allows it to look different at each stage of its life so that it can be protected from other animals that want to eat it.

Mr. A: That sounds reasonable. How many other groups discussed this benefit of metamorphosis? [Several students raise their hands.] Good! Then we'll make that our first item on the list. [Mr. Anderson writes a summary of Ellie's statement under the "Benefits of metamorphosis" heading on the board.] Did any groups have a different benefit of metamorphosis to share? . . . Sarah?

Sarah: We noticed that the caterpillar and the butterfly ate different kinds of things.

Bob: Wait a minute. They both fed on thistles!

Sarah: Yeah, but the caterpillars ate thistle leaves, and the butterflies drank nectar from thistle flowers.

Mr. Anderson realized that Bob spoke out of turn, something that often needs to be discouraged. However, in this case, the comment was on topic and well mannered. Additionally, it provided an opportunity for student-to-student interaction. Mr. Anderson believes it is beneficial for students to challenge and defend each others' ideas, as long as they treat each other respectfully.

Mr. A: And what good is it for caterpillars to eat different kinds of food than butterflies? . . . Alex?

Alex: Well, one of the things we were talking about in our group was that there's less chance of all the food getting eaten if the butterflies and caterpillars eat different things.

Mr. A: So there's less competition for food between the larvae and adults? [Mr. Anderson summarizes Alex's statement on the board.]

Alex: Yeah. If there are a lot of caterpillars and butterflies and they eat the exact same food, then there might not be enough for everybody to eat. This doesn't happen with metamorphosis, because the caterpillars eat one thing and the adults eat something else.

Mr. A: Good point. How many groups discussed this benefit of metamorphosis? [Most of the students raise their hands.] So, you've stated that metamorphosis is beneficial to the painted lady in that it allows each stage of the butterfly's life to have different characteristics that help it survive. You've also pointed out that it cuts down on competition for food between the adult and larvae. Did any of you discuss other benefits of metamorphosis?

Leah: Our group talked about something related to what the caterpillars and adult butterflies eat. Leaves are around for caterpillars to eat before there are any flowers. The caterpillars can't eat flowers that haven't bloomed yet, but by the time the caterpillar grows, becomes a chrysalis, and then turns into a butterfly, the thistle flowers are blooming. There are plenty of flowers for the butterflies then.

Mr. A: That's an excellent idea, and one that I hadn't considered. [Mr. Anderson summarizes Leah's point on the board.] Metamorphosis allows time for different foods to become available during different stages of the painted lady's life cycle. Did anyone else have something to share?

This question is met with silence. It appears that the students have exhausted their ideas about the benefits of metamorphosis. Nevertheless, Mr. Anderson waits for several seconds, just to be sure. Often a little extra wait time is all that is needed to encourage a reluctant responder. However, even after this additional wait time, there are no further responses from the students. Mr. Anderson is satisfied with the list his students have developed and begins the closure for the lesson.

Mr. A: You folks have made this a very interesting lesson today! Not only have you described the life cycle of the painted lady, but [Mr. Anderson refers to the "Benefits of metamorphosis" list on the board] you've also come up with some compelling reasons for why metamorphosis may be beneficial to butterflies. That brings another question to mind. If life cycles with different stages (like metamorphosis) are so beneficial, do you think butterflies are the only organisms that have them? Can you think of any other organisms that look differently at different stages of their lives?

Sarah: I know that lots of other insects do metamorphosis, like flies and honeybees.

Mr. A: Good point. Can you think of anything besides insects that look really different at different stages of their life cycle?

Adam: What about tadpoles and frogs?

Ellie: Yeah, and even baby animals, like kittens, look kind of different and eat different things than adult cats.

Mr. A: Good thinking! What I want you to consider is that every organism goes through some kind of life cycle. In many cases, the organism looks and behaves much differently in the younger stages than it does as an adult. In other cases, like the cat, the young do not look that much different than the adults. Even humans have life cycles.

Sam: That's right! We start out as babies, then we grow older and become children and teenagers, and then we get to be adults.

Mr. A: At each of these different stages we play a different role in our families, just like the painted lady plays different roles in its environment.

Ellie: I never thought of it like that before.

Mr. A: It's a pretty interesting concept and I'd like for you to think about this idea some more. Tomorrow we're going to do some brainstorming to see how many examples of life cycles we can come up with. Until then, be thinking about all the different kinds of plants, animals, fungi, and so on that you know and what their life cycles might be like.

As a final step to the lesson, Mr. Anderson takes a minute to focus students' attention on the butterfly investigation itself. Although students had made and recorded lots of observations, they had not actually done an experiment, per se. Even so, what they had done was very similar to the work of many scientists, including those who study animal and plant life cycles. Sometimes the scientists' questions are best answered through observation and description rather than testing hypotheses in an experiment. In this discussion, Mr. Anderson emphasizes that not all scientific investigations follow a set sequence of steps. There is no such thing as *the* scientific method.

Assessment

So far, Mr. Anderson only had anecdotal evidence from the students who responded in class that they had met the two objectives for today's lesson. It would be important to include a more formal assessment of these two objectives to be certain that all of his students understood the benefits and universal nature of life cycles. Certainly, Mr. Anderson could assess students' understandings of the benefits of life cycles through verbal questioning during their poster presentations. It would be informative to ask the presenters to explain how each organism's life cycle was linked to its survival. Assessment of students' understandings of the universal nature of life cycles could not come from the poster presentations alone, however, since each student pair would be focusing on a single organism's life cycle. Therefore, Mr. Anderson decided to follow the presentations with a writing assignment in which students could demonstrate their knowledge of both the benefits and universal nature of life cycles. To assess student progress toward his objective on scientific inquiry, Mr. Anderson would also require the students to explain why or why not they were doing science when they observed and described the painted lady's life cycle. The information gleaned from their writing would enable Mr. Anderson to decide whether his students had met his life cycle objectives or whether additional instruction was necessary.

Reflection

After the last of the students had left for home at the end of the day, Mr. Anderson took a few minutes to reflect on the metamorphosis lesson. Based on his students' responses to his questioning, Mr. Anderson was convinced that they were well on their way to constructing rich understandings of the concept of metamorphosis. To be honest, he had been a little concerned about how his more energetic students would behave during the lesson, since it was more minds-on than hands-on. He was pleasantly surprised by their active participation in both the group work and class discussions and attributed their good behavior primarily to the high level of interest that the butterfly project had generated.

Mr. Anderson was also pleased with the way his students seemed to respect each other's ideas and contributions. These days, he seldom had to remind students not to interrupt their classmates. In fact, the rule to raise your hand before you speak was gradually becoming unnecessary for these students. Certainly, the students had come a long way since the beginning of the year when they were prone to interrupt and speak over one another.

Despite his overall good feelings about the lesson, there was one aspect that he would like to have changed. A good portion of the lesson centered on class discussion, which was dominated by quickly responding students. The more timid and reluctant students did not participate as well as Mr. Anderson would have liked. He had been able to mitigate this to a degree by specifically calling on some of the more reluctant students and by breaking up the class into small groups for a portion of the lesson. However, experience had taught him that the best way to involve reluctant and timid students was to provide plenty of opportunities for them to work in pairs with less dominant partners. Fortunately, the metamorphosis presentation activity that students would begin tomorrow provided just such an opportunity.

Suggested Literature Connections

The Big Tree by Bruce Hiscock
    Macmillan Publishing Company, New York, 1991

Both Sides Now by Joni Mitchell
    Scholastic Inc., New York, 1992

Sophie by Mem Fox
    Harcourt Brace & Company, San Diego, CA, 1994

Once There Were Giants by Martin Waddell
    Delacorte Press, New York, 1989

Each of these books illustrates a different life cycle. They can be used together or individually to reinforce this concept. Have students compare and contrast these cycles. Using the timeline in *The Big Tree* as a guide, they can create their own timelines for themselves or other family members.

Environmental Science

We have emphasized several key biological concepts in this chapter. We have explored how life is defined, the incredible diversity of life, life cycles, and the relationship between structure and function in living organisms. Our primary focus has been on the individual organism and its characteristics, behavior, cycle of life, how it is adapted to its environment, and how it undergoes change. However, in the natural world organisms do not live in isolation but constantly interact with other organisms and the physical environment. In this section, we will explore some of the concepts of environmental science—the science that addresses the interactions of living things with each other and the physical environment.

Some Major Concepts in Environmental Science

Environmental scientists have developed many concepts that they use to describe and explain the complex interactions they observe among and between living and nonliving components of nature. These principles range from the intuitive to the esoteric and complex. For our purposes, we will focus on some of the ecological principles of environmental science that are both relatively easy to understand and relevant to elementary science instruction.

Habitat. Think of a particular species of animal or plant. It could be a bald eagle soaring over a mountain lake, a sugar maple tree on an Appalachian mountainside, or a brook trout in a creek. In fact, now that you have learned to appreciate the life cycle of the fern, it could even be a prothallus growing in a dark, moist woodland. The key concept here is that when we think of a specific animal or plant, we almost always picture it in a particular setting. Ecologists label this setting the organism's habitat. There are many kinds of habitats on earth, and scientists have grouped them (remember the human tendency to classify things?) into rather broad categories. For example, on land we see desert, woodland, urban, tropical rainforest, grassland, and tundra habitats, just to name a

A bald eagle is shown in its natural habitat. Ferns are also shown growing in their natural habitat.

few. Aquatic habitats include stream, lake, pond, estuary, marsh, and saltwater environments. Each of the land-based and aquatic habitats contains a diversity of organisms adapted to survive and reproduce in these environments.

Populations. Think back to your example of a specific kind of plant or animal in its habitat. Now, consider whether this organism leads a totally solitary life, or more likely, whether it has at least occasional contact with others of its species. Organisms seldom occupy a habitat as individuals. Instead, we usually find a number of the same species living and reproducing in any particular habitat. *Population* is the term ecologists use to describe a group of interbreeding organisms that live in the same time and place. For example, we might speak of a population of white-tailed deer living in a particular drainage of the Allegheny Mountains or a population of Saguaro cacti living in the Sonoran Desert.

Most habitats contain a rich mixture of populations. For example, a garden habitat may contain dozens of populations of animals, including earthworms, various beetles, pill bugs, centipedes, spiders, and so on. It is also likely to include several populations of plants. Some of these plant populations are cultivated (corn, beans, cabbage, etc.), whereas others may have moved in on their own (weeds). In addition to plant and animal populations, the garden habitat would contain populations of fungi, soil bacteria, and protozoa. As we shall see, this diverse mixture of organisms interacts in a habitat in various ways and these organisms are often interdependent on one another.

Communities. Interdependent populations of organisms make up the *community*, a term ecologists use to collectively describe the living portion of an ecosystem. A good analogy to natural communities is the local community in which you live. Your community consists of various groups of people with different skills and needs. Teachers, students, grocers, bankers, businesspeople, scientists, and consumers are just a few of the groups that interact to sustain the community. Each group plays a specific role and occupies its own place in the community structure. In fact, it is the interaction of the roles played by the various groups that make a community greater than the sum of its individual parts.

Just as in human communities, the populations in a natural community interact in complex ways to sustain its structure. Organisms compete for resources such as space to grow, sunlight, water, food, nest sites, and so on. Plants produce food (sugar) from available sunlight and are eaten by other organisms, like deer, which are collectively known as herbivores (plant eaters). Still other organisms, called carnivores (meat eaters), eat the herbivores for food. Cats, foxes, mountain lions, and hawks are all examples of carnivores. Some organisms are parasitic. They obtain the food and space they require by taking it from other organisms. Fleas, ticks, and tapeworms are just three of the countless examples of parasites. There are even examples of organisms that cooperate with each other.

For example, flowers offer nectar to bees and other insects in exchange for the transfer of pollen. The familiar lichens found growing on rocks and tree trunks are actually a close association of two different organisms, algae and fungus. Algae produce enough food from sunlight for itself and the fungus, while the fungus collects water and nutrients for itself and the algae. Just as the community where you live is the result of many different roles and interactions, the ecological concept of community describes the roles and interactions of the different populations of organisms.

Food Chains and Food Webs. Food (nutrients) provides energy and the chemical building blocks for growth and development. Interactions that involve eating or being eaten can be depicted in food chains and webs. Food chains show the linear connection between producers (usually green plants) and consumers (organisms that eat other organisms) in an ecosystem. For example, a food chain might start with a particular kind of plant (see Figure 7.10). Caterpillars that eat the plant's leaves could form the next link in the chain. The following link could be the birds that eat the caterpillars, followed by a link that includes the cats that eat the birds, and so on.

Are caterpillars the only organisms that feed on plants? You can probably think of lots of different kinds of insects that you have seen munching on plant leaves. The linear connections depicted in food chains may be useful in showing how energy flows through an ecosystem, but they do not reflect the complexity of the interactions that occur in nature. For example, leaves are eaten by many different organisms in addition to caterpillars. Caterpillars may be consumed by wasps as well as birds. Cats may kill and eat birds, but so do hawks and falcons. To more accurately reflect the complexity of interactions between populations in an ecosystem, ecologists construct food webs (see Figure 7.11).

Food webs consist of several interconnected food chains and usually depict three distinct levels: producers (usually plants), consumers (usually animals), and decomposers (fungi and bacteria). As we have already seen, consumers may be further classified as herbivores (plant eaters) and predators (animal eaters). Most animals and plants in a population never complete their life cycles because they are consumed by organisms higher up on the food chain. What do you suppose happens to the matter and energy tied up in living organisms that do live out their life cycles? Do they hold on to the matter and energy they have accumulated even after death? It turns out that even those that do complete their life cycles eventually become food for somebody. In this case, it is the decomposers. Decomposers, like fungi and bacteria, consume dead organisms in order to gain energy and nutrients for themselves. In the process, they release minerals to the soil and water and gases back into the air where they are once again available to growing plants. Thus, energy (in the form of food) and matter (in the form of water, gases, and minerals) move through the ecosystem in endless cycles.

Figure 7.10   Food Chain

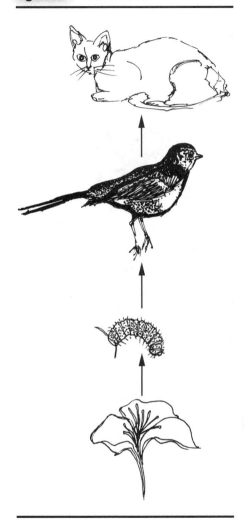

Figure 7.11   Food Web. A food web consists of many interconnected food chains. How many food chains can you identify in this web?

Ecosystems. A system can be thought of as an integrated set of parts that function as a unit. By now, you should be able to see how the populations of organisms in a community (including plants, animals, fungi, protists, and bacteria) depend on interactions with each other for survival. It should also be clear that the physical environment, including air, water, soil, heat, light, and minerals, contributes to the sustenance of life. The set of relationships within and between a community and its physical environment is called an ecosystem.

Figure 7.12 **Energy in a Food Web.** The energy that cycles through an ecosystem ultimately comes from the sun.

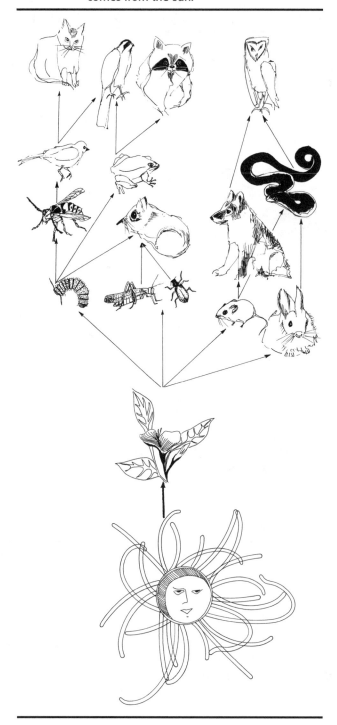

Energy is the driving force of ecosystems. In our discussion of food chains and webs, you have seen how it is transferred through the ecosystem. Energy is transferred when plants are eaten by animals, animals by other animals, and when whatever is not eaten is eventually decomposed by fungi and bacteria. However, we have yet to identify the ultimate source of energy involved in these transfers. Can you think of what it must be? Where do green plants, the producers in the ecosystem, obtain their energy? (See Figure 7.12.)

The Teaching Cycle

Mrs. Bird was beginning an environmental science unit that would include the development of her fourth-grade students' understanding of the concept of ecosystem. She was a little concerned about the topic, since most of her inner-city students had very little exposure to natural settings. Thus, the abstract concept of ecosystem would likely be exacerbated by her students' lack of knowledge and experience with the animals, plants, and environmental factors that are typically presented in textbook discussions of the topic. It would certainly be a challenge for her to find ways to make the concept concrete for her students to understand.

Goal Setting

Mrs. Bird started by carefully considering what she wanted her students to learn. Setting appropriate goals for instruction was important to Mrs. Bird because they helped focus her planning and guide assessment throughout the unit. To this end, she found the recommendations of the *National Science Education Standards* to be particularly helpful. The grade 5–8 standards under Populations and Ecosystems included:

- A population consists of all individuals of a species that occur together at a given place and time. All populations living together and the physical factors with which they interact compose an ecosystem (p. 157).
- For ecosystems, the major source of energy is sunlight. Energy entering ecosystems as sunlight is transferred by producers into chemical energy through photosynthesis. That energy then passes from organism to organism in food webs (p. 158).
- The number of organisms an ecosystem can support depends on the resources available and abiotic factors, such as quantity of light and water, range of temperatures, and soil composition. Given adequate biotic and abiotic resources and no disease or predators, populations (including humans) increase at rapid rates. Lack of resources and other factors, such as predation and climate, limit the growth of populations in specific niches in the ecosystem (p. 158).

It was apparent to Mrs. Bird that her students would be moving toward these goals rather than completely achieving them during this particular unit. Although Mrs. Bird believed that it was too early in the unit for her students to tackle the complete concept of ecosystem, she was sure that they could grasp the general notion that species depend on one another and on the environment for survival. By heightening their awareness of the kinds of relationships that exist among organisms and the physical conditions that organisms must cope with, she would be preparing them for a more formal understanding of the ecosystem concept that they would later develop.

Mrs. Bird's next step was to write instructional objectives for each outcome she wanted her students to achieve. Mrs. Bird always wrote objectives by considering what she wanted her students to be able to do after they completed the lesson. This ruled out ambiguous terms like *know* and *understand* because she had no direct way to determine whether a student knows or understands a concept. Instead, her objectives focused on behavior. For this particular lesson, students would be using their knowledge of the interactions of animals, plants, and their environment to develop more formal understandings of the concept of ecosystem. Students who developed the desired level of understanding should be able to define the term and describe examples of ecosystems in the wild. Therefore, Mrs. Bird included the following objectives in her plan:

1. Students will be able to describe an ecosystem as containing both living and non-living components.
2. Given an appropriate example, students will be able to list at least five living and nonliving components of an ecosystem.
3. Students will be able to define ecosystem as "the interactions of organisms with each other and their environment."
4. Given an appropriate example of an ecosystem, students will be able to describe at least five interactions among living and nonliving components.

It was clear to Mrs. Bird that students would not be able to master all of these instructional outcomes in a single lesson. It would be important to give students several opportunities to construct these understandings, so these objectives would guide instruction over the next few days.

Materials Development and Selection

Next, Mrs. Bird needed to choose an activity for the lesson. Mrs. Bird suspected that her students were somewhat familiar with the term *ecosystem* but were unlikely to have developed any formal understanding of the concept since they lived in an urban environment. She also knew that although her students had only a vague notion of the examples of ecosystems presented in textbooks, many had pets and would be familiar with the requirements of keeping animals in the home. Therefore, Mrs. Bird decided that she could build on her students' prior knowledge and experience with animals they had raised as pets to help them formalize their understandings of the concept of ecosystem.

What would be the best way to get students to share and apply their knowledge of the daily requirements of their pets to the concept of ecosystem? The first idea that came to mind was to ask students to bring in their pets and present a short talk about what it takes to keep the pet healthy and happy. No doubt this would lead to discussions about physical requirements, such as food and shelter, as well as interactions with other living

A Picture Is Worth a Thousand Words

Field trips are great, but you cannot always take your students to the environment you are studying, and it is not always possible to bring plants and animals into your classroom. Is it possible to use technology to bring the outside world into your classroom? You bet!

BOX 7.4

It has often been said that a picture is worth a thousand words. This is also true when teaching science. A picture, slide, or video clip can make a topic come alive for your class. Technological tools, such as traditional or digital cameras, video cameras, and tape recorders can provide images and sounds that will grab students' attention, especially when you are introducing a new topic.

How often have you documented your vacations through your photographs, only to have them sit unused in a photo album on your shelf? Begin a library of photos that can serve as a great resource for your science classroom. Film pictures can be developed into slides or scanned and stored on a computer disk. Today's digital cameras offer an easy way to collect pictures from school field trips and student projects for later presentations. You can use an Internet search engine to find photos or multimedia sites. (Remember to ask the photographer for permission when copying these photos.)

Mrs. Bird was concerned that her inner-city students had little exposure to natural settings. One way to address this issue would be to take students on a virtual field trip to various environments. Even better, using the digital camera, Mrs. Bird could record her walk through a dense forest, photographing different trees and organisms she finds along the way. Once she returns to school, she could use these photos in a slide show presentation, creating an economical virtual field trip for her students.

If Mrs. Bird cannot locate an environment within her area, there are many good websites she could have her students visit for another type of virtual field trip. *National Geographic* and the Smithsonian Institution have websites that offer a wide variety of photographs covering many different environments.

Your field trip possibilities are no longer bounded by limited funding and resources. You can take your students to places across the world without ever leaving your classroom.

things, like people. The children could then use their shared experiences to construct the analogy of an ecosystem in the home.

However, this approach presented a couple of difficulties that made it less than ideal. It was doubtful that many of her students had pets small and tame enough to bring to class. Of course, it would be possible to simply talk about pets without bringing any in, but Mrs. Bird feared that the lesson would lose much of its appeal without live animals. Furthermore, having conducted a few sharing times, Mrs. Bird knew that these sessions could be very time consuming. Giving each student a couple of minutes to talk about pets could easily require more than an hour, yet not giving each student an opportunity to speak could make them feel left out. It was a difficult situation. In the end, Mrs. Bird decided that such sharing sessions required far too much time up front, leaving little opportunity to address the content that she wanted to teach.

Mrs. Bird thought of another possibility for using her students' experiences to address the concept of ecosystem. Instead of having students give talks about their own pets, they could help her design and set up a suitable environment for a classroom pet, guppies, for instance. Such a project would provide ample opportunity for students to share what they know about the physical requirements of fish (e.g., water, food, oxygen). Adding some aquatic plants and a few snails would also lead to a discussion about the interactions of organisms. Furthermore, guppies were easy to keep alive and small enough for many to be easily raised in an aquarium.

The next step in Mrs. Bird's planning involved making a list of materials for the lesson. Whether she needed to gather all of the supplies for the guppy aquarium before the first lesson depended on which approach she used. She could have students generate a list of necessary supplies for the guppy ecosystem. She could then purchase the supplies at the pet store. This would require her students to wait a day before they could put the aquarium together, which might prove difficult for her enthusiastic fourth graders. For this reason, she thought it would be better to try to anticipate her students' suggestions for the supplies and purchase them ahead of time. This way, the class could put the aquarium together while their enthusiasm for the task was high and she could always make a return trip to the pet store if students made suggestions she had not anticipated. She made the following materials list to help her in gathering supplies over the weekend for Monday's lesson.

Material List for Guppy Aquarium

1. guppies (pet store)
2. fish food (pet store)
3. fresh water snails (pet store)
4. aquatic plants (pet store)
5. dechlorination tablets (pet store)
6. aquarium (school supply room)
7. gravel or sand, thoroughly rinsed to remove sedimentation (pet store)

Pedagogy

By Monday, Mrs. Bird had gathered all of the supplies for the ecosystem lesson. She hid everything from view, except for the plastic bag containing the guppies, which was displayed prominently on her desk. This generated lots of excitement and interest among the arriving students. After Mrs. Bird took roll, she asked students what they were so excited about. The students' enthusiastic references to the bagged fish on her desk let her know that she had successfully captured their attention and piqued their curiosity. Mrs. Bird told the students that she just purchased the guppies and the sales clerk had put them in the plastic bag. She did not think that the guppies could live for long in the bag, and hoped that the class could help her prepare a more suitable place for them to live.

She then asked, "What do guppies need to survive?" Two dozen hands immediately went up. Mrs. Bird began calling on students to answer, being careful not to bias her selection toward gender or ability level. Knowing that it would be difficult for students to remember a long list of items, she summarized their responses on the board (see Figure 7.13).

The last item required some prompting from Mrs. Bird, but several students were familiar with the way that fish use their gills to breathe underwater and were eager to explain this to the class.

Once students had exhausted their ideas for items to add to the list, Mrs. Bird decided to move on to the next segment of the lesson. She pulled out the aquarium and displayed it on the front of her desk where it could be seen throughout the room. Mrs. Bird asked the class if they thought it would do as a place for the guppies to live, and her students assured her that it would. She placed a check mark beside aquarium and pointed to the next item on the list. "Where shall we get the water to fill the aquarium?" asked Mrs. Bird. "Will tap water do?" Several students responded that tap water would not be good for the guppies because it had chemicals in it. Mrs. Bird wanted to determine if any of her students knew what these chemicals were in the tap water. By probing her students with more questions, she found out that a couple of students knew that the chemical was chlorine and that it was put into tap water to kill germs. "The chlorine kills the germs, but it can also kill the fish," said Sally, who happened to keep a fish aquarium at home. Mrs. Bird asked Sally what kind of water they should use. Sally said that you could use water from outside, like rainwater or water from a ditch, but these can be hard to get in the city. "They make chemical tablets that you can put into the water to take the chlorine out, and that's what we use at home," said June, another girl who had pet fish. Mrs. Bird showed the class the dechlorination tablets she had purchased and asked Sally and June to show the class how to get the chlorine out of the water. June filled the aquarium with water and Sally added the proper number of tablets as Mrs. Bird read the directions printed on the package out loud.

Once the girls had dechlorinated the water, Mrs. Bird placed a check on the board beside "water" and proceeded to the next item. "Does anybody know what guppies

**Figure 7.13   Student List of Items That
Guppies Need to Survive**

Guppies need:
- a bigger place to live, like an aquarium or a fish bowl
- water to live in
- food to eat
- light so they can see
- places to hide
- oxygen to breathe

eat?" asked Mrs. Bird. Various answers were given, including fish food, plants, animals, and potato chips. Mrs. Bird presented the package of fish food and read the ingredients to the class: ground fish, rice, soybean meal, and fish oil. Mrs. Bird wrote "fish and grain" in parentheses on the board beside "food" and checked the item off. "This next item is interesting. Why do guppies need a place to hide? What are they hiding from?" This question generated a lot of responses. Some students said that guppies might be eaten by other fish. Others said that the guppies would feel better if they had a place where they could not be seen by everyone. A few had raised guppies before and pointed out that the babies need to hide from the adults until they grow large enough to no longer be considered food. When Mrs. Bird asked what kinds of things would be good for the guppies to hide in, the students suggested plants, rocks, and caves. As each hiding place was mentioned, Mrs. Bird pulled out samples for the students to see. She had both floating and attached plants, some flat rocks that could be stacked to form a cave, and a large whelk shell that provided additional hiding space. Bobby pointed out that the attached plants would need something to grow in, at which point Mrs. Bird produced a bag of fine gravel that she had carefully rinsed to remove sedimentation. Andy noted that the plants would not only provide a place for guppies to hide but would also add oxygen to the water for them to breathe. "I saw a program on the Discovery Channel that talked about that." Mrs. Bird agreed that it was an important point and added the words "from plants" to the list beside "oxygen to breathe." Next, Mrs. Bird had volunteers place the plants, rocks, and shell in the aquarium while the class supervised and offered suggestions. When completed, the students agreed that the aquarium looked like an ideal fish home.

"I suppose we're ready to drop the guppies in?" asked Mrs. Bird. Bobby's hand went up immediately and when called on, he explained that the first time his family brought fish home from the pet store several of them died because they immediately dumped them in their aquarium. When they returned to the pet store, the owner said that the fish died from the shock of being dumped into water of different temperature than what was in the bag. The next time, the owner explained, they should float the bag of fish in the aquarium for half an hour or so to give the temperature of the water in the bag a chance to equalize with that in the aquarium. Sally and June agreed that this was important to do. Mrs. Bird floated the bag of guppies in the aquarium and added "proper temperature" to the list of guppies' needs on the board.

While the temperature of the bag of guppies was equalizing with that of the aquarium water, Mrs. Bird asked students for their attention as they discussed what they had put together. She reminded the class that in yesterday's lesson they had learned a new word for the kind of place that an organism lives. She asked students to write that word on a piece of paper. After students had finished writing, she called on Leah to share what she had written. Leah responded with "habitat." Mrs. Bird asked for thumbs up if you agree, at which point every student in the class raised their thumbs.

Mrs. Bird wrote the term on the board and then asked, "What single word would you use to describe the guppies' habitat?" Mrs. Bird called on several volunteers who shared such answers as water, aquarium, pond, and stream. Mrs. Bird explained that habitat descriptions were usually fairly general and that a more general word often used to describe the habitat of organisms that live in water is *aquatic.* As she wrote the term on the board, she asked if anyone noticed any similarities between the words *aquatic* and *aquarium.* A couple of students pointed out that the two words begin with the same four letters. Mrs. Bird followed this up by explaining that words with similar meanings sometimes have similar spellings. Both *aquatic* and *aquarium* refer to water, and they begin with the same four letters.

Referring to the list of guppy requirements on the board, Mrs. Bird asked, "So the guppies live in an aquatic habitat, but why did we have to add so much other stuff to the aquarium? Why wasn't it enough to simply add water?" After their participation in designing the aquarium, students were more than ready to answer this question:

Guppies need to eat.

They need places to hide, too.

If guppies do not have the right temperature, they could die.

Even though they live in water, they still need oxygen.

The plants add oxygen to the water, which makes it better for the guppies.

It takes a lot more than water to keep guppies healthy.

Mrs. Bird felt that it was appropriate to spend as much time as necessary on this portion of lesson development. She wanted to be sure that students had an opportunity to build on their own knowledge and experiences rather than her simply presenting students with the correct answer.

Mrs. Bird summed up these responses with, "So you're telling me that while habitat tells you something about where guppies live, it doesn't tell you how they interact with their surroundings. When we talk about the interactions of the guppies with their surroundings, we're describing what scientists call an *ecosystem.*" Mrs. Bird writes, "ecosystem: the interactions of organisms with each other and their environment" on the board and asks students to copy the term and definition on their paper. Mrs. Bird continues, "The guppies' ecosystem includes both the living and nonliving things that they use, give off, and come into contact with. In fact, one useful way to analyze an ecosystem is to list its living and nonliving parts." Mrs. Bird writes, "living" and "nonliving" on the board and challenges the students to list the components of the guppies' ecosystem under the correct category. Again, her students are ready for the task, listing water, oxygen, waste, rocks, and seashell under "nonliving" and guppies and plants under the "living" headings. There was some debate as to whether store-bought fish food should be listed under "living" or "nonliving." In the end, the students decided to list it under "living," since it was primarily made from fish parts and, therefore, had once been alive.

Mrs. Bird brings the discussion to a conclusion by getting students to restate the definition of ecosystem and that ecosystems have both living and nonliving components. Next, she asks students if they can think of any examples of an ecosystem in nature. Mrs. Bird believes this is an important question, because it gives students the opportunity to apply (and for her to assess) their understandings of the ecosystem concept.

Additionally, the question directs them to consider the idea that their guppy ecosystem is really just a simplified version of what typically occurs in nature.

Several students answer the question, all with fairly generalized examples, such as forests, ponds, and streams. Mrs. Bird focuses on the forest example and continues the line of questioning by asking various students to list living and nonliving components of the forest. Once again, students have little difficulty categorizing the living and nonliving components of the ecosystem. Finally, Mrs. Bird explains that they will be considering the guppy ecosystem in more detail in future lessons, especially in regard to how its various components affect, and are affected by, each other. She then releases the guppies and allows the students a few minutes to watch them explore their new home.

Assessment

As a more formal assessment of student learning, Mrs. Bird assigns a homework assignment requiring students to consider the addition of snails to the guppy ecosystem. She tells students that she would like to add snails to the aquarium, but before doing so it will be important to consider the snails' requirements and possible interactions with other things in the aquarium. She assigns students the task of listing on a sheet of paper at least five things that snails need to survive and to categorize these requirements as "living" and "nonliving." Additionally, they should consider how the snails might interact with the guppies and other components of their aquarium ecosystem and be prepared to discuss these things in class tomorrow. Mrs. Bird knew that some students in her class would know very little about snails and might have difficulty completing their lists. To remedy this, she showed several books that they could use in class that included information about snails. She also suggested that they use either the printed or computer versions of encyclopedias that were available in class to search for information on snails.

Mrs. Bird believed this to be an appropriate assessment because it challenged students to apply their understandings of ecosystem components and interactions to a different organism. Furthermore, she planned to use her students' ideas by actually adding the snails to the aquarium. This made the activity more authentic and gave her an opportunity to show her students that she valued their contributions. Also, the addition of snails would increase the complexity of the system, which would bring it that much closer to a real-life situation and permit students to observe more interactions.

Reflection

Mrs. Bird mentally reviewed her lesson at the end of the school day. She was always amazed at the usefulness of hindsight and used it regularly to improve her instruction. Mrs. Bird thought that the strong point of the lesson was using students' ideas to help them construct an understanding of the ecosystem concept. She much preferred this approach over simply telling them what she wanted them to learn. Overall, Mrs. Bird thought her students had participated well and was satisfied from their responses that they were able to recognize that there are both living and nonliving components of ecosystems. The homework assignment would further illuminate their understandings.

Mrs. Bird was happy that she had been able to introduce the topic of ecosystems by constructing a simple example in the classroom. Setting up the aquarium was a far better way to explore the components of an ecosystem than simply looking at pictures or books. Even so, it had not been possible for very many students to actually manipulate the materials. Mrs. Bird saw this as a weakness. It might have been better if students could have worked in small groups to construct their own ecosystems. She had attended a session at the National Science Association Teachers convention a couple of years ago in which the instructor demonstrated the construction of an ecosystem in a jar. She liked this idea and considered using it as an assessment activity toward the end of the unit.

There were a couple of other issues about the lesson that concerned Mrs. Bird. For one thing, none of the students had mentioned bacteria as a component of the aquarium ecosystem. This is understandable, since bacteria are too small to be seen and easy to overlook. However, bacteria play a critical role in decomposing waste materials and are an important component of any ecosystem. Mrs. Bird would need to prepare some questions for the next day's lesson to guide students to this realization.

A second concern was that there was no discussion of the reciprocal effects of the guppies on their environment. For example, the students clearly understood that clean water is a requirement for the guppies' well-being. However, they had not discussed the fact that the guppies produce waste, which reduces the water quality. This bidirectional aspect of ecosystem interactions would need to be addressed in subsequent lessons. Mrs. Bird intended to begin by emphasizing such interactions among the snails, guppies, and plants in the next day's lesson. In fact, Mrs. Bird was beginning to see that the guppy aquarium would provide many opportunities to guide her students' development of rich understandings of the ecosystem concept. She looked forward to using it in many lessons to come.

Suggested Literature Connections

My Little Island by Frane Lesse, Harper Trophy, New York, 1985.

The Great Kapok Tree by Lynne Cherry, Harcourt, Brace, Jovanovich, Orlando, Florida, 1990.

The Desert Is Theirs by Byrd Baylor, Macmillan Publishing Company, New York, 1975.

Learning to Swim in Swaziland by Nila K. Leigh, Scholastic Inc., New York, 1993.

A Small Tall Tale from the Far Far North by Peter Sis, Knopf, New York, 1993.

This combination of books addresses a variety of habitats. Although each represents very different ecosystems, they all illustrate the special relationship between living things and their physical environment.

Summary

You should now be feeling a bit more confident about your knowledge of form and function, life cycles, and environmental science, not to mention being able to define/characterize the distinction between living and non-living. These are all topics that have a significant role at all levels of the life science curriculum. More importantly, you should be feeling more confident about how to teach these topics. This chapter provides you with numerous opportunities to consider the interaction between subject matter and instruction. Specifically, you were asked to consider how best to maximize student learning of particular life science topics while maintaining a productive and inquiry-oriented classroom atmosphere. Rather than being asked to follow a magic algorithm that is expected to work for all students regardless of background and ability, you were asked to carefully consider the goals of your instruction and how they mesh with your students' needs and the resources available.

The decisions you were asked to make are the same decisions that the experienced teacher makes on a daily basis. And, the types of information you used to inform your decisions are what distinguish the expert teacher from the beginner. Yes, you are on your way to developing a functional understanding of the complexity of teaching. The following chapters will guide you down a similar path with other commonly included science concepts.

Physical Science

You are likely sitting at a desk, or maybe an easy chair, as you read this chapter. Perhaps you have a pen and some paper at hand to take notes and a bag of potato chips to munch on. Have you ever stopped to consider that the wood fibers that make up your paper, the petroleum products that make up the plastic in your pen, and the starch and salt of your potato chips are all made up of matter? These items possess different types of matter, certainly, but it's matter all the same.

Now, reach into your bag to pull out a chip or use your pencil to jot down a note. In doing so, you will have expended a small quantity of energy. The lightbulb in the lamp that illuminates the pages of this book, the sound that emanates from your stereo speakers, and even the sunny day that you enjoyed earlier this afternoon are all made possible by the expenditure of energy in one form or another.

Physical science is often defined as the study of energy and matter. If you have a curious nature, you might have already found yourself asking "why" and "how" questions about the objects in your immediate surroundings. Why does the wood in my paper burn but not the metal tip of my pen? How can I predict whether other objects in my room will burn or not? Why do some things dissolve in water, whereas others do not? How can I predict whether an object will dissolve in water? Why are some things harder or heavier than others?

Physical science has its roots in just this kind of speculation about the nature of matter and how it behaves. The physical sciences began with the nearly limitless curiosity of men and women and their quest for understanding their surroundings. As a teacher of elementary science, you will have many opportunities to lead students to investigate the physical world. The primary goals of this chapter are to provide background information and examples of the teaching cycle being used to teach selected inquiry-based physical science lessons. Four major physical science topics are included in the chapter:

- Properties of Matter
- Forces and Motion
- Energy
- Physical and Chemical Change

Properties of Matter

Understanding Properties of Matter

Pour yourself a glass of water. Look at the water very carefully and make all the observations you can. Remember from our previous discussions, observations only include what you can ascertain from your senses (e.g., see, touch, hear, etc.). If it helps, you can pour the water from one glass into another. Feel free to touch the water or even place objects, such as a toothpick or penny, in the water. Your list of observations probably contains some of the following:

1. clear
2. liquid
3. cold
4. changes shape
5. evaporates (disappears) if left on my hand
6. moderate weight

Your list may very well be much longer than what we have presented. Nevertheless, your observations have shown that water is matter. Matter is anything that has mass and occupies space. You already know that water is made up of many atoms. The atoms, hydrogen and oxygen, are combined into water molecules in the ratio of 2 hydrogen to 1 oxygen giving water the familiar chemical formula H_2O. These molecules give water substance or what we more commonly refer to as mass. By the way, since you were not able to observe these atoms of hydrogen and oxygen in the water, this would not have counted as a valid observation for your list. You knew about the atoms of oxygen and hydrogen because you learned about them when you studied chemistry or physical science. As far as taking up space, it is not too difficult to notice that the water filled the glass to some level. It took up space. If you look around your room, every object you see is matter of one type or another. If you can touch it, it is matter. You also know that one problem with continually increasing the matter in your room is that you have less and less available space.

If you did not try it before, pour the water from one glass to another glass of a different size. What do you see? Does the water occupy the same amount of space? You know that the amount of water has remained the same, but it appears to take up a different amount of space when it is poured into a different glass. By the way, if you are teaching very young children, you may notice that they will think the amount of water has changed because it appears to take up a different amount of space. Young children will think the same amount of water in a tall skinny glass is actually more than an equal amount of water in a wide and shallow glass. Although the amount of space being occupied appears to be different, it is really the same. It is just in a different shape. We will talk more about this later.

Now, notice the weight of the glass when it is filled with water. Pour the water into the sink. What did you notice? The glass is now lighter because the water has been removed. This is because water also has weight. There is no need to discuss what weight is. We all spend far too much time thinking about how much we weigh. Weight is a characteristic of matter that results from the earth's gravitational pull on any mass. The more massive the object, the greater the pull of gravity and the more the object weighs. Your body mass, it you have not already guessed, comes from all the molecules that make up your body structures. Mass is added, and so is weight, when we eat more food than we need.

Interestingly, one way to lose weight may be to live on the moon. The moon is a less massive object than the earth so it exerts less gravitational force on your body mass. Unfortunately, even though you would weigh less on the moon, you will still feel the need to diet because your body mass would not have changed. Weight is a function of gravity, whereas mass is independent of gravity. You will have the same amount of matter in your body on the moon as you did on the earth. Thus, there is no easy alternative to exercise and eating appropriate amounts.

So far we have briefly discussed two characteristics of water and all other matter. These characteristics are mass and weight. The mass and weight of the water in a glass can easily be changed by increasing or decreasing the amount of water. However, you would still have water. The amount of space taken up by the water would also change. This change in the amount of space would be more than just appearance, as in the case of the tall and short glasses. There would be more water and it would occupy more of what is commonly called volume. The volume of any substance is the amount of space it actually occupies. However, even with an increase in volume, you would still have water.

Some characteristics or properties of matter can change in the manner that weight, mass, and volume can be changed. These properties are not unique to the substance or matter and changing one or more of these properties does not change the matter. In all cases, we still had water, just different amounts. This is not true of all properties of matter. Some properties are unique to a particular substance and a change in the property is often indicative of a change in the substance. Let us show you what we mean.

Get a very large bowl or jar, one that is deep enough to hold a can of soda. If you happen to have a small fish aquarium that is not in use, this would be even better. You will also need a can of Coke Classic and a can of Diet Coke. If you prefer Pepsi and Diet Pepsi, this is okay as well. Fill the bowl, jar, or aquarium with water. Fill it most of the way but not completely. You will be placing two cans of soda in the bowl, jar, or aquarium and you do not want it to overflow. Turn the can of Coke Classic or Pepsi sideways and place it in the water. What happened? Did it float or sink? Now do the same with the Diet Coke or Diet Pepsi. Does it float or sink? You should notice that the diet soda floats while the regular soda sinks to the bottom, but why? Look at each can and determine how much soda is inside. It should be 355 milliliters or 12 ounces. Whatever the amount, it should be the same for both the regular and diet versions of the soda. This means that each can has the same volume of soda. Why would one float and one sink? Are the cans the same size? They should appear to be the same and, in this case, you can trust your senses. Perhaps the diet and regular soda have different ingredients. Wouldn't this be what makes one diet and one regular?

After closely inspecting the ingredients in the two cans, you will notice that the regular soda has much more sugar, or carbohydrates, than the diet soda and the diet soda has an additional ingredient, an artificial sweetener called Nutra-Sweet. The sweetener has significantly less mass than the sugar it has replaced. Consequently, the diet soda actually has less mass than the regular soda. This means that the regular soda has more mass in the same volume of soda, 355 mL. The ratio of mass per volume is known as density ($D = m/v$, where D = density, m = mass, v = volume), and it is because the diet soda is less dense than the regular soda that it floats. Let's try another example.

For the next activity you will need four liquids from your kitchen and bathroom, such as rubbing alcohol, cooking oil, water, and soy sauce. The water can come directly from your tap. Carefully pour a small amount of each of these liquids into the tallest glass you can find in the following order: soy sauce, water, cooking oil, alcohol. What did you observe? Did the liquids mix together? If you look carefully, you will notice that the liquids remain separate with the soy sauce on the bottom, followed by the water, cooking oil, and alcohol. The liquids have layered themselves according to their respective densities. Soy sauce is the densest and alcohol is the least dense. Now mix the contents of the glass and watch what happens. Carefully describe what you see. The liquids will separate again into layers after about five minutes, but you may not see all the layers you saw before. If you have ever mixed vinegar and oil for salad dressing, you have probably noticed something very similar. The oil tends to float on top of the vinegar. If you have salad dressing in your refrigerator, look at the contents of the bottle without shaking. You should see that the oil has floated to the top.

Density is a property of matter that is very different from mass, volume, and weight. Each substance has a specific density that does not change. Therefore, if you have a glass of vinegar, the density of the vinegar will remain the same no matter how much additional vinegar you add or remove. In addition, if you put the vinegar in a container with a different shape, the density will still remain the same. You can add water to the vinegar to change the density, but you no longer have pure vinegar. Instead, you have a mixture of vinegar and water, a mixture with a density different from the density of pure water or pure vinegar.

There are numerous other properties of matter, like density, that remain constant. Elasticity is a property that allows a substance to change shape and then return to its original shape. For example, a rubber band can be stretched but will then snap back to its original shape. The alcohol in a thermometer will expand and shrink in response to changes in temperature. This property is known as thermal expansion. If you strike certain metals with a hammer, the metal will change its shape and the change in shape remains. This is how copper bowls used to be shaped. The copper does not return to its original shape as in the case of the stretched rubber band. This property of matter is known as malleability.

Fill two glasses with a cup of water each. Put one teaspoon at a time of table sugar into the water, stirring after each addition. Do this until the sugar no longer dissolves and you can see it collecting at the bottom of the glass. Do the same thing with the salt in the other glass. What did you find? Were you able to dissolve more of one than the other? You should have found that you were able to dissolve more sugar than salt. This is because sugar has a higher solubility in water than salt. The property of matter that describes the ability of a certain amount of one substance to dissolve into a certain amount of another, at a specific temperature, is called solubility.

There are two final properties of matter with which you are very familiar, melting point and boiling point. The melting point of a substance is the

Adding salt to water raises its boiling point, and adding salt to ice lowers its melting point.

temperature at which it changes from a solid to a liquid. The boiling point is the temperature at which a substance boils. (Boiling is a rapid change from liquid to gas.) As with elasticity, thermal expansion, malleability, solubility, and density, the boiling point and melting point are unchanging and specific to a particular substance. Pure water boils at a temperature of 100 degrees Celsius at sea level. No matter how much you heat water once it has reached its boiling point, the temperature remains the same. One cooking trick that you may have tried is adding a little bit of salt to the water when cooking spaghetti. This raises the boiling point of water so that the spaghetti can cook at a higher temperature. However, the boiling point of water has really not been changed. You have added salt to the water and you now have a mixture of two substances, salt and water.

We commonly add salt to water for reasons other than cooking. Putting salt on icy roads and sidewalks helps melt the ice by lowering its melting point. Again, we have not really changed the melting point of the ice (i.e., solid water). Rather, we have mixed salt and water to create a solution with a lower melting point. In summary, the properties of matter we have discussed other than mass, volume, and weight are all constant and common to particular substances or matter. If you are curious, every chemistry laboratory has a *CRC Handbook* that lists the specific values we have spoken about for thousands of substances.

The Teaching Cycle

Ms. Dickinson teachers a sixth-grade class located in a rural community. Most of her students are from farm families and typically remain involved with the family farm throughout their lives. In short, many of Ms. Dickinson's students will not attend college and will not move far from their current community. Regardless, Ms. Dickinson believes that her students should participate in a strong science curriculum that will not place them at any disadvantage in the future, while at the same time being relevant to students' lives. She believes that the best way to motivate students is to show how science is related to their everyday experiences.

Goal Setting

Ms. Dickinson's students enjoy science, especially life science. Her students experience many aspects of life science while performing their daily chores and, for whatever reason, younger students appear to like studying animals and other living things. Ms. Dickinson is concerned that her students receive a balanced science curriculum and she is also aware from the visions of the *National Science Education Standards* and *Benchmarks for*

Science Literacy that it is important for students to see the interconnectedness of the physical and life sciences. She remembers a talk she heard at a recent meeting of her state's science teachers association that density is a physical property of matter that is difficult for students to understand, but it is a physical property that is quite pervasive in the natural world. She is a bit concerned that the topic may be too abstract for her students' age level (i.e., sixth grade) so she looks in the *National Standards for Science Education* for some guidance. She is pleased to find the following standard for physical science at her students' grade level:

> *Content Standard for Physical Science (5–8):*
>
> Properties and Changes of Properties in Matter—A substance has characteristic properties such as density, a boiling point, and solubility, all of which are independent of the amount of the sample.

Although the written standard lends support to her desire to teach the concept of density, she also notes that her students are at the lower end of the grade range advocated for addressing this important concept. Therefore, she is especially concerned that the experiences she designs for her students are particularly concrete and relevant. The last thing she wants to do is intimidate her students and "turn them off" of the topic. She calls one of the middle school science teachers to find out what she teaches on the topic of density and to hopefully get some teaching ideas. The colleague describes several activities that she does with density columns and measuring relative densities with hydrometers. The colleague also lends her several resource books bought at a convention of the National Science Teachers Association (NSTA). Ms. Dickinson wants to begin her students' experiences with density as concretely as possible. Therefore, her objectives for this first lesson are modest:

1. The students will be able to explain that liquids in liquids and solids in liquids will float or sink based on their relative densities.
2. Given liquids of different densities, students will be able to predict the sequence in which the liquids will form layers.

Ms. Dickinson will also be addressing several thematic goals related to scientific inquiry and process skills, such as deriving hypotheses from data, testing hypotheses, and drawing conclusions based on data. In addition to these inquiry skills, she will also be addressing knowledge *about* inquiry (e.g., there's no single scientific method) and the nature of science (e.g., scientific knowledge is subject to change). These are goals and objectives that she will not be able to completely accomplish during this particular lesson, but she addresses them throughout the year because she is aware of how difficult they are for students to achieve.

Materials Development and Selection

Ms. Dickinson is overwhelmed by the amount of activities she finds in the resource books. She is not sure where to begin because all of the activities seem so good. She is beginning to feel that her limited knowledge of science is making it difficult to decide which activities to use and how to sequence her approach to the topic. In particular, Ms. Dickinson decides that it makes the most sense to approach the topic of density by first having her students experience the density interactions of matter within particular phases of matter (e.g., liquids with other liquids, solids with other solids, etc.). She would do this before her students work with density gradients and their interactions across phases of matter. On the other hand, Ms. Dickinson is also concerned about what activities would be most interesting to her students. She wants to get things off to a good start. If she can grab students' interest initially, they will be more likely to be engaged with other activities that may, on the surface, be less interesting. In such situations, Ms. Dickinson usually opts for activities that involve or relate to things most familiar to her students. She read about one particular activity involving eggs floating and sinking in water based on whether there is salt in the water. Ms. Dickinson feels this activity would have obvious relevance for her students, given their agricultural backgrounds and general familiarity with the topic due to the prevalence of eggs as a food item.

The activity is written as a demonstration done at the front desk. It involves the use of three raw eggs decorated with hand-drawn faces. One egg has a frown, one a smile, and one with a neutral expression. Three 1,000-milliliter (mL) beakers are placed on the front desk, one filled with 500 mL of water, another with 500 mL of concentrated salt water, and a third beaker filled with 250 mL of concentrated salt water and 250 mL of water. In the last beaker, the salt water is added first and then the water is carefully layered on top of the salt water. The water will float on top of the salt water because it is less dense than the salt water. The demonstration calls for the placement of the egg with a frown into the beaker of plain water, the egg with a smile to be placed in the salt water, and the egg with a neutral expression into the remaining beaker. Because of the relative densities of the liquids and the eggs, the smiling egg floats, the frowning egg sinks, and the neutral egg sinks only part way in the beaker. Ms. Dickinson thinks her students will really enjoy the activity, but she is concerned about visibility. Even though 1,000-mL beakers are large, she has thirty students in her class and it may be difficult for some students to see from the back of the room. She could have students come up to the front desk for a closer view, but she does not want to face the potential management problems of having thirty students surrounding her front desk.

She is also concerned about student involvement in the lesson. The demonstration calls for extensive questioning of students in order to solicit their explanations of the eggs' behaviors. However, Ms. Dickinson is well aware how difficult it is to get all students involved in a whole group discussion. She constantly has to prevent certain students from dominating discussions and she also has a difficult time getting certain shy students to participate at all. Ms. Dickinson would rather have her students engaged both mentally and physically and so she considers whether to modify the demonstration into a laboratory activity. Primarily for reasons of maximizing student involvement and classroom management, Ms. Dickinson decides to do this lesson as a laboratory activity. She now carefully plans how she will group students, distribute materials, and collect materials.

Eyes-On versus Hands-On Activities

BOX 8.1

The decision to use a demonstration or a laboratory activity often revolves around classroom management. A demonstration is teacher directed and allows the teacher to more directly control the pace of the lesson and monitor safety. On the other hand, students tend to become more highly engaged in the topic of a lesson if they are working with their own materials at their own pace. Consequently, management decisions are often made within the context of desired student outcomes. In this particular lesson, the teacher was probably wiser to do the lesson as a demonstration as opposed to having to deal with the management issues that would no doubt result from students having their own eggs and beakers.

These are critical to the success of the lesson, but Ms. Dickinson has already spent a lot of time providing students with rules and expectations related to distribution and "cleanup" of materials.

Ms. Dickinson decides that it would be best to pair students with the individual seated next to them. This will be quick and it will minimize student movement around the room. Also, the nature of the activity is such that having more than two students in a group would leave several individuals with nothing to do. She decides to have pairs of students instead of individuals because Ms. Dickinson knows how important it is for students to discuss their ideas with a peer and test their speculations in a low-risk environment. This approach will allow students to struggle with the development of explanations for the observations they are making. Hopefully, this struggle will have a positive impact on student learning, as they will be given maximum freedom in constructing their own meanings for the phenomena they have observed. Ms. Dickinson believes this is much more effective than simply telling the students what has occurred.

Ms. Dickinson plans to follow this initial laboratory activity with a second laboratory involving the layering of liquids and a third involving the placement of solid objects in the layered liquids. This will be followed by a demonstration that will reinforce what the students have learned. Ms. Dickinson feels that this sequence of activities provides students with some initial exploratory experiences that build on what students may know and then some more focused experiences that will help them construct an understanding of density.

Pedagogy

Ms. Dickinson begins her introduction to the concept of density by asking students to predict whether eggs float or sink in water. She asks this question to immediately engage students in the lesson and to find out students' backgrounds and beliefs regarding the topic. She is always careful to involve boys and girls equally in every class discussion. Although the topic to be addressed is specifically density, Ms. Dickinson believes she can gather information about relevant student knowledge by asking about floating and sinking. She never mentions the word *density* but rather focuses her attention on ideas and terms with which students are familiar. As students make predictions, Ms. Dickinson sometimes asks for the reasoning that led to their prediction. She also keeps a cumulative class total for the "sink" and "float" predictions. She then tells the students that they will now have a chance to test their predictions. Ms. Dickinson knew that by having the students make predictions in advance, they would have a vested interest in the activity and this would serve as additional motivation.

The introductory portion of the lesson has indicated to Ms. Dickinson that most of the students' predictions were based on whether they thought the egg was lighter or heavier than the water. This is not surprising to Ms. Dickinson, because she has previously read in one of the resource books she borrowed that most students believe objects float or sink based on weight rather than density. Ms. Dickinson now directs students to work as a pair with the person seated at the same desk (students are seated at desks that accommodate two students) and that one person should be selected to gather three eggs and draw faces on them while the other is responsible for gathering three 1,000-mL beakers and filling them with the appropriate liquids. Ms. Dickinson has placed the eggs and marking pens for drawing at the front left of the room and she has placed the beakers and jugs of liquids at the front right. She has decided to place jugs of water and premixed salt water at the front instead of asking students to mix the solutions themselves or get regular water from the sink. She does not feel the time needed for students to mix the salt water is a wise use of time and she also wants to be sure that all students are using the same concentration of salt water. Ms. Dickinson's room also has only one sink and this would create a "logjam" of students if they were expected to get water directly from the tap.

Students are requested to gather their materials by rows. This limits the number of students gathering materials at the stations at any one time and it decreases traffic flow throughout the room. Ms. Dickinson is able to monitor student behavior by positioning herself at the front of the room between the two materials staging areas. As the students appear to be completing the gathering of materials, she reminds them to draw pictures of the setup for this inquiry activity in the science section of their notebooks. Once the students are ready to begin, Ms. Dickinson has each pair select the egg with a frown and gently place it in the beaker filled with regular water. Before having them actually perform this task, Ms. Dickinson illustrates what she means by careful placement of the egg into the beaker and then asks a few students to repeat the critical points she made in the instructions. Ms. Dickinson also brings students' attention back to the predictions that were previously placed on the board. The students are then told to place the egg in the beaker.

Ms. Dickinson questions students throughout the room about what they observed. Eventually, a class total is recorded that indicates all student pairs observed the egg sink to the bottom of the beaker. This does not surprise most students because most had predicted the egg would sink. Ms. Dickinson wants the students to reconsider their predictions now that they have had a chance to observe what actually happens. She once again has students throughout the room offer their explanations. She is careful to ask students who predicted correctly, as well as those who predicted incorrectly, to explain why the egg sank. This is important because Ms. Dickinson does not want her students to get the incorrect message that explanations are only required when incorrect answers are given. She also draws attention to the fact that different students may have had different explanations for the same observation. She stresses that this does not mean that any of the students did anything wrong but that such differences are typical in science and are one of the reasons why scientific knowledge is subject to change. Ms. Dickinson now focuses students' attention on the egg with the smile and the beaker with salt water. She asks students for a prediction of what will happen. Although a majority still thinks the egg will sink, more students are now predicting the egg will float. This is a curious response given the data the students collected with the first egg. However, Ms. Dickinson knows that students are probably changing their predictions because they are anticipating a different result. She is well aware of such "class wise" students and she is more careful than ever to ask students to explain the reasons for their predictions. After all, the students have experienced nothing that would have caused them to change their minds about the relative weights of the egg and water. Ms. Dickinson's suspicions are correct. Most students still feel that the egg is heavier than the water. However, several of the students predicting the egg will float provide the reason that the egg has a smile and that because the frowning egg sank the smiling egg should float.

Ms. Dickinson is careful not to immediately reject such reasoning. It is quite possible that the students somehow think the smile drawn on the egg influences the egg's ability to float. She asks the students if they think the smile affects the egg's subsequent behavior. The students do not hold this view; they were just trying to figure out Ms. Dickinson's lesson plan. Nevertheless, she asks the students to think about how they would test the idea that drawing a smile or frown on an egg would influence its subsequent behavior. After acknowledging students' suggestions for the testing of these ideas, Ms. Dickinson draws explicit attention to the different approaches and uses it as an opportunity to stress that there is no single set of steps that scientists all follow when performing scientific investigations.

The students are now instructed to place the egg into the salt water. Again, Ms. Dickinson surveys the students on what they observed. This time, all groups observed that the egg floated. The students are asked to explain the results. As might be expected, many students now feel that what was drawn on the egg influenced its behavior. Although it was not part of her original plan, Ms. Dickinson pursues the idea of how to test the students' new conclusion. She knows how important it is for students to play with these ideas and to test their speculations. It is much more important for the students to convince themselves than simply to be told they are incorrect. After a short discussion, the class decides that they could just switch the eggs in the beakers to see if the one with the smile stills floats and the one with the frown still sinks. The students are allowed to proceed and observe what happens. Contrary to student predictions, the egg with the frown is now floating and the egg with the smile has now sunk. Ms. Dickinson asks the students what this means. In general, the students now realize that what was drawn on the egg is not responsible for whether it floats or sinks. However, they appear to be unable to offer any further explanations.

Ms. Dickinson is not discouraged by the students' inability to explain the discrepancy between the sinking and floating eggs. The students do not appear to be frustrated but rather are intrigued and actively engaged. In a way, Ms. Dickinson has some evidence that the students are struggling to make sense of their observations. Again, this struggling is the good kind. It is the kind that keeps students engaged in learning activities. The last thing Ms. Dickinson wants to do now is tell the students the answer. How consistent with scientific inquiry would that approach be?

The students are now asked to predict what will happen when the egg with a neutral expression is placed in the final beaker. The class is evenly split between floating and sinking. None of the students predict that the egg will float in the middle of the beaker. As before, the students' reasons for the predictions have to do with the relative weight of the water and egg. The students are told to place the egg in the beaker and all are totally baffled by the observation that the egg sinks halfway in the beaker and floats in the middle. At this point the students are so excited that the noise level begins to rise as they converse with each other. Ms. Dickinson is glad to see the excitement, but she also sees the need to focus students' attention in a productive way. She calls the class to order and tells the students to spend a few minutes with their partner investigating how the various eggs behave in each of the beakers. Ms. Dickinson knows that this will focus students' attention, as well as reinforce the idea that what is drawn on each egg is irrelevant to the behavior. This is important because she wants the students to eventually focus on the nature of the liquid in each beaker, not the egg.

As the students switch eggs among the beakers, Ms. Dickinson circulates around the room asking students questions about what they are finding. She is careful to ask specific questions that require answers other than "yes" or "no." This way she can gather information on student understanding and learning during the activity. As she circulates, Ms Dickinson realizes that none of the students are keeping systematic records of the results. She realizes that she should have said something before letting the students freely investigate, but she now has no choice but to interrupt. She calls for the students' attention and waits for the class to quiet down before speaking. She does not want to have to repeat the important instructions she is about to give. Ms. Dickinson reminds the students to make a chart of their observations as they have learned to do in previous activities.

Ms. Dickinson gives the students several more minutes to investigate and then moves to the front of the room and asks the students what they found. She quickly draws a data table on the board that contains beaker contents and egg behavior. It does not take long for the students to see that the all three eggs floated in the salt water, all sunk in the regular water, and all three eggs floated halfway down in the beaker with salt water and regular water. The students readily admit that the expression on the egg had nothing to do with the eggs floating or sinking. The students quickly surmise that it must have something to do with the liquid in the beaker. Ms. Dickinson is very pleased with her students' conclusions, not because they provided the correct answer, but because they carefully used the data they collected to arrive at a valid conclusion. Ms. Dickinson uses this as an opportunity to stress the empirical basis of scientific knowledge and how the students are performing skills and procedures analogous to what scientists do in their investigations. For Ms. Dickinson, how students develop their knowledge is as important as the knowledge itself. The students are told to write their conclusion in their science notebooks as Ms. Dickinson wheels out a cart with more materials.

The cart contains small beakers of colored liquids, blue, orange, green, and red. The liquids are labeled 0%, 10%, 20%, and 30%, respectively. The percentages denote concentrations of salt water but this information is not given to the students. The students have previously discussed concentrations of liquids so the percentages should be somewhat familiar. The students are asked to work with the same partner as before and their task is to place the four liquids in the graduated cylinder in such a way that the colors stay separate with no mixing. Ms. Dickinson provides no further information except for the usual precautions about safety and the handling of materials. The students are allowed to freely experiment for 15 minutes. Ms. Dickinson is hoping the students will eventually be able to make the connection between the layering of the colored liquids and the percentage values. As originally written, this activity recommended that the teacher not provide the percentage values. However, Ms. Dickinson felt that approach would require her students to make inferences they were not capable of making.

The atmosphere in the classroom is much like a competition as students attempt to solve this problem-oriented task more quickly than their neighbors. At the end of 15 minutes, Ms. Dickinson calls the students to order and asks which groups accomplished the stated task. Some students are not close to being finished, whereas others have just two of the liquids mixed. Several groups, however, have created columns of clearly separated liquids in the following order from bottom to top: red, green, orange, and blue. The students are amazed to see the separated colors and Ms. Dickinson asks the students to explain what they have observed. The students continue, as before, to provide answers concerning relative weights. But Ms. Dickinson challenges them by asking if the situation is different than the egg and water because in this case all they had was water. Ms. Dickinson wants the students to really think about what the important variables are in this situation. She pauses for a long time so students have a chance to think and compose their answers. She knows how important it is to provide students enough time to process her question and then compose an answer. The students seem puzzled and Ms. Dickinson is now more convinced than ever that her decision to provide students with percentages in advance was a good idea.

She asks the students to think back to their final conclusion in the egg activity. The students quickly recall the conclusion that the liquid in the beaker was important. She asks if the liquids in this activity are different in any way other than color. Numerous students call out that the percentages are different. She quickly follows by asking if there is a relationship between the percentages and the layering of the liquids. The students readily note that the highest percentage was at the bottom and the lowest percentage was at the top. Ms. Dickinson now tells the students that the percentages pertain to salt concentration. She further explains that the salt concentration in the salt water was 35 percent in the egg activity. She asks students what the salt concentration was in the regular water. Several students answer that they do not know, but several others volunteer 0 percent.

Ms. Dickinson now thinks that the students have enough information to offer some explanations. She asks the students to think about the egg activity and the layering of liquids in terms of salt concentrations. She writes the following questions on the board:

1. How did the liquids in the beaker with salt water and regular water form layers? Which was on top?
2. How did the salt concentration of the water relate to the eggs floating or sinking?
3. How is the layering of the liquids similar to the floating of the eggs?

The students are asked to discuss these questions with their lab partners and write the questions and their answers to them in their science notebooks. After approximately 15 minutes, Ms. Dickinson asks the students to share their responses. Ms. Dickinson calls on two groups that volunteer and two that do not. Following each answer, Ms. Dickinson asks the other students to comment and ask questions. She takes this approach because she wants her students to question each other's ideas and arrive at a class-negotiated understanding of the phenomena investigated. Ms. Dickinson also enters the discussion by asking pertinent questions of the students. After a discussion of about 15 minutes, Ms. Dickinson is convinced that her students understand that the layering of the liquids and the behavior of the eggs were influenced by certain physical properties related to concentration of matter. The students had already studied the concept of concentration so it was not difficult for them to realize the relationship of concentration to amounts of matter in a given substance. At this point, Ms. Dickinson introduces the word *density* and tells the students that the relative densities of the materials cause the phenomena they have been observing. She does not mind providing the term to the students because she is convinced the students understand the concept. The term *density* is something the students would never have come up with themselves. Ms. Dickinson understands the difference between knowing the name of something and knowing something. She further defines density as the relative amount of matter in a given volume of a substance as she writes the definition on the board. She further states that 20 percent salt-water solution is denser than 10 percent salt-water solution because it contains more salt relative to the amount of water. Ms. Dickinson then asks students, "Does denser material float on top or below a less dense material?" She draws students' attention to the layered liquids activity and repeats the question. The students answer correctly.

Ms. Dickinson asks the students what they can say about the density of the eggs relative to the densities of the liquids in the beakers in the first activity. The students are quickly able to describe what occurred in the beaker with regular water and the beaker

Technology Does Not Have to Be So Technical!

When you think of technology, complicated devices like computers, graphing calculators, digital microscopes, or spectrophotometers might come to mind. In reality, any tool, from pencils and paper to the most complex networked computer system, is an example of technology. In the science classroom, technology can be introduced in the earliest grades as a way of extending the senses of the students. Rulers, thermometers, balances, and volume measuring devices are all examples of appropriate technology that can be included in the elementary science classroom.

BOX 8.2

Ms. Dickinson could include technology in her density activity by having students make volume and mass measurements of the water and salt solutions. Kitchen measuring cups or graduated cylinders are appropriate tools for volume measuring. A balance may be used to make mass measurements, or a scale may be used to measure weight. As an extension to the density activity, Ms. Dickinson could ask her students to make predictions about the mass of equal volumes of the different salt solutions. Does a cup (8 ounces) of water have the same mass (or weight) as an equal volume of 10 percent salt solution? Does a cup of water have the same mass (or weight) as an equal volume of 30 percent salt solution? How can students find out?

with salt water. They are slower to grasp what occurred in the beaker with salt water and regular water, but with several hints and a diagram on the board, the students appear to understand. Ms. Dickinson finishes the lesson by describing to the students the fact that scientists used to believe that objects floated or sank in water for reasons other than density. This is just another opportunity for her to explicitly stress that all scientific knowledge is subject to change.

Assessment

At this point in the lesson, Ms. Dickinson is reasonably confident that her students have a good introductory grasp of the concept of density. However, she is too experienced a teacher to believe that a concept this abstract can be learned so quickly. She is also cognizant of the fact that the students have been working hard for a long period of time and she feels the need to bring the science lesson to a close. However, she wants the students to be thinking about what they learned when they go home at the end of the day. The assignment that she describes is a more formal method that Ms. Dickinson will use to assess the understanding of each student as well as provide data for the next day's instruction. She informs the students that tomorrow they will be asked to recreate the layered liquids in the same graduated cylinder. She then adds that they will be given five objects with different densities. Their task will be to determine the densest to the least dense of the objects. The students are asked to think about this at home and write what approach they will use in their science notebooks. Before completing the lesson, Ms. Dickinson asks several students to explain various parts of the homework assignment and what will occur in tomorrow's lesson. She wants to be sure that the students have understood her instructions so that confusion can be avoided the next day.

Ms. Dickinson has decided to assess students in this manner because she feels that it is an authentic application of the activities students experienced in today's lesson. If they can successfully determine the relative densities of the mystery objects and provide a sound explanation in terms of the concept of density, she will feel comfortable that her lesson was a success.

Reflection

Ms. Dickinson feels that her lesson went fairly well. The students seemed to be productively engaged in each of the activities and they seem to have a basic understanding of what they observed. She is particularly happy with her decision to do the egg activity as a laboratory instead of as a demonstration. This activity was a good way to get students physically and mentally involved immediately. The two activities did take longer than anticipated, but the students appeared to remain engaged throughout the lesson.

In retrospect, Ms. Dickinson feels she missed some good opportunities to stress scientific inquiry and the nature of science. These are goals and objectives that Ms. Dickinson strives to include throughout the year and she could have done more during the present lesson. The students did have plenty of opportunities to develop hypotheses, collect data, and analyze data but there was virtually no discussion of how these activities are similar to science in general. She also missed an opportunity to discuss cause and effect when the students were considering the possible influence of the eggs' expressions on the eggs' behavior. In short, Ms. Dickinson knows that simply doing science does not necessarily mean that students will come to understand scientific inquiry and the nature of science.

As Ms. Dickinson replays the lesson in her head, she is very concerned about one critical point. The students held the expected view that weight was the primary reason why the eggs floated or sank and the same was true for the layering of the liquids. Although Ms. Dickinson has moved the students toward a rudimentary understanding of density, none of the activities or discussions actually eliminated the idea that weight, as opposed to density, is the critical factor. Without an activity that involves the same amount of a substance occupying different volumes students cannot come to such a conclusion. Thus far, they have only dealt with materials with different amounts of matter. In the same gravitational field substances with more matter or equal volumes of substances with greater density do weigh more. Ms. Dickinson needs to find an activity that allows students to see density changing in response to a change in volume and not a change in the amount of matter. Presently, she has allowed students to develop and accept a conclusion that they have no strong evidence to support. Does this accurately portray science as it was presented in Chapter 1?

Forces and Motion

Understanding Forces and Motion

For the following discussion all you will need is your book and a pen or pencil. Put the book on your desk if you are holding it in your hands. Observe carefully what happens. What did you see? You should have observed, as you would have predicted, that nothing happens. The book just sits there. Why did you anticipate that nothing would happen? How could you make the book move? Most likely you are well aware that something needs to be done to the book, like pushing it, if you expect it to move. This is an idea we all know quite intuitively from everyday experiences. Unless something is pushed or pulled, it does not move. Even living things move because, in a way, they are pushing or pulling themselves (e.g., muscles contracting and relaxing). Do the same with your pencil. Again, nothing happens. Push the pencil softly with your finger. What happens now? It rolls and then stops. What you have observed is the pencil's response to your push and its motion eventually stopping. Now, push your book with the same effort you used on the pencil. Most likely, nothing happened, or you observed that the book only moved slightly. If it did move, it definitely did not move as much as the pencil. The book is clearly more massive than the pencil and this is why it did not move as far when pushed. Why is this the case? We will discuss this in a little more detail later.

We have not used formal scientific language for what you have just observed, but now is the time. The push you gave the pencil and book is an example of a force. In science, a force is defined as a push or a pull and nothing moves unless a push or pull (i.e., force) is applied. The movement you noticed can also be referred to as motion. We experience these ideas so commonly in our everyday lives that we hardly ever notice. For example, when you walk from your kitchen into the living room, your body is in motion because you are actually pushing against the floor. At the anatomical level, your calf muscle is contracting, pulling your heel upwards, resulting in the ball of your foot pushing against the floor. There are actually numerous other muscles involved, but ultimately what you have is a lot of pushing and pulling. Some motion may be less obvious in terms of the force involved. If you pick your pencil up from the desk and drop it to the floor, it is actually moving downward in response to the pull of gravity. There is something else you may have noticed from these few examples and that is that motion continues unless another force is applied. The pencil stopped rolling and the book stopped moving because of friction, which is another force with which you are probably familiar. The pencil you dropped stopped falling because it confronted the force of the floor. These ideas probably sound very simple, but the ideas that objects do not move unless a force is applied and that they continue to move unless another force is applied is actually Newton's First Law of Motion, which can more simply be called inertia. What we have just done has some instructional implications for you to think about. If we began this discussion stating that we were going to explain Newton's First Law, you would have likely experienced some trepidation.

You now need some additional materials for this next activity, which we call "Crash Test Barbie." If you don't have a Barbie doll, a GI Joe or any small stuffed animal will do just fine. You also need something with wheels that Barbie can ride on, such as a plastic car, skateboard, or single roller skate. Place Barbie (or another object of your choice) on the "vehicle" with wheels and watch it go. You probably have already guessed that nothing happens unless you apply a force (i.e., a push or pull). What happens if you push the vehicle with a different amount of force? Try it and observe as carefully as you can. You probably notice that the vehicle goes further and moves faster when you push harder. With a softer push, the vehicle moves more slowly and does not travel as far across the room. Another way to describe these observations is to say that the result of a harder push is greater speed. Technically, speed is the rate of motion or motion per unit of time. In everyday language, this is really how far something travels in a certain amount of time. You are probably familiar with this from the speedometer in your car. When it reads 60 miles per hour, it is telling you how far you will travel in one hour. It is indicating your *current* speed. We emphasized *current* in the last statement because you are probably aware that your speed is not constant throughout the last car trip you took, and neither is the speed of Barbie's vehicle constant as it moves across your floor. At first, Barbie's car has a speed of zero—it was not moving at all. Then you push her vehicle and she begins to travel very quickly, eventually slowing down as she moves across the floor and comes to a stop. You could calculate the speed of her vehicle at each moment of her trip or you could focus on the changes in speed from one part of the trip to another. These changes in speed are referred to as acceleration. At the beginning of Barbie's trip her speed is zero and her acceleration is zero. After you apply a force, the speed increases and so does the acceleration. Eventually, the speed of Barbie's vehicle becomes constant (even though this is only for a short period of time). As long as Barbie's speed remains constant, her acceleration returns to zero. Once friction begins to slow Barbie's vehicle, the speed decreases and this change in speed actually results in what can be called a negative acceleration, or deceleration.

Let's now return to the difference between the two forces you apply to Barbie's vehicle. One is a stronger force and one is a weaker force. What did you notice in terms of acceleration? That is correct; the harder push produces a greater acceleration than the weaker push. This relationship between force and acceleration for a given mass (Barbie plus the vehicle) is Newton's Second Law. Scientists often express this law with the expression: force = mass × acceleration.

What do you suppose would happen if the mass is changed instead of the force? Let's try it and see. You can increase the mass of Barbie's vehicle by adding a heavy weight of any type (e.g., a book or a jar of jelly). What would you predict if you were careful to apply the same force as before? You should have predicted and observed that the acceleration was less. In this case, as you increase the mass the acceleration decreases. This is another way of expressing Newton's Second Law. It is also why the pencil moves further than your book when you push each with the same amount of force. We are about to move on from using Barbie and her vehicle. However, if you are not ready to put her away yet, you can use the same materials to illustrate Newton's First Law of Motion (i.e., inertia). If you place Barbie on the hood of the car, parade style, or on a skateboard without being fastened down and strongly strike the back of the vehicle, Barbie will fall off of the car as the car continues to move across your room. This is because the vehicle receives a strong force but Barbie does not, and so she does not move. Actually, the vehicle moves out from under Barbie. Alternatively, if Barbie remains in the vehicle until it smashes into your wall, she will be thrown forward after the car stops. In actuality, the vehicle confronts the force of the wall, but Barbie does not and continues to move. Believe it or not, this is the idea behind seat belts.

Incidentally, you should recall that we mentioned scientific laws and theories as two types of scientific knowledge in Chapter 1. Scientific laws identify relationships among observable phenomena. In the case of Newton's laws, this is exactly what he did. He specified the relationships among observable phenomena such as force, motion, and acceleration. It is for this reason that Newton's descriptions are called scientific laws. They are not called laws because they have been proven in any absolute sense. Recall that all scientific knowledge, including laws, is tentative. At this point you may be curious about the definition of scientific theory. Theories are inferred explanations for what we observe. Theories would be used to explain why we observe Newton's laws.

We now need you to put on a pair of roller skates or use the skateboard that was used for Barbie's vehicle. Go outside and find your car. Open the door. While standing on the skateboard or with your roller skates on, quickly slam the door shut. What happens? If you are unable to do this activity, at least attempt to predict what would happen. You should have started to roll backward or in the direction opposite to the direction the door slammed. This illustrates Newton's Third Law, which states that forces always come in pairs that are equal and opposite. In other words, every force has an equal and opposite force. If you have ever shot a gun, you are probably quite familiar with the recoil or "kick." The bullet is fired in one direction under a force and the gun recoils in the opposite direction. In the case of a rocket ship, gases are expelled from the engine with a downward force while the rocket is pushed upward with an equal and opposite force. Can you think of any other examples? Examples of all three of Newton's laws are common in your students' daily lives. It might be a good idea to start making a list now in preparation for lessons you will eventually be teaching on the topic of forces and motion.

The space shuttle launching is an example of Newton's Third Law of Motion.

The Teaching Cycle

The twenty-two first graders in Mr. Caduto's class are excited and curious learners. They touch and play with everything and ask endless questions. He encourages this behavior. He wants his students to freely explore, manipulate, and observe their world. Therefore, he makes sure their classroom environment is rich with resources. Goldfish, hamsters, plants, books, toys, puzzles, crayons, and computers are basic supplies in the room. These materials are organized in five different learning centers located around the room. Each center has a name: Computer Central, Book Bank, Toy Chest, Design Center, and the Science Corner. These centers are stocked with different materials to reflect the concepts that are being taught at different times in the school year.

Mr. Caduto has used the first quarter of the school year to establish classroom protocols and procedures. He knows that it usually takes this long for his young students to adjust to first grade and to being in school for a whole day. Activities are varied throughout the day. Besides students working together as a whole class or in groups, the students always have a daily free choice period.

They can go to any of the classroom centers during this time, but they have to make sure they visit each of the five centers during the week. This classroom rule ensures variety and exposure to the benefits of each center, as well as developing responsibility. One of Mr. Caduto's favorite units at this point in the school year is his science unit on forces and motion. He plans to use this unit not only to teach his students about forces and motion but also about how to ask questions and design experiments to help answer their questions. He knows that there is a difference between free exploration and inquiry and plans to use this topic to introduce this distinction to his students.

Goal Setting

The first time Mr. Caduto checked his science curriculum, he was very surprised to find that a unit on forces and motion was included for first graders. He didn't remember studying these concepts before ninth grade, and all he could recall were lots of mathematical formulas and complicated definitions. How could he possibly teach these sophisticated concepts to 6-year-old children? Did someone make a mistake? To make sure, he borrowed copies of the science reforms and checked the sections on Physical Science for primary-level students. Sure enough, the *National Science Education Standards* for K–4 included:

- An object's motion can be described by tracing and measuring its position over time.
- The position and motion of objects can be changed by pushing and pulling. The size of the change is related to the strength of the push and pull. (p. 127)

The *Benchmarks for Science Literacy* for grades K–2 stated:

- Things move in many different ways, such as straight, zigzag, round and round, back and forth, and fast and slow.
- The way to change how something moves is to give it a push or a pull.

He was relieved to see how simply these concepts were presented. These were concepts he knew he could teach and were developmentally appropriate for his students. He felt it was most appropriate for his first-graders to understand that objects could move in many different ways and that things only move by pushes and pulls called forces. Through the years he developed lessons that allow his students to freely explore forces and how they make things move. He begins the unit by introducing the concept of motion. His students are already familiar with the notion of movement. They observe many examples of moving things, themselves included, all the time. The objectives he sets for this first lesson include:

>Students will be able to identify several examples of things that move.

>Students will be able to demonstrate several ways to move an object.

These objectives will allow him to assess their background knowledge and establish a foundation for future lessons that introduce the concept of forces.

Materials Development and Selection

The afternoon before he begins the new unit on force and motion, Mr. Caduto restocks the individual learning centers with topic-related items. Both fiction and nonfiction trade books that deal with motion and things that move are placed in the book center. He includes picture books, books with text suitable for beginning readers, and books that he will read to students during the unit. Wind-up toys, balls, a small train set, play cars, trucks and planes, a wagon, and a child-size shopping cart are added to the toy center. In the design center, Mr. Caduto puts a stack of old magazines and newspapers. He plans to have the students create a "motion mural" during the course of the unit and they will be able to cut pictures out of these materials as well as bring in their own pictures from home. He is excited about a new software program about animal locomotion that his students will explore in the computer center. This will be a good connection with an item he added to the pet corner in the science center. He cannot wait for his students' reactions to the treadmill he put in the hamster's cage! In this center, he also added sets of magnets and slinkies.

Pedagogy

As Mr. Caduto suspected, the students were delighted to discover the new additions to their classroom. He encouraged them to move around the room and explore. He wanted them to become somewhat familiar with the new materials, since he was planning on referring to some of the items later in the lesson. He also knew that it would be difficult to focus their attention if they did not have time to examine the changes to the room. Before he started the lesson, he let them touch, observe, manipulate, and play with everything for a little while. He also reminded them about the class rules for appropriate behavior during these free exploration periods—no running or pushing and they were to use their "quiet" voices. He did not want their excitement to interfere with learning possibilities.

Once students have had a chance to play with the toys for several minutes, Mr. Caduto instructs them to gather around him at the front of the room and take a seat on the floor. Mr. Caduto sits down on a low stool and asks them to tell him about their discoveries. They eagerly tell him about the toys and books and materials they found. They are especially excited about the addition to the hamster cage and describe in detail how

The Learning Cycle

BOX 8.3

The learning cycle is a student-centered model of instruction developed by researchers in the 1960s. It is designed to guide students from concrete, hands-on learning experiences to the more abstract formulation of concepts and the ability to apply these concepts to new situations. Although many variations to the model have been developed in the past three decades, all have a common core structure consisting of the following three elements:

Explore: In the first phase of the learning cycle, students are given opportunities to actively manipulate objects and experience phenomena *before* they are introduced to new concepts and vocabulary. This provides them with a common base of experiences on which they can build concepts and principles.

Explain: During this phase of the instructional model, the teacher focuses students' attention on a particular aspect of their exploration experiences in order to help them recognize relationships between objects and events and to develop accurate explanations. It is at this time that the teacher introduces formal labels and definitions.

Apply: The application phase provides opportunities for students to apply their newly developed ideas to other situations. The goal is for students to reinforce their learning through the generalization of concepts and practice of skills.

Now, see if you can apply your understanding of the learning cycle by identifying the "Explore," "Explain," and "Apply" phases in Mr. Caduto's motion lesson.

their classroom pet is running around in it. This sharing time is important because not all the children get to see and/or do everything during the free exploration time period. Some children run from one center to another, quickly checking everything out but spending very little time in any one place. Other children are fascinated with one item and spend all of their time exploring it. Most of the children divide their time between two or three centers. So this preliminary discussion serves as a way to introduce all of the new resources to everyone. It is also a method for him to get a sense of the novelty of these experiences for his students.

After the children talk about what they found, Mr. Caduto asks them if they think these things have anything in common with each other. Some of the students mention that a lot of the items have wheels. Someone else says that many of the things were yellow. The students come up with many connections and Mr. Caduto acknowledges them all. Then one of the students says she could move the wagon and truck around the room. Another student adds that the hamster is moving around in the wheel really fast. Then someone says that he can move fast, too! Mr Caduto told them they are all good observers and thinkers and that they have all come up with great connection ideas. He reminds them, as he always does, that they are acting like scientists when they make their observations and connections. He tells them that all the new additions have something to do with the next area of science they would explore—motion.

Next, he begins to read them a story. The students love to be read to and they know their teacher expects them to be very quiet now. Mr. Caduto plans on using the book to begin a more focused discussion on motion. This activity also helps to continue to settle the students down. The book is *Gilberto and the Wind* by Marie Hall Ets. This is a story about a little boy, Gilberto, and his playmate, the wind. To Gilberto's delight, his whirling friend moves bubbles, leaves, and kites around. After the story, Mr. Caduto asks his students if they would like to have the wind for a friend. They all agreed that this would be wonderful. He asks them what objects they would like the wind to move around for them. They come up with many suggestions.

Then, from behind his desk, Mr. Caduto takes out a giant beach ball. He tells the students to pretend for a moment that they are the wind. He asks them how they would move the ball. "How many ways could you move it?" he asks. They immediately begin to call out suggestions, but Mr. Caduto stops them quickly. He tells them that they all need to quietly think about this question and keep all of their ideas in their heads and that they cannot even whisper to their friend. He wants all of them to consider ways to move the ball and he wants to give them all the time they need.

When some of the students seem ready before others, he asks them to try and think of more ways to move the ball. After giving them a long time to think about the question, he finally asks them what their ideas are. He calls on different children to come up and demonstrate different ways to move the ball. After each child moves the ball, he asks them to describe what they did. "I picked it up," "I rolled it around," "I bounced it," "I pulled it toward me," "I threw it to my friend," "I pushed it into the corner," are some of the responses that accompany their demonstrations. "Wow," said Mr. Caduto, "you already know a lot about motion!" Then he tells them that during the next science unit they will be studying even more about motion. The students all agree that this will be great!

Literature Integration

Using children's literature is an excellent way to introduce and reinforce science concepts for students of all ages, in addition to its ability to help students develop reading and writing skills. However, it is critically important, when integrating literature into a science lesson, that the focus remains on science concepts in a productive manner. Simply reading a story about a tree is not effective science instruction. Note how carefully Mr. Caduto uses literature to connect a familiar experience to the lesson's focus on forces and motion. It is also important to note that the book chosen focuses on a Hispanic child and helps to establish an instructional approach that celebrates diversity.

BOX 8.4

Curriculum
Connections

Assessment

Mr. Caduto designs an assessment for this lesson that sustains the children's enthusiasm and also provides him with insight into their understanding of the concept of motion. Since most of the students cannot yet read or write, he relies on verbal feedback and direct observations of concept application. He divides them into groups of three students and gives each group a toy car. He tells them that, just as they did with the ball, he wants them to move the car in as many ways as they can. Mr. Caduto develops the following observation checklist for this assessment:

Students move and describe the movement of the toy as:

1. _____ back and forth
2. _____ side to side
3. _____ zigzag
4. _____ round and round
5. _____ up and down
6. _____ fast and slow

As the children play with their cars, Mr. Caduto observes their actions and interactions. He moves from group to group and asks them to show him and tell him about the ways they could move the car. The students have all played with cars before and are familiar with how real cars move, so they all move them back and forth first. Mr. Caduto asks them to show and tell him about other ways to move the car. He also reminds them to make sure everyone in the group has a turn to move the car around. He visits each group several times and makes sure he speaks with every child in the class.

Reflection

Soon after the students finish with the science lesson, they leave for a music class with another teacher. Mr. Caduto uses this time to record his observations of his students while they are still fresh in his mind. All of the students moved the cars back and forth. Some students moved them around in circles and zigzags but all of the students kept the wheels of the car on the floor. Mr. Caduto assumes this is a reflection of the students' experiences with real cars. He decides that the next day he will have them repeat this activity using two new objects, slinkies and balls.

He hopes the students will move these in more creative ways. In future lessons on forces, he plans to refer back to these activities and have the students consider the pushes and pulls they had to apply to the objects to get the cars and slinkies and balls to move. All things considered, Mr. Caduto feels this lesson is a good introduction to the motion unit. The students have a notion about the new topic, he is able to assess some of their prior knowledge about motion, and it includes experiences to refer to for future lessons during the unit. From these initial activities, inquiry investigations will be developed that challenge the students to test variables involved in making objects move.

Energy

Understanding Energy

What is energy? Write down a definition for it right now. Did you find it diffi-cult to come up with a comprehensive definition? Most people do! Even though the term is familiar to most of us and we see evidence of it in our daily lives, it is a general concept, like love or justice, which is hard to describe. If you chose to look up the definition of energy, you may have written down this classic de-finition that is found in many textbooks, "Energy is the ability to do work." What does that statement really mean?

Evidence of Energy. We suggest that it is more useful to have an understanding about energy than to recite a meaningless definition. To help understand the concept, let's first think about how it affects us, how we use it, and what evi-dence we have of it. Make a list of how you used energy or experienced it in any form during the last two days. It is probably a pretty long list. Your list may include using some type of electrical appliance, such as a hair dryer or computer, light from a lamp, heat from a stove, chemical reactions from cooking, a flag blowing in the wind, the sound of music from a CD player or television, or your own body moving as you exercise or walk around. Each list is different, of course, but all include a number of experiences with energy in many forms. What do they all have in common? As you compare and analyze them, you should begin to see that they each produce a change of some sort in the system in which they are operating. These changes can be measured. From your list you should also be able to identify different forms of energy: heat, chemical, electri-cal, mechanical, sound, and light. Probably the only form of energy that is not on your list is nuclear energy.

Kinetic and Potential Energy. In general, all of these forms of energy can be de-scribed as potential or kinetic. Potential energy means energy that is capable of coming into action but is presently stored away. A wound spring in a wind-up toy, a raised hammer or golf club, and water at the top of a falls all have poten-tial energy. Kinetic energy is energy in motion. Imagine yourself on a play-ground swing. A friend raises your seat up as far as she can. She has given you and the swing potential energy, the higher you are lifted, the more potential en-ergy you have. Then she lets go and you are in motion. The potential energy you started with is changing into kinetic energy. As you drop you have less and less potential energy, but you are going faster and faster so your kinetic energy is increasing. On the second part of the ride, you start rising up again and your speed is decreasing. Your potential energy is increasing now but your kinetic en-ergy is decreasing. Throughout the entire trip your total energy is constant. That is, the sum of potential and kinetic energies is the same at any point in the ride. Kinetic energy is sometimes referred to as mechanical energy, or energy of motion. Whenever you see the wind blowing, water flowing, a ball bouncing, or a plane flying, you have evidence of energy of motion.

Energy Transformations. If you check your list once again, you probably noticed that many of your experiences involved several different forms of energy. For instance, a hair dryer uses electrical energy and transforms it into heat, sound, and motion. The chemicals in a battery provide electrical energy to run a portable radio, producing sound. A moving car uses chemical energy and converts it into heat, sound, and motion. A power plant uses the chemical energy in fossil fuels to produce electricity.

Energy Conservation. Over and over, we see evidence of one energy form transforming into another. Just as with potential and kinetic energy, the total amount of energy in a system remains the same. Whenever we consider conservation of energy, we refer to a closed system. Picture an imaginary bubble or boundary around the region in which the energy exchanges occur. This bubble prevents none of the energy in it to escape and allows no new amounts of energy to enter. When we say something is conserved, we mean that it cannot be destroyed or created but only exchanged within the boundary. We could consider the whole universe to be the region in our closed system and consider the total amount of energy in it to be conserved. Let's look at a smaller closed system to get a better understanding of this concept. Remember the playground swing set?

Imagine a bubble around it, making it a closed system. The original amount of energy was the amount that was imparted to it by your friend when she lifted the swing up into the air. When she let go, most of the energy was converted to motion, but as you continue to swing back and forth your speed decreases and you eventually come to a stop. Is the energy destroyed? No, it is just converted to other forms. Some is converted to heat where the chains of the swing came in contact with the top support bar of the swing set. There is also heat due to friction between you and the air you move through, and some of the original energy is converted to sound. If we could measure the amounts of each of these energy forms, they would add up to the total amount of energy with which we started.

Entropy. You may be wondering then, if the total amount of energy is constant, why is there so much concern about conserving our energy resources? When we speak of energy, we are usually referring to useful or usable energy. This is energy that is readably available to do a particular job or task for us. The portion of the total energy in the swing set system that was converted to heat and sound goes off in a disordered manner. This energy becomes less available to us and, therefore, less useful to do further work. This trend toward disorder in a system is called entropy. Because entropy happens, if new, usable energy is not supplied to a system, eventually all of the energy in it will be discarded and useless. Remember the swing ride? If your friend does not continue to push you, your ride will eventually come to an end. The total amount of energy in the system remains the same but none of it will be available to do the job of keeping you swinging back and forth!

The Teaching Cycle

When Mrs. Berg's fifth-grade students return to school after their spring break, they are surprised to find a large banner across the front of the room with the word "Transformations!" written across it. They immediately begin to ask their teacher what this means. Mrs. Berg explains that "Transformations" will be the theme for their last quarter in her class. This is also the students' last quarter in this elementary school. Next year they will be attending one of the district's middle schools. She feels that this is an important and appropriate time for the students to reflect on their growth, physically, emotionally, and intellectually, and all the other changes that have taken place in their lives while they have been in elementary school. She plans to use this theme to also have the students consider their futures and help them prepare for the changes of going to middle school.

Mrs. Berg is aware that many broad thematic units often do not accommodate the goals and objectives of specific disciplines. In the past, she has chosen to exclude certain subjects from her theme rather than make strained fits and inappropriate connections. However, this theme is an appropriate fit for her fourth-quarter, fifth-grade science curriculum, which includes energy transfer. In earlier grades, the students learned and explored the concept of energy in the forms of light, sound, heat, motion, and electricity. As she begins this unit, she plans to first assess their prior knowledge about these forms and then continues on to energy transfer.

Goal Setting

When Mrs. Berg prepares for this unit, she first refers to the grade 5–8 physical science *National Science Education Standards.* She finds a content standard on Transfer of Energy that includes the following fundamental concept:

> Energy is a property of many substances and is associated with heat, light, electricity, mechanical motion, nuclei, and the nature of a chemical. Energy is transferred in many ways. (p. 154)

In the *Benchmarks for Science Literacy,* the Energy Transformation section for grades 6–8 states:

> Most of what goes on in the universe from exploding stars and biological growth, to the operation of machines and the motion of people, involves some form of energy being transferred from one form to another.

Although this is suggested for higher grade levels, she feels her students are capable of understanding the concepts in this benchmark at this point in their fifth-grade class. During the introductory lesson for this unit, she reviews the different forms of energy with her students. This lesson not only gives her insight into their prior knowledge of each energy form but also reveals any misconceptions they might have about these difficult concepts.

This lesson also serves as a beginning discussion of energy transfer. Now she wants them to understand how these different forms are used in energy transfer systems to do work. Her objectives for the lesson are as follows:

> Students will be able to give examples of simple energy transfer systems.
>
> Students will be able to identify the different forms of energy in an energy system.
>
> Students will be able to analyze an energy system and trace the pathway of energy as it is transferred through the system.

To meet these objectives, Mrs. Berg plans a number of different activities. Collectively, they will present her students with a wide variety of energy systems to explore. Through the activities of the lesson, Mrs. Berg wants the students to realize that they are already familiar with many energy transfer systems.

Materials Development and Selection

Mrs. Berg often tries to extend her teaching environment beyond the classroom to include the entire school facility and its surrounding neighborhood. The school is located on the main street of a small town. It has a large playground and tree-studded lawn on its property. Just beyond the boundaries of the school are a number of different shops, restaurants, and businesses that service the town. Mrs. Berg is planning to take her students on an energy scavenger hunt though the neighborhood. For this to be a successful learning experience, she knows that advance planning is necessary. She creates the following prelesson checklist:

- Inform her principal about her plans. She prepares a written outline of the activity that includes her goals and objectives as well as specific details about the outing.
- Design, distribute, and collect signed parental permission forms. These forms not only include the date and time of the scavenger hunt but also a rationale for the activity and how it is connected to classroom instruction. She invites parents to come along if they wish.
- Contact each business to tell the owners about her lesson and ask their permission to have her students visit. She assures them that the students will be spending no more than 10 minutes in each location sometime between 12:30 to 2:30 P.M.
- Go on a trial run of the trip. She plans out the best route, designs a time schedule, and makes notes of any safety issues she needs to caution her students about before the trip. As she goes along, she also makes her own list of energy transfer systems in the neighborhood.

- Gather clipboards and pencils for the students to use on the trip. Clipboards help to secure worksheets on windy days. They also supply the students with a sturdy surface to write on instead of using store windows and counters. Even the most supportive businesspeople won't appreciate 24 sets of fingerprints all over their stores!

Pedagogy

On the morning of the trip, Mrs. Berg asks her students to look around the classroom and make a list of all the forms of energy they can find. She then puts them into groups of four students and has them share their lists with each other. Each group is instructed to combine all the individual lists, disregarding overlap, and come up with one list for the group. Each group can pick a spokesperson to report their final energy list to the rest of the class. The students are surprised to hear all the different forms of energy that are evident in the room. All of their lists include electricity, light, heat, sound, and motion. One group also includes chemical energy. The other groups challenge them about this, but they explain that chemical energy is going on inside them as they digest their breakfasts. Mrs. Berg encourages these types of challenges because they encourage the students to explain their answers.

Next, she asks them how the energy forms on their lists are being used in the classroom. Again, she gives the students time to brainstorm answers to this question with the other students in their groups. Again, each group shares their answers. They include the use of electricity to light the fluorescent ceiling lights and to operate the computers, the clock, the filter in the aquarium, the VCR, and the television. Sound is involved in speaking, as well as the fire alarm, and the bell that indicated the start of school and the beginning of the lunch period. Of course, they mention the use of motion by their own bodies. One group includes the motion of the hands on the clock, and another adds the movement of the air bubbles from the filter through the water in the aquarium.

Now Mrs. Berg asks the groups to pick one of these applications and write down all the forms of energy that are involved in making this happen. She also asks them to organize their work in some way to show how they are related to the application. She is tempted to give them an example but decides to wait. She knows that teachers' examples can often direct the way students proceed with problem solving and influence how they work. She does not want all group responses to be revisions of her example. Instead, she moves around from group to group to answer any question they have and make suggestions. She notices that one group has decided to examine the energy that is involved in making the clock work. They have drawn a picture of the clock with a wire coming out of it. The other end of the wire is connected to a plug in an electrical socket on a wall. Another group wrote out the word *television* in the middle of their page. Then they drew one arrow pointing to it with the word *electricity* at the end. On the other side of the word *television* they drew three arrows with the words *light, heat,* and *sound* at the ends. A third group wrote out their solution in paragraph form. Mrs. Berg has the

Nature of Science

Convergent versus Divergent Activities

BOX 8.5

Too often, students learn science through lecture, text, and activities that promote the idea that there is always one "right" answer in science. These can be thought of collectively as *convergent* activities. Taken to an extreme (as students are inclined to do), this can lead to the misconception that scientific knowledge is absolute. Certainly, science has provided many concepts and explanations that have withstood the test of time and that we can be certain about, but science instruction should promote the understanding that even the most cherished scientific ideas are subject to change should contradictory evidence emerge.

One way to achieve this is to regularly provide students with opportunities to respond to questions and participate in activities for which there are multiple "correct" answers. Often referred to as *divergent,* such questions and activities stimulate more personal and creative responses while emphasizing that there is often no single correct answer or approach to a problem. Coupled with the type of explicit nature of science instruction illustrated in Chapter 1, divergent activities and questioning can go a long way toward helping your students achieve a more accurate view of science and scientific knowledge.

students share not only their answers but also their strategies for solving the problem and what they wrote and drew on their papers. She wants the class to see that there are many methods to solve a problem rather than one single "right" answer.

The students are surprised to see how each group approaches the problem and how differently they illustrate their solutions. Mrs. Berg explains that their solutions are examples of energy transfer systems. She tells them that after lunch they will be going on a hunt through the neighborhood to look for more of these systems. They will visit five different businesses. In each, they are to observe how energy is being used. At each business, they should identify one energy transfer system.

Assessment

The students' work as a result of the community field trip provides Mrs. Berg with insight into their understanding of energy systems. When they return to the classroom, she asks them to share the results of their energy transfer hunts. Their homework assignment for that night is to choose one of these systems and trace the pathway of energy forms that are involved in it.

Reflection

At the end of this full day, Mrs. Berg is exhausted but very pleased with her lesson. However, upon thinking back over the entire day she realizes that she missed some oppor-

tunities to discuss the nature of science with her students. Because energy transfer cannot be experienced directly, it would have been appropriate to talk about observation versus inference. She knows that it is necessary to teach the nature of science explicitly and makes a note in her plan book to bring up this discussion during the next day's science lesson. She makes one final note to send thank-you letters from her and her students to the businesses and parents who helped during the day.

Physical and Chemical Change

Understanding Physical and Chemical Change

Earlier in this chapter, we explored some of the physical properties of matter, such as mass, weight, volume, density, elasticity, and boiling point. We also examined the various forms of energy and the ways that energy may be transformed from one form into another. In this section, we will look at two ways matter can change and the role energy plays as these changes occur.

Physical Changes. If you look around, you cannot help but notice that matter constantly undergoes change. Sometimes the appearance of matter changes but not its substance. For example, cloth can be torn or cut, pencils wear down, and modeling clay can be molded into various shapes. These are all examples of physical change—when the physical properties of a substance are altered but the substance remains the same kind of matter. Copper is copper whether it takes the shape of a penny, electrical wire, or a frying pan. Paper is still paper, even when cut in two or folded into the shape of an airplane.

A good example of this type of physical change is provided in the children's book *Something from Nothing,* by Phoebe Gilman. In the story, Joseph's grandfather makes a beautiful blanket for him when he is just a baby. As Joseph grows older, the blanket grows older too and becomes tattered and worn. It undergoes physical change. Joseph's mother declares that it is time to throw the blanket out, but Joseph is not ready to give it up. Instead, he takes it back to his grandfather, who uses his sewing skills to make the old blanket into a new jacket. He uses the same material but gives it a new appearance. Again, this is an example of physical change. As the story progresses, Joseph continues to grow and the jacket, like the blanket before it, becomes tattered and worn. Eventually, Joseph's grandfather turns it into a vest, and then a tie, handkerchief, and button in succession, as each reincarnation of the blanket becomes too worn. All of these changes are physical changes, since Joseph's grandfather is only changing the appearance of the material, not the material itself.

Eventually, Joseph loses the tiny button his grandfather made from what was left of the original blanket. He runs to his grandfather's house to have him fix it but learns an important lesson instead. Not even his grandfather can make something from nothing. No one can. This is just a simple way of stating the law of conservation of matter. Stated more formally, the law declares that matter cannot be created or destroyed. You can change its forms and even convert it into energy, but you cannot make something from nothing.

Not all physical changes are as simple as cutting paper or mending a blanket. Earlier we mentioned that the melting point of a substance is the temperature at which it changes from a solid to a liquid, and the boiling point is the temperature at which it changes from a liquid to a gas. These types of changes are physical changes because you are changing the appearance of the substance (from solid to liquid to gas) but not the type of substance. Solid ice appears to be very different from liquid water and water vapor, but all three are still made up of the same kind of matter—water molecules. What, then, causes a substance to be in one phase rather than another? At the heart of the explanation is the kinetic molecular theory. This theory assumes that all matter is made of extremely small particles that are constantly moving and colliding. These particles may be atoms or combinations of atoms called molecules. As more energy is applied, the particles speed up and move farther apart. Conversely, as energy is taken away, the molecules slow down and move closer together.

The kinetic molecular theory provides a way of looking at the phases of matter in terms of energy. Thus, a liquid tends to have more energy than the same substance in the solid phase. The particles making up the liquid are moving faster and are farther apart. Likewise, a gas tends to have more energy than the same substance in the liquid phase. Water vapor, therefore, has more energy than both liquid water and ice. The greater energy content of water vapor explains why vegetables cook faster steamed than boiled and why steam burns more than hot water.

Because the different phases of matter are dependent on energy content, you can change the phase of a substance by adding or taking away energy. The most common way to do this is to heat or cool a substance. Try it for yourself. Place several ice cubes in a pot and let them sit at room temperature. After a short while, you should notice that the ice is beginning to melt. This takes energy, of course, but where is the energy coming from? You probably realize that the ice is absorbing energy from its surroundings. Heat energy from the air and the pan is causing the ice to melt, changing it to liquid water. If you further allow this liquid water to sit, it will continue to absorb heat energy from the room and gradually evaporate into water vapor. You will not be able to see the water vapor, but you will be able to see that the liquid water is gone. This process is called evaporation.

You can speed the process up considerably by adding energy, say, by heating the water on a stove. If enough heat is applied, the water will boil, which may be thought of as very rapid evaporation. Of course, you can reverse the whole process by cooling the water vapor. One way to do this is to hold a cool glass a few inches above the boiling water. What do you see forming inside the glass? How did the water get there? The cool glass absorbs energy from the water vapor, causing it to condense into liquid water. If you cool the liquid water by placing it in the freezer, even more energy is removed, causing the liquid water to freeze. It is important to remember that throughout these changes the energy (and speed) of the particles change but the substance of the particles remains the same. Whether we are talking about ice, liquid water, or water vapor, it is still water. Therefore, phase changes are considered physical changes.

Another less than obvious case of physical change is dissolving. Place a teaspoon of sugar in a glass of warm water and stir. What happens to the sugar? At first glance, it appears to have disappeared, but you know this cannot be true. Remember the law of conservation of matter. Matter (including sugar) cannot be created or destroyed. So what happens to it?

Taste the water. Go ahead, take a sip. How would you describe the taste? The sweetness you taste is a physical property of sugar. Thus, the sugar is still there, even though you cannot see it! The water has simply broken the sugar up into pieces that are too small to see. The sugar has changed its appearance but not its substance. You can easily verify this by allowing all of the water to evaporate to see what is left behind (go ahead and try this). Dissolving is also a physical change.

Chemical Changes. When you bake a cake, you combine flour, eggs, sugar, oil, water, and baking soda in the batter to form a mixture. Certainly, the batter has a different appearance (different properties) than the separate ingredients, but the individual ingredients are still in there. If you had a way to separate them, you would end up with the same materials you started with. When you bake the cake, however, something amazing happens. The heat energy from the oven causes the individual ingredients to combine to form cake, an entirely new kind of matter. The baked cake not only appears different from its batter but also actually contains different kinds of substances. This type of change, resulting in an entirely new substance (or substances), is called a chemical change or chemical reaction.

If you could look at the particles making up the cake, you would see that they are new combinations of the original atoms of the ingredients that went into the cake. No new atoms were produced and none of the previously existing atoms disappeared. The atoms that you started with were simply rearranged into new combinations (molecules), resulting in a new substance, cake.

Let's apply the law of conservation of matter to baking the cake. What do you predict you would find if you compared the weight of the batter to the weight of the cake it produces? If you said that they would be the same, you are catching on to the general principle. Nevertheless, you would be incorrect. The cake would actually weigh less than the batter. The total weight of the materials

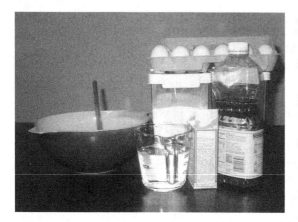

The ingredients used to make a cake are mixed together to form the cake batter. When the ingredients are baked in the oven, they undergo a chemical change to become finished cakes.

going into a chemical reaction does, indeed, equal the total weight of the materials produced by the chemical reaction. However, cake is not the only material produced by the reaction. Certain gases (like carbon dioxide) are produced and dissipate into the atmosphere as the cake bakes. Additionally, a good portion of the water that went into the batter evaporates (a physical change) as the cake bakes. You would have to capture all of the gases produced by baking the cake before you could adequately apply the law of conservation of matter. If you did, you would find that the total weight of the reactants (materials in the batter) equals the total weight of the products (cake, water vapor, and carbon dioxide gas).

Now let's see if you can apply your understandings of physical and chemical change to the processes of eating and digesting the cake. Cutting the cake with your fork certainly changes its appearance, but is the change physical or chemical? Hopefully, you recognized that the cake on your fork is simply a smaller piece of the cake on your plate and identified this as a physical change. Now place the bite of cake in your mouth and chew. Now, you have really changed its appearance (if you do not believe us, just open your mouth and have a look in the mirror). Is the cake in your mouth the same as the cake on your plate? It is certainly mashed up and there is some saliva added, but other than that, it is just cake. The change is, therefore, a physical one. (OK, some of you may have recognized that this is not technically correct. Saliva contains an enzyme that begins to digest starches in the cake, changing them to sugar. So there is some chemical change going on in your mouth, too.) Now, swallow your bite of cake and predict what kind of change goes on in your stomach and intestines. If you guessed chemical, then you guessed correctly, but how do you know it's a chemical change? In what way is the cake altered? What new substance is produced?

The Teaching Cycle

Mrs. Patla's fifth-grade class is nearing the end of a unit on physical and chemical changes. The unit began with a review of physical properties, a topic they covered during the previous unit. Next, students are introduced to the concept of physical change, starting with the general changes in the appearance of a substance. Students grind up sugar cubes, tear paper, and form mixtures of sand and sugar as examples of physical change. From these examples, they are able to see that physical change involves changing the appearance, but not the substance, of a sample. The class then explores phase changes by melting ice, boiling the resulting water, and condensing some of the water vapor produced by boiling back into liquid water (accomplished by Mrs. Patla placing the bottom of a cool glass just above the pot of boiling water). After some discussion about these latter demonstrations, the class reaches consensus that phase changes are examples of physical change because they also result in the same substance that they started with.

Mrs. Patla uses an inquiry approach to teach the final example of physical change at the end of the first week. In this activity, she asks students to explain whether dissolving salt in water matches their definition of physical change. She gives her students appropriate materials and lets them devise their own methods for answering the question. Mrs. Patla often provides opportunities for students to design their own investigations because she considers this an important inquiry skill. Most students are convinced that dissolving the salt in the water is a physical change simply by tasting the saltiness of the resulting solution. Others go a step further by placing their solutions in saucers and letting the water evaporate in a sunny window over the weekend. It is clear that when the water is gone, nothing but salt is left behind. These results lead students to believe that dissolving salt in water is a physical change.

Science as Inquiry

Assessing Levels of Inquiry

Scientific inquiry is a complex concept possessing many nuances and facets. Because of this, teachers often become confused about exactly what it means to teach and do scientific inquiry. Hopefully, we have been able to clear up some of this confusion through earlier discussions of teaching students the skills necessary to *do* inquiry and teaching them knowledge *about* inquiry. Now we would like to clear the matter further by providing a means of assessing the level of inquiry in a particular activity.

BOX 8.6

In the late 1960s and early 1970s, researchers developed a tool for determining the level of inquiry promoted by a particular activity. Known as Herron's Scale, the assessment tool is based on a very simple principle: How much is "given" to the student by the teacher or activity? Using this question as a framework, Herron's Scale describes four levels of inquiry:

Level 0: The *problem, procedure,* and correct *interpretation* are given directly or are immediately obvious. This type of activity involves confirmation of a principle through an activity in which the results are known in advance.

Level 1: The *problem* and *procedure* are given directly, but the students are left to reach their own conclusions. In this type of activity, students investigate a problem presented by the teacher using a prescribed procedure.

Level 2: The *research problem* is provided, but students are left to devise their own methods and solutions.

Level 3: Problems as well as methods and solutions are left open. This type of activity involves students in formulating their own research questions and developing procedures to answer their research questions in addition to reaching their own conclusions.

Obviously, the four levels of Herron's Scale are hierarchical. In other words, students cannot be expected to successfully complete a Level 2 activity without plenty of experience with Level 0 and Level 1 activities. Furthermore, although it may be desirable for upper elementary students to eventually participate in some Level 2 and Level 3 activities, we do not mean to imply that the ultimate goal is to make all of your hands-on activities Level 3. Rather, you should strive for a mix of inquiry levels appropriate to the abilities of your students. Having said that, we hope that you will agree that providing your students only with activities at inquiry Level 0 denies them the opportunity to develop and practice important inquiry skills and gives them an incomplete view of how science is done.

Apply Herron's Scale to Mrs. Patla's lesson on dissolving salt in water. What level of inquiry did this lesson provide?

For chemical change, Mrs. Patla emphasizes to her students that something new is produced. She does this with several demonstrations. She brings in nails that have been soaking in water for several days for students to examine. Students are able to determine that the rust on the nails is a new substance, because it has totally different properties than the nails. As another example of chemical change, Mrs. Patla burns a piece of paper and lets students examine the ashes that are left behind. Again, it is clear that the chemical change produces new substances, in this case, ashes and gases. Finally, Mrs. Patla lets students mix baking soda and vinegar in small cups and observe the production of bubbles. This time change is not so easy to detect because both baking soda and vinegar appear to remain in the cup after the reaction occurs. However, the students decide that this was a chemical change as well, because the production of bubbles indicates a gas, which is a new substance.

Mrs. Patla is now anxious to see whether her students can apply what they have learned about physical and chemical changes. Although she could address this question in a written assignment, Mrs. Patla wants the students to gain firsthand experience with physical and chemical changes. Therefore, she decides to set up a number of stations where students will be asked to identify changes in various materials as physical or chemical. Such an assignment will reinforce the activities and demonstrations that students have experienced, as well as provide her with an assessment of their understandings.

Goal Setting

The primary goal for the unit is for students to understand physical and chemical changes at a developmentally appropriate level. Mrs. Patla and the other two fifth-grade teachers at her school developed this goal for fifth-grade science last year while attending a curriculum planning workshop. The goal is based on the grade 3–5 benchmarks in *Benchmarks for Science Literacy:*

> When a new material is made by combining two or more materials, it has properties that are different from the original materials. For that reason, a lot of different materials can be made from a small number of basic kinds of materials.

A complete understanding of chemical changes requires knowledge of the making and breaking of bonds between atoms, a topic the elementary teachers believed more appropriate for middle school science. However, students could begin developing their understandings of chemical changes by exploring such changes in their everyday lives. Certainly, developing the understanding that chemical changes always produce new substances was an appropriate goal for fifth-grade students.

Students began to develop conceptions of physical and chemical change in the earlier lessons of the unit. For the sake of simplicity, these lessons focused on the definitions and recognition of physical and chemical changes separately. Now it is time to enrich students' understandings by allowing them to apply and contrast their concepts of physical and chemical change.

Mrs. Patla chose the following objective to guide the next day's lesson:

1. Given a set of appropriate hands-on examples, students will be able to distinguish between examples of physical and chemical changes.

Being at the application level of Bloom's Taxonomy, this objective builds on the comprehension-level objectives of the previous lessons:

2. Students will be able to describe physical change in their own words.
3. Students will be able to describe chemical change in their own words.

Mrs. Patla believes that the best way to address this goal would be to give students the opportunity to apply their understandings of physical and chemical change to familiar phenomena, such as melting ice, burning matches, and baking cookies. This is especially important because she used demonstrations exclusively during the previous lesson on chemical change.

Material Development and Selection

The first step in selecting the materials is to decide how many stations will be necessary. Two primary factors influence this decision. First, Mrs. Patla needs to have enough stations to allow for several different examples of physical and chemical change. Second, she needs to consider the number of students in the class and provide enough stations to keep all of them busy. After all, students with idle time are more prone to misbehave.

Mrs. Patla believes that eight different sample demonstrations split evenly among physical and chemical changes would provide an adequate assessment of students' ability to distinguish between these types of changes. Given that she has twenty-four students in the class, she needs to set up three replications of each sample demonstration if students are to work alone. Fortunately, the arrangement of her room can accommodate this many stations because students are arranged four to a table at eight separate tables. Mrs. Patla can place two stations at each table, for a total of sixteen. The other eight stations could be spaced along the counter at the back of the room.

Now that she knows how many stations she needs to put together, her next task is to choose the materials for each station. This choice has to be made carefully because she needs to choose sample demonstrations comparable to the ones she used during the unit and they have to be safe, inexpensive, and easily obtained. With so many students working at different stations, she could not possibly keep a close eye on each one, making safety an important consideration. Therefore, the stations had to involve materials and activities unlikely to cause injury, even if exposed to the eyes or skin.

After considering these factors, Mrs. Patla decided on the following materials and demonstrations for the eight different stations:

Station 1: Physical Change

Materials for three stations: 1 box of sugar cubes

3 spoons

30 paper towels

At this station, students will use a spoon to smash and grind a sugar cube into a fine powder. They will record whether the change is physical or chemical on their answer sheets, along with an explanation for their choice.

Station 2: Chemical Change

Materials for three stations: 3 matches

3 burnt matches

3 cards labeled "Before"

3 cards labeled "After"

Combustion is an important chemical reaction, but it would be unacceptably dangerous for students to burn their own matches during the assessment. Therefore, Mrs. Patla plans to set this station up as an observation station rather than as an activity. She places a match on a card labeled "before" and a burnt match on the card labeled "after."

Station 3: Chemical Change

Materials for three stations: 3 boxes of baking soda

3 dropper bottles of vinegar

24 paper cups

24 paper towels

3 pairs of safety goggles

At this station, students will be asked to place a small amount of baking soda (½ teaspoon) in a paper cup and then add a small amount of vinegar to the cup. Students will then record their observations and decide whether the change is physical or chemical. Students will be reminded that safety goggles must be worn during this activity.

Station 4: Physical Change

Materials for three stations: 24 small sheets of paper

At this station students will be asked to tear a piece of paper in two. They will then identify the change as chemical or physical and provide an explanation for their choice.

Station 5: Chemical Change

Materials for three stations: 3 pieces of steel wool

3 rusty pieces of steel wool (steel wool can be made rusty by placing it in a jar with a small amount of water for a few days)

6 index cards, 3 labeled "before" and 3 labeled "after"

Students will observe the steel wool (labeled "before") and the rusty steel wool (labeled "after"). They will be asked to record whether the change they observe indicates a physical change or a chemical change and explain their answer.

Station 6: Physical Change

Materials for three stations: 3 1-liter bottles of soda

3 clear plastic cups

3 large bowls of ice cubes

Students will be asked to place a couple of ice cubes in the cup, then pour about ¼ cup of soda over the ice, observing any changes. Students will then record whether they believe the change to be physical or chemical and explain their answers.

Station 7: Physical Change

Materials for three stations: 3 glasses, each filled with ice cubes

Students will be informed that the glasses contained only ice when the demonstration began. They now obviously contain ice and water. Students will be asked to record whether the change is chemical or physical and to explain their answer.

Station 8: Chemical Change

Materials for three stations: 3 small bowls of cookie dough

3 dishes containing 8 cookies

24 napkins

Students will be asked to compare the cookie dough to the cookies and explain whether the change from dough to cookie is a physical or chemical change. Once students have finished their answers, they may each have a cookie.

In addition to the material for the eight stations, Mrs. Patla prepares an answer sheet on which students could record their responses (see Figure 8.1). This sheet includes space for students to indicate the type of change at each station, plus space to write out the explanations for their choices.

Mrs. Patla is aware of the possibility that students might get the stations confused on the answer sheet and record their answers in the wrong places. To help avoid this problem, Mrs. Patla uses a descriptive title for each station on the answer sheet in addition to a number.

Figure 8.1   Student Answer Sheet for Physical and Chemical Change Assessment

Name _____

Date _____

Physical and Chemical Changes

Part A. Follow the directions posted at each station and determine whether the change is physical or chemical. Circle your choice for that station on the answer sheet and explain why you selected that choice. You may use the back of this sheet if you need more space.

Station 1: Sugar Cubes   Physical   Chemical
Reason for choice:

Station 2: Matches   Physical   Chemical
Reason for choice:

Station 3: Fizz   Physical   Chemical
Reason for choice:

Station 4: Paper   Physical   Chemical
Reason for choice:

Station 5: Steel Wool   Physical   Chemical
Reason for choice:

Station 6: Soda   Physical   Chemical
Reason for choice:

Station 7: Melting Ice   Physical   Chemical
Reason for choice:

Station 8: Cookies!   Physical   Chemical
Reason for choice:

(continued)

Figure 8.1   Continued

Part B. Answer the following questions while you wait for a station to become free and/or when you have finished your work at all eight stations, using the back of this sheet if you need more space.

Use your own words to describe what is meant by physical change.

Use your own words to describe what is meant by chemical change.

Make a list of as many physical changes as you can think of.

Make a list of as many chemical changes as you can think of.

On the evening prior to the lesson, Mrs. Patla gathers the materials for each of the stations, prepares the batter, and bakes the cookies. She decides to give the assignment first thing in the morning so she can set up the stations before students arrive. Spacing the twenty-four stations is an important concern for Mrs. Patla because she knows that students will need room to complete their work, and she wants to discourage talking and shared work. Therefore, she places stations at the ends of each of the eight tables in the classroom. The remaining six stations are spaced along the counter at the back of the room. A descriptive title and number corresponding to those on the answer sheet identify each station. Mrs. Patla includes a short list of instructions for the activity at each individual station.

Pedagogy

The school where Mrs. Patla teaches opens its doors to students at 8:00 A.M., with classes starting 15 minutes later. This means that she needs to provide something to keep the early arrivers occupied and away from the assessment stations until all students are present. Experience has taught Mrs. Patla that a good warm-up activity is effective in such situations. Ideally, the activity should not only serve to keep students who arrive early busy but should also help prepare them for the day's lesson. Therefore, she decides it would be a good idea to have students work together on a warm-up task before beginning the lesson: As students enter the room, she places them in groups of three or four at the carpeted area in the front of the room. She writes the following instructions on the board:

> Work in your groups to list as many physical and chemical changes as you can. Be prepared to explain why you identified each change as chemical or physical.

By 8:15, all of her students are present and working in groups to complete the warm-up task. Mrs. Patla gives them an additional 5 minutes to complete the task as she takes roll. Next, she leads a discussion to wrap up the activity, listing the examples that students give on the board under the appropriate headings of "Physical Change" and "Chemical Change." As each group provides an example, she asks a different group member how their group decided whether their example represented physical or chemical change.

Next, Mrs. Patla erases the board, passes out the answer sheets, and goes over the directions to the task. Mrs. Patla has learned through experience that giving good directions to an activity is critical to its success. Although it is obvious that students need to know what they are supposed to do to successfully complete a task, the amount of detail that is necessary to pull this off is not always as obvious. She begins by reminding students to write their names in the appropriate space (it is so easy for students to forget to do this). She lists this direction on the board as students write their names. Next, she points out the eight different stations around the room and briefly describes what students will be doing at each station. She points out that there are three copies of each

Special Needs for Special Students

Today's teachers should expect to have students with special needs, including learning disabilities, visual or hearing impairments, or other physical impairments. Federal laws [Education for All Handicapped Children Act Public Law 94-142 (1975); Disabilities Education Act Public Law 101-476 (1990), and Americans with Disabilities Act Public Law 101-336 (1990)] require the "least restrictive environment" for the education of these students. Beyond the legal issues, however, you will want to give all of your students the best possible learning environment. With careful planning, Mrs. Patla can provide an active and safe classroom environment for exceptional needs students in her regular classroom. What suggestions would you offer to Mrs. Patla to help her make the physical and chemical changes activity safer and more accessible to special needs students?

BOX 8.7

The following list should help you get started, but feel free to add your own ideas.

- When using chemicals, be careful to set out only small quantities at each station.
- Minimize the amount of walking students need to do with chemicals in their hands.
- Have safety goggles, aprons, or rubber gloves available when appropriate.
- Plan in advance for cleanup, disposal procedures, and personal hygiene (hand-washing with soap after handling chemicals).
- Provide a "talking partner" for visually impaired students whose job is to provide a running narrative of each activity.
- Be sure that individual stations are easily accessible to any students in wheelchairs or on crutches.
- Take advantage of school resources, such as special education teachers, to work with students diagnosed with learning disabilities.
- Maintain high, but reasonable, expectations for all students.
- Remember the "golden rule" of teaching: "Treat special needs students as you would have other students treat them."

station, so three students can work on the same task at once. Mrs. Patla explains that there are spaces on their answer sheets that correspond to each of the stations. She also explains that students should be careful to write their answers in the appropriate spaces. Mrs. Patla directs students to do their own work and to wait until the station is free before moving to the next one. Also, she reminds students that they probably will not be able to complete the stations in order. Rather, they should plan to move to whatever station is free that they have not yet completed.

Because she knows how important it is for students who finish early to have something to do while they wait on a station, she directs students to complete part B of the assessment during this time. When they have completed their work at all of the stations, Mrs. Patla instructs students to return to their seats and work on part B. When they complete the entire assessment, they should turn in their answer sheets and work quietly on other assignments or read. Finally, she reminds students that they can have one cookie when they complete station 8 and asks if students have any questions before they begin.

Mrs. Patla realizes that the length of the directions she is providing for the activity can make it difficult for students to remember them. Therefore, Mrs. Patla writes the directions on the board, so that students can refer to them as they complete the assessment. At the end of the discussion, the board contains the following list of directions:

1. Write your name on your answer sheet.
2. Begin work at one of the eight different stations.
3. Follow the written directions at each station.
4. Move to the next station only when the previous student completes his or her task.
5. Use your own words to answer the questions.
6. Have a cookie when you finish station 8!

Mrs. Patla reminds students that they should refer to these directions during the activity and to be sure to raise their hands if they have questions as they complete the eight tasks. To cut down on congestion and confusion, she directs individual students to their first stations and instructs them to begin. As students begin their work, Mrs. Patla circulates around the room to make sure they are getting off to a good start. After she completes this initial circuit, she continues to move from station to station, asking questions about what the students are finding. She is careful to avoid asking questions that can be answered with one word or phrase, in order to better gauge student understanding.

Normally, Mrs. Patla gives students a time estimate for completing the activity at hand before students begin their work. However, it is difficult to say how long it will take students to complete all of the stations, especially since each one will require different amounts of time. Instead, Mrs. Patla pays close attention to her students' progress and gives them a "10-minute warning" when she notes that the majority of students are working at their last stations.

Assessment

Mrs. Patla collects the answer sheets from her students as they complete their work and gives students the choice to either read or work on other assignments while they wait for their classmates to finish. Once all students' work is handed in, Mrs. Patla leads a class discussion on their results. She feels this is important because students have been working individually for a long time during the activity. Mrs. Patla believes that giving students an opportunity to verbalize their experiences will facilitate learning and provide her with a chance to informally assess the outcome of the lesson.

She leads the discussion by progressing through a series of planned questions chosen to review the results of the activity and help students synthesize their learning of the past few days. She begins by asking what they had learned about physical changes.

Then she asks about chemical changes to contrast the two. Finally, she asks students to identify the type of change represented at each of the eight stations. Throughout the discussion, Mrs. Patla calls on both volunteers and nonvolunteers for each question. She also encourages students to question each other and to discuss their understandings. In fact, Mrs. Patla sees her role as that of facilitator, rather than leader, and tries to keep the lesson closure student centered.

The students' participation in the discussion leads Mrs. Patla to believe that they have, indeed, been able to successfully apply their conceptions of physical and chemical change. She knows better, however, than to depend on a class discussion as the sole assessment of students' attainment of the lesson objective. There is simply no way to question each individual student and, even if you could, the students would eventually fall into the pattern of repeating their classmates' answers. The class discussion provides her with a general view of the class's progress. Mrs. Patla plans to individually assess students' ability to distinguish physical and chemical changes as she grades their answer sheets later that day.

One significant point of confusion emerges during the discussion having to do with station 6. This station includes the activity where students have to decide whether the fizz produced by soda was a physical or a chemical change. The class is about evenly split on this issue. Rather than try to resolve the question for her students, Mrs. Patla decides to use it as a basis for further inquiry. Mrs. Patla knows that using student-generated questions is a powerful way to encourage student involvement and helps her provide instruction that is relevant to students' daily lives. Therefore, she tells students to write a brief description of how they could resolve the issue for their homework assignment. She adds that the description should include a sentence describing the problem, followed by the approach students suggest the class use to solve it. Finally, in order to avoid confusion about the homework, Mrs. Patla asks a student to explain the writing assignment and then addresses student questions about what they're supposed to do.

Reflection

Later that evening, Mrs. Patla evaluates her students' answer sheets, which constitute her formal assessment of the lesson. After grading the assignment, Mrs. Patla is pleased to note that it supports the initial impression she gained during the discussion used to close the activity. Most of her students understand physical and chemical changes well enough to distinguish between the two and apply the concepts to novel situations. In fact, approximately three-fourths of the class can accurately distinguish between the two types of change at nearly every station and are able to explain their choices based on whether a new substance is produced. That still leaves one-fourth of the students who are not able to distinguish physical and chemical changes consistently. These students are likely to become more confused during the next unit on chemical reactions, unless Mrs. Patla provides further instruction on physical and chemical changes. Therefore, Mrs. Patla decides to provide an additional activity before moving on to the next topic.

The activity she has in mind is for her to bring an electric skillet into the classroom and actually cook pancakes. The process of mixing the ingredients for the batter would provide good examples of physical change, whereas cooking the pancakes would be a chemical change. Students can readily compare the differences between the batter and pancakes to see that a new substance is produced. Mrs. Patla likes this activity because it will give her students an additional opportunity to apply their understandings of physical and chemical change, and because it is based on cooking, a process that is relevant to students' lives. Between the pancake activity and the inquiry into soda fizz that students would be pursuing, Mrs. Patla decides that it is going to be a very busy week!

Summary

As this chapter comes to a close, you should ask yourself: "What have I learned about physical science and how to teach it?" Hopefully, you can think of several things, including knowledge and understandings about physical science and how the teaching cycle applies to physical science instruction. For instance, we included several activities designed to help you explore key physical science concepts, including the definition and physical properties of matter, Newton's three laws of motion, energy transformations, and the differences between physical and chemical changes. If you completed these activities, you should now have a better understanding of matter and energy, as well as a deeper appreciation for the power of inquiry in exploring the world around you.

In addition to this focus on physical science content, we have included examples of using the teaching cycle to design effective, inquiry-based lessons related to these "big ideas" in physical science. Hopefully, reading these examples of the teaching cycle being used to teach physical science in a variety of contexts has brought you to a greater understanding and appreciation of the components of effective teaching, including:

- Careful and detailed instructional planning (*setting goals* and *selecting materials*).
- Effective classroom practice (*pedagogy*).
- Appropriate *assessment* of learning.
- *Reflecting* on the effectiveness of instruction and making revisions where necessary. To the degree that this introduction to teaching physical science has increased your understandings of matter and energy and reinforced your commitment to the critical concepts of teaching, your hard work during the chapter has been worthwhile.

Suggested Literature Connection

Properties of Matter

Who Sank the Boat by Pamela Allen, Putnam & Grosset, New York, 1996.
When friends decided to go for a boat ride in the bay, they did not anticipate the boat sinking! This book could complement any activity on sinking and floating. Have the students make aluminum foil or clay boats and test to find out how many paper clips they can hold before they sink.

Too-loose the Chocolate Moose by Stewart Moskowits, Simon & Schuster, New York, 1982.
This moose is unlike any other moose because he is made of chocolate. As a result he has different characteristics and properties. What if he were made of ice cream or mud? How would his properties and behavior change?

The Three Little Pigs (any edition)
Why are some materials better than others for house construction? Any version of this classic folk tale can reinforce the lesson on physical properties. Students can draw pictures or make models of houses in their own neighborhoods and compare the properties of the materials from which they are constructed.

Force and Motion

Gilberto and the Wind by Marie Hall Ets, Puffin, New York, 1963.
Gilberto plays with his friend, the wind. This story can be used to begin a discussion of motion. It could also be part of an assessment lesson by having the students identify examples of motion from the story.

Pretend You're a Cat by Jean Marzollo, Dial books, New York, 1990.
No unit on motion is complete without including animal locomotion. Have the students act out the animal actions described in this book filled with action words.

Energy

Two Bad Ants by Chris Van Allsburg, Houghton Mifflin Company, Boston, 1988.
This story is about the adventures of two ants as they move through a household. They experience the effects of a variety of energy forms. Students could be asked to identify different energy forms as an assessment. This story is a model as they create their own tale that includes energy forms and transformations.

Barbra's Mystery by Laurent de Brunhoff, Random House, New York, 1978.
   The busy illustrations in this mystery story provide students with many examples of energy systems.

Physical and Chemical Changes

Amelia Bedelia by Peggy Parish, Harper and Row, New York, 1963.
   This is the first in the series of Amelia Bedelia books. In this story, Amelia is given a list of chores to do. In the process of doing these, she creates physical and chemical changes throughout the house.

Something from Nothing by Phoebe Gilman, Scholastic Inc., New York, 1992.
   Joseph's grandfather reconfigures his baby blanket into many different forms as Joseph grows and the blanket material frays. Each of these has a different shape and different use, such as jacket, vest, tie, handkerchief, and button, but are still made out of the same blanket material. This book can be used to begin a discussion of physical change.

Pancakes, Pancakes! by Eric Carle, Scholastic Books, New York, 1990.
   All the ingredients and steps to make pancakes are included in this story. Students could identify each step of the recipe as either a physical or chemical change.

Snowflake Bentley by Jacquelin Briggs Martin and Mary Azarian, Houghton Mifflin Co., Boston, 1998.
   This book, which won the Caldecott Medal Award, tells the true story of a Vermont farm boy, Wilson Bentley, who was mesmerized by snowflakes. Bentley spent his life taking exquisite photographs of these tiny crystals and their delicate structures. This beautifully illustrated book is an excellent introduction for children to the scientific secrets and ephemeral beauty of these winter delights.

Earth Science

Whether you take a teaching position in the city, in the suburbs, or out in the country, you will find that earth science is both relevant and readily accessible to you and your students. Rocks are underfoot, the moon and stars are out at night, and, of course, the weather is always a topic of conversation. In fact, the earth, sky, and weather combine to make a wonderful interactive laboratory just waiting to be explored by you and your students. Here you will find applications of the fundamental principles of the physical and life sciences, including how evaporation and condensation impact weather and how humans' propensity to find patterns has led to the creation of constellations. The earth and space sciences also provide a meaningful context for addressing the interrelationships between humanity and the earth system (e.g., global climate change and the environmental impacts of mining), a critical aspect of scientific literacy.

The primary goals of this chapter are to provide relevant background information on selected earth science topics and to provide examples of the teaching cycle being used to teach hands-on, inquiry-based lessons that capture the excitement of discovery in the earth and space sciences. The content will include the following major earth science topics:

- Nighttime astronomy: Stars and constellations
- Daytime astronomy: The solar system
- Geology: Rocks and the rock cycle
- Meteorology: The water cycle

The Universe: Stars and Constellations

Step outside on any clear night and you will likely see hundreds of stars. In fact, it has been estimated that on a moonless night far away from city lights, a careful observer may see as many as 3,000 individual stars. What a sight! However many stars are visible in the night sky where you live, you will notice that the brighter stars tend to form patterns in the sky. Go ahead, take a look and see! On any given night, you are likely to see a variety of geometric figures, including lines, triangles, and squares. If you have a vivid imagination, you may even make out figures of plants, animals, and humans. Are these patterns really there or are they the result of human creativity and imagination? That is a good question and one that is related to the nature of science. In this section we will consider some common star patterns or constellations and how they came to be.

The Constellations

Since the beginning of civilization, people have used the stars to mark the seasons, to aid in navigation, and to serve as a reflection of their heritage through myth and folklore. Because of the importance of stars and the need to communicate about them, ancient peoples grouped the brighter stars into patterns they could recognize and remember. These patterns became known as constellations. Different cultures saw different patterns in the sky, reflecting their unique cultures and mythologies. Consider, for example, the familiar group of stars known as the Big Dipper. Not every culture has seen this group of stars as a dipper. In France, it is known as the saucepan. To the British, it's the plough. The Chinese saw it as a chariot, while runaway slaves during Civil War times saw a drinking gourd pointing the way north to freedom.

The seven stars that make up what we call the Big Dipper are actually only part of a larger group of stars that make up the modern-day constellation, Ursa Major, or Great Bear. Our modern constellation system is based on the names and mythologies developed long ago by the ancient Greeks. In all, astronomers officially recognize eighty-eight constellations in the skies of the northern and southern hemispheres. Most of these constellations do not bear much resemblance to the people, animals, and mythological figures they represent. For example, the principle stars of the constellation Cassiopeia look more like a "W" or "M" than the Ethiopian Queen they are meant to represent (see Figure 9.1). It is more accurate to think of them as symbolic rather than literal representations, much as the state of Washington is meant to honor, rather than look like, America's first president.

Another important point to consider about constellations is that, with few exceptions, the stars that make up a constellation are not actually connected to one another. In fact, more often than not, they differ widely in their distance from the Sun. Thus, the patterns we recognize in the sky are the result of chance alignment. Although the patterns that we recognize today are much the same as they appeared when they were first named nearly 3,000 years ago, this will not always be the case. Even the seemingly fixed stars are moving rapidly through space. Because they are so far away, it takes thousands of years to see significant changes in the star patterns (see Figure 9.2).

Figure 9.1   The Principle Stars of the Constellation Cassiopeia

Figure 9.2   The Big Dipper in the Distant Past, Present, and Remote Future

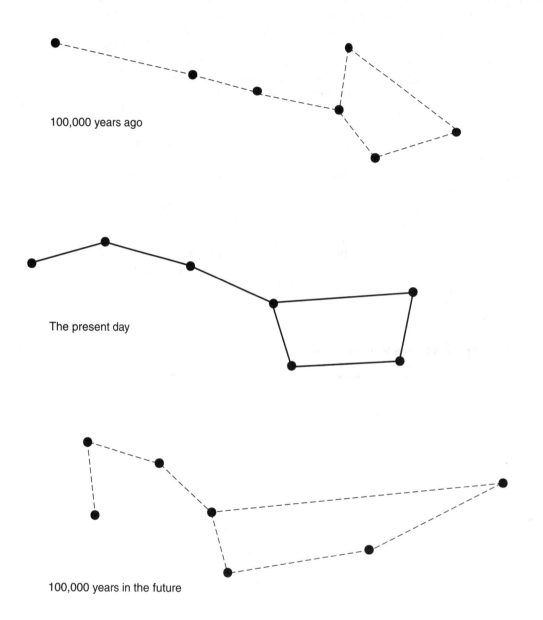

100,000 years ago

The present day

100,000 years in the future

Star Watching

One of the best and easiest methods of becoming familiar with the night sky is simply to step outside on a clear night and look up. To be sure, a little preparation will make your star watching more enjoyable, but you do not have to be an expert to enjoy the night sky and learn more about it. For starters, bring a pencil and some paper for recording your observations. Next, consider the season and dress accordingly. If the weather is cold, be sure to wear several layers of clothing, and do not forget your hat and gloves (more heat is lost through your head and hands than any other parts of your body). If it is warm out, you will likely need to contend with mosquitoes, so do not forget the insect repellant. Try to observe from an area as far away from lights as possible that has a wide view of the sky.

Note that it takes your eyes more than half an hour to become fully adjusted to the dark, so do not expect to see a lot of stars at first. In fact, it is interesting to note just how few stars you can actually see when you first step outside. Then watch the dimmer stars become more visible as your eyes become more adapted to the dark. Beware of light once your eyes are adapted. It only takes a flash of bright light to cause your eyes to lose their sensitivity. That is why, if you bring a flashlight, you will want to cover the lens with some type of red filter, say a balloon, or a couple layers of tissue paper. This will both dim and redden the beam. It turns out that red light impacts your night vision much less than any other color.

Now that you have found your spot, lay flat on your back (it is much too tiring to crane your neck back while standing) and enjoy the view. Try to take in all you can of the night sky above you. Do you see stars of different brightness? Are they all the same color? How do they appear to be arranged? Open your eyes and your mind and enjoy the spectacle above you!

Now, imagine that you want to point out a star or group of stars to a friend. How would you do it? Using your finger to point does not help much. After all, it's dark! You could try to use a landmark, particularly if the star you are interested in lies near the top of a tall tree or chimney. This could be a good method for a particular star at a particular time, but there is a problem with using stationary objects as star pointers. Can you think of what it is? If not, try it and see. Locate a star near a landmark such as a tree, post, or top of a building. Try to position your head so that the star is right over the landmark you are using. Now, watch it carefully for the next 5 or 10 minutes. What do you notice about its position? Notice how far the star appeared to move in just a few minutes, and imagine how far it will have appeared to move in an hour or two. Obviously, your landmark will not always mark the position of a particular star, simply because the earth is rotating, making the stars appear to gradually move toward the west.

Another way to identify stars is to group them together into easily re-membered patterns. This is what people have been doing for thousands of years. As you observe the heavens, see if you can make out any star patterns or constellations. Even if you don't know any of the official constellations, you can always make your own. Give it a try! Once you have identified a few star patterns, you can point stars out to your friend by telling her to look at, for in-stance, the bright, reddish-looking star at the base of the kite shaped group of stars.

After you have spent some time making out star patterns in the sky, you will want to try to identify some real constellations. A good constellation to start with is the Big Dipper. Many people are familiar with its distinctive shape, but even if you are not you will likely recognize it if you look to the north (see Fig-ure 9.3). Keep in mind that the Big Dipper may appear upright, on its end, or upside down, depending on the season and the time of night. Once you find the

Figure 9.3   The Big Dipper and Polaris

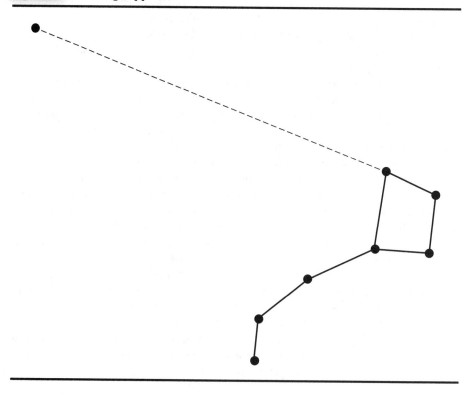

Big Dipper, pay particular attention to the two stars that make up the end of the cup of the dipper.

These two stars are sometimes referred to as pointer stars, because an imaginary line extended from them intersects Polaris, the North Star. This star is very important for navigation for two reasons. The first reason is because it happens to lie very close to the north celestial pole. Thus, when you are facing this star, you are facing north. With this information, you can also easily derive the other directions. Which direction will be to your right, to your left, behind you? If you said east, west, and south to these questions, then you have a good sense of direction! The second reason that Polaris is important for navigation is that it is always visible in the northern sky. It never sets! You can verify this by making some careful observations. Take a moment to sketch the Big Dipper and Polaris. Try to position them in your sketch as they appear in the sky. Now predict how the Big Dipper and Polaris will appear later in the night, say six hours from now. (As a hint, think about how far the hour hand travels around the face of a clock in six hours.) You may go inside after you have made your prediction, but do not forget to check the position of the Big Dipper and Polaris again six hours later to see if your prediction was right.

Figure 9.4 shows the position of the Big Dipper and Polaris at six-hour intervals on December 10 and 11. Notice how the Big Dipper appears to rotate around Polaris, just like the hands of a clock! And because Polaris lies near the celestial north pole, it appears to be the pivot point, so its position does not change. Now, make another prediction. Where do you think the Big Dipper will appear in the sky *at the same time of night* three months from when you made your observation? How about six months? Nine months? One year? Think about the hands of the clock again, and the fraction of year that is covered in three, six, nine, and twelve months. The answer to this challenge is provided in Figure 9.5, if you do not want to wait until you make a full year of observations.

The Big Dipper is also useful as a guide to help you find bright groupings of stars in other constellations. For example, if you look toward the opposite side of Polaris from the Big Dipper at about the same distance, you will find a bright, compact grouping of five stars that look like an "M" or "W," depending on when you look (see Figure 9.6). These are the five brightest stars of the constellation Cassiopeia, the Ethiopian Queen. In late winter or early spring, you can follow the pointer stars of the Big Dipper in the opposite direction (away from Polaris) to arrive at the constellation Leo the Lion (see Figure 9.7). In summer and fall, you can trace the arc of the Big Dipper's handle to Arcturus, the brightest star in Bootes, the bear hunter (see Figure 9.8). Once you have added these constellations to your repertoire, you can use them as jumping off points to other constellations. Armed with a star map or guidebook from your local library or bookstore, you can add to your night watching fun by star-hopping from one constellation to the next.

Figure 9.4 The Big Dipper and Polaris on December 10

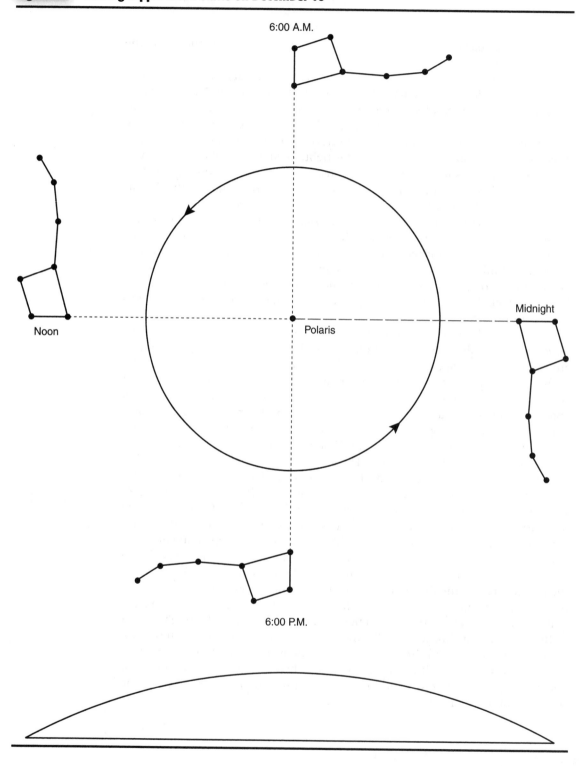

Figure 9.5 The Big Dipper and Polaris at 8:00 P.M. throughout the Year

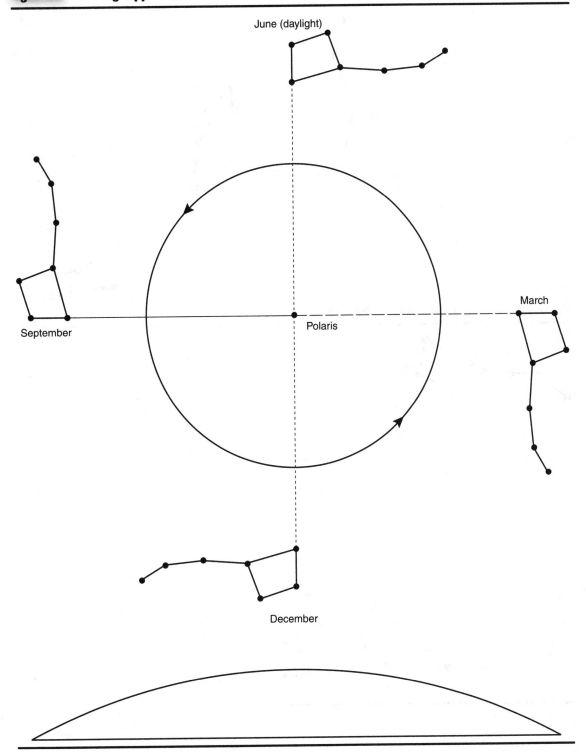

Figure 9.6   The Big Dipper and Cassiopeia

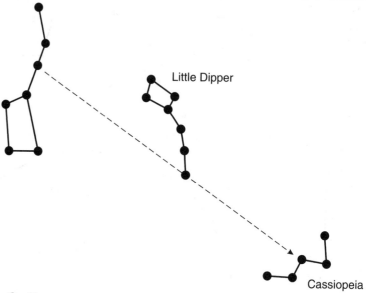

Little Dipper

Cassiopeia

Figure 9.7   The Big Dipper and Leo the Lion

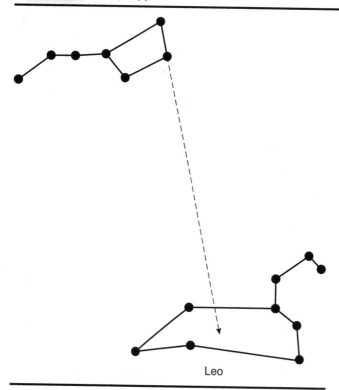

Leo

Figure 9.8   The Big Dipper and Bootes

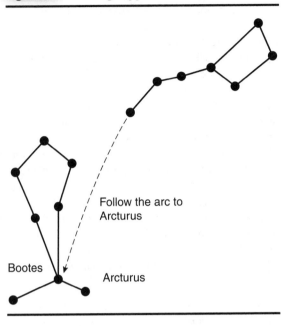

Follow the arc to
Arcturus

Bootes

Arcturus

The Teaching Cycle

For the past several years, Mrs. Simpson's class has joined the school's other fifth graders on a field trip to a local museum each spring. The students always seem to enjoy the field trip. However, it is not very organized, and Mrs. Simpson believes they are not taking full advantage of the learning potential the museum affords. This year, she is determined that her students will get a greater educational benefit from the field trip, especially from the planetarium program, which has usually tended more toward entertainment.

Goal Setting

No one had thought much about setting learning goals for this field trip. Instead, the primary focus had been to simply provide an opportunity for students to experience the museum. Mrs. Simpson believed that it was imperative that she develop specific learning outcomes for the field trip. Her overall goal was for her students to learn a new science concept from the planetarium experience.

Since she had been to the program several times before, she knew what to expect. The director always showed students the mythological figures represented by the constellations, along with the current positions of the sun, moon, and planets. Students seemed to enjoy the presentation but were always puzzled that the star patterns do not really look much like the figures they are supposed to represent.

Mrs. Simpson thought there could be a lesson there that could be related to multiculturalism and the nature of science. A recent in-service workshop at her school had emphasized the importance of addressing the multicultural aspects of whatever subject matter was being taught. The speaker said that students tended to look at things only from the viewpoint of their own culture. The workshop convinced her of the value of helping students view knowledge as created by all cultures and to understand that everyone has value, no matter what their cultural background.

In addition, at a state science education conference she had attended for the first time last spring, a speaker emphasized the importance of teaching students *about* science itself, as well as science content. According to the speaker, most students see science concepts as absolute, being read directly from the "book of nature." Students must be taught explicitly to realize the more accurate view of scientific knowledge is that it is constructed by humans and at least partly influenced by the cultural background of the people who do the constructing.

Mrs. Simpson finds the following related standard in the *National Science Education Standards:*

- Many individuals have contributed to the traditions of science. Studying some of these individuals provides further understanding of scientific inquiry, science as a human endeavor, the nature of science, and the relationships between science and society.

She also notes the following in the grades 3–5 benchmarks in the *Benchmarks for Science Literacy:*

- Science is an adventure that people everywhere can take part in, as they have for many centuries.

After considering what she has found in the national reform documents related to the intent of her lesson, Mrs. Simpson developed the following three specific objectives. Students should be able to do the following:

- Explain that constellations represent patterns of stars created by humans.
- Give an example of two different constellations people have created from the same set of stars.
- Explain how people's cultural backgrounds can influence the patterns they see and create.

Materials Development and Selection

To meet these objectives, Mrs. Simpson would have to go beyond textbook instruction because none of the science textbooks with which she was familiar addressed these con-

Issues in Technology

Science That Is Virtually Real

Sometimes you want to take your students places or have them do things in the classroom that are too costly, too dangerous, or just plain impossible to do. Fortunately, there are many excellent computer simulations available that can give students 90 percent of the experience with 0 percent of the associated dangers and at much less expense in terms of time and cost.

BOX 9.1

Teaching supply catalogs carry a variety of simulation software that allows you, for example, to conduct plant growth experiments, travel to different planets, conduct dissections, and explore chemical reactions. Sometimes simulations help you visualize abstract science concepts that are difficult to see. For instance, ExploreScience.com offers free online simulations that enable you to manipulate and observe abstract concepts, such as the motion of sound waves and the Doppler effect, and even breed different-colored mice to explore basic principles of genetics.

Mrs. Simpson wanted to use star maps during her astronomy lesson, but she was not able to find a book that included the constellations she needed. Planetarium simulation software is available that not only provides the maps she was interested in using but also simulates the motion of the night sky just like in a planetarium. Many of these programs include a wealth of information and can be used by both novice and advanced learners. Mrs. Simpson's students could observe the motion of the stars in class during the day and then watch the stars in their backyards at night.

cepts. She thought one good approach would be to read a book about how another culture viewed a well-known constellation. The book that immediately came to mind was *Follow the Drinking Gourd* by Jeannette Winter. It tells the story of a slave family seeking freedom in the North and followed the constellation we know as the Big Dipper to find their way.

After reading and discussing the story, students could work in pairs to invent their own constellations from maps of the stars. The difficulty here would be coming up with constellation maps. She wanted several different constellations for the current season (spring). Plus, she wanted each map to show a lot of stars to give students plenty of possibilities. She looked in the school library. A couple astronomy books there had star maps, but the constellation lines were already drawn in.

She decided to try searching the Internet. She went to a popular search engine and typed the word "constellation." From that search, she got a list of sites that mostly included books about constellations, histories of constellations, and mythological figures of constellations. None of the sites appeared to have star maps. She tried a new search with the words "star map." This time the sites focused on books about star maps and some even showed star maps for specific areas of the sky. However, she could not tell which season they represented.

Starry Night

An excellent software program that can be used for star mapping in your local area is called Starry Night™ and is available at the website www.starrynight.com. If you have an LCD projector for your computer, you can display various aspects of the night sky and have an interactive discussion. The software is also available for a free download!

BOX 9.2

She next typed the words "constellation AND star map AND spring." Now she quickly found a site posted by a commercial astronomy software company. It had a demonstration showing the night sky for any date in time and allowed her to zoom in on particular constellations. From this, she cut and pasted a series of star maps for her location and season and printed out the general areas of six different constellations. Finally, she called ahead and talked to the planetarium director to make sure he would talk about at least two cultures' views of the Big Dipper. He had done this in the past, but Mrs. Simpson wanted to leave nothing to chance.

Pedagogy

It is now the day after the museum field trip and, as usual, students had a lot of fun. The planetarium session seemed to be a success as well. Students enjoyed the animation and simulation of the night sky. The director addressed two cultures' views of the Big Dipper, as Mrs. Simpson had requested. He even had images of a Roman chariot and the Greeks' Big Bear superimposed on the constellation to illustrate this difference.

Mrs. Simpson wanted to begin the lesson by reviewing what students remembered about the planetarium. In doing this, she hoped to set the context for the present lesson and informally assess what her students had learned and experienced on the trip. She began the review by asking a series of questions, moving from the general to the more specific.

"What did you enjoy about the museum?" As she called on individual students, Mrs. Simpson received a range of answers, from the live animal displays to the Native American artifacts. Eventually, one student mentioned the planetarium.

"What do you remember about the planetarium program?" Mrs. Simpson asked. Several students responded enthusiastically as she called on them one at a time.

"Seeing thousands of stars."

"Watching the sun move across the sky."

"Seeing the moon go through its phases."

"Seeing different constellations."

Mrs. Simpson then asked, "Was there a constellation that you found particularly interesting?" Most students agreed that the Big Dipper was particularly impressive.

"Do you remember anything the director said about the Big Dipper?" Mrs. Simpson asked. Again, she called on the students who had their hands raised: "It's the easiest constellation to recognize." "You can use it to locate the North Star." "It's not the whole constellation but part of a bigger group of stars called the Great Bear." "Not everybody saw it as a bear."

Mrs. Simpson asked a nonvolunteer student to elaborate on this last statement. "The Romans viewed the Big Dipper's stars as a chariot, and the Greeks had a whole story about how the Big Bear was created." Mrs. Simpson added a third example by introducing the children's book *Follow the Drinking Gourd.* She told them she was not going to give them any background information about the story, but she would ask them to figure out when and where the story took place as she read. This is a device she used to help kids pay attention. By giving them a task up front, Mrs. Simpson knew her students would have a reason to listen closely.

After reading the story, she asked students to tell her what it was about. Various students reiterated the major portions of the story. As promised, she also asked students to tell her the setting of the story. Students eagerly complied because they had been thinking about it and looking for clues throughout her reading of the story. Once she saw that they understood the story and its setting, she asked how the story related to the planetarium director's discussion about the Big Dipper. From their answers, it was obvious her students recognized that different people or cultures viewed the stars in different ways.

Mrs. Simpson then asked for more detail, and the students described what they had learned about the Romans, Greeks, and slaves. "What was it about the Romans, the Greeks, and the slaves in the story that may have caused them to see different patterns in the same set of stars?" Mrs. Simpson asked. Various students responded that the people lived at different times and different countries, they had different situations, and their parents probably told them different stories.

Mrs. Simpson elaborated on their responses, adding that there are other factors that can also influence how we view the world: for example, art, music, and religion, which together make a culture. "Why would the Romans see chariots in the sky?" she asked. "Why would the slaves see drinking gourds?" Mrs. Simpson was pleased that her students could make connections between everyday objects people were familiar with and the different patterns they saw in the sky.

To make the point even more clear, Mrs. Simpson paired up students with their pre-assigned partners (the strategy she had decided on in advance for a smooth transition). She gave each pair of students one of the star maps, which were printed on overhead transparencies rather than paper. The six different star maps were labeled 1–6. She instructed students to study the stars and make up their own constellation from the set of stars. Like real constellations, the lines do not have to include all the stars, but the constellation should include the brightest stars. The students were to give their constellation a name and then be prepared to tell the class why they chose the name and figure they did. To check that her students understood the assignment, she asked a student to repeat her directions and asked if anyone had questions. To encourage students to use their time efficiently, she told them that they would have 10 minutes to complete their task of creating a constellation.

Once each student pair had completed their task, they presented their work in numbered order. The two pairs with star map 1 shared theirs first, and so on. For each star map, Mrs. Simpson had a transparency outlining the constellation recognized by astronomers, which she presented after each pair.

Assessment

After all the pairs had presented, Mrs. Simpson was ready to assess the students' understanding. "You notice we have three different patterns formed by the same set of stars," she said. Picking up a set of transparencies, she commented, "Sarah's group came up with a question mark. Bobby's group came up with a mouse. Astronomers call this Leo the Lion. On a sheet of paper, list the image you created, as well as the other two images imposed on the same set of stars. Then write a paragraph explaining why three different patterns were obtained from the same set of stars. I want you to spend the next 10 minutes writing everything you can think of that might explain this." Again, Mrs. Simpson asked a student to repeat the directions for the task. She then instructed students to begin work and, after 10 minutes had passed, she collected their papers.

Reflection

As Mrs. Simpson reflected on the lesson later that evening, she thought about her objectives and whether the students had met them. Certainly, each pair of students had been able to create star patterns from the maps she had provided. She knew from the planetarium show and the class discussion that her students understood that constellations were patterns of stars created by humans. As she read her students explanations for why different people might create different patterns, it was obvious that her students understood that one's background can influence the patterns one sees. Their responses included discussions about specific aspects of this idea, such as how people are raised, what stories they are familiar with, and what religious ideas they hold may affect the star patterns they see.

Although she was pleased with these responses, Mrs. Simpson did not want her students' understanding of background influences to stop with their views of constellations. Pattern creation is common to many aspects of science, as is the influence of background knowledge on the patterns scientists create out of data. She believed it was crucial to connect the specific example of star patterns in constellations, which students appeared to understand, to a more general application to science as a whole. Therefore, she determined to try to help students see that pattern creation is common to other areas of science by discussing specific examples with them during tomorrow's science lesson.

Patterns

As you teach other lessons or come up with other examples of how scientists use or create patterns to make an interpretation or explanation, you may want to create a bulletin board area in the classroom that can be developed throughout the school year.

Discussions about patterns that scientists use, patterns that students **BOX 9.3** create on their own, or newspaper clippings about patterns and interpretations can all be added to the bulletin board. The bulletin board can also be divided into scientific disciplines so that as the year progresses students can observe and discuss the patterns and possible interpretations or explanations. The critical use of this bulletin board idea is that it will make explicit the idea that scientists impose patterns on nature and use these patterns to offer explanations for how the universe works.

One such example is the field of meteorology, where scientists attempt to identify patterns in weather data (including temperature, humidity, atmospheric pressure, etc.) in order to model and predict future weather patterns.

Another good example is the various interpretations that scientists have come up with regarding the demise of the dinosaurs. Scientists from different backgrounds interpret the available data differently, leading to such divergent explanations as a catastrophic asteroid impact, climate-altering volcano eruptions, and disease and sickness as likely candidates for the cause of the extinction of dinosaurs. The main point she wants to emphasize is that although scientific endeavor represents an attempt to be objective and unbiased, the patterns, interpretations, and explanations scientists create are all influenced by the scientists' background and culture. In some ways this can be seen as limiting, but she preferred to look at it as a strength. In Mrs. Simpson's experience, understanding the human element in science makes it more relevant, accessible, and interesting to students.

The Solar System: Daytime Astronomy

When considering the topic of astronomy, most people think of starry nights, the moon, and the planets. These celestial objects are typically thought of as nighttime objects and astronomy as a nighttime activity. This poses difficulties for the teacher who wants to teach astronomy through inquiry activities because most astronomical objects are not visible during the day when class is in session.

Fortunately, the notion that astronomical inquiry is confined to the night sky is too limited a view. There are a lot of things to do and learn about astronomical objects during the day. In this section, you will learn about some of these activities, as well as develop understandings of several important astronomical concepts relevant to elementary instruction.

Spinning and Speeding through Space

How fast are you traveling as you read this text? At first, this may appear to be a trick question, especially if you are seated. Even if you appear to be motionless relative to your surroundings, you can still be moving, providing your surroundings are moving with you. For example, the earth and everything in or on it (including the atmosphere and clouds) spins on its axis once in approximately 24 hours. Considering that the earth is about 25,000 miles in circumference at its equator, an otherwise motionless person on the equator travels approximately 25,000 miles in 24 hours. Do the math and you will see that this works out to more than 1,000 miles per hour!

25,000 miles/24 hours = 1,042 miles per hour

Few of us live at the equator, so this calculation must be adjusted for more temperate latitudes. For example, consider a position halfway to the North Pole from the equator (45 degrees latitude), say, Salem, Oregon. The circumference of the earth at this latitude is half that at the equator, or about 12,500 miles. Once again, do the math to see how fast citizens of Salem are spinning. If you calculated correctly, you will note that they are spinning half as fast as a person at the equator, or about 500 miles per hour. Who would have guessed that we are so speedy?

Our actual motion is complicated by the fact that we're not just spinning in place. As you know, the earth travels around the sun once each year. It turns out that the earth's orbit is roughly circular with a circumference of about 584,337,600 miles. Considering that there are approximately 365 days in a year and 24 hours in a day, how fast is the earth traveling in miles per hour? Can you do the math?

Dividing 584,337,600 miles by 365 days yields 1,600,925 miles traveled each day. Dividing this number by 24 hours results in the number of miles traveled per hour, or 66,705 mph. And you thought you were sitting still!

How can this be? Because the rest of the earth is spinning and moving with us, we have the impression that we are stationary while celestial objects like the sun, planets, and stars are moving. This is similar to riding a carousel or merry-go-round. Your movement on the ride causes the sensation that your surroundings are spinning around you. Because of this, we can never directly observe the earth's spin or its motion around the sun from a position on the earth. Instead, we observe the resulting apparent motion of the sun, moon, planets, and stars as they rise in the east and set in the west. It took a long time for people to develop the concept that the sun, rather than the earth, is the center of the solar system. This concept developed as the result of inferences that were drawn from countless observations. We see the nature of science popping up once again (see Chapter 1 for a discussion of observation, inference, and the nature of science).

You may not be able to infer the sun-centered model of the solar system, but you can make observations and inferences about the apparent motion of celestial bodies. In doing so, you will be performing a form of science similar to that of great scientists in the past. Additionally, teaching students to make such observations and inferences will help them understand and experience scientific inquiry.

Shadow Sticks

What do you know about the sun's position and apparent motion in the sky? Take a moment to consider the question and write down everything you can think of. You have probably heard that the sun rises in the east and sets in the west. You have probably also noticed that it changes its altitude as the day progresses. What time of day is it at its highest? Is it ever directly overhead? The answer to this last question may differ from what you have heard. Try this simple activity to investigate.

For this investigation you will need a pencil or pen, a large sheet of paper and a stick (a broomstick or dowel rod 12" to 18" long is best, but a pencil will work also). A compass will make things easier if you do not already know north from south at your particular location. On a sunny day, place one end of the stick into the ground in a location exposed to the southern sky and safe from disturbance for a few hours. Take care to position the stick as close to vertical as possible.

On the north, or shadow, side of the stick, place a large sheet of paper on the ground so that the middle of the long edge of the page touches the base of the stick. Mark this spot with an *X*. To aid subsequent data interpretation, it helps to mark the cardinal points on the paper. So, you should mark the edge of the paper directly opposite the *X* you made earlier as north, the lower right corner as east, and the lower left corner as west. The paper now forms a screen on which you can trace the stick's shadow throughout the day. Make sure the paper is long enough to contain the entire length of the stick's shadow. Beginning early in the morning and at regular intervals (say, one hour) throughout the day, record the shadow length by placing a mark on the paper at the tip of the shadow. For each observation, record the time next to each mark.

At the end of the day, pull up your stick and bring your data sheet indoors. Connect each dot on the paper to the *X* mark you made earlier. Each of these lines now is a replica of the stick's shadow at the recorded time. Look at your data. When did the shadow point toward the west, toward the east? When was the shadow longest? When was it shortest? Did it ever point toward the south?

Now, let's consider our original question. When is the sun directly overhead? First, we must consider the question, what would the stick shadow (or any shadow, for that matter) look like if the sun were directly overhead? If you answered that there would be no shadow visible, you answered correctly. Do any of your data points indicate a time when there was no shadow? How does this match your prediction? Was the sun ever directly overhead? If the sun was not directly overhead at noon where you live, is it directly overhead anywhere else on earth?

To investigate further, gather a globe, a compass, a small bit of modeling clay, and a toothpick. Take the globe outside on a sunny day and orient the globe by

Shown here is the set-up described for the Shadow Sticks activity. The shadow of the toothpick can be seen over Russia on the globe.

pointing the North Pole due north. Then tilt and turn the globe so that your location on the earth is pointing straight up. For example, if you live in Kansas City, locate the city on the globe and then tilt and turn it so that Kansas City is the highest point. Now, using the modeling clay, place the toothpick on your location. If you have done this correctly, you should notice that the shadow cast by the toothpick onto the globe is proportional and in the same direction as the shadow cast earlier by your shadow stick. Now, turn the globe toward the east (counterclockwise) and notice that the toothpick shadow creates a pattern proportionally equivalent to what you observed in your daylong observation with the shadow stick. You will also notice that the shadow moves clockwise. Incidentally, the term *clockwise* was originally used to describe the motion of the shadow of a sundial, an ancient timekeeping device that works on the same principle as your shadow stick.

Back to our question of interest, is the sun directly overhead anywhere on earth at this moment? Reorient your globe so that your location is straight up. Now, pick off the clay-mounted toothpick and move it to another location on the sunlit side of the earth. Is the shadow now longer or shorter? If it's shorter, you are moving in the right direction. Keep moving the toothpick until no shadow appears. This is the only spot on earth at this instance where the sun is directly overhead! If you have aligned your globe carefully as directed, you'll note that the spot is within the tropics. Furthermore, you will see that it is closer to the Tropic of Capricorn if it is near the beginning of winter and closer to the equator if it is near the beginning of spring or fall.

If you were to repeat this exercise throughout the year, you would confirm that the sun can be directly overhead in only a relatively narrow band around the earth. This band is 23½ degrees north and south of the equator, corresponding to the 23½-degree tilt of the earth. Every other place on earth, including North America, lies outside the zone where the sun can be directly overhead. Therefore, rather than defining local noon as the time of day when the sun is directly overhead, it is more accurately defined as when the sun is at its highest point, or due south.

The Teaching Cycle

Mr. Reyes is really excited about teaching astronomy to his second graders, because it is one of his favorite topics. The first unit in the astronomy section of the teacher's guide is on the solar system.

Goal Setting

Because he has been working to make his lessons more inquiry oriented, Mr. Reyes found the encyclopedic description of the solar system in the teacher's guide uninspiring and sterile. He wanted to do something that would permit students to explore and inquire, but how could they explore with the sun and planets millions and millions of miles away?

He first turned to the *National Science Education Standards* to see what was covered under earth and space science for K–4 students. Under "Objects in the Sky," he finds the following: "The sun, moon, stars, clouds, birds, and airplanes all have properties, locations, and movements that can be observed and described."

Under "Changes in the Earth and Sky," the *Standards* read:

> Objects in the sky have patterns of movement. The sun, for example, appears to move across the sky in the same way every day, but its path changes slowly over the seasons. The moon moves across the sky on a daily basis much like the sun and the observable shape of the moon changes from day to day in a cycle that lasts about a month.

His students would certainly be able to observe motions of the sun, moon, and stars, as suggested in the *Standards,* but since school is during the day, it made more sense to focus on the sun. How could they observe the motion of the sun? More importantly, what questions could they ask to guide their inquiry on the motion of the sun?

Mr. Reyes decided on the following objectives for his lesson:

- Students will be able to state that the sun appears to move across the sky during the day.
- Students will be able to infer the apparent motion of the sun from changes in their shadow length and direction.
- Students will be able to predict what their shadows will look like and where the sun will appear in the sky later in the day.

Not long ago, Mr. Reyes had read a children's storybook about shadows to the class and then allowed them time to experiment with shadows indoors using action figures and flashlights. In this lesson, they discovered that shadows changed direction when the light source moved. This knowledge could be helpful in learning about the sun's apparent movement.

Materials Development and Selection

Mr. Reyes always keeps an eye out for good publications, like the National Science Teachers Association's *Science and Children,* that contain science teaching ideas and activities for elementary children. He remembered reading somewhere an activity description in which children inferred the apparent movement of sun from the changing length and direction of a shadow. This seemed like a good way for second graders to make observations. What objects should they use to make the shadow? In the article he had read, he recalls that they used sticks driven into the ground or the school's flagpole. Gathering twenty sticks of the right length seemed too time-intensive and using the flagpole would not allow all students to directly participate. What would be easy for each child to use but would not take a lot of preparation?

What if they observed their own shadows and had a partner measure them? They could record the length and direction of their shadows using meter sticks, but that would be too advanced for many of his students. They could make a mark on the pavement at the end of their shadow, but that might be too boring. Mr. Reyes had a better idea. The students could sketch the outline of their partner's shadow on the sidewalk. He suspected that after only a few minutes the direction and length would change enough that the shadow would no longer fit exactly in the outline.

Mr. Reyes had enough experience with Murphy's Law to try this out ahead of time. At lunchtime, he grabbed a teacher from across the hall, and she traced his shadow with chalk. His shadow moved outside the outline within 3 minutes. Within 5 minutes, the change was really obvious.

Once he knew his idea would work, he gathered materials for the lesson. Well ahead of time, he gathered 10 pieces of sidewalk chalk for his 20 students and cut out 10 small black paper dolls (each numbered 1–10) and 10 short, fat pencil shapes (also numbered 1–10). He set out a box of paper clips for attaching one tag to the shirt of each student. These would facilitate quick pairing of the students.

Pedagogy

The timing of this activity is important. First thing in the morning, the shadows will be too long to draw. Too close to noon, shadows will be too short. Midmorning is best.

Around 9:30, Mr. Reyes hands out the tags and tells the students to find the person with the same number. "That person will be your partner for the rest of the activity," he tells them. To introduce the activity, Mr. Reyes positions himself so that when the children are facing him, their shadows are directly in front of them. "Point with your finger in the direction your shadow is and hold it," Mr. Reyes instructs. He makes a quick assessment that everyone is pointing in the right direction. As he directs the students' discoveries about their shadows, his questioning is as follows:

Stand still for now, but think about where your shadow would be if you turned around backward. Point to where you think it will be.

Now turn around.

Is your shadow where you thought it would be?

Turn to the side. What happens? [shadow gets skinnier].

Point in the direction of your shadow. Is it in a different direction than it was before?

Turn to the other side. Now where is it?

Face me again and touch your toes. Where is your shadow?

Wiggle your body. What happens to your shadow? [This helps them expend energy and gives them further opportunity to explore in an open-ended way before they need to be still.]

Take two steps to the left. What happens? Take two steps to the right.

What can you say about the direction the shadow points when you move?

Does it always point in the same direction?

[Mr. Reyes takes a couple of answers, then asks the class to raise their hands in answer to the following question.]

Who thinks the shadows stay in the same direction?

Who thinks they move? Let's see.

Mr. Reyes first demonstrates the activity with a student. He instructs the student to stand with her arms at her sides. "Don't hold your arms out to the side," he says. "It's too hard to hold perfectly still." He traces around the student's feet first. That way, if she gets fidgety and moves, she can move back into her original position.

He notes to the students that he will start tracing their shadows at the head end and then go back toward the feet. This is because the head end of the shadow is furthest away and will move the furthest. "It is important to draw this as quickly as you can," he tells them. "Don't worry if it isn't perfect." Time is of the essence, because the shadow will move within minutes.

Mr. Reyes checks for understanding by quizzing other students about what they are supposed to do. He asks questions such as, "What is the first thing to do? What do you do after that? How do you hold your arms? Where do you begin tracing?" He instructs the students to stand beside their partners and spread out an arm's length apart. Then he says, "If you have a paper doll tag, face me and stand very still. If you have a pencil tag, move around to the front of your partner and first trace around your partner's shoes like I showed you."

"The students with the paper doll tag should keep their feet in those prints at all times," he continues. "Once that is done, quickly begin tracing the shadow of your partner." As the students are tracing, Mr. Reyes circulates among them and checks to make sure they are doing it right. He encourages a couple of them to speed up. "It doesn't have to be perfect," he reminds them. Another couple of students need reminders to hold still or stand straight. "Remember to keep your arms down," he tells one student.

As they are finishing up, Mr. Reyes tells them, "When you're finished, continue to stand in the same spot and hold still. You did a good job and I could see that you were careful to draw right on the edge of the shadow."

"Remember how in the activity before, no matter how you moved, the shadow stayed the same direction? Now you're standing still for a longer period of time to see if your shadow still points in the same direction. You and your partner decide if your shadow is still in the same direction." After a couple of seconds of discussion, Mr. Reyes calls on a nonvolunteer and asks whether the shadow stayed still and how they can tell. [The shadow is no longer exactly in the outline they drew.] "Raise your hand if your shadow is a little outside the outline," Mr. Reyes says to the entire class. All the students raise their hands.

"Hmm . . . let's try it again. Trade tags with your partner. The students who are now holding the pencil, remind me what you're supposed to do." The process is repeated with additional discussion at the end to give the shadows plenty of time to change. "Now, raise your hand if your shadow is outside the tracing," Mr. Reyes says. "Did you move?"

he asks one student. Then he asks a second and third student whether they had moved. Once they establish that nobody moved, he asks, "So how did the shadows move?"

Adair: I think I moved a little bit.
Mr. R: That's certainly a possibility.
Joey: Maybe we didn't draw very well.
Mr. R: That's another reasonable answer. But I saw most of you taking care to stand still and to draw the shadows accurately. So if you didn't move, and your partner drew the outline carefully, why is your shadow outside the outline now?"

He reminds them of their earlier lesson on shadows.

Mr. R: How did you make shadows change direction when we were using the flashlights?
William: We moved the flashlight.
Mr. R: That's right. Scarlet, you look excited. What do you think?
Scarlet: Maybe, the sun moved.
Mr. R: [As the students turned to look at the sun, Mr. Reyes reminded them that it was dangerous to look directly at the sun.] So you're saying that the sun appeared to move. How would that change the appearance of your shadow? What do you think, Sam?
Sam: [pointing to the sky] When we first drew the shadow, the sun was over this way. But then it moved a little over that way.
Mr. R: And how could that make the shadow move, Kristen?
Kristen: When we used the flashlights, we made the shadows move by moving the flashlight. So if the sun moved, I guess the shadow would move, too.

Mr. Reyes thanks Kristen for her answer and asks the rest of the class whether they agreed with her. After several students express agreement with Kristen, he asks if anyone had actually seen the sun move. No one had, but they were all sure that the sun must have moved, based on what they had done so far. Mr. Reyes points out that a lot of science is based on observations, what we can see, but that some science is based on what we think is happening, rather than what we see. In this case, we did not see the sun moving by looking at it, but we thought that it had moved in the sky based on our shadow observations. Scientists often do the same kind of thing when they cannot observe something directly. Mr. Reyes could have carried this discussion about observation and inference much further, but he did not want to overload students with this abstract concept. He would, however, revisit the concept in the future as he provides other opportunities for them to observe and infer.

Upon returning to the classroom, Mr. Reyes hands each student a piece of blank paper and instructs the students to fold it in half. He draws a simple stick figure on the board and then adds a shadow by sketching a straight line of the appropriate proportional length facing the appropriate direction (see Figure 9.9). He instructs the students to draw on one half of the paper a picture of themselves and their shadow.

"We talked about our shadows moving because the sun is moving," he says. "If we went out today at noon, how would our shadows appear differently?" After drawing a

Figure 9.9   Shadow Observation and Prediction Sheet

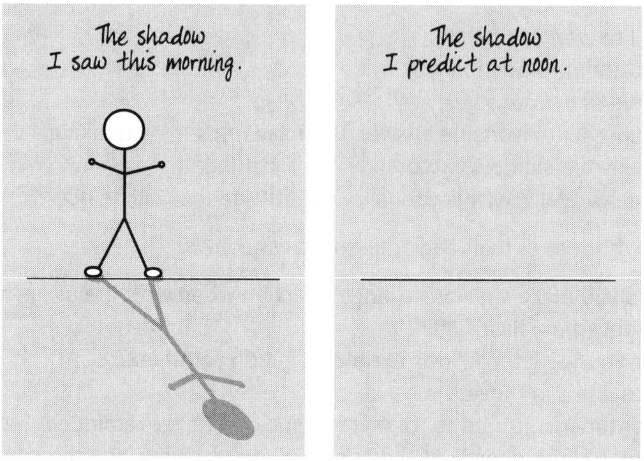

few examples on the board to demonstrate how to adjust perspective in their drawings, he instructs the students to work with their partner and draw their predictions on the other half of the paper.

When they are finished, Mr. Reyes has several students share their predictions. Then he asks how they can test their predictions. "Go outside and try it out," they suggest.

Right after lunch, the class goes back outside to test their predictions. Mr. Reyes emphasizes that the test has to be fair and asks them how to accomplish that. They have little difficulty coming up with idea of standing in the same spot and posture as before and facing the same direction.

Most of the students are excited to find their predictions had been correct, although some predictions were off. All the students are amazed at how much their shadows had changed in only two hours. As a final step to the activities, Mr. Reyes has the students compare the length of their shadow to the relative position of the sun in the sky.

Assessment

Mr. Reyes had his students fold a second sheet of paper and draw a picture of their shadow in the morning on one half and their actual shadow at noon on the other half. When most had completed their drawings, he told them to add to both drawings the sun in its appropriate location in the sky.

As they were drawing, he spoke with the students at each table asking them to compare their predictions to the drawing of the actual shadow at noon. He carried a flashlight and pencil with him as props to help students who were having trouble understanding the

> ## Just the Story
>
> **A**t this point you may also want to integrate language arts into the lesson by having the students write their own short stories based on the constellations that the various small groups created. The short stories could describe the figure that is formed by the constellation and how it represents some aspect of their own class-room culture.
>
> **BOX 9.4**

concept. He did not get a chance to talk with everybody, so he made a point to talk with remaining groups at choice times later that afternoon.

Reflection

Mr. Reyes collected all the student drawings, both before and after versions. As he looked over them, he noted their ability to record what they had seen and done, as well as their ability to explain the concept during his earlier discussions at each table. A few students had difficulty connecting the change in their shadow to the sun's changing position in the sky, but talking with them at their tables and using the flashlight prop helped them understand the concept. All the students' drawings and verbal descriptions reflected the appropriate understandings of the sun's apparent motion and how this affected their shadows. Furthermore, most students correctly predicted that their shadows would be shorter and pointing toward the north at noon. However, a significant number of students had predicted no shadow at all, believing that the sun would be directly overhead at noon. Mr. Reyes's conversation with these students had indicated that they were quite surprised to see their shadows at noon but had correctly inferred that the sun was not directly overhead, even at noon. This conclusion led to a discussion regarding when and where the sun is ever directly overhead, and the class had decided to pursue this topic further in subsequent investigations.

To add closure to this activity, he decided to make a bulletin board with some of their drawings that depicted shadows getting shorter with the rising sun. He also planned to add students' drawings to their portfolios. He thought a good extension would be to ask students to make predictions about their shadow's appearance in the afternoon and let them come up with a method for testing their predictions.

The only thing that concerned him about the lesson was that he realized he had only focused on the sun's position and not on what made its position change. Although it looks like the sun is moving in the sky, the earth is actually rotating, and Mr. Reyes wanted to be careful not to reinforce a misconception. However, he thought it was appropriate to focus on the apparent motion of the sun first and deal with the more abstract notion of the earth's rotation after they understood the first concept well.

The Earth:
Rocks and the Rock Cycle

Look along the edges of a creek, a road bank, or even a gravel pile and you are apt to encounter rocks of many sizes, colors, and textures. Rocks can be large or small, light colored or dark, and even speckled or unspeckled. As discussed in Chapter 7, humans have a tendency to classify objects, and rocks are no exception. For example, it would be relatively simple to devise a classification scheme for rocks that focused on their physical appearance, such as color, size, shape, and so on. However, this classification system would tell us very little about the rocks themselves. A more useful way to classify rocks is by the way in which they were formed. Such a classification scheme has the advantage of not only telling us something about how rocks appear to be related but also tells us about their origins. In this section, some activities will be presented that will allow you to explore the classification and formation of rocks.

Understanding Rock Formation

For the first activity, locate two or three different rocks to compare, making sure they are as different in appearance as possible. If you still have a pet rock from

These are the three major types of rock: igneous, metamorphic, and sedimentary.

your childhood, you can use that. Otherwise, it should not be difficult to step outside and locate two rocks to compare.

Look at the rocks and describe their differences and similarities (e.g., color, texture, pattern, presence or absence of crystals, shape, and hardness). Think about how these rocks must have been formed. If they are different in appearance, then they probably formed through different processes. Scientists recognize three major processes by which rocks are typically formed. Rocks formed from hot molten material (magma) are referred to as *igneous,* from the Latin root meaning "fire" (think *ignite*). Rocks formed from small pieces of other rocks are called *sedimentary* rocks (think *sediment*). Most sedimentary rock is formed from sediments that settle and accumulate in the bottom of large bodies of water. *Metamorphic* rocks form when igneous or sedimentary rocks are subjected to just enough heat and pressure to cause their crystal structure to change, but not enough heat to cause the rocks to melt. The word *metamorphic* is formed from Greek roots, including *meta-* (to change) and *morph* (form).

In nature, each of these three rock types is related to the others and, in fact, may be derived from the same materials. This relationship between rock type and formation is commonly known as the rock cycle. In the next activity, you will investigate the rock cycle using everyday materials to model the processes.

Gather the following materials for the activity:

- several crayons of different colors with the paper wrappers removed (old, broken ones are fine)
- a crayon sharpener or knife to make crayon shavings
- several 12" square pieces of heavy-duty aluminum foil
- an electric skillet lined with aluminum foil for protection
- a stack of heavy books and a hard surface

Sedimentary Rocks. Sedimentary rocks, such as sandstone and shale, are formed when sediments are transported to new locations where they can accumulate in vast quantities. Typically, the sediments are washed by streams and rivers into larger bodies of water, where they accumulate, although wind and glaciers may also transport them. As these sediments pile up, they create incredible pressure on the sediments at the bottom of the pile. Over long periods of time (anywhere from thousands to millions of years), the sediments fuse together into rock. Where do you think the sediments come from?

Sediments are simply small pieces of big rocks. As rocks are exposed to forces of nature, such as wind, running water, gravity, freezing, and thawing, they are broken into increasingly smaller pieces, which geologists refer to as gravel, sand, and silt. Wind, water, and gravity then transport these sediments to new locations, such as lakes and seas, where they may accumulate in vast quantities. Given enough time and pressure, the accumulated sediments may cement to form sedimentary rock.

You cannot replicate the natural conditions necessary to create real sedimentary rocks in your kitchen, but you can model the process. Models are useful because they help us visualize objects and processes that are not easily viewed directly. It is important to remember that models, although useful for understanding, are not exact copies of the real thing. Rather, they are simplifications that make the complex more understandable.

Select five different color crayons as models of large rocks. Using your crayon sharpener or knife, shave about two-thirds of each crayon into different piles of "sediments," one for each color. Which forces of nature does the act of shaving the crayons represent?

The next step in the rock formation process is to transport the sediments to a new location where they can accumulate. For our model, we'll use a piece of aluminum foil. You can accumulate your sediments randomly or by layering the colors. Once you've accumulated all your sediments, fold the edges of the foil over to make a square packet with your sediments completely sealed within. To simulate the vast pressure necessary to form sedimentary rock, stack a number of large, heavy books on top of your foil packet. What in nature do the books represent? While additional sediment does the heavy work in nature, you could never pile on enough crayon shavings to replicate this amount of pressure, so in this case the books do the job. After a few moments (simulating thousands or even millions of years), you may remove the books and observe the "sedimentary rock" you have created inside the foil. Note that the size of the original "grains" and the color of the "parent material" (crayon) are readily identifiable. It should be relatively easy to identify the sources of the sediments, just as it would be in real sedimentary rock.

Igneous Rocks. Igneous rocks are formed from molten material, called magma, that originates deep within the earth. When hot magma cools, it changes from a liquid into a solid, which we call igneous rock. There are two types of igneous rock, depending on how quickly the magma cools. Igneous rocks that form beneath the surface of the earth are call intrusive igneous rocks. These rocks cool slowly because they are insulated by other rocks and are characterized by readily visible interlocking crystals and minerals. Granite is an example of an intrusive igneous rock.

Magma that reaches the earth's surface in volcanic eruptions is called lava. Because lava is exposed directly to air or water, it cools very quickly, not allowing time for large readily visible crystals to form. Rocks formed in this manner are called extrusive igneous rocks. Common extrusive igneous rocks include basalt and obsidian.

To form igneous rocks from crayon, you'll need to start with molten material. In other words, you have to melt some crayons. Choose two or three crayons—you decide whether to use different colors or the same color—from which to make your "magma." Remove any paper from the crayons and place them in a "pot" made from a sheet of heavy-duty aluminum foil. To facilitate quicker melting, break the crayons into small pieces. Line an electric skillet with foil to protect it from leaks. Place your pot with the crayons in the skillet and heat until all the crayon pieces have melted. While the crayons are melting, form another piece of aluminum foil into a small rock mold. Make sure your mold sits upright without being held so you don't have to hold it while pouring the melted crayon into it. Alternatively, you could use a pair of pliers to hold the mold—just don't burn your fingers! Now, pour the magma into the mold (be very careful, liquid crayons are hot!), placing the mold over another piece of foil to catch spills. After the magma cools, remove the foil and you'll have formed a model of an igneous rock.

Let's analyze the process. The heat from the skillet simulates the high temperature deep within the earth produced by radioactivity in the core of the earth. The melted crayons, of course, represent magma deep within the earth, and the mold represents cracks and crevices in which the magma can invade. Given this information, which kind of igneous rock did you form, extrusive or intrusive? This model simulates intrusive igneous rock. For extrusive rock, you could pour your crayon magma on a flat surface to let it cool. This simulates lava being poured out on the earth's surface.

Metamorphic Rocks. Metamorphic rocks are an intermediate link in the rock cycle. They are made of either sedimentary or igneous rocks (or even other metamorphic rocks) that have been deformed by high temperature and pressure. It differs from igneous rock in that it is not completely melted—just hot enough to be pliable. As rocks are buried underneath huge depths of other rocks, pressure and heat increase, transforming the original igneous, sedimentary, or metamorphic rock into new rock. Metamorphic rock can also be formed when rocks are transported by earthquakes or other forces downward into higher-temperature regions of the earth or when rising magma comes into contact with existing rock and heats it up.

To make crayon metamorphic rocks, place a piece of your "sedimentary rock" and a piece of your "igneous rock" into a foil pot in an electric skillet. Heat them slowly until they *just begin* to melt. Notice that changes in the rock structure, especially the sedimentary rock, occur slowly at first but quicken the pace as the temperature increases. This is consistent with what happens with real metamorphic rocks. When your rocks have been deformed to your liking, you can remove them from the heat. Notice that the original structure of the sedimentary rock is still visible but deformed. This is true in real metamorphic rock, such as marble or gneiss. If you get careless or do not monitor your rock heating carefully, you may melt the metamorphic and sedimentary rock completely, leaving you with which kind of rock? This is analogous to rocks that are buried extremely deep in the earth being melted into magma and eventually forming igneous rocks, allowing the rock cycle to start once again (see Figure 9.10).

Figure 9.10   The Rock Cycle

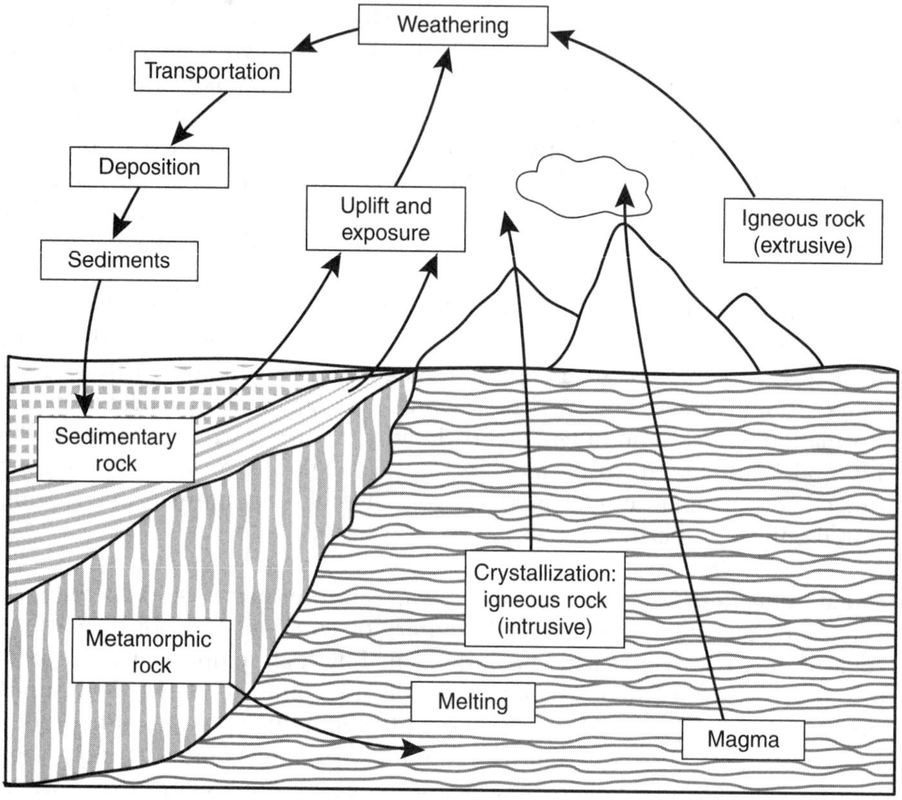

The Teaching Cycle

Several students in Mrs. Taylor's fourth-grade class had been clamoring to learn about volcanoes ever since they had seen the previous week's television special on the subject. Fortunately, Mrs. Taylor's science lessons were currently focusing on earth science, including volcanoes, so the class didn't have long to wait. Furthermore, the previously covered earth science topics, including lessons about the earth's crust and interior, magma, and lava, provided good background material for studying volcanoes.

Goal Setting

As was her habit when beginning any new topic, Mrs. Taylor reviewed her state's standards of learning before preparing for her lessons. Looking over the earth science standards for fourth grade, Mrs. Taylor noticed that students were not only expected to learn about volcanic eruptions (the topic students always found most exciting) but were also supposed to be able to identify different types of volcanoes and how they form. Mrs. Taylor's commitment to hands-on, inquiry-based instruction meant that students would need to be doing more than simply reading about volcanoes in the textbook or watching volcanic eruptions on television. She wanted her students to explore on their own. This hands-on, minds-on approach always required more planning and preparation on her part but resulted in students' developing greater understandings about the topics they were learning.

Mrs. Taylor's years of experience teaching earth science made her realize that viscosity was a key concept for understanding volcano formation. Viscosity is a measure of a liquid's "thickness," or ease with which it pours. Different magmas have different viscosities, which impact the explosiveness of volcanic eruptions and the ultimate shape the volcano takes. For students to truly understand volcano formation, they first need to understand the concept of viscosity. Therefore, Mrs. Taylor wrote the following objectives for her introductory lessons about volcanoes:

- Students will be able to define viscosity as a liquid's resistance to flow.
- Given five different liquids, students will be able to design and perform a controlled experiment to rank them from highest to lowest viscosity.
- Students will be able to describe how the viscosity of magma in a volcanic eruption affects the ultimate shape of the volcano.

By attaining these objectives, Mrs. Taylor believed that her students would be building a foundation of understanding on which additional detail about volcanoes and volcanic eruptions could be added in subsequent lessons.

Materials Development and Selection

Mrs. Taylor's introductory lesson on volcanoes included three related activities. For each of these, she had to prepare and collect specific materials. First, she wanted to provide an exciting introduction to volcanoes by having students watch a video about volcanic eruptions. Because so many students expressed interest in the Discovery Channel volcano program, she decided to watch it herself the next time it aired in order to assess its appropriateness for her fourth-grade students. After viewing the program, she decided that it would work as an introduction in that it was visually exciting, not too technical, and focused on the impact of volcanoes rather than their formation. This last point was critical because subsequent lessons were designed to help students construct their own understandings of volcano formation through simulations and hands-on exploration. Starting with a video that presented volcano formation in a didactic manner would undermine her constructivist approach to teaching. Given the appropriateness of the program, she decided to record it on videocassette to show in class on the first day of the volcano unit. To comply with copyright requirements, Mrs. Taylor wrote the date of the program on the videocassette label so she would know when the license expired and the tape had to be erased (nine days in this case).

As a way to involve her students and to pique their interest further, she asked the class to look for pictures of volcanoes in magazines and on the Internet that they could bring into class for the bulletin board. She made this request about a week before the unit was to begin, so the bulletin board would already be started when she began teaching about volcanoes. As students brought in pictures, she let them choose where to display them on the board and let them staple the pictures themselves. She was pleased to see that the bulletin board project really got students excited about volcanoes, and they were already asking questions before the unit began.

The third activity involved an investigation about viscosity. To investigate viscosity, she wanted to have students set up a race to see which liquids flowed fastest down a ramp. The necessary materials for this activity included:

- liquids of different viscosity (vegetable oil, pancake syrup, molasses, white glue, and rubber cement)
- a cookie sheet for each pair of students (to serve as the ramp)
- aluminum foil to cover the cookie sheet (to make cleanup easier)

Even though Mrs. Taylor had in mind what she wanted students to do, she wanted to let students develop their own investigations regarding the viscosity of the different liquids. Therefore, she determined not to tell students how to set up their investigations, but rather, she would act as facilitator to help them come up with their own methods (using the materials she would provide) to answer their research question about viscosity.

Pedagogy

As an introduction to the volcano video, Mrs. Taylor asked students a few questions designed to provide an overview and focus their attention on specific aspects of the program. First, she asked who had already seen the program, and when five hands went up, she asked these students to describe what it was about. One by one, each student highlighted different aspects of the program, such as the violent explosions, the destructiveness, and how "cool" the hot lava appeared as it streamed down the mountain. Mrs. Taylor agreed that the program included a lot of exciting footage that would give students a feel for what volcanic eruptions are like. She asked students to pay particular attention to any differences in the intensity of the eruptions and the shapes of the volcanoes and to be prepared to discuss their conclusions after the video.

After students had finished watching the video, Mrs. Taylor instructed students at each table to work together as a group to discuss whether they had observed any differences in the shapes of the volcanoes and the explosiveness of their eruptions. Mrs. Taylor often had students work in small groups as a way to increase participation. She found that the tactic was an especially effective way to involve students who were too shy to participate in whole class discussions. After a couple of minutes, when most of the groups appeared to have finished discussing the issue, Mrs. Taylor asked volunteers at each table for their group's conclusions. As each reporter spoke, she recorded their observations on the board under the headings of "Shape" and "Eruptions," resulting in the table shown in Figure 9.11.

As she had expected, most students were focusing on the more spectacular eruptions. She wanted students to consider the less violent eruptions, too, so she asked students whether all of the eruptions on the video were violent and whether all of the volcanoes were tall and steep. In response, several students described other volcanoes that were less steep and whose eruptions were less violent. Mrs. Taylor added these observations to her list and separated them from the first set of observations with a line (see Figure 9.12).

After completing the table, Mrs. Taylor pointed out that the volcanoes described above the line appeared very different from those described below the line. She solicited student ideas about why these differences existed. After acknowledging several students' suggestions, she told the class that the answer was based, in part, on an unfamiliar property of liquids they would be exploring after they returned from recess.

Upon returning from recess, Mrs. Taylor's students found that she had rearranged the seating into four stations, each consisting of two tables back to back, with six chairs around each table. The stations were covered in newspaper and in the center of each were containers of vegetable oil, pancake syrup, molasses, white glue, and rubber cement. Individual stations also included two cookie sheets and ten plastic spoons. As the students seated themselves, Mrs. Taylor directed students not to touch anything until she gave them further instructions.

Once everyone was seated, Mrs. Taylor directed the students' attention to the five different bottles of liquid at each station. Next, she instructed students to take a couple of minutes to make observations about how the liquids differed from each other. She further explained that, although it was all right to pick up the bottles, shake them, and even take the lids off to smell them, they were not to pour the liquids out or taste them. After a few minutes of observing, shaking, and smelling the liquids, the students were ready

Figure 9.11 Student Observations of Volcano Differences

Shape	Eruptions
Steep	Powerful
Craggy	Showers of lava
Crater	Lots of smoke and ash
Gentle slope	Fast-moving streams of lava
Smoother appearance	Less violent Less smoke and ash

Figure 9.12 Additional Student Observations of Volcano Differences

Shape	Eruptions
Tall	Powerful
Steep	Showers of lava
Crater	Lots of smoke and ash

to share their answers. As the students described the differences they had observed, Mrs. Taylor listed their observations on the overhead projector (see Figure 9.13).

After recording these observations, Mrs. Taylor told students that scientists used a different word for what students called "thickness," and the word was *viscosity.* Next, she asked if anyone knew what the word meant. When no one responded, she told them that viscosity is defined as "the resistance of a liquid to flow" and wrote the definition on the board. To see if her students comprehended this definition, she asked the class to re-state the definition in their own words. After a bit of discussion, the class agreed that the viscosity of a liquid describes how easily it pours or flows. High-viscosity liquids are thick and do not pour easily; low-viscosity liquids are easy to pour.

To see if her students could apply the definition, she asked which of the five liquids had the most viscosity and which had the least. One student volunteered rubber cement as the most viscous and another student suggested that the white glue was the least vis-cous. A third student disagreed; stating that the vegetable oil would flow fastest and, therefore, had less viscosity.

This disagreement was exactly what Mrs. Taylor was looking for. "How could we find out?" she asked. The class agreed that a test was in order. Mrs. Taylor knew how impor-tant it was for students to know her expectations, so she reviewed the procedure for cre-ating a test, even though the class had done it many times before. Mrs. Taylor asked a nonvolunteer for the first step. "Make a prediction" was the reply. Mrs. Taylor told them to work in groups of three to list the five liquids in order from the least to the most vis-cous. After each group had completed its list, she asked, "Then what?" "We need to de-sign a fair test," half the class said in unison." "OK, then, using only the materials at your desk, work with your group to design a fair test," said Mrs. Taylor. As the students de-signed their tests, Mrs. Taylor circulated to each table to check their progress, answer questions, and offer suggestions. Because she wanted her students to feel that they had designed the tests themselves, she was very careful not to give too much help.

As each group decided on a fair viscosity test for the five liquids, Mrs. Taylor reviewed the group's procedure before giving the group permission to begin. This way, she could be certain that the students' plan was safe, not too messy, and really was a fair test. In the cases in which these criteria were not met, Mrs. Taylor asked questions that directed the group's attention to the specific problems. Generally, these focused on critical issues

**Figure 9.13   Student Observations
of the Liquid Differences**

Liquid Differences
Color
Smell
Stickiness
Thickness

the students had failed to address, such as not considering what criterion to use to determine the fastest-running liquid. On this latter point, Mrs. Taylor was pleased to see that students designed a variety of measures. Most decided to separately time how long it took for each liquid to run from top to bottom of the tilted cookie pan, but a few chose to measure the length that each liquid ran over a particular time interval.

One by one, each group developed an approved procedure for the test and was allowed to begin. As the tests proceeded, Mrs. Taylor continued to circulate, offering encouragement and help as needed. When a group finished its tests, Mrs. Taylor instructed all members to clean up their workstation and begin writing a brief report of the group's results. Even though these reports were part of the science investigation routine they had followed throughout the year, Mrs. Taylor provided a worksheet to help them structure their reports (see Figure 9.14).

When the last of the groups had completed their tests and worked on their lab reports for a few minutes, Mrs. Taylor asked a few key questions to close the lesson. First, she had called on nonvolunteer students to give examples of what they had written for each section of the report worksheet. This provided her with a chance to address any confusion the students had about their reports, as well as an initial assessment of their understandings of the results of the investigation. It turned out that all of the groups' viscosity rankings were consistent, even though they had used different procedures to test the viscosity of the liquids. She took a moment to praise students for their creativity and ingenuity and pointed out the scientists use the same types of creativity and ingenuity in their work. As she had done several times throughout the year, Mrs. Taylor emphasized that there is no single way to do science; there is no single "scientific method."

Mrs. Taylor listed the results on the board, from least to most viscous. For the most part, the students' predictions had been correct, owing to the fairly obvious differences in the viscosity of the samples Mrs. Taylor had selected. Mrs. Taylor reminded students to address any differences between what they thought would happen and what actually had happened in the conclusion section of their reports. Next, she asked students to think about how this activity related to the formation and shape of volcanoes and informed them that this was the issue they would address in the next day's activity. Finally, she reminded them that their investigation reports were to be completed as homework to be turned in the next morning.

Assessment

Mrs. Taylor taught her students to use a common format (see Figure 9.14) when reporting the results of their investigations. This reduced the need to address procedural questions during class time, since once students learned to use the format early in the school year, they did not need to review what to include in their reports for each investigation.

Reflection

At the end of the day, Mrs. Taylor reflected on the effectiveness of the science lesson and jotted some notes on her lesson plan. She used these notes to help her remember from

Figure 9.14 Mrs. Taylor's Investigation Report Worksheet

Investigation Report Worksheet

Name _____ Date _____

Investigation Report

Question (Write out the question the investigation was designed to answer):

Prediction (What did you think would happen?):

Method (Briefly state how you tested your prediction):

Results (Describe what actually happened when you tried it. Use graphs when appropriate):

Conclusion (What is the answer to your research question? How does this compare to your original prediction?):

year to year what worked and what needed improvement for each lesson. In general, she felt good about the way the introduction to volcanoes had progressed. The video was an effective aid to student observation about the differences in eruptive force and shape of volcanoes. In fact, none of her students had personal experience with an erupting volcano, so without video, they would have been unable to refer to any personal experiences. However, in regard to personal experiences, Mrs. Taylor realized after the fact that students did, indeed, have ideas about volcanoes even before they had seen the video. These ideas were the result of other magazine articles, books, TV news clips, and so on that students had seen and read. It would have been informative for her to have assessed in some way her students' ideas about volcanoes prior to showing the video. This would have helped her identify any misconceptions her students had, as well as provided a set of student-generated ideas that she could refer to during the lesson.

The worksheets the students were to turn in the next day would provide a formal assessment of their understandings of viscosity. However, Mrs. Taylor already had a good idea of what her students had learned. Students' answers to her questions during the video debriefing, the procedures they had come up with during the viscosity investigation, and the discussion of their results together provided an informal assessment of her objectives for the lesson. She knew that most of the class had at least a basic understanding of the different shapes and types of eruptions of volcanoes, that they comprehended the concept of viscosity, and that they were able to design a controlled experiment. Of course, the size of the class and time limitations prevented her from verbally questioning each student on each topic they had covered in class, so her informal assessment did not provide a complete view of what each student had learned. The students' lab reports would help fill in the missing pieces when she collected them the next day.

Finally, Mrs. Taylor thought about how she would connect today's lesson on viscosity to the next lesson in which students would connect the viscosity of the lava erupting from a volcano to its ultimate shape. The textbook she used in class talked about the shapes of volcanoes but did not relate these shapes to the viscosity of magma. Mrs. Taylor wanted her students to understand that the viscosity of the magma determines the shape of the volcano. Free-flowing, low-viscosity magma tends to produce the gentle slopes of shield volcanoes, whereas sticky, high-viscosity magma tends to produce the steep, imposing peaks of composite volcanoes.

Mrs. Taylor realized that it would be important for students to be able to investigate and manipulate materials on their own; otherwise, the connection between magma viscosity and volcano shape would likely be too abstract. Therefore, in the next day's activity, students would be making models of shield volcanoes and strato volcanoes. To do this, they would need to make "magma" out of white glue (for shield volcanoes) or rubber cement (for composite volcanoes), each mixed with various other materials like sand and/or aquarium gravel. Mrs. Taylor prepared a materials list for this activity as follows:

- Aluminum pie tins (she had each student bring one in)
- Several large bottles of white glue and rubber cement
- Several grades and colors of sand and aquarium gravel from a local pet shop
- Paper cups and plastic spoons for mixing the glue and sand

She made a mental note to pick up several of these items after school because they were not available in her regular classroom supplies. Mrs. Taylor decided that she should set up a station in a corner of the room for students to work on their volcanoes.

Sign Up

BOX 9.5

It is important to monitor the students at the science station. Allowing no more than a few students to be at the science station at once will allow students to more effectively use their time at the station. You may also want to provide the students with a sign-up sheet for the use of the station. In this way, you will be able to monitor who was at the station and for how long. This information may also be added to your files for later reflection in terms of student time management.

The station would have to be located near a window that could be opened for ventilation whenever students were working with the rubber cement. The volcano-making activity would take several days to complete, but Mrs. Taylor did not want to spend class time each day for students to work on their volcanoes. The station would provide a place where students could work on their volcanoes when they had free time.

At the conclusion of this activity, in conjunction with the students' investigations today, Mrs. Taylor was confident that her students would have the necessary background and experiences to understand how volcanoes form and how their ultimate shape was related to the viscosity of magma. In addition, she knew that the experiences and investigations her students performed while learning these concepts would help them develop meaningful, rich understandings of the phenomena of volcanoes.

Forces of Nature: Weather

You are probably familiar with the fact that in winter dew often forms on windows, and, if you have observed carefully, you may have noticed that the dew always forms on the inside surface of the window and never on the outside. Can you explain why? The answer to this simple question is more complicated than it first appears and involves many important scientific concepts related to the water cycle and weather, such as cloud formation and precipitation. In this section we will explore these concepts using several activities you can perform at home.

Evaporation and Condensation

To begin our exploration of why dew forms on the inside surfaces of windows, we need to first consider how water gets into the air in the first place. You can answer this question by conducting a simple activity. First, you will need to gather some materials, including a small glass of water, a watch, and something with which to write on a sidewalk, such as a crayon or a piece of chalk. When you have collected these items, go outside and create a small puddle of water. You can make your own puddle by pouring the glass of water where you find a small depression on a sidewalk or driveway, being careful not to select a site with any holes or cracks from which the water can leak. If the weather is not favorable, or if it is dark outside, you can perform the activity indoors by pouring a small amount of water in a pan or dish. When you have created a suitable puddle, mark the puddle's boundary by carefully tracing its circumference with your chalk. What do you think the puddle will look like half an hour from now? Your answer will likely be influenced by current conditions—whether it's warm, cold, overcast, or sunny. Keeping these variables in mind, go ahead and make a prediction.

The next step is to test your prediction by observing the puddle again after an hour or so has passed. You can make productive use of your wait time by conducting a second activity related to the question about dew formation. For this activity, you will need a pot, some water, a stove, a hot pad or mitt, and an empty glass that has been cooled in the refrigerator. Begin by heating the pot containing a small amount of water on the stove. As the water heats, you will soon begin to see steam in the air above the water. It may be tempting to think that the steam you see is evaporated water from the pot, but this is not the case. Evaporated water, also called water vapor, is an invisible gas and, therefore, impossible to see. So if it's not water vapor, what is the steam that you see? You can answer this question by taking the glass from the refrigerator and placing it a few inches above the hot water (be sure to use the hot pad or mitt to avoid burning yourself). What do you observe?

When we tried it, we noticed that a kind of haze developed immediately where the hot water vapor contacted the cold glass. If you look carefully at the haze on the glass, you will notice that it consists of tiny droplets of water. The process of water vapor changing from the gaseous to the liquid phase is called **condensation.** Condensation can form steam, fog, or clouds in the air, as well as dew on the ground or other surfaces. Essentially, the haze of tiny water droplets on the glass is dew. How is the dew on the glass related to the steam you saw above the pot? If you are not certain, focus on the relative temperatures of the water vapor, glass, and air. In both cases, the hot water vapor from the pot came into contact with something cooler—cool air in the case of the steam and cool glass in the case of the dew. Water, in the form of steam or dew, forms when warm air comes into contact with cooler air, or a cool surface, but is this always the case?

Place a second glass in the refrigerator to cool. After it has had time to cool to roughly the same temperature as the first glass, take it out and blow warm air onto it using a hair dryer. Does dew form on the glass? Why not? After all, you brought warm air into contact with a cool surface, just as you did in the first activity.

Holding a cold glass over a pan of hot water is one way of demonstrating condensation to students.

If your answer to this question focused on the presence of water in the air above the pot of hot water and the lack of water in the dry air from the blow dryer, you are on the right track. But how does the water get into the air in the first place? To answer this question, it's time to return to our puddle. Observe it again, paying particular attention to its size relative to the boundary you drew earlier. Do you notice any changes? Unless the weather is very cold or very damp, you most likely observed that the puddle has shrunk significantly in the short amount of time since you first observed it. Now, we know that the water doesn't just disappear (remember the law of conservation of energy and matter), and you were careful to select a site where the water could not leak away. So what happened to the water?

You probably already know the answer has to do with evaporation. Evaporation refers to the physical change in which a liquid changes into the gas phase. In this case, liquid water from the puddle evaporates to form gaseous water (or water vapor) in the air above the surface of the puddle. You can confirm this by inverting a chilled glass in the puddle. Although it will take a little longer than it did with the heated pot of water, you will likely see dew form inside the glass, confirming the presence of water in the air above the puddle.

So what have you learned thus far from these activities? You've learned that water changes from a liquid to a gas when heat energy from the sun or the stove is added. You've also learned that this process is called evaporation. You've learned that the process can be reversed, by cooling water vapor in the air. When this happens, either by coming into contact with cooler air or a cooler surface, water condenses, forming steam, fog, clouds, or dew.

Now apply this information to the original question we posed at the beginning of the chapter. Why does dew form only on the inside surface of a window in winter? By now you should realize that your answer involves several components, including where the water comes from that forms on the window, why it forms only on the inside surface, and why it only happens in cold weather. Our answer to the question is diagrammed in Figure 9.15. How does your answer compare?

Figure 9.15   A Winter Indoor Water Cycle

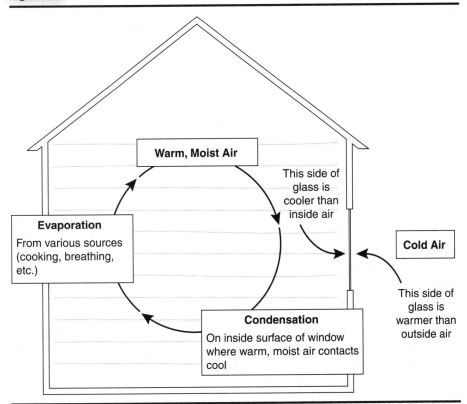

Using the Dew Point Concept to Go a Little Farther

As Figure 9.15 shows, during winter, temperatures inside a house are typically warmer than those outside. The window may be thought of as a sort of bridge between the inside and outside temperatures. Because of its conductive properties, the window's inside surface is cooler than the air temperature inside the house, while its outside surface is a little warmer than the outside air temperature.

Dew, or condensation, forms when the temperature drops below the dew point. This is the temperature at which the air is holding all of the water vapor it can. Although it is tempting to think of evaporation and condensation as occurring under different conditions, this view is misleading. In fact, evaporation and condensation always occur concurrently. It is the relative rates of evaporation and condensation that determine whether we observe *net* evaporation (shrinking puddles) or *net* condensation (dew formation). At the dew point, the rates of evaporation and condensation exactly balance. If the air temperature is raised above the dew point, the balance is shifted in favor of evaporation. If it is lowered below the dew point, it is shifted in favor of condensation and dew forms.

Because the outside temperature of our winter window is higher than the outside air temperature, the rate of evaporation is higher than condensation. Therefore, no dew can form. The temperature of the inside surface of the window, however, may be lower than the dew point of the air inside the house, allowing dew to form.

You may well ask that if this is the case, why do we not typically see the process reversed in air-conditioned homes in the summer? In this case, the air temperature inside the house is cooler than the outside temperature. Heat conducted through the window would result in an inside window surface warmer than the inside air temperature and an outside window surface temperature cooler than the outside air. If this were all there were to it, we would expect to see windows in air-conditioned houses dew up on their outside surfaces during the summer. But this is not typically the case.

It turns out that the dew point (the temperature at which air is saturated with water vapor) does not occur at a fixed temperature. Instead, it falls along a sliding scale, relative to the humidity of the air. The lower the humidity, the larger the difference between the air temperature and the dew point. The temperature difference between air-conditioned air and outside air is seldom greater than 25°F in most of the United States. This combined with the relatively low humidity of hot summer days means that the dew point is not reached and no condensation forms. On the other hand, winter differences between inside and outside temperatures are typically much greater (on the order of 40°F or more), allowing the dew point to be reached.

The Water Cycle

The water cycle is the natural cycle in which water continually leaves the earth's surface through *evaporation* and returns to the earth's surface through condensation and precipitation. These processes are driven by the wide variety of temperatures on earth. Just like there is a variety of temperatures in your house, different places on earth experience different temperatures, depending largely on the amounts of solar energy they receive and the various rates at which different materials heat and cool. Places that are relatively warm experience net evaporation. When the resulting water vapor comes into contact with air or surfaces whose temperatures are below the dew point, net condensation occurs. The condensation is typically deposited onto the earth's surface in the form of dew, rain, snow, and so on, and the cycle continues.

The water cycle is critical for life on earth, because it is the primary mechanism by which water is transported. Without it, water would be much less available to organisms living on land. A typical water cycle is depicted in Figure 9.16, but there are many variations that could be included. For example, evaporation

Figure 9.16   An Example of a Water Cycle

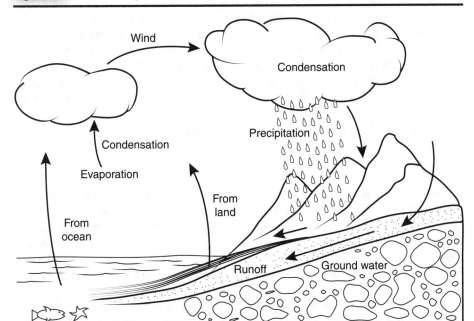

from large bodies of water such as oceans and lakes is not the only source of water vapor. Other sources include evaporation from smaller bodies of water, such as streams and puddles. Even plants and animals are sources of water vapor. Plants release water through pores in their leaves (a process called transpiration) and animals release water through exhalation and perspiration.

It can also be informative to depict the water cycle on a smaller scale. For instance, you could construct a water cycle for your house. Consider the many sources of water inside your house, the different places where net evaporation and condensation might occur, as well as ways in which water might leave your house. Put all of these into a diagram and you'll have your own water cycle.

The Teaching Cycle

Ms. McNall teaches third grade in an inner-city school in the Boston area. The majority of her students are from low-income, often single-parent, families. This is true for the school in general, where greater than 65 percent of the students are enrolled in the reduced/free lunch program. Additionally, several of her students are designated ADD (Attention Deficit Disorder) and have difficulty focusing on a task for more than a few minutes. These factors combine to create a class that is significantly behind national norms in reading comprehension and language skills, and all of them crave Ms. McNall's attention.

With these challenges and maybe even because of them, Ms. McNall loves teaching her students. Rather than seeing them as "problem children," she views their behavior and learning difficulties as challenges and opportunities for her to make a real difference in their lives. She has made a concerted effort to make her class an emotionally safe place to learn, and her students have responded to her care. She especially enjoys teaching science to her students, because she has found that hands-on, inquiry-based activities are a great way to expend their excess energy and enthusiasm.

Goal Setting

Ms. McNall is in the middle of reorganizing her science program. During the previous summer, she had attended an in-service sponsored by her district that focused on science instruction. Specifically, the workshop had introduced her to one of the science education reform documents, *Benchmarks for Science Literacy,* and had stressed the importance of using it to guide science instruction in the district's schools. She was impressed by the inquiry-oriented vision of science instruction described in the document and came to believe it would be a good guide for her science instruction.

Across the district, students were typically introduced to basic concepts of weather in the third grade, including evaporation, condensation, and precipitation. Ms. McNall was pleased to see that both reform documents included standards related to these concepts for the primary grades:

Benchmarks in Science (Grade 2)

Some events in nature have a repeating pattern. The weather changes some from day to day, but things such as temperature and rain (or snow) tend to be high, low, or medium in the same months every year.

Water can be a liquid or a solid and can go back and forth from one form to the other. If water is turned into ice and then the ice is allowed to melt, the amount of water is the same as it was before freezing. Water left in an open container disappears, but water in a closed container does not disappear.

Based on these recommendations, Ms. McNall decided that she would teach her students about evaporation and condensation so that they could eventually relate these concepts to weather patterns. She wrote the following objectives as a first step in developing her instructional plan:

- Students will be able to define evaporation as water changing from a liquid to an invisible gas in the air.
- Students will be able to define condensation as water changing from an invisible gas in the air into a liquid.
- Students will be able reach an appropriate conclusion from an investigation.

Additionally, Ms. McNall believed that the lesson would provide a good opportunity to learn something about the nature of science. Although students would be reaching conclusions during the lesson, they would be unlikely to connect this with what scientists do unless she addressed the issue explicitly. She, therefore, decided to add the following nature of science objective:

- Students will be able to state that scientists use observations to reach conclusions.

Materials Development and Selection

Ms. McNall wanted her students to understand the relationship between relative humidity and precipitation. She decided on a long-term project in which students observe temperature, humidity, and precipitation patterns to see if there are any relationships among them. Additionally, Ms. McNall wanted to build a solid foundation that would assist students' learning of the water cycle, an important concept to which they would be introduced in middle school. For students to be successful at this, however, Ms. McNall realized that they would first have to understand the concepts of evaporation, condensation, and relative humidity. She knew these concepts describe abstract processes that cannot be easily observed. She also knew the importance of carefully choosing activities that would give students hands-on activities. These activities should lead them to construct concepts, help them to develop the right concepts, and reinforce the right concepts they were developing about these ideas.

She remembered a lesson she had had in high school in which the teacher used a sponge as an analogy for relative humidity. Her teacher had used it to show the processes of evaporation and condensation and how these processes were related to temperature.

By using a sponge, which is something the students were very familiar with, Ms. McNall could model phenomena students cannot see and make the abstract concepts more concrete. She wanted to show them more than the analogy. If they could not see the process of evaporation, they could at least see the products.

Ms. McNall had participated in a teacher workshop once where they demonstrated these processes with a container of warm water with plastic wrap loosely fitted across the top and held in place with a rubber band. An ice cube was placed on top of the plastic wrap. Using the sponge as a demonstration and the bowl activity, which the students could work on in pairs, Ms. McNall could prepare students for the class project of tracking temperature, humidity, and precipitation. The day before the lesson was to begin, she gathered materials: one extra-large sponge, a measuring cup, plastic wrap, rubber bands, a dozen large containers, and ice cubes.

Pedagogy

As is typical for Ms. McNall's lessons, she started with an activity to assess her students' knowledge and experiences. This is standard practice for her, because she knows that students' background knowledge profoundly influences what they learn. In this case, she wanted to build on students' prior knowledge of evaporation and condensation (concepts they had been introduced to earlier in the year) to help them develop conceptions of how evaporation and condensation contribute to weather.

She began the lesson by swiping a damp sponge across the blackboard and asking students to observe what happens. She reminded students to raise their hands if they wanted to contribute an observation. She called on volunteers, making a conscious attempt to select students who typically do not participate in discussions. As expected, several of these shy students volunteered answers, partly because of the concrete nature of the task. As usual when soliciting observations, Ms. McNall found it necessary to remind students to focus on what they can observe rather than infer. This became an issue this time as well, when one student stated that the water evaporated. She asked this particular student what he saw, rather than what he thought was happening. Next, she summarized the students' responses on the board as a means of focusing their attention on the salient points (see Figure 9.17).

Figure 9.17   Student Observations on Evaporation

Observations
Wet sponge wiped on board
Water sticks to board
Wet board is shiny
Water eventually goes away

Next, Ms. McNall asked the class where they think the water went. Most students believed that the water went into the air, but a few said that it "disappeared." Ms. McNall knew that this was a common misconception. Furthermore, she knew that such misconceptions were not likely to be corrected through superficial lessons in which students are told the "correct" answers. Instead, she knew that students needed to confront their naïve conceptions about evaporation and learn whether they actually worked. Therefore, Ms. McNall asked how they could settle the debate. One girl suggested that, if they could get water back from the air, it would show that it did not just disappear. Ms. McNall commented that this was an excellent idea, and that they would next perform an activity to see whether they could get water back from the air.

Next Ms. McNall directed students' attention to the large plastic bowls at each table. Earlier, she had instructed students to keep their hands off the bowl and materials inside it, but now she told them that it was time to use them. She instructed students to work in their table groups to make some observations and reach a conclusion about whether water could be made to reappear from the air. These groups are heterogeneous in composition with respect to ability, gender, and personalities. Ms. McNall rotates these groups throughout the year because she believes it to be important for all students to have opportunities to interact with all the other students in the class. She filled each bowl about one-third full with some very warm (but not hot) water she had prepared in the microwave in the teachers' lounge. She asked students how they might capture water that was going into the air, if indeed that was what was happening. She accepted a range of ideas, but focused on one student's notion that they could use a lid to capture the water in the air before it escaped from the bowl. Ms. McNall gave each group

A bowl of warm water covered in plastic wrap with ice cubes on top is another way of demonstrating condensation and evaporation to students.

a piece of plastic wrap and rubber band and demonstrated how to fashion a cover from these materials. She emphasized that the cover should be loose so that it could sag a bit in the middle. Next, she gave each group three ice cubes to place on the lid. They were to observe what happened and record their observations.

Before the students began their work, Ms. McNall called on a student to summarize the directions for the activity as a check for understanding. While students were doing this, she circulated to address questions and help those who needed assistance in setting up their materials.

It did not take long for students to notice that water was forming on the underside of the plastic wrap. As she circulated to each table, Ms. McNall encouraged students to look carefully at where the water was forming and what it was doing. She also asked each group to summarize their notes into a written statement about what they had observed. After students had accomplished this, she called on a member of each group to share their observation statements. As the students did this, it became clear that all of the groups had observed water forming on the underside of the plastic wrap. The water began as small droplets, which then ran down the plastic to the low spot formed by the weight of the ice cubes and dripped back into the water in the bowl.

Ms. McNall asked the class where the water on the underside of the plastic wrap came from. Several students suggested it came from the air inside the bowl, but a few pointed out that a small puddle of water formed where the ice cubes were melting and that this may have leaked through the wrap. Ms. McNall asked each group to brainstorm ways that they could test whether this was the case. Some groups suggested turning the containers upside down to see if any water leaked through. These students first had to dump the ice in the sink and dry the plastic so they could tell if any water leaked through. Other students suggested that they could try placing the plastic wrap and ice over a bowl with no water. When Ms. McNall asked them to explain their reasoning, a volunteer explained that if water showed on the underside of the plastic stretched over an empty bowl, it could only come from the ice. Students who wanted to try this poured the water in their bowls down the drain. They then placed a new plastic cover and ice over the empty bowl to see if any water leaked through.

When the groups had finished their testing, Ms. McNall asked a student from each group to report which test they had performed and the results. She was careful to ask a different student to report than had reported the first time. None of the students had observed any water leaking through the plastic. While the results were being reported, she summarized them on the board:

What happened:

1. No water leaked through when the bowl was turned upside down.
2. No water appeared on the underside of the plastic in the empty bowl.

"So, what do you conclude—did the water leak through the plastic?" "No" was the consistent answer from the students she called on. "And why did you conclude this?" She called on several students to offer their reasons, ending the discussion when she was certain that the students were basing their conclusions on the results of their tests.

Experience had taught Ms. McNall that it was always important to revisit the main concept she wanted students to learn from each activity. It was all too easy for students to focus on the activity itself and miss the purpose for which it was done. She wanted to be sure that her students focused on the condensation of the water on the cold plastic wrap, rather than the observation that water cannot seep through the plastic wrap. So she asked a question to focus their attention on the reason they performed the tests.

"Now I want you to use your observations about the water and the plastic wrap to reach a conclusion, much as scientists use their observations to reach conclusions. If the water did not leak through the plastic, what does this tell you about where the water came from that appeared underneath the plastic covering of the bowl of warm water?" To make this question more concrete, she directed students' attention to her plastic wrap covered bowl of warm water and carried it around for students to see the water that had formed on the underside of the wrap. Ms. McNall knew that some students would be very quick to answer the question, not allowing students who were slower the time they needed to relate the results of the activity to her question. Therefore, instead of answering out loud, she instructed students to discuss possible conclusions as a group.

Assessment

Furthermore, because she wanted to assess each student's understanding individually, Ms. McNall instructed students to write their group's conclusion on a sheet of paper. While the ideas the students would be writing about were shared and discussed by the group, the wording would come from each individual student. Ms. McNall knew that reading individual responses would provide her with critical information as to whether each student was "getting it." Ms. McNall circulated to each group, checking to see that they were on the right track and asking key questions to those groups that were having trouble.

When everyone had finished writing, Ms. McNall had a member of each group share his or her group's conclusion. These were discussed by the class until consensus was reached that their investigations indicated that water moved from the warm water into the air in the bowl, and then from the air back into water on the cool plastic wrap. Ms. McNall commended her students for their work and then wrote the following definitions on the board:

Evaporation: water changing from a liquid to an invisible gas in the air

Condensation: water changing from an invisible gas in the air into a liquid

Ms. McNall knew that these two concepts and terms would be used in subsequent lessons on cloud formation and weather, so she wanted her students to gain some familiarity with these terms. Therefore, she instructed students to write these definitions on their conclusion sheets. Next, she asked each student to use the word *evaporation* in a sentence describing what happened to the water she wiped on the blackboard at the beginning of class. After students had finished writing, she asked them to answer one final question, which she wrote on the board: "What do scientists base their conclusions on when they do investigations?"

Reflection

Later that day, after school was over and the students had all left, Ms. McNall took a few moments to reflect on the evaporation/condensation lesson. First, she considered the major parts of the lesson. She had assessed students' prior knowledge about evaporation with the initial activity of wiping the wet sponge across the blackboard. The subsequent inquiry-oriented activities related to condensation provided students with opportunities to test their own ideas and to interpret the results. Additionally, Ms. McNall was pleased that she was able to provide students with opportunities to explore the concepts of evaporation and condensation before she gave them the specific terms and definitions. All in all, she believed that the lesson was structured appropriately and that students had responded well to it.

However, had they actually learned anything? To answer this question, Ms. McNall looked at the conclusion sheets each student had turned in. The first part of this assignment was a brief conclusion in each student's own words about whether the water appearing on the underside of the plastic wrap in the condensation activity had seeped through or whether it had come from the air within the bowl.

Most students appropriately concluded that the water had not seeped through the plastic, based on the results of the two activities the class had performed to test this. Ms. McNall was not surprised that most of the class performed this task well because the students had worked in groups to reach the conclusion and she had helped groups that were having trouble. However, in reviewing students' written responses, she identified five students who had difficulty putting the conclusion into words. Additionally, two other students did not connect their conclusions to the results of their investigations. Ms. McNall noted that she would need to spend some extra time with these students the next day to make sure that they understood the purpose of the condensation activities and why the class had reached the conclusion that it did.

Next on the assignment were the definitions of evaporation and condensation. That everyone had copied these correctly came as no surprise to Ms. McNall because from the beginning of the year she had emphasized the importance of carefully writing the definitions of new terms. Students were able to apply the term *evaporation* in a sentence about what happened to the water on the board at the beginning of the lesson as well. However, most of these sentences were superficial, such as:

The water on the board evaporated.

In these sentences, students simply stuck in the word *evaporation*. Unfortunately, this did not provide Ms. McNall with the information she needed to assess whether students understood the concept of evaporation and were able to apply it. She realized that this problem was created by her need to rush the lesson a bit at the end because it was running long. She had forgotten to instruct students to explain what they meant by evaporation in their responses. Realizing this omission, Ms. McNall determined to call on a few students to explain what they meant by these sentences when she reviewed today's activities at the beginning of the next day's science lesson. Thinking of this reminded her that she would need to get a sponge for tomorrow's science lesson, which would use a sponge as an analogy of the water-holding capacity of the air to build on students' understandings of evaporation and condensation and would allow her to introduce the concept of precipitation.

Finally, she looked at students' answers to the question, "What do scientists base their conclusions on when they do investigations?" The purpose of this question was to help her assess students' understandings of the concept that scientific conclusions are often based on observation. Based on the answers they provided, most students appeared to understand this concept. Their answers included discussions about scientists making observations, predicting and trying things out, and doing experiments. All of these reflected at least some understanding of the concept that science is based, in part, on data. Although her students' answers were technically correct, Ms. McNall was concerned that they did not emphasize the observational aspect of reaching conclusions in science to the exclusion of inference. Therefore, she determined to revisit the importance of inference in reaching conclusions in science in a subsequent lesson.

Summary

In this chapter you were introduced to the study and teaching of earth science. You explored some basic concepts developed by earth scientists from their investigations of the characteristics of rocks and the earth's interior, the far reaches of space, and the impact and workings of weather. In addition to providing background content knowledge, we hope the chapter has given you lots of ideas for teaching earth science in an engaging, inquiry-oriented manner.

Hopefully, this brief introduction to earth science will inspire you to learn more about this fascinating topic. The books listed at the end of the chapter have been specifically selected to provide background information and activities related to teaching the earth science topics of astronomy, geology, and weather. Hopefully, you'll be able to add many of these books to your personal library. Regardless of whether you are able to obtain some or all of these books, we certainly hope that you will continue to observe and question the world around you. In so doing, you will be modeling two of the most important characteristics of science to your students as you develop a deeper understanding and appreciation of the earth and its position in space and time.

Suggested Literature Connections

Snowflake Bentley by Jacqueline Briggs Martin and Mary Azarian, Houghton Mifflin Co., Boston, 1998.

This biography of Wilson Bentley describes his fascination with snowflakes and documents his life work of photographing snowflakes. Included in the text of this book is a clear description of the water cycle and how snowflakes are formed.

Weather Report edited by Jane Yolen, Boyds Mills Press, New York, 1993.

This collection of poems about weather celebrates the work of over three dozen poets. As an assessment activity have students identify poems that deal with each part of the water cycle or have them pick a poem that best illustrates the weather they are experiencing on that particular day.

The Big Rock by Bruce Hiscock, Aladdin Library, New York, 1999.

Trace the development of a big rock from a molten stone to a granite rock in a present-day forest. The rock cycle, timelines, and succession are other topics that can be developed with this richly illustrated book.

The Sun's Day by Mordicai Gerstein, Harper-Collins Children's Books, New York, 1989.

This happily illustrated book follows the passage of time through a day and illustrates children's activities as the day progresses.

The Story of the Milky Way: A Cherokee Tale by Joseph Bruchac and Gayle Ross, Dail Books for Young Readers, New York, 1995.

How did the Milky Way come to be? This traditional Cherokee legend tells the story of the formation of the Milky Way that was passed down through generations. Have the students research other cultural fables about the stars and sky and then have them write their own.

Follow the Drinking Gourd by Bernardine Connelly, Simon & Schuster, New York, 1997.

Based on the traditional American folk song "Follow the Drinking Gourd," this story recounts the daring adventures of a young girl and her family as they use the "Drinking Gourd" (the Big Dipper) as a navigational aid to help them escape slavery in the Deep South.

40 Nights to Knowing the Sky: A Night-by-Night Skywatching Primer by Fred Schaaf, Owl Books, New York, 1998.

This book offers a simple, interactive, step-by-step program for new skywatchers of all ages. Starting with simple instructions on learning one's way around the night sky and progressing to more challenging concepts, each of the forty activities takes the reader to a deeper level of knowledge and understanding of the night sky.

Nightwatch: A Practical Guide to Viewing the Universe by Terence Dickinson with Timothy Ferris, Firefly Books, Toronto, Canada, 1998.
Nightwatch is a well-illustrated handbook for the beginning astronomer. Terence Dickinson covers most of the problems beginners face, starting with the fact that the night sky does not look the way a modern city-dweller expects. He discusses how to find planets and constellations, how to choose binoculars and telescopes, how to pronounce the names of stars and constellations, and why the harvest moon looks especially bright. Dickinson's star charts will help the beginner find particular stars and constellations.

Keepers of the Night by Michael J. Caduto and Joseph Bruchac, Fulcrum Publishers, Golden, CO, 1998.
This well-illustrated book combines Native American wisdom and science to teach children about the night sky and the outdoors. The authors feature eight carefully selected Native American stories, scientific explanations, and hands-on activities to teach lessons about the natural world.

Transcendent Themes

Quick . . . name the first three science topics that you can think of off the top of your head! Your list might include topics such as plants, animals, electricity, digestion, the solar system, rocks and minerals, volcanoes, evaporation, forces and motion, and ocean or desert habitats. Most likely, the items on your list could be categorized as life, physical, earth, or space science. These are the traditional areas that are most often considered scientific disciplines and are the content areas we discussed in previous chapters. However, there are other important ideas that can and should be taught in a science program that do not fall within the exclusive domain of any one science discipline and can in fact be taught in all of them.

Nature of science, science as inquiry, common or unifying themes, and science and technology are all content areas that are considered important components of any science curriculum. In Chapters 1 and 2 we discussed the nature of science and inquiry as content and suggested how they should be taught in the science classroom. These concepts should be explicitly included within the instruction of the major science disciplines in a curriculum.

The *National Science Education Standards* and the AAAS *Benchmarks* have also identified several common themes and unifying concepts as content to be taught throughout a student's K–12 science education. These are not the standard concepts that one thinks about as science content. They include transcendent themes such as:

- Form and function
- Systems
- Change and constancy
- Scale
- Models

These themes are important ideas that help connect, explain, and complement the other science disciplines. Your students will need to have an understanding of them in order to have a better understanding of the other science content areas.

Right now, you might also be thinking, "Oh, no! Not more content to teach!" but look over the list again. You will see that these concepts are also components of many other science content areas. For instance, systems are discussed in chemistry, astronomy, physics, and biology when studying energy systems, the digestive system, the solar system, ecosystems, and weather systems. You may recall studying models while learning about cells, atoms, and gravity. Life cycles, water cycles, and rock cycles all illustrate patterns of change. They are referred to as common themes or unifying concepts because they are integral parts of many different science units. They are most often taught in conjunction with these other topics and not as exclusive units. The *National Science Education Standards* reinforce this integrated instruction by presenting the same K–12 standards for the unifying concepts suggesting that they be taught in conjunction with the other grade-appropriate content areas. Consider the three science topics you named at the beginning of this chapter. Can you connect any of these themes with your topics? Most likely, a particular theme is repeated in all three of your topics. By highlighting these common ideas while teaching other science disciplines, you not only help your students develop a better understanding of them, but you are also making important connections between what often seem to be unrelated and disconnected science concepts.

Teaching Transcendent Themes

Go back and review the lessons in the last three chapters. Can you identify how and where transcendent themes were incorporated into the lessons? It is important to point out that although we often use themes such as models, change, systems, nature of science, or inquiry to teach other science concepts, the themes themselves were not being taught in these lessons. There were no specific student objectives or assessment plans for the learning of these themes in the lessons. Remember, just as with any other science concept, the teaching of transcendent themes should be explicitly planned for, taught, and assessed.

In the next sections of this chapter we will revise lessons from previous chapters to illustrate how the teaching of transcendent themes can be woven through several science disciplines and taught in conjunction with a variety of topics to students in different grade levels. In each example, the basic lesson will remain the same and all of the components of the teaching cycle will still be employed. The lessons will be modified to also include the teaching of a particular theme.

Models

Models are representations of something else. They can present a physical, mathematical, or conceptual example for an idea, process, phenomenon, or object. Throughout your life, you have used models to help make sense of the world and learn new things. You could consider a lot of the toys you played with as a child as models of real objects, such as stuffed animals, action toys, spaceships, toy trucks, or ovens. You may have built replicas of real things by making models of airplanes, trains, or houses. Look around the room you are sitting in right now. Can you identify any models? Do you see any artificial flowers or plants, sculptures, photographs, drawings, or posters of real places, people, or things or clocks that represent time passing? Do you have any souvenirs from trips that are small versions of a landmark like the Statue of Liberty or the Washington Monument? All of these things are models of something else.

As we are writing this page, a little girl has walked into the room. She is about 6 years old, with brown eyes and long, black hair that is pulled back in a ponytail. Her freckled face is smiling, revealing a grin with two missing front teeth. She is wearing jeans and a yellow t-shirt and is bouncing a big red ball. Draw a picture of the little girl we just described. Your picture is a model of how you imagined the little girl to look from the description we gave you. You designed it from the evidence we provided. You probably included details that reflect fine points about the little girl that would distinguish her from other

The toy plane is one example of a model. In this case, it is a model of a real airplane. The teddy bear is another example of a model. It can also be considered a model of a real bear.

children, but it is a two-dimensional line drawing of a three-dimensional, living person and not the real thing. If you had some clay, you could build a three-dimensional representation of the little girl, but it would still be a small, nonliving version of the child. It is important to remember that your drawing is a model of your interpretation of the evidence. Even though everyone who reads this has the same written description to follow, their drawings are all probably a little different. Their conceptual models of the girl are somewhat different and this will be reflected in their physical interpretations.

Besides representing how things look, models can be used to help understand how things work. Do you remember learning about DNA in your biology classes? It was described as a double helix, and your textbook illustrated this large turning molecule in drawings and diagrams. Your teacher may have had you build a replica of a section of DNA by adding the appropriate pairings of nucleic acids. The model became a useful tool to help you better understand how this molecule duplicates and replicates itself.

You will find that using models with your own young students will help them to conceptualize scientific notions by making connections to real things with which they are already familiar. For all of these reasons, we use models to help teach life, physical, and earth and space concepts in many of the lessons described in the last three chapters.

Lessons from Previous Chapters Modified to Teach Models

Earth Science Example

Forces of Nature, Chapter 9 on Earth Science

Lesson Overview

The primary focus of this lesson was to teach about the concept of condensation as part of the water cycle. During the lesson, Ms. McNall used models to help her students learn about this aspect of the earth's water cycle. However, she did not explicitly teach about models during this lesson. To do so, she would need to modify the original lesson slightly by adding the following details to the teaching cycle.

Goal Setting

To include the teaching of models in the lesson, it would be necessary for the teacher to identify the supporting benchmarks and/or standards and student objectives for this content. The following additions should be made to the original lesson:

Benchmarks and Standards:
Benchmarks (K–2)

- A model of something is different from the real thing but can be used to learn something about the real thing.
- One way to describe something is to say how it is like something else.

Objective:

- Students will be able to compare and contrast their models for condensation to other models of condensation.

Materials Development and Selection

No changes or additions are necessary.

Pedagogy

As the students are examining the results of their plastic bowl demonstrations of condensation, Ms. McNall asks, "Have any of you ever seen this happening before?" Some students may answer that this is the same thing that happens when their moist breath hits a cold window, when their mom puts the heat on in the car on a cold day and the windshield fogs up, or when water drops form on a cold cup of soda in the summer. The teacher congratulates them for all these great examples and goes on to say their desktop experiments are models of these naturally occurring events. She tells them that models like these are often used to help people understand things they cannot see.

Later in the lesson, Ms. McNall introduces the word *condensation* to the students. Condensation is water changing from an invisible gas in the air into a liquid. Once again she refers back to their plastic wrap experiments and tells them this was a model of condensation.

Assessment

Ms. McNall needs to assess her students' initial understandings of models. This was the first lesson in which she introduced the concept of models to them. She knows she will be using models throughout the rest of the weather unit, especially during this section on the water cycle. She also plans to continue to teach about models during this unit. Just before she ends the lesson, she tells her students that they will create another model of condensation at home. She tells them to go into their bathrooms with a parent or older brother or sister, close the door, and turn on a hot shower. After waiting a few minutes, they are to observe what happens to the bathroom mirror. For homework, she would like them to write in their science journals about what happens to the mirror and whether it is the same or different from the experiment they did in class that day.

Reflection

As Ms. McNall planned for the next lesson, she decided to use a sponge as an analogy for the water-holding capacity of air in order to build on students' understandings of evaporation and condensation. This would also allow her to introduce the concept of precipitation. To continue to teach about models, she decided to explicitly point out that this sponge demonstration is a model of what happens in nature. By doing so she will not only show her students another example of a model, but she will also begin to make a connection between these classroom activities and naturally occurring weather patterns.

A sponge can be used as a model of the water-holding capacity of air.

Life Science Example

What Is Life? Chapter 7, Life Sciences

Lesson Overview

Mr. Evans is introducing the concepts of living and nonliving to his second-grade class. The idea of motion being connected with living things is considered through the use of toys and physical science demonstrations. Both of these model the motion we associate with living things. Mr. Evans could easily revise his lesson in the following way to introduce his students to the use of models to help teach and understand science concepts.

Goal Setting

The following benchmarks that support the teaching of models should be added to the lesson plan:

- Many of the toys that children play with are like real things only in some ways. They are not the same size, are missing many details, or are not able to do all the same things.

Mr. Evans adds the following objective to his original list:

- Given a particular model, students will be able to identify how it is like and unlike a real living thing.

Materials Development and Selection

No additions are necessary.

Pedagogy

Mr. Evans uses models twice during this lesson to teach his students about characteristics of life. Both the wind-up toys and the bouncing pasta in club soda modeled the motion usually connected with living things. When Mr. Evans asks the class whether the ability to move is a characteristic that distinguishes the living from nonliving, students answered that it is and he responded with the question, "So, does that mean your toy is alive?" The class unanimously agrees that the toys are not alive. At this point in the lesson, it would be appropriate for him to explicitly explain to his students that these toys were models of the way living things move. He would go on to explain that many of the toys that children play with are like real things in some ways. Next, he asks the students for other examples of toys that they are familiar with and that act like living things. The students tell him about toy trucks and cars that move and toy dolls that eat, talk, cry, and even poop! Once again, he asks the question, "But are they alive?" and, again, the students answer no. Mr. Evans explains that these only model the actions of living things, like the wind-up toys they just played with. He would go on to explain that these toys are not able to do all the other things that living things could do.

Later in the lesson, he has the students observing the up-and-down motion of pieces of pasta in club soda. After hearing the students' discussions of what they observed, he again asks, "Are the pieces of pasta alive?" The students who volunteer do not think that the pasta is alive. This is another appropriate point in the lesson to mention that the pasta that is moving in the soda is a model for the way living things move and are really not alive. Mr. Evans could then go on and teach the original lesson as described in Chapter 7.

Assessment

Originally, Mr. Evans told the students to look around their yard, neighborhood, or home at the end of the day and list five living and five nonliving things that move. To assess his students' learning of models during this lesson, Mr. Evans needs to make only one adjustment to this homework assignment. He adds the request that the students pick one item from their nonliving list and write about why it is not living, even though it models the way living things move.

Mr. Evans was particularly pleased with the science lesson because he thinks the students recognized that nonliving things can move, but there is something missing from the nonliving things that is present in the living things. He felt that use of the wind-up toys and the bouncing pasta helped develop his students' understanding of these concepts. He wanted the initial activity to be very familiar and accessible to his second-grade students. For these reasons, he felt this was a good lesson to introduce models to his students. Toys are very useful models for many science concepts and he uses them often in his science lessons. Conversely, toys are equally useful tools to teach children about the concept of models and the important role they play in understanding science.

Physical Science Example

Energy and Energy Transformations, Chapter 8, Physical Science

Lesson Overview

This lesson introduces a unit on energy transfer and energy systems to Mrs. Berg's fifth-grade students. During the lesson, she has the students describe an energy transfer system of their choice with drawings, diagrams, and written descriptions.

Goal Setting

Mrs. Berg identifies the following benchmark for grades 3–5 that supports her plans to teach the concept of models to her fifth-grade students:

- Geometric figures, number sequences, graphs, diagrams, sketches, number lines, maps, and stories can be used to represent objects, events, and processes in the real world, although such representations can never be exact in every detail.

During her planning, Mrs. Berg also decides to add the following objective for her lesson:

- Students will be able to explain how their system diagrams are representations of energy systems but are not exact replicas.

Materials Development and Selection

No changes or additions are needed.

Pedagogy

Mrs. Berg is aware that these fifth graders are already familiar with the concept of models. In earlier grades, they used toys to model characteristics of living things and made model volcanoes and model fossils. They had learned that even though models were like the real things they represented in some ways, they were not the same as the real things in many other ways. Earlier in the school year during a lesson on speed, her students designed model paper airplanes, tested them, and changed them to determine what they needed to do to make them go faster. During those lessons, Mrs. Berg took the opportunity to discuss with the students the idea that by changing their models they were able to better understand how a real airplane might behave if similar changes were made. For example, many of the students said they changed the shape of their paper airplane wings to increase their speed. Mrs. Berg showed them a video of scientists testing different airplane wing models in wind tunnels. Afterward, the students concluded that models are valuable tools to scientists.

Even with this background knowledge, Mrs. Berg was not sure if the students recognized their drawings, diagrams, and written descriptions were models, too. After all, the students' connection with models had always been with three-dimensional objects. During this lesson, Mrs. Berg had the students identify and describe an energy transfer system. Then Mrs. Berg had the students share their answers and strategies for solving the problem and what they wrote and/or drew on their papers. The students were surprised to see how each group approached the problem and how differently they illustrated their solutions. It is at this point in the lesson that Mrs. Berg brings up the concept of models. She explains that each of their representations were examples of an energy transfer system. She then asks if they thought these examples could also be considered models of energy transfer systems. Just as she suspected, some of the children immediately said no because they were not "whole" objects. Some of the other children said that they were models. When asked why they thought so, one student answered, "Because they represented an action not a noun." When Mrs. Berg asked her to explain what she meant, the student replied that energy transfer is a verb, an action, and not a thing. Their drawings and diagrams modeled how the energy passed between a number of different things. The teacher asked the other students what they thought about this idea and they all agreed that this made sense. At this point, Mrs. Berg continued with the rest of the planned lesson.

Assessment

The original homework assignment required the students to choose one of the energy transfer systems they identified during their "community energy hunt" and trace the pathway of energy forms that are involved in it. To assess their knowledge of models, Mrs. Berg added to the assignment by asking the children to also write a brief explanation about how this pathway is a model for the real thing.

Reflection

At the end of this full day, Mrs. Berg was exhausted but very pleased with her lesson. She was especially glad she took the opportunity to develop the concept of models with her students. The energy transfer diagrams were a perfect example of a different type of model than the kind her students were used to using. After reading their homework assignments, she will have a better idea of how many students made this connection. She plans to continue to weave the teaching of two-dimensional models into the rest of this unit whenever it is appropriate.

Systems

One of the most interesting ideas that the scientific study of our natural world has developed is that many of the objects we observe interact with one another.

In addition, many of the objects we use (e.g., a watch) contain parts that interact with one another to produce a particular effect. You can easily illustrate what we are talking about using your own body. Find your pulse by placing your middle and first fingers along the outside surface of your wrist (i.e., directly below your thumb and below the end of your hand where your wrist begins). Count the number of "beats" you can count for 15 seconds. Do this three times and calculate the average. Take the average and multiply by four to determine the number of beats per minute. We say "beats" because the pulses you are counting directly correspond to the beating of your heart.

Next, count how many times you inhale in 15 seconds. As you did with your pulse, do this three times and calculate the average. If you multiply this average by four, you will arrive at the number of breaths you take each minute. What you have done in the last few minutes is calculate your heart rate and breathing rate while at rest.

We now want you to stand up and do some exercises. You have the choice of doing jumping jacks or simply running in place for one minute. Once you have decided, exercise for one minute and then calculate your average pulse rate and breathing rate. The average should be the number of each per minute. These averages represent your heart rate and breathing rate after exercise. Compare the difference between the heart rate at rest and the heart rate after exercise. Do the same for your breathing rate. Which was larger? You most likely had a resting heart rate (pulse rate) of about 70 beats per minute and a breathing rate of about 18 breaths per minute. Following exercise, your rates most definitely increased for each. How much of an increase you noted is a function of your physical fitness, as is the length of time it would take your heart and breathing rates to return to the level you found when at rest.

More importantly, for our purposes, you have just demonstrated what we mean by a system. You were actually able to show the interrelationship of different parts of your body. When you exercised, you increased your cells' need for oxygen. In addition, as your cells became more active, they produced more waste, which needed to be carried away. The oxygen is carried to cells and the waste is carried away from cells by blood. As you noticed, the blood supply to and from cells was created by an increased heart rate. The extra oxygen carried in the blood was supplied by an increased rate of breathing and some of the wastes produced by the cells (e.g., carbon dioxide) were removed from the body by the same increased breathing rate. This short activity has illustrated the defining characteristics of a system. A good definition for *system* that can be used with your students is a combination of two or more parts that interact to produce one or more specific effects. In this case, the parts are your heart, blood vessels, blood, lungs, and cells. Your body, in some sense, is one large system with millions of interacting parts. Another way to look at what you observed is to say that it involved an interaction between your circulatory, respiratory, and muscular systems. In reality, the parts of the body can be further subdivided into smaller systems than the body

The inside of a watch is one example of a system, and the solar system is another example of a system.

as a whole. What constitutes the extent of a system is arbitrary, but the critical idea is that the parts of a system are interdependent and the functioning of one part affects the functioning of one or more of the other parts.

Can you think of any other systems in your life? Take a moment to make a list. Also, think about why each of the items on your list is a system. Here are some of the items we put on our list: solar system, weather system, computer system, ecosystem, and stereo system. Can you explain why we called each of these a system? It should be clear to you that systems can exist among living things, nonliving things, or between the living and nonliving. Consider your watch. We consider it to be a system. Why? If you open your watch (we advise you not to do so) or have seen an opened watch, it is immediately obvious that the watch is made of many parts, all of which must function appropriately if the watch is to keep accurate time. If any one of the parts works incorrectly, the watch will run too fast, too slow, or not at all. The functioning of one part clearly affects the functioning of the other parts. The effect can be limited to a single other part or to the overall functioning of the watch.

One of the most obvious systems you see every day on television and probably never notice is the weather system. All of those wind patterns, highs and lows, and so on the weather person talks about as you wait to hear the forecast function as a system. It is the complex interaction of the parts of this system that is used to predict the weather. We do not know all the parts and/or the nature of all the interactions, which is why weather forecasts are occasionally inaccurate. You may be interested to know that the parts of the weather system have been put into forecasting models for purposes of predicting the weather. These models have all the characteristics discussed earlier in this chapter.

Just as with models, systems are among the big ideas in science that serve to connect all of the more foundational ideas. It is for this reason that they are included in this section on transcendent themes. Systems and models are not unique to any of the areas of science (i.e., life, physical, and earth and space) but rather transcend the traditional subject matter disciplines of science.

Lessons from Previous Chapters Modified to Teach Systems

Earth and Space Science Example

Solar System Lesson, Chapter 9, Earth Science

Lesson Overview

Mr. Reyes is introducing his second-grade students to the concept of the sun's apparent motion. By observing changes in the appearance of their shadows over time, students infer the apparent motion of the sun across the sky. The shadows students observe in the lesson may be thought of as a system consisting of two components: a light source (sun) and an opaque object (student). It takes both components to create a shadow—neither a light source nor opaque object can cast a shadow by itself. A few simple modifications to his original lesson would allow Mr. Reyes to teach some important ideas about systems.

Goal Setting

The following K–2 benchmarks address the unifying theme of systems:

- Most things are made of parts.
- Something may not work if some of its parts are missing.
- When parts are put together, they can do things that they couldn't do by themselves.

Mr. Reyes adds the following objective to his original lesson:

- Students will be able to explain that both a light source and an object to block the light are necessary to create a shadow.

Materials Development and Selection

No additions are necessary.

Pedagogy

Mr. Reyes knows that when people think of systems, they typically think of complex systems consisting of many interacting parts. The human digestive system, a stereo system, and even political systems are common examples of this type of complex system. When introducing primary students to the concept of systems, however, Mr. Reyes wanted to focus on very simple systems that would be easy to understand. Shadows, although not commonly thought of as systems, represent a good example of a simple system that even his second-grade students would be likely to understand.

To meet the two system objectives for the lesson, Mr. Reyes needed to get his students to think about their shadows in a different way. He accomplished this by using a few key questions to focus their thinking while they were making shadows. For instance, when Mr. Reyes circulated among the pairs of students observing their shadows on the playground, he asked, "What two things does it take to make your shadow?" It generally required very little prompting for students to respond that both the sun and their bodies were necessary to create the shadow on the pavement. Mr. Reyes followed up this question by asking whether the shadow would be there in the dark without the sun. He also asked whether the shadow would be present if the student was not there. These questions were intended to help students begin to realize that shadows are produced by a system consisting of two interacting parts: a light source and something to block the light.

Students' understandings of this concept were further developed later in the lesson when Mr. Reyes reviewed the activity during the lesson closure. Although the main focus of this portion of the lesson was to model the sun's apparent motion, Mr. Reyes also asked students to describe two things that were necessary for creating a shadow. After students had revisited the concept that both a light source and something to block the light were necessary to make a shadow, Mr. Reyes discussed the concept of systems a bit further. He pointed out that a system exists whenever separate parts work together to do things that they could not do alone. Next, he discussed some examples of systems including a bicycle, a plant, and even a pencil. Mr. Reyes asked students to name the parts that make up each of these systems and challenged them to explain why the system would not work if a particular part were missing.

Assessment

Mr. Reyes had students compare drawings of their shadows and the sun's position in the morning and afternoon to assess their understandings in the original lesson. To assess student attainment of the systems objective, Mr. Reyes simply asked students to list on their papers the two things that were necessary to create the shadows they observed outside.

When Mr. Reyes looked over the shadow drawings his students completed, he noted that most were able to list the sun and their own bodies as necessary for creating the shadows they had observed on the playground. Although Mr. Reyes was satisfied with his students' understandings for now, he realized that the concept of components of a system working together to do something that they could not do on their own was a very big idea for his second graders. Therefore, he would need to revisit the "big idea" on other occasions throughout the year.

Life Science Example

Ecology, Chapter 7, Life Science

Lesson Overview

Mrs. Bird introduces the concept of ecosystem to her inner-city fourth-grade class. Wanting to make the lesson as concrete as possible, she has the class help her construct a mini-ecosystem for guppies. The lesson involves students sharing ideas about living and nonliving components of their mini ecosystem, as well as discussion and explicit instruction on the ecosystem concept itself. To address the transcendent theme of systems in the lesson, Mrs. Bird would need to make some additions to the lesson.

Goal Setting

Mrs. Bird refers to the grades 3–5 benchmarks on systems as she begins to consider addressing the transcendent theme of systems in her lesson:

- In something that consists of many parts, the parts usually influence one another.
- Something may not work as well (or at all) if a part of it is missing, broken, worn out, mismatched, or misconnected.

The concept behind the first of these benchmarks was covered in her original objectives, which state that students will be able to list five parts of the mini-ecosystem and state how these parts interact. The second benchmark was not covered directly in her original objectives, so she added the following objective:

- Given their lists of five living and nonliving components, students will be able to discuss the negative consequence(s) of removing any of the components.

Materials Development and Selection

No additions are necessary.

Pedagogy

To address this new objective Mrs. Bird simply needed to have her students consider what might happen if specific components of their mini-ecosystem were removed. She decided to do this at the point in the lesson when students were listing the living and nonliving components of the mini-ecosystem under separate headings on the board. Once the list was complete, she pointed sequentially to each item in the two lists, asking specific students what would happen if this particular item were missing. Often, after a student had answered the question, she would ask other students what they thought. The ensuing discussion allowed for a lot of student-to-student interaction and further served to reinforce the concept that separate components of the ecosystem interacted in complex ways. The students quickly began to understand that the ecosystem would not be as healthy (or support life at all) if one or more components were missing.

Assessment

In the original assignment, students were asked to list five living and nonliving items necessary for snails to live in the class aquarium. To assess students' attainment of the new systems objective, Mrs. Bird simply added the task of describing the negative consequences of individually removing at least three of these ecosystem components.

Mrs. Bird reviewed her students' assignments the following evening. All the students had adequately completed their lists of five living and nonliving requirements for snails to live in the aquarium. However, a few students had not completed their descriptions of the negative consequences of removing three items from the list. A few students included only two such descriptions on their assignment and three students failed to do this part of the assignment at all. On each of these assignments, she wrote a note for the student to see her during "choice" time, when she intended to work with the students as a team to come up with the missing descriptions. This would allow her to ascertain whether the students did not understand the task, the concept of interdependence and interaction of individual components of an ecosystem, or had simply forgotten to do this part of the assignment.

Physical Science Example

Energy and Energy Transformations, Chapter 8, Physical Science

Lesson Overview

This lesson introduces a unit on energy transfer and energy systems to Mrs. Berg's fifth-grade students. During the lesson, she has the students describe an energy transfer system of their choice with drawings, diagrams, and written descriptions. Before the lesson ends, Mrs. Berg takes her students on an energy hunt through the neighborhood.

Goal Setting

To include the teaching of systems into this lesson, Mrs. Berg refers to the following benchmarks about systems for grades 3–5:

- In something that consists of many parts, the parts usually influence each other.
- Something may or may not work as well (or at all) if a part of it is missing, broken, worn out, mismatched, or misconnected.

She decides to add the following new objective to her plan:

- Students will be able to predict what might happen to a system if one or more parts of it are changed.

Materials Development and Selection

No changes or additions are necessary.

Pedagogy

Mrs. Berg knows the students are already familiar with the concept of systems. In earlier grades, they learned that systems are made of parts and that a system may not work properly, or at all, if one or more of its parts are missing. This year she has been developing the idea that a system can also be affected if one of its parts was modified or changed in some way. She feels it is appropriate for her to review this aspect of systems again within this last physical science unit on energy systems. During the lesson, Mrs. Berg has the students consider all the types of energy that are involved in making an appliance work and then asks them to describe all the different transfers of energy involved in making it work. After the students present explanations of their energy pathways to their classmates, Mrs. Berg explains that their solutions are examples of energy transfer systems. In the original lesson, she goes on to discuss energy systems, but in this modified lesson she would first take a moment to discuss systems with her students. She reminds her students that they have discussed systems in the past and asks them what they remember learning about them. They tell her that systems are made up of parts that work together to produce some effect. Then she asks them if what they just described are examples of systems. They all agree that these are systems because they are made of a number of different parts or steps working together to accomplish a task. She then asks them what they think would happen if one part of their system is removed. The students say that the pathway would be interrupted and most think the system would probably stop. Next, she asks them what they think would happen to the system if one of the parts just changed in some way. The students ask her what she means by "changed." She uses a television as an example. Many of her students also use a television for their pathway example. Mrs. Berg asks what would happen to the system if the sound went off on a television. How would the system be affected, would it work in the same way, would it be somehow changed, or would it stop entirely? The students all have their opinions about what would happen to the system as a result of this change. Most agree that it would still work but not as well without the sound. One girl in the class says that this system would all but stop for her grandmother because her grandmother has a visual disability and depends on the sound to help her understand what is going on. After more discussion, the students agree that this slight change in the system could greatly alter the system in general.

Assessment

Their original homework assignment for that night was to choose one of the energy systems they identified on their energy hunt through the neighborhood and trace the pathways of energy forms that are involved in it. She modified this assignment to include an assessment of their understanding of systems. After describing their energy pathways, she asked them to choose one part of the system and describe how it might be changed in some way. They then needed to write a prediction of what they thought would happen to the entire energy transport system as a result of this change.

Reflection

At the end of this full day Mrs. Berg was exhausted but very pleased with her lesson. She was looking forward to receiving the students' homework assignments. She was curious to see how they changed a part of their systems and how this change would affect the entire system. She thought the students might need more concrete examples of the effects of change within a system. She remembered she had some old household appliances such as a mixer, toaster, hair dryer, blender, alarm clock, and a radio in her garage that she was planning to sell some day in a yard sale. Instead, she decided to bring them to school. After examining the appliances, she would ask the students to pick one thing to change, make a prediction about how this change would affect the system, and then let them modify their appliance to see what actually happens.

ERIC Tutorial

The ERIC database is one of the most comprehensive educational information sources in the world, containing more than 1 million abstracts of documents, lesson plans, and journal articles on educational research and practice. ERIC, an acronym for Educational Resources Information Center, was begun in 1966 and is supported by the United States Department of Education, Office of Educational Research and Improvement, and administered by the National Library of Education.

New abstracts are added monthly to the database including extensive collections of literature located in education-related journals and magazines. ERIC also has abstracts from lesson plans, conferences, and published research. Some articles are available in full text from ERIC's document supplier, the ERIC Document Reproduction Service (EDRS), and may be ordered online through the ERIC website. Many articles can also be located in your university library.

Items in the database include an ERIC assigned number, title, author's name, publication data, journal title, abstract, major and minor keyword descriptors, type of document, clearinghouse number, International Standard Serial Number (ISSN), language of document, and ERIC issue identifier (see Figure A.1).

ERIC lesson plans can provide new ideas, inspirations, and guidance as you prepare for daily instruction. However, it's important to remember that no one knows your students, curriculum, and classroom situation as well as you do, so be prepared to modify any lesson plans found in the ERIC database to fit your particular context.

How Do I Find Lesson Plans Using the ERIC Database?

Where do you begin? You can go directly to the AskERIC lesson plan archive by pointing your Web browser to http://www.askeric.org/Virtual/Lessons/. Alternatively, you can locate the ERIC lesson plan database by searching for "ERIC lesson plans" with one of the many search engines available, such as Google, AltaVista, Infoseek, or Yahoo! If several sites appear in your search results listing, click on the one with the words AskERIC Lesson plans in the title (see Figure A.2). Click on the hyperlink to get to the Ask ERIC Lesson Plan home page.

Figure A.1   An Example of an ERIC Database Entry

OBTAIN

ERIC_NO: EJ572543
TITLE: Exploring Geology on the World-Wide Web--*Volcanoes* and Volcanism.
AUTHOR: Schimmrich, Steven Henry; Gore, Pamela J. W.
PUBLICATION_DATE: 1996
JOURNAL_CITATION: Journal of Geoscience Education; v44 n4 p448-51 Sep 1996
ABSTRACT: Focuses on sites on the World Wide Web that offer information about *volcanoes*. Web sites are classified into areas of Global Volcano Information, *Volcanoes* in Hawaii, *Volcanoes* in Alaska, *Volcanoes* in the Cascades, European and Icelandic *Volcanoes*, Extraterrestrial Volcanism, Volcanic Ash and Weather, and Volcano Resource Directories. Suggestions for classroom activities using the Web sites are included. (PVD)
MAJOR_DESCRIPTORS: Computer Uses in Education; Earth Science; Information Sources; *Volcanoes*; World Wide Web;
MINOR DESCRIPTORS: Computer Networks; Geology; Higher Education; Natural Disasters; Plate Tectonics; Science Activities; Science Education;
PUBLICATION_TYPE: 080; 132
CLEARINGHOUSE_NO: SE560502
ISSN: ISSN-0022-1368
LANGUAGE: English
ERIC_ISSUE: CIJMAY1999

Figure A.2   From the search listing, select AskERIC Lesson Plans

There are at least two ways to locate science lesson plans using the ERIC lesson plan database. If you know the science discipline (earth science, for example) but don't have a particular topic in mind, you might begin with the Science link on the Lesson Plan home page (see Browsing for a lesson? in Figure A.3).

At the Science Main Index page, you may choose the science discipline that interests you, for example, earth science or astronomy (see Figure A.4).

At the next screen that you view, an alphabetical listing of earth science lessons with appropriate grade levels allows you to browse through lesson plans for your students (see Figure A.5).

If you already have a lesson topic in mind, using the Search feature might be a more efficient way of finding appropriate lesson plans. Click on the search tab (near the top of any page in the AskERIC Lesson Plan site, see Figure A.3) to take you to the Ask ERIC Web Site Search Options screen (Figure A.5). Select Simple Search Page to get to the AskERIC Simple Search screen (see Figure A.6).

Figure A.3 Ask ERIC Lesson Plans Page: www.askeric.org/ Virtual/Lessons/index.shtml

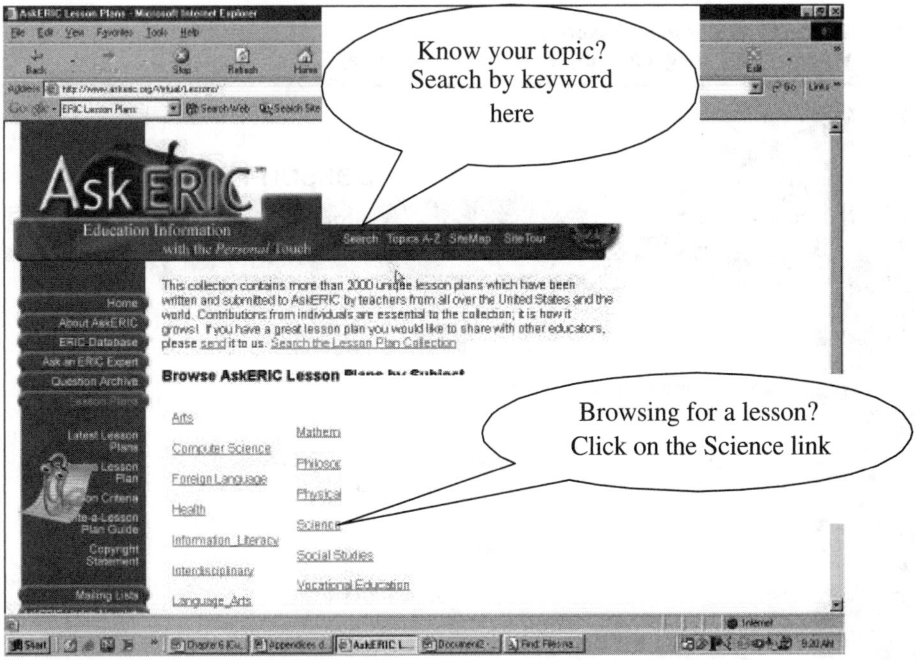

Figure A.4   ERIC Lesson Plan Science Index Page:
www.askeric.org/cgi-bin/lessons.cgi/Science

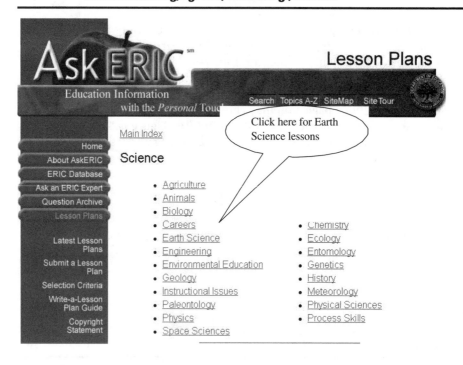

Figure A.5   ERIC Earth Science Lessons:
www.askeric.org/cgi-bin/lessons.cgi/Science/Earth_Science

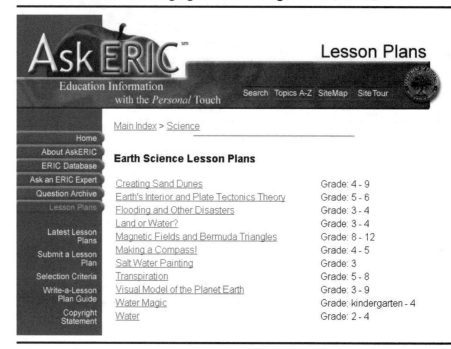

Figure A.6   Ask ERIC Website Search Options Screen: www.askeric.org/Search/

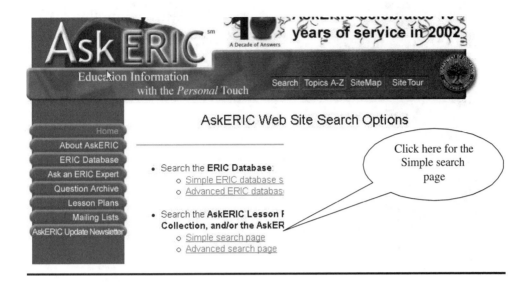

Select the resources you want to search (all boxes are checked in Figure A.7), and type in the keyword for your search. In the example shown in Figure A.7, notice the keyword *volcano*. Once the search information is entered, click on the search button. Documents that match your search term will be listed below the Simple Search screen features. Be sure to scroll down the screen to check them out. You may need to look at more than one page in order to see abstracts of all the lessons. There are thirteen volcano lessons indicated in the results of a simple search. Figure A.8 shows the first three entries.

Use the advanced search to include several keywords or phrases and to limit your search to particular grade levels. If you are interested in volcanoes, plate tectonics, and lava for kindergarten through third grade students, an advanced search would help you locate relevant lesson plans more efficiently (see Figure A.9).

Finally, consider submitting lesson plans of your own to the AskERIC Virtual Library Lesson Plan Collection. After all, writing good lesson plans is hard work—why not extend the benefit of your efforts to teachers around the world? For information on how to write and submit lesson plans, click on the Write-a-Lesson Plan Guide on the left side of the screen.

Figure A.7   Simple Search Page: www.askeric.org/Search/simple.shtml

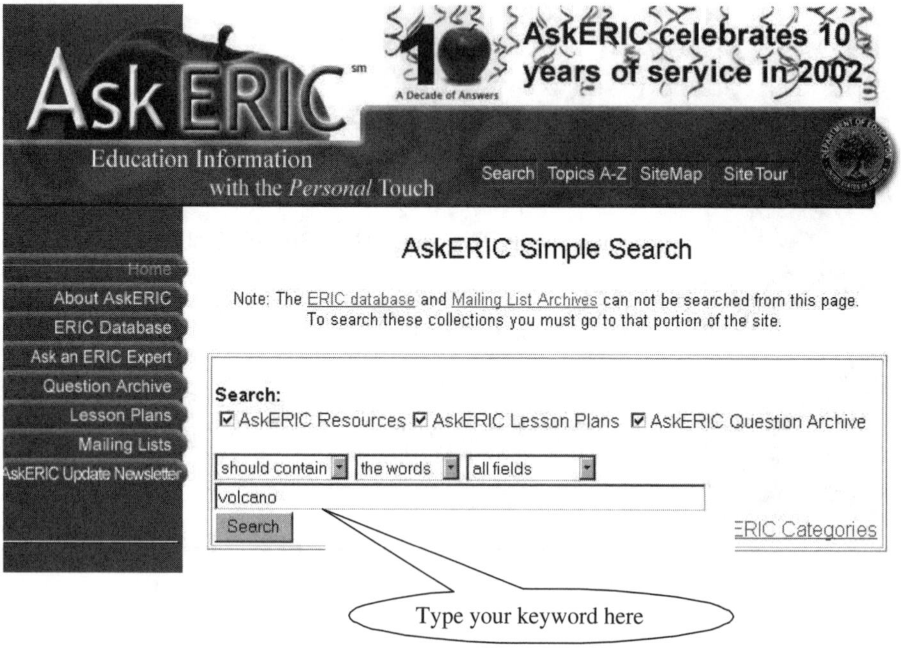

Additional Websites for Science Lessons and Activities

National Science Teachers Association
www.nsta.org/programs/laptop/grade.htm

National Science Teachers Association offers science, mathematics, and technology lessons designed for laptops at its site. The site is searchable by subject and grade level.

United States Department of Agriculture
www.usda.gov/news/usdakids/index.html

The United States Department of Agriculture sponsors a USDA for Kids Page with topics such as food-borne illnesses, gardening, backyard conservation, ecology, fire prevention, the food pyramid and weather.

U.S. Environmental Protection Agency (EPA)
www.epa.gov/teachers/curriculum_resources.htm

This site offers activities and lesson plans covering topics such as air and air pollution, conservation, ecosystems, human health, waste and recycling, and water.

Figure A.8   Documents Listed for the Volcano ERIC Simple Search

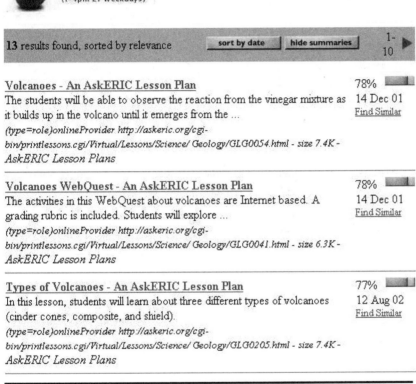

Document count: volcano (13)

Results for: volcano

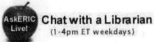 Chat with a Librarian
(1-4pm ET weekdays)

13 results found, sorted by relevance | sort by date | | hide summaries | 1-10

Volcanoes - An AskERIC Lesson Plan   78%
The students will be able to observe the reaction from the vinegar mixture as   14 Dec 01
it builds up in the volcano until it emerges from the ...   Find Similar
(type=role)onlineProvider http://askeric.org/cgi-
bin/printlessons.cgi/Virtual/Lessons/Science/ Geology/GLG0054.html - size 7.4K -
AskERIC Lesson Plans

Volcanoes WebQuest - An AskERIC Lesson Plan   78%
The activities in this WebQuest about volcanoes are Internet based. A   14 Dec 01
grading rubric is included. Students will explore ...   Find Similar
(type=role)onlineProvider http://askeric.org/cgi-
bin/printlessons.cgi/Virtual/Lessons/Science/ Geology/GLG0041.html - size 6.3K -
AskERIC Lesson Plans

Types of Volcanoes - An AskERIC Lesson Plan   77%
In this lesson, students will learn about three different types of volcanoes   12 Aug 02
(cinder cones, composite, and shield).   Find Similar
(type=role)onlineProvider http://askeric.org/cgi-
bin/printlessons.cgi/Virtual/Lessons/Science/ Geology/GLG0205.html - size 7.4K -
AskERIC Lesson Plans

In addition, EPA provides links to other sites that may be useful in planning science lessons.

Discovery School.com K–5 Lessons Plans
http://school.discovery.com/lessonplans/k-5.html

Discovery has a database of hundreds of science lessons for K–12 teachers including topics such as plants and animals, ecology and the environment, astronomy and space, and many more. The K–5 Lesson Plan page organizes lessons according to topic. Each lesson includes web links to useful resources and connections to *Benchmarks for Scientific Literacy*.

**Figure A.9   AskERIC Advanced Search:
www.askeric.org/Search/advsearch.shtml**

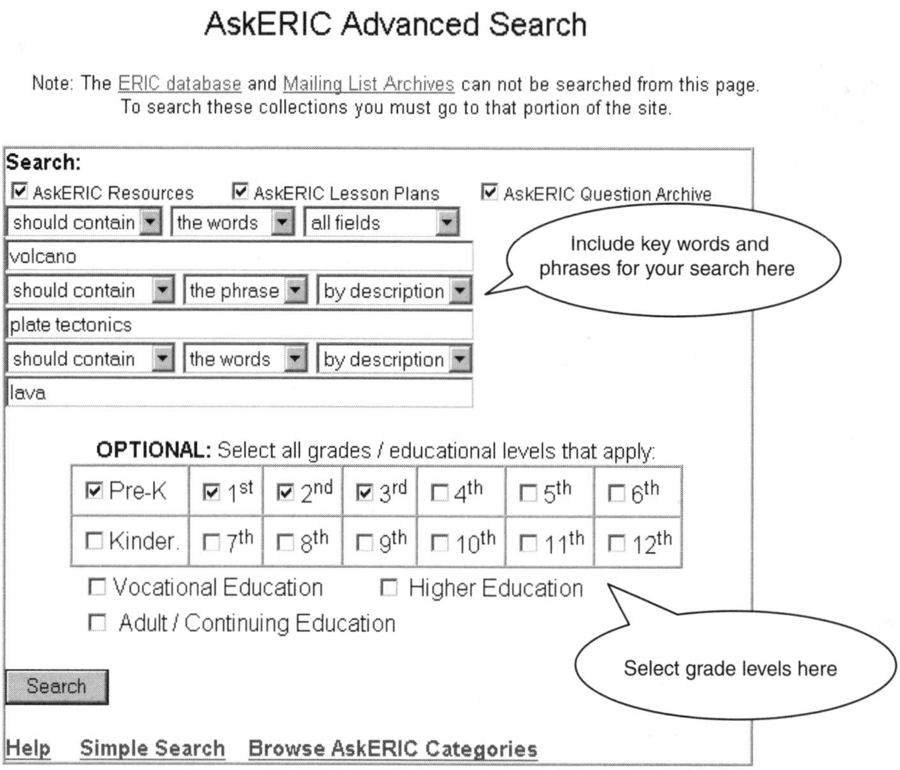

AskERIC Advanced Search

Note: The ERIC database and Mailing List Archives can not be searched from this page.
To search these collections you must go to that portion of the site.

Search:
☑ AskERIC Resources   ☑ AskERIC Lesson Plans   ☑ AskERIC Question Archive

| should contain ▼ | the words ▼ | all fields ▼ |

volcano

Include key words and phrases for your search here

| should contain ▼ | the phrase ▼ | by description ▼ |

plate tectonics

| should contain ▼ | the words ▼ | by description ▼ |

lava

OPTIONAL: Select all grades / educational levels that apply:

| ☑ Pre-K | ☑ 1st | ☑ 2nd | ☑ 3rd | ☐ 4th | ☐ 5th | ☐ 6th |
| ☐ Kinder. | ☐ 7th | ☐ 8th | ☐ 9th | ☐ 10th | ☐ 11th | ☐ 12th |

☐ Vocational Education   ☐ Higher Education
☐ Adult / Continuing Education

Select grade levels here

| Search |

Help   Simple Search   Browse AskERIC Categories

Space Science Education Resource Directory
http://teachspacescience.stsci.edu/cgi-bin/searchkey.plex
This NASA site provides hundreds of lesson plans and activities covering space, physical, and earth science topics, including lessons for grades K–12. Lessons are easily accessed using a database search engine found on the site.

Public Broadcasting Service Teacher Source
www.pbs.org/teachersource/teachtech.htm
PBS Teacher Source includes more than 3,500 lesson plans and activities on a wide selection of topics. The site is searchable by subject, topic, and grade level.

APPENDIX

B

Item Analysis

Once you have scored the items from a test or students' performance on a task, you should check to see that the item or task has been a fair assessment. The technique for doing this is called an **item analysis.** Our discussion will assume that you have given a multiple-choice test, but this technique can be used whether you have used a test with different item formats or any of the other varied approaches to assessment. Let's also assume that you have a class of thirty students. The first task is to rank-order students' scores on the test. The focus of your attention, for statistical reasons, will be on the top and bottom third of the scores, a total of twenty in this case. For each question on the test, a table similar to Table A.1 is created.

The table indicates how many of the high and low scorers (i.e., top third and bottom third) in your class responded to each of the multiple-choice item options. So, for test item 5, three of the high scorers answered with choice B and two of the low scorers answered with choice B. The "*" above the choice of C indicates which answer was keyed as correct. Having the data for each test item in this format easily allows you to note some potential problems. For example, it seems that choice D was a clear preference for those low scorers getting the question incorrect, whereas none of the high scorers selected it. This particular choice may provide you with some valuable information about your teaching and student learning. Although this rather informal "eyeballing" of trends may be useful, there are some formal analyses that you can now perform.

Table A.1   Test Item 5

	A	B	C *	D	E
High Scorers	0	3	6	0	1
Low Scorers	0	2	3	4	1

Index of Difficulty. This value tells you the average proportion of your students (i.e., top third and bottom third) who answered a particular item correctly. The calculation is quick and simple:

$$\text{Difficulty} = \frac{\text{Proportion of High Scorers Answering Correctly} + \text{Proportion of Low Scorers Answering Correctly}}{2}$$

$$D = \frac{.6 + .3}{2} = .45$$

Interpretation Guide

>.75   → Too Easy
.25–.75 → O.K.
<.25   → Too Difficult

The results of the calculation indicate that .45 (i.e., 45 percent) of the students scored correctly on this test item. Using the interpretation guide, we find that the item has an "O. K." index of difficulty. The interpretation guide is derived from the recommendations of the Educational Testing Service and it assumes that you will be grading using a norm-referenced approach, a curve. In norm referencing, the goal is to spread students' scores out across the range of possible scores. Remember, in norm referencing a student's grade is determined by how well the student does relative to the other students in the class. This decision is facilitated if students score differently from each other as opposed to everyone doing about the same. Consequently, in a norm-referenced system, a difficulty index of .50 is best because it will spread out the scores as much as possible. If, however, you are grading with a criterion-referenced approach, the interpretation guide would not be very useful. In a criterion-referenced approach, you will be comparing students' scores with an a priori standard. Depending on the question, you may expect a large proportion of students to get the answer correct. Consequently, an index of difficulty of .85 may simply indicate that you did an excellent job of teaching what you intended to teach. In fact, supporters of criterion-referenced grading would argue that your goal should be for all students to get the highest score possible, and a high index of difficulty should be viewed as a success instead of an indication that a test item was too easy. So, whether you choose to eliminate a test item, based on an item analysis, is intimately related to the evaluation approach you are using.

Item Discrimination. A second calculation will provide you with a measure of how well each item discriminates between students who score well with those who do not score well on a test. Ideally, if you are evaluating with a norm-referenced approach, you would expect the top third of your scorers to answer correctly, with none of the low scorers answering correctly for any particular item. Using the data in Table A.1, the discrimination of test item 5 is calculated as follows:

$$\text{Discrimination} = \frac{\text{Proportion of High Scorers}}{\text{Answering Correctly}} - \frac{\text{Proportion of Low Scorers}}{\text{Answering Correctly}}$$

$$D = .6 - .3 = .30$$

Interpretation Guide

$>.40 \quad \rightarrow$ Good
$.30–.39 \rightarrow$ O.K., but needs improvement
$.20–29 \quad \rightarrow$ Marginal
$<.20 \quad \rightarrow$ Poor

The results of our calculation indicate that the item does a reasonable job of distinguishing between the high scorers and low scorers on the test. Once again, the discrimination index is primarily used in norm referencing because the total calculation is based on how students perform relative to each other, an idea not consistent with criterion-referencing. If you are grading with a criterion referenced approach, item discrimination is of interest if the lower-scoring students actually do better on an item than the high-scoring students. Have you ever given an incorrect answer to a question because you knew too much? This does happen, and the item discrimination can identify such problematic questions. One other instance in a criterion-referenced approach that you would expect an item to discriminate is with respect to pretests and posttests. You would expect students to do better on the posttest than the pretest, and item discrimination should indicate that test items discriminate when pretest and posttest are compared (as opposed to high and low scorers being compared).

Given the results of the two analyses for item 5, it appears that the item does okay on both difficulty and discrimination. There is no reason to consider the item problematic or unfair. It is important to note that a test item can have a good difficulty index but a poor discrimination index. Notice what happens if you alter the data for item 5 so that four high scorers and four low scorers answered correctly. What happens to the difficulty and discrimination indices? It is important that you perform both analyses and make no assumptions based on the calculation of just one or the other.

The overall purpose of doing an item analysis is to alert you to potentially unfair test items that you want to eliminate from consideration before making evaluation decisions. Items should be eliminated for reasons of either poor difficulty or poor discrimination, or both, when using a norm-referenced approach to evaluation. If you are using a criterion-referenced approach, item difficulty will be the more important calculation. However, instead of using the guides we provided, you will need to decide on the importance of the subject matter addressed by the test item, the wording of the item, the amount of instructional time provided, and so on when making decisions concerning the retention or deletion of an item.

What about Other Types of Assessment Items?   Although the example used for item analysis was a multiple choice test, the same procedure can be used for all other test item formats as well as for projects and alternative forms of assessment. For example, if you have true–false or matching-type items, the response options are basically a dichotomy. This means instead of including many choice options in the table, you will only have two, true and false or correct and incorrect. The same would be the case for completion items.

Essays, projects, and alternative assessments present a different problem than various test item formats because they typically will involve partial credit. Multiple credit assessments are easily handled by the procedures we described. The only variation is that you will use "proportion of points earned" instead of "proportion of students answering correctly." For example, consider an individual science project on which a student can earn 20 points. You still rank-order student scores on the project. Then you calculate what proportion of the total available points the high scorers received and the same for the low scorers. The total possible points would be 200 (i.e., 10 students × 20 points) and you just need to calculate how many of the 200 possible points were achieved by the high-scoring and low-scoring students. So, regardless of assessment format or approach, the item analysis procedures can be used to further ensure that the scores you use to make evaluations of students' performance are as accurate and as fair as possible.

Determination of Grades: Additional Perspectives

Evaluating students using a **normal curve** is a formal, systematic approach to norm referencing. For obvious reasons, the normal curve is sometimes referred to as the "bell curve." Its distinguishing characteristics are having a single mode (the single high peak in the center), being symmetrical, and being asymptotic (i.e., each of the tails never reach the horizontal axis). The space underneath the drawn curve represents frequencies of events or data points. When a grading scale is aligned with the curve, the result is an equal number of As and Fs, Bs and Ds, and approximately two-thirds of the grades being Cs. It is the vestige of this model that often has teachers carefully considering if they are giving enough or too few of a particular letter grade. The dashed vertical line represents the mean (average) of scores and the other vertical lines separating different grades are spaced according to the standard deviation of the distribution. Generally speaking, the standard deviation of a curve represents the average distance individual scores are from the average of all scores. As you can see from the figure, 68 percent of the scores fall between a range of one standard deviation from the mean. The reason why many teachers think that more students should get Cs than any other grade on a test is derived from the model of the normal curve.

There is one critical point we would like to make about the normal curve that is much more important than the characteristics you have just observed. The normal curve is a model that represents the frequencies of certain observable events. There are two assumptions, however, about the types of events that should be distributed as a normal curve. These assumptions are that the event occurs **by chance** in any **random sample.** In terms of classrooms and evaluation, the event is learning. The sample is the class. If your grades conform to a normal curve, this means that learning occurred by chance and that your students are a random sample. Classes are not formed randomly for reasons of school and individual scheduling constraints. And, if learning occurs in your class by chance, you may need to reconsider whether you should accept your next paycheck. It is our contention that obtaining a normal distribution of grades for a single test, unit, or course is indicative of a serious problem.

You should more appropriately expect to see what is commonly known as a bimodal curve. The name comes from the distinguishing characteristic of two modes, as opposed to the single mode of a normal distribution. Alternatively, the bimodal curve actually looks like two normal curves that have been placed side by side. When a grading scale is aligned with a bimodal curve, you find that the lowest grade frequency is a C. You will also note that there appears to be a normal distribution around the Fs and Ds and around the As and Bs. This makes sense because whether a student achieves an A or B is often due to chance. The same is true for the distinction between F and D. The element of chance we are talking about is the infamous luck of the draw. How often have you felt that you could have done better on a test if the teacher would have asked more questions about the stuff you knew? Or you felt you were lucky to do as well as you did because the teacher just happened to ask what you spent most of your time studying.

Naturally, your goal as a teacher should be to reduce the size of the curve around the Fs and Ds as much as possible. In the ideal world, all of our students would get either As or Bs. Unfortunately, none of us lives in the ideal world. Although teachers are an extremely important influence on students' lives, we are but one of a multitude of influences. Try as we may, the best we can hope for is a minimization of poor student performance. It is unrealistic to think that a quality science education alone will eliminate less than desirable student achievement.

Professional Development

Throughout your career as a teacher, you have a responsibility to yourself and your students to continue to develop yourself as a science educator. Would you want to be examined by a doctor who doesn't keep updated on treatments, procedures, or prescriptions, or have your taxes done by an accountant who doesn't learn about the annual changes in the tax laws, or have your car repaired by a mechanic who is unfamiliar with your problem? Of course, you wouldn't! For the same reasons your students deserve to be taught by a teacher who is equally well informed about his or her profession. Professional development will keep you updated on current thinking and trends in science education, familiarize you with the latest teaching materials and resources, and increase your science content knowledge. Engaging in professional development endeavors will also put you in contact with other teachers with whom you can share ideas and techniques. More often than not, you will find that this networking will be a very valuable aspect of any professional development activity and will result in reflection and consideration of your own teaching practices.

You might be thinking that professional development is appropriate for a classroom teacher but isn't particularly necessary for you right now as a preservice student. However, you may find yourself in need of information, resources, and professional contacts during your student teaching experience. You might also be surprised to find that many organizations offer professional development experiences and opportunities specially designed for preservice and new classroom science teachers. So, how do you continue your education as a science teacher? Where do you find workshops and classes to learn more science content and methods to teach it? How do you meet other science teachers? Which professional journals and organizations are appropriate for elementary-level science teachers? There are many ways to keep updated on current ideas in science education. Reading professional journals and publications, joining local and national organizations for science teachers, attending science education meetings, and enrolling in workshops and graduate courses are all valuable methods to continue your education as a science teacher. In the next section we list national and state organizations and agencies dedicated to improving the teaching and learning of science. We encourage you to contact them, investigate their websites, and use their resources to improve yourself professionally.

State Education Agencies and Science Teacher Organizations

The departments of education in each state offer professional development programs, produce resource materials, and coordinate events for teachers. They often maintain contact directories and calendars of statewide professional development opportunities. Each state also has its own organization for science teachers that sponsors meetings, publications, and support for new teachers. Not every state teacher organization has a web page or mailing address so you may need to contact the education department to obtain information about that state's science teacher organization. Get in touch with these agencies and organizations to find out more about the opportunities available to you as a teacher of science in your state. They may also be able to connect you with other agencies unique to your state that also offer professional development such as environmental centers, museums, zoos, and other informal facilities.

Alabama

Alabama State Department of Education
50 North Ripley Street
P.O. Box 302101
Montgomery, AL 36104
www.alsde.edu

Alabama Science Teachers Association
Route 4, Box 4260
OPP, AL 36467
www.teachscience.net

Alaska

State of Alaska Department of Education
801 West 10th Street, Suite 200
Juneau, AK 99801-1878
www.edu.state.ak.us

Alaska Science Teachers Association
P.O. Box 210361
Anchorage, AK 99521
www.aksta.org

Arizona

Arizona Department of Education
1535 West Jefferson Street
Phoenix, AZ 85007
www.ade.state.az.us

Arizona Science Teachers Association
3301 E Ft Lowell Road
Tucson, AZ 85716
sapphire.ucc.nau.edu/~smlc/azsta

Arkansas

Arkansas Department of Education
4 Street Capitol Mall
Little Rock, AR 72201
arkedu.state.ar.us

Arkansas Science Teacher Association
2705 North Fillmore
Little Rock, AR 72207
www.aristotle.net/~asta

California

California State Department of Education
P.O. Box 944272
Sacramento, CA 94244-2720
www.cde.ca.gov

California Science Teacher Association
3800 Watt Ave., #100
Sacramento, CA 95821
www.cascience.org

Colorado

Colorado Department of Education
201 East Colfax Avenue
Denver, Colorado 80203-1799
www.cde.state.co.us/index_home.htm

Colorado Association of Science Teachers
17395 Jurassic Rd.
Morrison, CO 80465
www.mines.edu/Outreach/
    Cont_Ed/cast1.htm

Connecticut

State Department of Education
165 Capitol Avenue
Hartford, CT 06145
www.state.ct.us/sde/

Connecticut Science Teachers Association
P.O. Box 1811
Wallingford, CT 06492
www.csta-us.org

Delaware

Department of Education
Townsend Building
P.O. Box 1402
Dover, DE 19903
www.doe.state.de.us

Delaware Teachers of Science
526 Kates Way
Smyrna, DE 19977
www.k12.de.us/science/dts/

District of Columbia

Education Program
D.C. Public Schools
415 12th Street, NW, Room 1004
Washington, DC 20004

Florida

Department of Education
Turlington Building, Suite 1514
325 West Gaines Street
Tallahassee, FL 32399
www.fldoe.org

Florida Association of Science Teachers
9851 N. Oak Knoll Circle
Ft. Lauderdale, Florida 33324
www.fastscience.org

Georgia

Georgia Department of Education
2054 Twin Towers East
Atlanta, GA 30334
www.doe.k12.ga.us

Georgia Science Teachers Association
P.O. Box 2668
Stockbridge, GA 30281
www.ceismc.gatech.edu/gsta

Hawaii

Board of Education
P.O. Box 2360
Honolulu, HI 96804
doe.k12.hi.us

Idaho

Idaho State Department of Education
650 West State Street
P.O. Box 83720
Boise, ID 83720-0027
www.sde.state.id.us/dept

Idaho Science Teachers Association
2119 Gourley Street
Boise, ID 83705-3308

Illinois

Illinois State Board of Education
100 North First Street
Springfield, IL 6277-0001
www.isbe.state.il.us

Illinois Science Teachers Association
College of Education
University of Illinois
1310 South 6th Street
Champaign, IL 61820
www.ista-il.org

Indiana

Indiana Department of Education
Room 229, State House
Indianapolis, IN 46204-2798
www.doe.state.in.us

Hoosier Association of Science Teacher
5007 West 14th Street
Indianapolis, IN 46224
www.hasti.org

Iowa

State of Iowa Department of Education
Grimes State Office Building
Des Moines, IA 50319-0146
www.state.ia.us/educate

Iowa Science Teachers Section of the Iowa
Academy of Science
175 Baker Hall
University of Northern Iowa
Cedar Falls, IA 50613
www.iren.net/ias

Kansas

Kansas Department of Education
120 SE 10th Avenue,
Topeka, KS 66612-1182
www.ksbe.state

Kansas Association of Teachers of Science
PO Box 751
Ashland, KS 67831-0751
kats.org

Kentucky

Kentucky Department of Education
500 Mero Street
Frankfort, KY 40601
www.kde.state.ky.us

Kentucky Science Teachers Association
PO Box 991236
Louisville, Kentucky 40269-1236
www.ksta.org

Louisiana

State Department of Education
P.O. Box 94064
Baton Rouge, LA 70804-9064
www.doe.state.la.us/DOE/asps/home.asp

Louisiana Science Teachers Association
P.O. Box 5097
Terrebonne School Board
Houma, LA 70364
www.lsta.info

Maine

Maine State Department of Education
State House Station #23
Augusta, ME 04333
www.state.me.us/education

Maine Science Teachers Association
41 17th St.
Bangor, ME 04401-3139
www.mainescienceteachers.org

Maryland

Maryland State Department of Education
200 West Baltimore Street
Baltimore, MN 21201-2595
www.msde.state.md.us

Maryland Association of Science Teachers
Maryland Science Center
601 Light Street
Baltimore, MD 21230
www.emast.org

Massachusetts

Massachusetts Department of Education
350 Main Street
Malden, MA 02148-5023
www.doe.mass.edu

Massachusetts Association
of Science Teachers
P.O. Box 87
West Side Station
Worcester, MA 01602
www.mast.nu

Michigan

Michigan Department of Education
608 W. Allegan
Lansing, MI 48933
www.michigan.gov/mde

Michigan Science Teacher Association
3300 Washtenaw Ave. Suite 220,
Ann Arbor, MI 48104.
www.msta-mich.org/index.php

Metropolitan Detroit Science
Teachers Association
School Center Building, Room 932
5057 Woodward Ave.
Detroit, MI 48202
www.mdsta.org

Minnesota

Minnesota Department of Education
1500 Highway 36 West
Roseville, Minnesota 55113-4266
education.state.mn.us

Minnesota Science Teachers Association
2395 University Avenue #222
St. Paul, MN 55114-1511
www.mnsta.org

Mississippi

Mississippi State Department of Education
P.O. Box 771
359 North West Street
Jackson, MS 39205
www.mde.k12.ms.us

Mississippi Science Teachers Association
1510 Oldfield Drive
Gautier, MS 39553
www.misssta.org

Missouri

Missouri Department of Education
PO Box 480
Jefferson City, MO 65102
www.dese.state.mo.us

Science Teachers of Missouri
1204 Fowler Street
Lebanon, MO 65536-4144
www.nwmissouri.edu/stom

Montana

Montana Office of Public Instruction
P.O. Box 202501
Helena, Montana 59620-2501
www.opi.state.mt.us

Montana Science Teachers Association
PO Box 191
Plevna, Montana 59344
www.opi.state.mt.us/msta

Nebraska

Nebraska Department of Education
301 Centennial Mall South
Lincoln, NE 68509
www.nde.state.ne.us

Nebraska Association of Teachers of Science
502 9th Street
Milligan, Nebraska 68406
www.neacadsci.org/natshp.htm

Nevada

Nevada Department of Education
700 E. 5th Street
Carson City, NV 89710
www.nde.state.nv.us

Nevada State Science Teachers Association
9509 Cynthia Joy Dr.
Las Vegas, NV 8913
www.geocities.com/nsstahome

New Hampshire

New Hampshire Department of Education
101 Pleasant Street
Concord, NH 03301-3860
www.ed.state.nh.us

New Hampshire Science
   Teachers Association
P.O. Box 1472
Concord, NH 03302
www.nhsta.net

New Jersey

New Jersey Department of Education
P.O. Box 500
Trenton, NJ 08625-0500
www.state.nj.us/education

New Jersey Science Teacher Association
14 Jill Drive
Princeton Junction, NJ 08550
www.njsta.org

New Mexico

State of New Mexico Department
   of Education
300 Don Gaspar
Santa Fe, NM 87501-2786
www.sde.state.nm.us/index.html

New Mexico Science Teachers Association
No contact information available

New York

New York State Education Department
89 Washington Avenue
Albany, NY 12234
www.nysed.gov

Science Teachers Association of New York
491 Oakdale Road
East Meadow, NY 11554
www.tier.net/stanys

Science Council of New York City
13-25(A) 31 Drive
Flushing, NY 11354-2664

North Carolina

North Carolina Department
   of Public Instruction
301 N. Wilmington St.
Raleigh, NC 27601
www.ncpublicschools.org/about_dpi

North Carolina Science
   Teachers Association
PO Box 1783
Salisbury, NC 28145-1783
www.ncsta.org

North Dakota

North Dakota Department
   of Public Instruction
600 E. Boulevard Avenue, Dept. 201
Bismarck, North Dakota 58505-0440
www.dpi.state.nd.us

North Dakota Science
   Teachers Association
301 Wallace St.
Burlington, ND 58722
www.ndsta.k12.nd.us/index.htm

Ohio

Ohio Department of Education
25 South Front Street,
Columbus, Ohio 43215-4183
www.ode.state.oh.us

Science Education Council of Ohio
PO BOX 349
Sharon Center, OH 44274-0349
www.secoonline.org/Default.htm

Ohio Council for Elementary
   School Science
P.O. Box 1013
Reynoldsburg, OH 43068
Members.aol.com/ocess

Oklahoma

Oklahoma State Department of Education
2500 North Lincoln Boulevard
Oklahoma City, Oklahoma 73105-4599
sde.state.ok.us/home/defaultie.html

Oklahoma Science Teachers Association
1707 S. Mansfield
Stillwater, OK 74074
www.angelfire.com/ok3/osta

Oregon

Oregon Department of Education
255 Capitol Street NE
Salem, OR 97310-0203
www.ode.state.or.us

Oregon Science Teachers Association
P.O. Box 80456
Portland, OR 97280-1456
www.oregonscience.org

Pennsylvania

Pennsylvania Department of Education
333 Market Street
Harrisburg, PA 17126
www.pde.state.pa.us/pde_internet/
   site/default.asp

Pennsylvania Science Teachers Association
PO Box 144,
Towanda, PA 18848-0144
www.pascience.org

Philadelphia

Philadelphia Area Elementary Science
Teachers Association
2209 Oakwyn Road,
Lafayette Hill, PA 19444

Rhode Island

Rhode Island Department of Education
255 Westminster Street
Providence, RI 02903
www.ridoe.net

Rhode Island Science Teacher Association
www.ids.net/rista

South Carolina

South Carolina Department of Education
1429 Senate Street
Columbia, SC 29201
www.sde.state.sc.us

South Carolina Science Council
P.O. Box 1783
Salisbury, NC 28145-1783
www.scscience.org

South Dakota

Department of Education
   and Cultural Affairs
700 Governors Drive
Pierre, SD 57501-2291
www.state.sd.us/deca

South Dakota Science Teachers Association
820 N. Broadway
Watertown, SD 57201
www.angelfire.com/sd/SDSTA

Tennessee

Tennessee Department of Education
Andrew Johnson Tower 6th Floor
Nashville, TN 37243-0375
www.state.tn.us/education

Tennessee Science Teachers Association
2133 Williamsport Pike
Columbia, TN 38401
cesme.utm.edu/TSTA/tsta.html

Texas

Texas Education Agency
1701 North Congress Ave.
Austin, TX 78701
www.tea.state.tx.us

Science Teachers Association of Texas
P.O. Box 4828
Austin, TX 78765
www.statweb.org

Texas Council of Elementary Science
2523 Carlow
Austin, TX 78745
www.statweb.org/TCES

Utah

Utah State Office of Education
250 East 500 South
P O Box 144200
Salt Lake City, Utah 84114-4200
www.usoe.k12.ut.us

Utah Science Teachers Association
174 East 1825 South
Orem, UT 84058
www.usoe.k12.ut.us/curr/science/
   usta/reg.html

Vermont

Vermont State Department of Education
120 State Street
Montpelier, VT 05620-2501
www.state.vt.us/educ

Vermont Science Teacher Association
www.uvm.edu/vsta

Virginia

Virginia Department of Education
PO Box 2120
Richmond, VA 23218
www.pen.k12.va.us

Virginia Association of Science Teachers
134 Twin Lake Circle
Newport News, VA 23608
www.vast.org

Washington

Washington State Office of Superintendent
   of Public Instruction
Old Capitol Building, P.O. Box 47200
Olympia, WA 98504-7200
www.k12.wa.us

Washington Science Teachers Association
Geology Dept., 9080
Western Washington University
Bellingham, WA 98225-9080
www.wsta.net

West Virginia

West Virginia Department of Education
1900 Kanawha Boulevard East
Charleston, WV 25305
wvde.state.wv.us

West Virginia Science Teachers Association
www.wvsta.org

Wisconsin

Wisconsin Department of Public Instruction
125 S. Webster St.
P.O. Box 7841
Madison, WI 53707-7841
www.dpi.state.wi.us

Wisconsin Society of Science Teachers
(WSST)
University of Wisconsin, Oshkosh
Office of Science Outreach
800 Algoma Blvd.
Oshkosh, WI 54901
www.wsst.org

Wisconsin Elementary and Middle Level
Science Teachers
Science Outreach-WEST
UW Oshkosh
800 Algoma Blvd.
Oshkosh, WI 54901
www.westsci.org

Wyoming

Wyoming Department of Education
2300 Capitol Avenue
Hathaway Building, 2nd Floor
Cheyenne, WY 82002-0050
www.k12.wy.us/index.htm

Wyoming Science Teachers Association
960 Road 20
Powell, WY 82435
wsta.1wyo.net

National Agencies and Organizations for Teachers of Science

The following are lists of national professional organizations dedicated to the
support of teachers of science. Visit their websites to find out how they can support and enhance your teaching.

National Science Teachers Association (NSTA)
The largest organization of K–12 science teachers promotes excellence
and innovation in science teaching and learning. It publishes journals for
elementary, middle, secondary, and college levels as well as news reports
on current issues in science education and sponsors regional and national
meetings.
www.nsta.org

Council for Elementary Science International (CESI)
The international organization for elementary and middle school science
educators is dedicated to excellence in the teaching and learning of
elementary-level science.
www.unr.edu/homepage/crowthers/cesi

Discipline-Related Science Organizations

The following is a list of organizations that promote and support the teaching and learning of specific science disciplines. These organizations produce publications, host meetings, and offer workshops and activities for teachers.

National Association of Biology Teachers (NABT)
   www.outcast.gene.com/ae/RC/nabt.org

Association of Physics Teachers (APT)
   www.aapt.org

National Earth Science Teachers Association (NESTA)
   www.aug.org

National Marine Educators Association (NMES)
   www.marine-ed.org

Association of Astronomy Educators (AAE)
   www.solar.physics.montana.edu/aae

American Chemical Society (ACS)
   www.acs.org

Index

Ability grouping, 72
Acceleration, 247, 248
Advanced preparation as key to successful whole group instruction, 58
Advance organizers in whole class instruction, 60
Affective domain, 87, 91–92
Alternative learning environments, 73–78
American Association for the Advancement of Science, 28
American Chemical Society (ACS), 378
Americans with Disabilities Act, 274
Animal life cycles, 199–202
Application level in Bloom's Taxonomy, 89
Aristotle, 24
AskERIC Virtual Library, 161
Assessment, in earth science, 331–332
Assessment in Science Education, 34
Assessments. *See also* Evaluation
alternative, 113, 124–135
authentic, 113, 124–125
conceptualizing, 106–109

developing, to match instructional objectives, 109–113
in earth science, 296, 306–307, 317
equality of, 121–122
in life science, 183–184, 195, 211–212, 226
making judgments from, 136–137
in physical science, 244–245, 254, 260, 275–276
traditional approach in developing, 113–121
Association of Astronomy Educators (AAE), 378
Association of Physics Teachers (APT), 378
Atlas of Science Literacy, 33
Authentic assessment, 113, 124–125

Back to the basics, 26
Behavioral expectations in whole class instruction, 59–60
Benchmarks for Science Literacy, xiii, 29–32, 33, 36, 85, 145, 177, 338
on energy, 257–258
on forces and motion, 189, 250

on life cycles, 203
on physical and chemical changes, 267
on universe, 292
on what is life, 177
Bimodal curve, 367
Birds, teaching about, 188–196
Bloom's Taxonomy, 87–94, 122
affective domain, 87, 91–92
analysis level in, 89
application level in, 89
cognitive domain, 87, 88–91, 109–111
comprehension level in, 88–89
evaluation level of, 90–91
knowledge level in, 88
psychomotor domain, 87, 92–94
synthesis level in, 89–90
Blueprints for Reform, 32–33
Boiling point, teaching about, 233–235
Book center. *See* Reading centers
Brainstorming, 207, 209, 210–211
Butterflies, teaching about, 202–213

Cells, teaching about, 174
Change and constancy as transcendent theme, 338

Chemical changes, 261–265
  literature connection, 279
  teaching cycle, 265–277
Class discussion, 212, 275–276,
  314–315
Classification schemes, 308
Classroom, arranging, 52–57
Classroom design
  alternative, 52, 54, 55, 56
  choosing, 52, 53
Closure, 96, 97
Cognitive domain, 87, 88–91
Communities, teaching about,
  215–216
Completion items, 116–117, 123
Complying, 91–92
Comprehension level in Bloom's
  Taxonomy, 88–89
Computer centers, 251
Computers in classrooms, 57
Concept maps, 102, 130
Conclusion sheets, 331–332
Condensation, 320–323
Condition component of instruc-
  tional objectives, 83
Constellation maps, 293
Constellations, teaching about,
  282–284
Constructivism, 40–42
Convergent activities, 260
Cooperative behavior-building
  activities, 73
Council for Elementary Science
  International (CESI),
  158–159, 378
Criterion component of
  instructional objectives,
  83–84
Criterion referencing, 107–108,
  137–138
Cultural literacy, 26
Curriculum
  defined, 141
  inclusion of science in, 24–26
  modification of, based on
    student prior knowledge,
    151
Curriculum integration, 155

Curriculum materials
  evaluating, 145–146
  revising, based on your
    analysis, 147–151
Curriculum Materials Resource, 33

Data analysis, 176–177
Data collection, 177
  in laboratory activities, 70
Demonstrations
  classroom, 52, 54, 238
  versus laboratory activity, 245
  in lesson plan, 96–97
  in teaching about life science,
    178–179
  in whole class instruction,
    63–66
Density, teaching about,
  232–233, 237, 238–245
Designs for Science Literacy, 33
Development, teaching about,
  173
Directions, importance of, 275
Disabilities Education Act, 274
Discipline-related science
  organizations, 378
Discussions
  keeping visual record of, 62
  in small group instruction,
    71–73
Dissolving, 263, 265, 266
Distribution deliberation, 194
Divergent activities, 260
Diverse backgrounds, assessment
  of students from, 124

Earth science, 281–335
  literature connections in,
    334–335
  models in, 310–311, 341–342
  rocks and rock cycle,
    308–312
    teaching cycle, 312–320
  solar system, 297–301
    teaching cycle, 301–308
  systems in, 349–351
  universe, 282–291
    teaching cycle, 291–297

weather, 320–326
  teaching cycle, 326–333
Ecosystems, teaching about,
  217, 220–222, 225–226,
  227
Education for all Handicapped
  Children Act, 274
Elastic clause, 206
Elasticity, teaching about, 233
Energy, 255–257
  conservation of, 256
  evidence of, 255
  kinetic, 255–256
  literature connection,
    278–279
  potential, 255–256
  teaching cycle, 257–261
  transformations of, 256
Entropy, 256–257
Environmental science, 213–219,
  213–227
  literature connections, 227
  major concepts in, 213–219
  teaching cycle, 219–227
ERIC database, 355
  finding lesson plans using,
    355–362
ERIC Document Reproduction
  Service (EDRS), 355
Essay questions, 120–121, 122,
  123–124
Evaluation. *See also*
  Assessment
  of alternative assessments,
    132–135
  conceptualizing, 106–109
  of curriculum materials,
    145–146
  determination of grades,
    137–139
  formative, 136
  making judgments from
    assessments and
    measures, 136–137
  summative, 136
Evaluation level of Bloom's
  Taxonomy, 90–91
Evaporation, 320–323

Exploratorium in San Francisco, 159
Eyes-on activities, 238
Eyewitness software, 195

Field trips, 77–78, 221, 260, 291
Fine motor skills, 92
Fine movement, 92
Flinn Scientific, Inc., 167
Food chains, teaching about, 216
Food webs, teaching about, 216
Forces and motion, 246–248
    literature connection, 278
    teaching cycle, 249–254
Form and function, 185–196
    teaching cycle, 188–196
    as transcendent theme, 338
Formative evaluation, 136
Fossil fragment activity, 9–12, 19
Free exploration periods, 250, 251

Gateway to Educational Materials (GEM), 161
Gender in small-group instruction, 67
Goal setting
    in earth science, 291–292, 301–302, 312–313, 326–327, 341–342
    in life science, 171–178, 189–190, 203–206, 217–220, 343–344
    in physical science, 235–236, 250–251, 257–258, 267–268, 345–346
Grades
    defined, 105
    determination of, 137–139, 366–367
Great Explorations in Math and Science (GEMS) Teacher's Guides, 161
Gross movement, 92
Growth, teaching about, 172–173, 175
Guided practice, 96, 97
Gukberti and the Wind (Ets), 253

Habitat, teaching about, 213–215
Hands-on activities, 54–55, 212, 238, 268, 313
Hands-On-Nature: Information and Activities for Exploring the Environment with Children, 161
Hearing impairments, 274
Herron's Scale, 266
Homework in assessment, 226, 227, 244–245, 260
Hypothesis, 88

Igneous rocks, 309, 310–311
Independent activities, 128
Independent practice, 96, 97
Index of difficulty, 364
Indispensable supplies, 165–166
Individualized Education Programs (IEPs), 111
Inertia, 248
Inference, 176–177
Inquiry, 176–177, 236, 250. *See also* Scientific inquiry
    assessing levels of, 266
    science assessment and, 184
Inspection method, 138–139
Instruction, interdisciplinary, 42
Instructional materials
    criteria in selecting, 142–143
    finding and selecting, 153–154
Instructional materials analysis
    as basis for revising curriculum materials, 147–151
    making sense of, 146
Instructional objectives, 82–94
    Bloom's taxonomy, 87–94
    condition component of, 83
    criterion component of, 83–84
    developing assessment items to match, 109–113
    of laboratory activities, 70
    performance component of, 83
    plan template, 98–100
    reform documents and, 84–87
Instructional outcomes, 44

Instructional planning, 81–104
Integration, 42
Interdisciplinary instruction, 42, 159
Internet, 160–161
Interviews, 127–128
Investigation report worksheets, 317–319
Item analysis, 138, 363–367
Item discrimination, 364–366

Journals, 130–132, 195–196

Kits, 167
Knowledge level in Bloom's Taxonomy, 88

Laboratory activities, 238–245
    versus demonstration, 245
    in small group instruction, 69–71
Laboratory practical, 125
Lavatories as learning environment, 74–75
Learning centers, 55–57
    in physical science, 251
    in studying physical and chemical changes, 268–273
    in teaching about forces and motion, 249–250
Learning cycle, 252
Learning disabilities, 274
    modifications of exams for students with, 111
Least restrictive environment, 274
Legal issues in laboratory activities, 70–71
Lesson plan, 94–102
    closure, 96, 97
    demonstrations in, 96–97
    finding, using the ERIC database, 355–362
    guided practice, 96, 97
    independent practice, 96, 97
    introduction, 96

Life, definition of, 171–176
  teaching cycle, 176–185
Life cycles, 196–213
  animal, 199–202
  literature connections,
      212–213
  plant, 197–199
  teaching cycle, 202–213
Life science, 171–228
  definition of life in, 171–176
    teaching cycle, 176–185
  environmental science,
      213–219
    teaching cycle, 219–227
  form and function, 185–196
    teaching cycle, 188–196
  life cycles, 196–202
    teaching cycle, 202–213
  models in, 343–345
  systems in, 351–352
Literature connections, 253. *See
      also* Reading centers
  for earth science, 334–335
  for energy, 278–279
  for environmental science,
      227
  for forces and motion, 278
  for form and function, 190
  for life cycles, 212–213
  for physical and chemical
      change, 279
  for properties of matter, 278
  for solar system, 307
  for what is life, 185
Living things, distinguishing
      from nonliving things,
      180–183

Magma, 310
Malleability, teaching about, 233
Mass, 232, 247–248
Matching questions, 119, 122,
      123
Materials development and
      selection
  in earth science, 292–294,
      302–303, 313–314,
      327–328

  in life science, 178–179,
      190–191, 206–207,
      220–222
  in physical science, 236–238,
      251, 258–259, 268–273
Matter
  conservation of, 263–264
  properties of, 230–235
    literature connection, 278
    teaching cycle, 235–246
Measurements
  conceptualizing, 106–109
  making judgments from,
      136–137
Melting point, teaching about,
      233–235
Mental discipline theory, 24–25
  validity of, 26
Metabolism, teaching about,
      174–175
Metamorphic rocks, 309, 311
Models
  in earth science, 310–311,
      341–342
  in life science, 343–345
  in physical science, 345–346
  as transcendent theme, 338,
      339–346
Modified true-false questions,
      114–116, 122–123
Motion. *See* Forces and motion
Movement. *See also* Forces and
      motion
  teaching about, 171–172, 178,
      181–182, 185–186,
      250–251
Multicultural knowledge, 59,
      292
Multiple-choice questions,
      117–119, 122, 123, 366
Multiple credit assessments, 366

National Academy of Sciences,
      28
National Aeronautics and Space
      Administration
      Educational Resources,
      160

National agencies and
      organizations for teachers
      of science, 377–378
National Association of Biology
      Teachers (NABT), 378
National Council for Teachers of
      Mathematics (NCTM), 33
National Earth Science Teachers
      Association (NESTA), 378
*National Education Technology
      Standards for Students:
      Connecting Curriculum and
      Technology,* 162
National Marine Educators
      Association (NMES), 378
National Research Council
      (NRC) of the National
      Academy of Sciences, 33
*National Science Education
      Standards* (NSES), xiii, 28,
      42–43, 106, 177, 338
  evaluation criteria, 143
  on forces and motion, 189,
      250
  instructional objectives and,
      84–85
  learning environment and,
      51–52
  on life cycles, 203, 206, 219
  on properties of matter, 236
  on solar system, 302
  on universe, 292
  on what is life, 177–178
National Science Teachers
      Association (NSTA), 33,
      156, 158–160, 160,
      377–378
Nature of Science, 4–18, 184,
      260, 297
Newton
  First Law of Motion, 246–247,
      248
  Second Law of Motion, 247,
      248
  Third Law of Motion, 248
Nonliving things, distinquishing
      from living things,
      180–183

Normal curve, 366–367
Norm-referenced approach, 108, 137, 138–139

Observations, 176–177, 182–183, 188, 328–331
checklist for, in assessment, 254
Online simulations, 293

Pairs, working in, 180–181, 205, 206–207, 238, 295–296
Paper-and-pencil tests, 113
Patterns, 296–297
Pedagogy
in earth science, 294–296, 303–306, 314–317, 328–331
in life science, 179–183, 191–195, 207–211, 222–226
in physical science, 238–244, 251–253, 259–260, 273–275
Performance assessment, 125
Performance component of instructional objectives, 83
Performance objectives, 83
Photographs, 221
Physical changes, 261–265
literature connection, 279
teaching cycle, 265–277
Physical science, 229–279
energy, 255–257
literature connection, 278–279
teaching cycle, 257–261
forces and motion, 246–248
literature connection, 278
teaching cycle, 249–254
models in, 345–346
physical and chemical change, 261–265
literature connection, 279
teaching cycle, 265–277

properties of matter, 230–235
literature connection, 278
teaching cycle, 235–246
systems in, 353–354
Piaget, Jean, 40
Planetarium, visiting, 294
Planetarium simulation software, 293
Plant life cycles, 197–199
Populations, teaching about, 215
Portfolios, 126–127, 207, 307
planning and production, 127
Poster presentations, 205, 206–207, 211–212
Prior knowledge
assessment of, 136, 179–180, 220, 254, 328, 332
curriculum modification based on student, 151
Problem-solving in small group instruction, 71–73
Professional development, 369–378
Project 2061 Curriculum Evaluation Criteria, 28, 29–33, 34–35, 39, 42, 126–127, 143–145
Psychomotor domain, 87, 92–94

Questioning
in teaching about life science, 176–177, 182–183
in whole class instruction, 60–62

Random sample, 367
Reading centers. *See also* Literature connections
in life science, 188–189, 190, 195, 204–205
in physical science, 251
Reflections
in earth science, 296–297, 307, 317–320, 332–333
in life science, 184–185, 195–196, 212, 226–227
in physical science, 245, 254, 260–261, 276–277

Reform documents, instructional objectives and, 84–87
Reinforcement of concepts, 100
Reproduction, teaching about, 175–176
Reproductions, 126
Resource card file, 154–163
Resources for Science Literacy: Professional Development, 32, 33
Responding, 92
Rock cycle, 309
Rocks and Minerals unit, goals for, 163–164
Rocks and rock cycle, 308–312
teaching cycle, 312–320
Rubrics, 132–135
Rutherford, F. James, 29

Safety
in the classroom environment, 56, 79, 320
on field trips, 258
food allergies, 191
goggles, 269
in laboratory activities, 56, 69, 70–71, 74
in material development and selection, 178, 179, 268
Scale as transcendent theme, 338
Scavenger hunt, 258–259
School kitchen as learning environment, 74
School laboratory, 74–75
School Science and Mathematics (journal), 159
School Science and Mathematics Association (SSMA), 159
Schoolyard as learning environment, 76–77
Science
body of knowledge, 7–8
defined, 4–6
gathering supplies for learning in, 163–168

Science *(continued)*
objectivity of, 12–18
reasons for teaching, 23–45
as requirement for all
students, 24–26
specific comparisons between
reforms, 42–43
teaching nature of, 19–20,
187
Science and Children (journal),
156, 158, 302
Science assessment, inquiry and,
184
Science Content Standards, 34
Science education
common themes in reforms,
39–43
contemporary reform efforts
in, 28–39
*Science Education Program
Standards*, 34
Science Education System Standards,
34
Science for All Americans, 29
Science Is . . ., 162
*Science on the Internet: A Resource
for K–12 Teachers*, 162
Science Scope (journal), 158
Science station, monitoring
students at, 320
Science Teacher (journal), 158
Science teacher organizations
national, 377–378
state, 370–377
Science Teaching Standards, 34
Scientific inquiry, 44, 121,
132–133, 151–152. *See
also* Inquiry
Scientific knowledge, 248
characteristics of, 7–12
Scientific laws, 248
Scientific literacy, 26
defined, 27–28
Scientific method, 12, 206,
211
Scientific theory, 248
Sedimentary rocks, 309–310
Self-referencing, 108–109, 137

Shadow sticks, 299–306
Sharing times, 221–222
Short-answer questions,
116–117, 123
Simulation software, 293
Single-variable concept, 89
Small group instruction,
66–73
discussion and problem
solving in, 71–73
laboratory activities in,
69–71
small group work in, 67–69
Small group work in small group
instruction, 67–69
Solar system, 297–301
teaching cycle, 301–308
Space travel, 298–299
Special students, special needs
of, 274, 326
Standardized tests, 108
*Standards for Professional
Development for Teachers of
Science*, 34
Star maps, 293, 294, 296
Starry Night™, 294
Stars, teaching about,
282–291
State education agencies,
370–377
State science teacher
organizations, 370–377
Student-centered model of
instruction, 252
Students, involvement of, in
teaching, 181, 185
Student-to-student interaction,
210
Subjectivity of scientific
knowledge, 9–12
Subject matter, knowledge of,
xi
Summative evaluation, 136
Supplies, gathering, for science
learning, 163–168
Supply companies, 166–167
Synthesis level in Bloom's
Taxonomy, 89–90

Systems
in earth science, 349–351
in life science, 351–352
in physical science, 353–354
as transcendent theme, 338,
346–354

Table of specifications, 110–111,
112–113, 138
Tables, 315, 316
*Teaching Chemistry with Toys:
Activities for Grades K–9*,
162
Teaching cycle, 169–170
assessment and evaluation in,
106
for earth science
solar system, 301–308
universe, 291–297
weather, 326–333
for life science, 171–228
environmental science,
219–227
form and function, 188–196
life cycles, 202–213
what is life, 176–185
for physical science,
229–279
energy, 257–261
forces and motion,
249–254
physical and chemical
change, 265–277
properties of matter,
235–246
*Teaching Physics with Toys: Activities
for Grades K–9*, 162
Technology in teaching, 244
Test banks, 118
Textbooks, 141–142
adoption of, 142
selecting, 141
Thinking outside the box, 159
Three-dimensional
investigations, 195
Traditional approach to
developing assessment
items, 113–121

Transcendent themes, 337–354
  models as, 338, 339–346
  systems in, 346–354
Transfer of knowledge, 26
True-false questions, 113–114, 122, 366
  modified, 114–116, 122–123

Universe, 282–291
  teaching cycle, 291–297

Valuing, 92
Vico, Giambattista, 40–42

Virtual field trips, 221
Visual impairments, 274
Visual representations and pictures, 129–130
Volcanoes, teaching about, 313, 320

Wait time, 61
Warm-up activities, 273
Water cycle, 196, 325–326
Weather, 320–326
  teaching cycle, 326–333
WebQuests, 160–161

Whizbangers and Wonderments: Science Activities for Young People, 162
Whole class discussions, 314–315
Whole group instruction, 57–66
  advance organizers in, 60
  demonstrations in, 63–66
  establishing behavioral expectations, 59–60
  preparing, 57–62
  questioning in, 60–62
Writing assignments in assessment, 212, 317

Photo Credits